A MULTICULTURAL ODYSSEY

*A Memoir
(almost) sans Regrets*

James Houston

COVENTRY
PRESS

Published in Australia by
Coventry Press
33 Scoresby Road
Bayswater Vic. 3153
Australia

ISBN 9780648145721

Copyright © James Houston 2018

All rights reserved. Other than for the purposes and subject to the conditions prescribed under the *Copyright Act*, no part of this publication may be reproduced, stored in a retrieval system, or transmitted in any form or by any means, electronic, mechanical, photocopying, recording or otherwise, without the prior permission of the publisher.

First published 2018

Cataloguing-in-Publication entry is available from the National Library of Australia
http:/catalogue.nla.gov.au/.

Design by Filmshot Graphics (FSG)

Printed in Australia

CONTENTS

Acknowledgments 7

Prologue 8

1. A New Dawn 10

2. A Born Romantic 17

3. Wellspring 21

4. A Forties Childhood 27

5. Long Day's Journey into Light 46

6. Embrace of the Alma Mater 51

7. Student Daze 58

8. Joining the Real World 65

9. Launch of an Odyssey 68

10. "Hullo, Cobber" 71

11. Migrating to Germany 79

12. Minden Days 88

13. Dicing with Death 93

14. Journey to the End of the Earth 100

15. Striking Root 104

16. Stirrings of Dissent 110

17. *'Let's Speak French'* 113

18. A Proper Bureaucrat 120

19. Citizens of No Mean City 124

20. A Nation Transformed 127

21. Taking the Ethnic Pulse 139

22. Courting Ethnic Allies 145

23. An Evolutionary Ferment 161

24. A Multicultural Society for the Future 171

25. "A Name to Conjure With!" 196

26. Fostering a Fairer Australia 206

27. "The Most Racist Town in Australia?" 220

28. Monitoring Rural Racism 233

29. A Tale of Two Towns 237

30. Ebb Tide 252

31. Explosion of Grace 261

32. Transitions 283

33. Sorting out ITEMS 296

34. Girdling the Globe 304

35. Charting New Waters 318

36. Journey to Parish Ministry 325

37. Sowing in Tears 336

38. Reaping in Joy 347

39. Dreams and Visions 364

40. Seeds Blowing in the Wind 368

41. The Heartache of Parting 375

42. Challenging the Church Establishment 379

43. Promoting Multiculturalism across the Churches 383

44. In Search of Meaning 390

45. Core of my Heart 410

Appendix – Publications 426

ACKNOWLEDGMENTS

A dilemma for the père de famille: writing a Memoir inevitably puts a family under the spotlight. So I record my grateful acknowledgment of the practical support and the many suggestions received from the members of my family. In a sense, we all wrote the story.

In addition, I acknowledge the enriching relationships within the Christian community that have contributed lifelong to my search for an over-arching meaning to life.

I am grateful to my high-school language teachers for opening my eyes to a wider world. Release from my monocultural prison would foreshadow the vision of an Australia beyond the British Empire. This would be greatly supplemented by my later research among hundreds of migrant leaders nationwide.

The outcomes of that research produced an alternative vision for an Australia of many – all equally humanising – cultures held together by a will to equality. I acknowledge my debt to visionary academic and community activists who would contribute to my initial draft of our national policy of multiculturalism.

In particular, I have to thank the first (and only) Commissioner for Community Relations, A J Grassby, for offering me a key role in the combat of racial discrimination, particularly suffered by the First Australians.

I gratefully acknowledge the calling to a role in Christian ministry by the late David Penman, Anglican Archbishop of Melbourne in the early 1980s, and my debt to the people of several parishes in offering opportunities for service.

Finally, I need to acknowledge the unstinting technical help received from Maarten Ligtvoet, my ever-patient computer mentor.

PROLOGUE

Canberra. 11th November 1975. Remembrance Day.
Another day unlikely to be forgotten.
Reacting to hints of a resolution looming in the stand-off over the Whitlam Government's accessing of Supply to keep the country running, my colleague George and I slip out of the Admin. Building and cut across the lawns to the original Parliament House not a hundred metres away, gleaming white in the warm afternoon sun.

Perhaps 100 people have beaten us to it, clustered in a tight hubbub of voices. Their bush telegraph must be a cut above ours. We join the back of the throng, twenty metres over the road from the front steps of Parliament and take up the spontaneous chant, *"We want Gough! We want Gough! We want Gough!"* But instead we get the Official Secretary to the Governor-General, Sir John Kerr.

Over a generation later, it still remains the stuff of a disordered nightmare. An eerie silence falls as he reads to the hushed crowd a proclamation dismissing from office the elected Prime Minister of Australia and appointing Malcolm Fraser acting Prime Minister, on the day styled 'Kerr's cur'. Impiously, the proclamation concludes *'God save the Queen'*.

Behind, towering over him and flanked by his Cabinet colleagues, the ex-Prime Minister steps forward to unleash a brief but pungent tirade concluding with the memorable –and prophetic – words *"Well may you say, 'God save the Queen,' because nothing will save the Governor-General!"*

Simmering in our impotent rage, George and I drive directly to 'Yarralumla', residence of the Governor-General, and order the gate attendant to admit us on government business. Bemused by our terrible resolve, he opens the gate and we drive right up to the main portal where George, adept at such legalisms, demands access to the Visitors Book. We are shown in and there we both record our outraged protest at Kerr's hubris, and sign our names in our best copperplate handwriting. Undoubtedly we are proffering the first officially recorded citizens' comment on the Dismissal. Or – unlike the PM – was the page *discreetly* removed?

Two weeks before his dismissal, I had been present at a brief ceremony where Gough Whitlam had proclaimed the *Racial Discrimination Act* as the law of the land and had formally appointed Al Grassby for a seven-year term as the first Commissioner for Community Relations. *It would prove to be the last legislative act of his Government.*

CHAPTER 1: A New Dawn

Al Grassby had been Whitlam's Immigration Minister until losing his seat of Riverina in the 1974 double dissolution election. Subsequently he was re-styled 'Special Consultant on Community Relations'. His role was to devise a new statutory authority modelled on a UK counterpart, with powers to examine complaints of racial discrimination and settle them through reconciliation, if need be backed by a compulsory conference, with Court action as the ultimate sanction. The Commissioner for Community Relations would be backed by two Assistant Commissioners: I would be responsible for planning and co-ordinating an Australia-wide program of community education to tackle racist attitudes and behaviour, while George would be responsible for handling complaints of racial discrimination lodged under the Act, as well as for the day-to-day running of the Office.

But for the next seven years the Dismissal would cast a long shadow over our day-to-day work lives by leaving us hamstrung and frustrated in playing the roles required of us. For the previous two months we had been helping devise an administrative framework for implementing the racial discrimination legislation, then still under debate in Parliament – and making heavy weather of it. It took its sanction from the *International Covenant against All Forms of Racial Discrimination* launched by the UN in 1965. Like the good international citizen that we were, Australia had signed up early. But in the absence of any legislation to give it effect, in this country ten years later there was still nothing to show.

After almost two centuries of open prejudice against the Aboriginal population, and more recent antagonism towards some non-English-speaking migrants, it would be a demanding process to bring about change in community attitudes. But in the brave new world of the early 70s hopes and visions abounded about Australia living down its racist past and building a truly humane society. We stood on the threshold of the Promised Land!

Al Grassby with Gough Whitlam at the proclamation of the Racial Discrimination Act

At the brief proclamation ceremony, Whitlam had contended:

"For the first time the nation has solemnly affirmed its opposition to all forms of racial discrimination, and established machinery to deal with it. Inadequate as it is in many respects, the Act is still the best guarantee that Australians have ever had that the dark forces of bigotry and prejudice which have so often prevailed in the past will never again be able to exercise influences far greater than their numbers in the community. The long-term and continuing need is to entrench new attitudes of tolerance and understanding in the hearts and minds of the people. The *Racial Discrimination Act* writes it firmly into the legislation that Australia is in reality a multi-cultural nation, in which the linguistic and cultural heritage of the Aboriginal people and of peoples from all parts of the world can find an honoured place."

Dreams in the dust

But beyond the Government's dismissal, George and I had waited in vain for the Attorney-General's Department to proceed with the recruitment of the staffing we envisaged. It was not to be. What saved us from total ignominy was the political consideration that, across the ethnic communities of the nation, Al Grassby was a *guru* – if not actually canonised.

In the end, as usual, political expediency and compromise would win the day. He would not be axed as Commissioner for Community Relations. After all, to dismiss him at the very beginning of his seven-year term would be extremely costly – he would have to be paid out his seven years' remuneration in full – and that would make a government committed to pruning back the 'runaway costs' of the 'prodigal'

Whitlam administration look hypocritical and vindictive. On the other hand to walk away from the awkward prospect opened up by the new legislation would be tantamount to announcing to the world that Australia had now *endorsed* racism and discrimination. Hence the wilful compromise to let us wither on the vine. For his part Grassby accepted as a key aspect of his role the maintenance of the balancing act against a basically hostile government, which as career public servants George and I nominally served – albeit with mutual distrust.

So our incipient Office (the notion of a 'Commission', UK style, now unthinkable) was only sullenly tolerated. For the next seven years, we subsisted on starvation rations, always just ahead of abolition as redneck elements in the government from time to time fulminated against Grassby's perceived – and occasionally overt – disloyalty (actually grounded on his adherence to the international norms). But with the Attorney-General's Department we lost all the arguments over the need for funds and staff to carry out our statutory obligations. So we were only granted three more staff: clerical *assistants* (not even clerks), to cope with the avalanche of typing relating to public correspondence and the cases of racial discrimination pouring in from across the land. Although a federal agency, outside Canberra in all six States we were only permitted to employ a single operator in Sydney and one in Melbourne, both functioning as lone rangers.

Really the situation was an absurdity, pure tokenism. For the seven years, George and I would act as members of the Senior Executive Division. But minus any of the accoutrements of office: a private secretary to take our dictation, do our typing and filter phone calls – nor any specialist staff to direct and supervise. Across the entire Commonwealth Public Service we must have been the only members of the Executive Division wasting much of our highly-paid time on the work of Clerical Assistants! And during my frequent interstate safaris I would take route buses to airports rather than the chauffeured Commonwealth cars. Among mandarins, unheard-of!

Inspirational leader

But Al Grassby possessed manifest talent and boundless energy. From the outset he launched into a veritable frenzy of public appearances at ethnic community gatherings, education conferences, seminars and special events, preaching the Gospel of cultural pluralism with all the spiritual fervour of a new convert endowed with a ministry of itinerant evangelism. By profession a journalist, he was also good on geographical and historical detail. When in his home base in Canberra, he churned out a spate of journalistic articles and the texts of speeches.

In the community at large, he was a proven performer for his charm, his verve and his popularity with the migrant voters then emerging as a key sector of the electorate, who viewed him as one of themselves. In fact he had been partly raised in Latin America, son of a civil engineer. Moving deftly among their diverse customs he sported a wide knowledge and respect for 'migrant' cultures. He became one of the most recognisable figures in Australian public life, projecting his colourful dress sense of purple suit and yellow tie against the politicians' garb of sombre dark suits and plain ties. Above all, he was genial, positive, a visionary. And a thoroughly likeable character.

Very often he wasn't in Canberra but travelling incessantly wherever he was invited to speak. From this, Australia-wide, he gained constant media exposure, maximising the modest impact of his Office with its important message that the old racist Australia was on the way out. But for all the popularity that he courted in ethnic community circles and amongst the chattering classes, he forfeited as much respect among many of the 'Ockers' – especially those who saw him as disfranchising them – and was denounced outright by some rural interests (*'upsetting the balance of the community'*) and business and industry heavies (*'can't afford it'*). Twenty years later, some of those rural stalwarts stoutly resisting the threatened *'take-over by the wogs'* would become foot-soldiers for Pauline Hanson's One Nation Party.

Prodigious output

Nevertheless during those seven years, despite its Lilliputian staffing complement of five (later eight – though four of them clerical support workers) – the Community Relations Office strove heroically to support Commissioner Grassby. My part involved co-ordinating the drafting of public education programs for countering racism, organising community-based public conferences on multiculturalism in several States and finally a national congress in Canberra, and advising other government agencies and Government Enquiries about fostering multiculturalism. All of it focused on acting as the champion of ethnic minority group interests across Australia. Not to mention the thousands of complaints of racial discrimination handled by George.

I was also responsible for co-ordinating the production of the blockbuster Annual Reports to Parliament required under the *Racial Discrimination Act*. For the whole seven-year term of Grassby's appointment, I aided and abetted him, sometimes deputising for him at short notice. It satisfied my thirst for adventure and travel, while furthering a manifestly Good Cause. It also saw me writing and editing a deal of creative material, much of it to be subsequently published. (See *Appendix* on Publications.) Frankly, I was in my element.

Historic post-script

Towards the end of the seven-year term, as I was working alone in the Community Relations Office beyond the close of day, in walked Gough Whitlam for a meeting with Al Grassby, who had not returned punctually. Overawed, I received him in Al's name, and we chatted to pass the time. I made so bold as to ask why he had not refused to accept Kerr's dismissal (as had often been publicly canvassed). He replied unequivocally that he could not trust the loyalty of the Armed Forces, and did not wish to go down in Australian history as having triggered an armed revolt[1].

Enigma

So how come a boy from working-class Punchbowl, born during the Great Depression to poorly educated Celtic-Australian parents, should emerge (without a patron) as a champion of migrant rights, a

---

[1] My letter to the editor of The Age recounting this episode was published on 22nd October 2014, the day after Gough Whitlam's death. The next day Geoff Walsh, former press secretary to Prime Minister Hawke, made a similar statement in an interview.

pioneer of multiculturalism, and an advocate against the crippling and entrenched racism suffered by Aboriginal people?

By profession a trained teacher of modern languages and classics who had worked in Australia, and later in England and Germany, on return home in 1964 I had been selected by the Sydney-based Commonwealth Office of Education to work in a small team producing an innovative new French course for Australian schools (for Years Seven to Twelve). Drawing on recent overseas experience I had written the creative passages in French for each chapter of the most senior volume, and also a beginners' French reader on an imaginative adventure in the Australian bush. On completion of the project, for several years I was to gain invaluable experience in the role of executive secretary to a government committee for UNESCO.

A unique opportunity

In 1969, newly relocated to Canberra with the Commonwealth Public Service, I transferred to the Immigration Department on being appointed as the Commonwealth Government's first (and last) *'Liaison Officer with National Groups'* (i.e. ethnic community organisations), tasked with forging positive relationships Australia-wide with migrant leaders. In this specialised role, I planned and carried out – later with a young assistant – a program of locating, identifying and interviewing the leaders of some 1,350 migrant organisations across the country and wrote up detailed accounts of my findings. Spending on average an hour and a half with each leader or committee, completing a questionnaire and making supplementary notes on insights gleaned, I amassed a mine of data and understandings of the emerging 'ethnic situation' in the Australia of the early 1970s. Arguably I gained a wider awareness of the range of ethnic community life than anyone in Australia – before or since. But my request to the leaders of the Department to be given time out, mentored by premier ethnic sociologist Prof. Jerzy Zubrzycki, to produce a book disseminating this knowledge was declined. What happened beyond migrants' initial settlement was not of interest. I remained a "voice crying in the wilderness", a prophet ahead of his time.

In my work with the Department, around 1973 I came across the Canadian policy of 'multiculturalism': the original two 'charter communities' from French and English roots broadening to embrace other more recent immigrant communities, typified by the Ukrainians of the prairie provinces, all held in equal esteem. Intrigued, I ordered the opening of a new file with the title *'Multiculturalism in Australia'*. It was the first Commonwealth Government file on multiculturalism.

Foundational document of multiculturalism

In 1973, I distilled these insights into a speech which the leaders of the Immigration Department asked me to prepare for their new Minister, Al Grassby, about the prospects for Australia in the year 2000. I entitled it *A Multicultural Society for the Future*. Subsequently it was published by the Government as an 'Immigration Reference Paper'. Though to me at the time unwitting, this would come to be seen as a historic moment. In the later literature, it would be hailed as the foundational document of Australian multiculturalism. And in the Queen's Birthday Honours in 2001 I would be awarded the Medal of the Order of Australia for my 'contribution to the development of our national policy of multiculturalism'.

After the presentation of the speech in Melbourne, I was summoned to Parliament House to the Minister's suite. Apprehensively (since public servants never related to Ministers) I met Al Grassby who queried where I had got such ideas from? I stammered *"I believe them"*, citing my intimate and protracted exposure to migrant leaders' opinions Australia-wide. His reply floored me, *"If that's how you feel I would like you to work with me"*.

But that would not come about until his appointment six years later as Commissioner for Community Relations. Then he would invite me to join him as his Assistant Commissioner (Education & Research) at the Senior Executive Level of the Public Service.

What would be my brief? *To alter the temper of the nation from redneck to urbane cosmopolitan* – no mean task! How can a law alone change what is in the human heart? As Grassby was wont to say, attitudes can only be changed by exposure to better ideas, through informal contacts and education programs. And these would have to become the driver of change.

CHAPTER 2: A Born Romantic

Some have romance thrust upon them. Well, I was born a romantic. A dreamer. And crippled by it. Or was it liberated? Already at three my first romance – with the cotton-wool sheep trailing across the sky beyond the backyard apple-trees, and musing why the world should end at the great high convent wall that framed our garden.

At then at four – romance with the azure infinity of the Pacific horizon so neatly framed between Cape Banks and Cape Solander, the Botany Bay Heads. And then romance with melody, in my open-air performance of songs picked up from my father, like *When I grow too old to dream,* or *I'm forever blowing bubbles,* loud enough for Mrs Gilmour two doors down to hail the songbird.

At five – romance with the notion of a God who might be up there over the clouds and beyond the Botany Bay horizon... but if not, could do no harm to an unbeliever. Ha! So you don't lose and you might win: OK, I believe in God. And closer at hand I believe in the glamorous sweater-girl with the ill-fitting name of Miss Foot, my kindergarten teacher. It wasn't her feet that I remember.... New romances, ever evoking memorable pictures. Will they go on forever?

Now the romance of travel, beckoning towards the ever-receding horizon. Beginning with the steam locos, on wet winter mornings out of breath with luminous clouds of fire, tackling the grade to Dulwich Hill through the long sandstone cutting at the foot of our street, and the silly electrics skating downhill to the city with their loads of morning workers. Romantic! Travelling to city offices every day, if not by train then maybe by tram or double-decker bus, sporting a suit and tie, with felt hat and carrying a Globite case full of lunch and the morning paper (of course the *Sydney Morning Herald,* a proper broadsheet. Only the working-class would buy the tawdry little *Daily Telegraph* – as my Mum who knew everything would tell me.)

And then even at home, the romance with Grandfather Hughan's great rolltop desk exuding status and authority, with Very Important Papers and receipt books with their magic blue carbon paper, stamp pads and stationery hidden away in its mini-compartments, in the 'front room' of our (his) Federation house in Challis Avenue. What bliss to be handling the very levers of power, until summary ejection by the dour old Scot, the ancestral Hughan after whom I was named – but discreetly, in a middle name that no one would ever use – except to be revived decades later for my son. And his son!

Mysteries of time and place

Then at six – face-to-face with history opening a new dimension: there was a time before I was born! In the NSW Sesqui-Centenary celebrations (1788-1938), in First Class at West Marrickville Infants' School (weird terminology that: at six are we still *'muling and puking in our mothers' arms'?*), all schoolchildren are awarded a bronze medallion attached with a blue and gold ribbon, plus a glossy coloured booklet with Governor Arthur Philip on the cover.

Hmm, so the Australian colonial saga began so close, at Kurnell just across Botany Bay from the ti-trees of Doll's Point where we sometimes go for a Sunday picnic with the mosquitoes. Turn a few pages. Now it's the drama of the convicts and the redcoats, and the heroic pioneer bushmen carving their Australian dream out of a hard, resistant land. And Aborigines brandishing spears – but only to re-enact the landing of the First Fleet at Sydney Cove. Pathetic but innocent stooges. Flick over further, to the triumphant recital of a century and a half's 'cavalcade of progress' – from bullock-drays to British Bedfords, from scythes to Sunshine harvesters – bestowing on the present moment the heavy accolade of the end of history. Concentric ripples of memories as the world of childhood expands.

The concentric ripples widen. Before long I stumble on the pregnant notion that the romance of history actually occurs within a geography, proffering a new dimension of romance. Wow! Dulwich Hill is a 'place'. But how come I was born *here?* Maybe everywhere there are 'places' waiting to be heard of, seen – experienced! Best you go there to find romance. It may take time because they say the world is big, so the sooner you start the better. So where better to start than the picnic spots of outer Sydney? How I loved the weekend outings in our rattly old Chev tourer, to Kentucky and Picnic Point on the George's River near Milperra (today a university campus), past Bankstown airfield with its flimsy Tiger Moths, or to the Sydney water supply dams, or Bobbin Head on Broken Bay.

Wraiths of romance

And then the glorious fortnight of summer holidays in the Blue Mountains. To little boys sheer wonderment, the fleecy morning mists snugly cocooned in the Jamieson Valley with cool wisps blowing up into your face. At Leura Cascades dank walks down ferny glades. Sheer escarpments daring you ever closer to eternity. The projecting platform at Echo Point with its aerial view. The spooky coalmine with its scary 'Scenic Railway' hauling you nearly vertically to the top like a load of coal.

And everywhere the fading glory of a once popular holiday resort whose half-empty guesthouses still traded on names from the Great War like *Villers Bret*. But to be wandering on a misty night pierced only by the pale haloes of the street lights – pure magic!

For us two rascals, brother Max and me, the delicious naughtiness of slipping out of the rented holiday house before anyone else was astir, making for the mecca of Katoomba railway station, with its mini-bustle and the hope of witnessing from our chosen vantage point – standing on the post-and-rail fence by the level crossing – the momentous arrival or departure of a steam train. Some came double-headed, panting up the ranges from the coastal plains assisted by a 'banking' engine, to be uncoupled at Katoomba, driven onto the finely balanced turntable and then swung around by driver and fireman pushing in opposite directions before nonchalantly chuffing off downhill. For the well-to-do, excursions to Jenolan Caves in eight-door char-à-bancs; for the plebs, picture shows on misty afternoons.

One misty afternoon we saw *Shipyard Sal* with England's favourite singer Gracie Fields. It is 1940 and a Greater War has broken out. *'Austerity for the duration'* (whatever that means) is the catchcry, and a world at war has little time for frivolity. Music-hall stars are now singing in the shipyards: *Wish me luck as you wave me good-bye*. Unwittingly, it would turn out to be the swansong for a doomed way of life.

Of course, childhood romantics never manage to disentangle the dream from the nightmare. Yet is it only the childhood romantics? Lifelong I have been dubbed a dreamer. No point in repudiating it now. Didn't Karl Marx urge the solidarity of interest groups through his heroic dictum, *"Romantics of the world, unite! You have nothing to lose but your dreams"?*

CHAPTER 3: Wellspring

I first encountered this world in November 1932 at Nurse Dawson's private hospital in Dulwich Hill. In view of my subsequent work with the Immigration Department this was a well-chosen entry point: decades later the old Victorian mansion would become a State Government migrant hostel.

I was born into the household of my Scottish grandfather, William Hughan, a retired stonemason, practising wobbly Presbyterian ethics though essentially unbelieving. I was the first son of John and Elsie Houston, née Hughan.

Child of the Great Depression

These were the grim years of the Great Depression following the Wall St bank crash of 1929. By 1932, local unemployment stood at 20%. Before he married, John Houston had been among the unemployed mine workers drafted away from the Cessnock coalfields in a bid to lower the temperature of industrial unrest. An asthmatic, his work had been at the pithead. He was packed off to a 'relief work' project on the construction of the new Pacific Highway to Gosford. Camping in the bush and working in damp clothes, with minimal medical services, he spent a cold, wet winter blasting and physically digging out a cutting through virgin sandstone.

However, the acquaintance he struck up with hand tools was to stand him in good stead for his working life over the next 35 years as a 'service layer' with the Australian Gaslight Co. in Sydney.

At the time of my birth, not long married but jobless and walking miles every day around the industrial zone of Botany and Alexandria, he was competing for work by knocking on factory doors. For unemployed workers, it was a time of bitterness and anger. Some were drafted into labour camps run with military discipline. The alternative was to face the degrading experience of 'going on the dole' for which the conditions were rigorous and demeaning. Many families were destitute. Some lived on 'sustenance payments' while working on useless public works.

For those in work, wages were cut across the board by 10%. The State Bank of NSW went insolvent. Bankruptcies, evictions from rental houses and the enforced sale of domestic possessions were the order of the day. Homelessness was rife, with shanty towns on racecourses and crude shelters scattered around government land on the northern foreshores of Sydney Harbour and in scrub near Botany Bay.

Begging and hawking cheap household wares and trinkets from door to door was a commonplace. Some offered skinned rabbits – two for ninepence (20c) or solicited odd jobs from householders. Others scraped little piles of horse manure off the roadways, hoping to sell it to households with big gardens.

Scottish roots

Both my parents had come from Scottish immigrant families of the previous generation, my father's from Ayrshire coalminers and my mother's from Galloway stonemasons – all of them Lowland Scots. Why did they emigrate? As whole families, by sailing ship, across perilous oceans to the ends of the earth? No wonder my mother's mother cried all the way. Were they imbued with hope and expectancy? Or maybe by the urge to escape? How shall we ever know?

For the day, my mother was moderately educated, before the advent of secondary education, completing her schooling at 14. But my father had had a disjointed experience of education in bush schools around Newcastle.

After her mother died young, Elsie Hughan had to forsake her chosen trade of milliner to keep house for the dour patriarch William and a maternal uncle Thomas Breakwell. By then they had acquired the family home at Dulwich Hill, a substantial new 'blue' brick, slate-roofed house in the emerging middle-class suburb of Dulwich Hill on the lower Belmore (later Bankstown) line. This was the household into which I would be born in 1932. But in the decade from 1914 her life, like that of all Australians, had been traumatised by the bloodletting of the 'Great War'. The crowded Rolls of Honour in every town of the land and in all the churches tell the story.

The resulting imbalance of the sexes meant she did not marry until late – in 1926 when she was 31 the proposal came from the unemployed mine worker four years her junior, met on a visit to a cousin in Greta on the Cessnock coalfield. Lacking means of his own, our father was granted the privilege of moving into his father-in-law's household – but I sense on sufferance. And on condition that he be a total abstainer, a commitment that I also inherited. The family must have been outraged at the southward social trajectory of her marriage defying gravity and common sense. I imagine that her patriarchal and by then *petit bourgeois* father would have had scant sympathy for the 'shiftless labourer' on whom she had recklessly thrown herself away. My sister's birth certificate cites his profession as fitter's assistant.

For his part, Grandfather Hughan, a master stonemason who had retired as Clerk of Works for the building of Sydney's Central Railway Station and other sandstone landmarks like the University's Fisher Library, had by then become a man of property owning a row of rental terrace houses in Paddington – today worth well over a million each. He would present each of his four adult children with a block of land on the expanding fringe of Sydney where my mother would build our own family home in Punchbowl, but as late as 1946 when I was thirteen.

An angular marriage

But for my father - by nature a non-assertive and non-communicative man - entry into this circle must have been daunting indeed. I have no memories of ever seeing him in conversation with my grandfather. The social cleft between my parents was yawning: she identified with the lesser colonial bourgeoisie of self-made Scots. At the time, it was customary for such families to employ a domestic servant, whereas Dad's mother Gwyllimia had been brought out from Wales to Newcastle as a (Welsh-speaking) domestic servant.

I have no memory of anyone ever expressing any views on society or the world. But of course Dad was a worker *(=Labor!)* and my mother's family were *nouveaux riches*. I suspect he must have paid a high price for his appetising mess of pottage. In a street of 25 year-old houses whose children had long since grown up and departed, we lived an isolated childhood: I had never heard of sleepovers or even playing at someone else's home. Children of the day were supposed to be *"seen but not heard"*. We got the message. Early on I learnt not to talk about what was going on inside my head. Dreams were safer.

Yet if under-educated, my father was an intelligent man, with a wide range of general knowledge: a reader of history and archaeology and Australiana, with a love of bush ballads and poems and also of our native flora. He was an Australian patriot, in a bourgeois British household, unashamedly on the Left. In later years, I would recognise my debt to him: in temperament, range of interests, sense of humour, whimsy. Many of his mannerisms live on. Not to speak of his genes for tallness and slimness and good health.

Nevertheless, I consider my childhood experience to have been rather impoverished, with no firm role model put before us: no values enunciated, no commitments, beliefs, not much interest in my achievements at school. No one took the time to school us in life. Consciously observing others to gauge appropriate behaviours, I used to sense I had little to offer in friendship. Beset by self-doubts, small wonder I often tended towards a semi-paralysing pensiveness.

But what I did internalise was the motif of escape – on family excursions by motor-bike and sidecar, and later in the Chev 'tourer'. It brought my Dad a sense of independence, even power over his new connections: not one of them could drive. It also conferred on us the freedom to seek an ever-receding horizon: beaches, cliffscapes, bushland, mountains. And for me ultimately an appetite for exploration beyond the horizon. And of our impoverished culture.

The regular visits to Newcastle opened my child's eyes to the realities of social and cultural differences: between educated and uneducated, city and country, and how this affects life chances, especially in hard times. On the other hand, I loved what I used to think were the deliberately defiant grammatical mistakes made by the northern brigade in their homespun English: *"Where was ya all? I never seen yez. Who done that? He must of went early"*, etc. At home, I still use them whimsically for special effect: imitation the highest compliment!

Preserving an ethnic culture

The tangible link with our ethnic background – in the Australia of the 1930s with immigration running at its lowest ebb ever, indeed an almost forgotten dimension – was through the Dumfries & Galloway Society's social evenings, especially at Hallowe'en. With the red lion rampant on the yellow flag of Scotland, the singing of folksongs, lads and lassies dancing in kilts, the piping in of the haggis, climaxing in Rabbie Burrrns' *Auld Lang Syne*, stirring the whole assemblage to clasp hands and surge back and forth while ethnic emotions soared. Foundational stuff.

It offered an uncanny portent for my later years of Australia-wide research with the Immigration Department, recording migrants' treasuring of their ethnic cultural heritages – subsequently recognised as the elemental stirrings towards our national policy of multiculturalism.

In grandfather Hughan's mind, I was destined to become a draftsman. Probably it triggered my lifelong interest in architecture. Once he presented some unused architectural-drawing books for me to copy facades of classical buildings, and in his latest years he gave me books on the history and geography of Britain. Though pitched far above my nine or ten years, I read them all avidly, whetting my appetite for cultural exploration in Europe. Of the third generation, I would become the first member of the two migrating families ever to 'go home' to Britain.

The rest of the story is one of humanisation into a confident, expressive and sociable being, triggered largely by my early discovery of the Christian faith. I suspect the initial impulse arose from the kindness shown me by the other older member of the household, Thomas Breakwell, my mother's uncle.

He was a scholarly and well-read man, possessing a collection of impressive hardbound, gold-lettered books on science, astronomy and technology, as well as poetry and great works of literature. He was kindly to us children: he owned a microscope and a telescope through which on clear nights I remember gazing at the moon.

His personal motto, *'True as Steel'* is engraved within the glass of a very large, fragile goblet especially crafted for him in England, in order to preserve within a glass bubble in the stem the first shilling he ever earned. It is my most treasured heirloom and a precious memento of this rather remarkable man. He died in 1935 when I was three

He had been a great Congregationalist and a lay preacher. I perceive him now as a man of considerable depth and spirituality, whom I would later recognise as a 'grandfather in Christ'. His reputation as a strong Bible student – I still have his well annotated Bible – and his role as a lay preacher implied a commitment to a living faith in contrast to the nominalism of the Presbyterian household.

Doubtless he prayed over, blessed and shared children's hymns with the little boy who reputedly sang like a blackbird in the back garden. Probably hymns have imparted much of the theology that I have imbibed lifelong. I think it likely that Uncle would have prayed that I too might become a preacher, and in God's good providence this was to be answered – beginning with my amateurish attempts as a university student about 1951. But my incipient calling would need all of 50 years to evolve.

CHAPTER 4: A Forties Childhood

From Day 1 at Infants Schools I was captivated by a passion for learning. Soon words and numbers were appealing enough but my favourite lessons were history and geography, plus the British folksongs that we learnt to sing: the melodious *Danny Boy* and *The Ashgrove*, and *The Road to the Isles* with its opaque Scots dialectal terms. In particular, the first European navigators to explore the African, Asian and American coasts captured my imagination: Columbus, Jacques Cartier, Diaz, Vasco da Gama, Magellan, Torres, Tasman *et al*. The courage to go beyond what others had dared!

Our 4th grade classroom had a big upright teaching aid like a Punch and Judy show which, as you wound the rollers, would display a series of colourful paintings on canvas of some key scenes from Australian history. I can still picture the landing at Sydney Cove on 26th January 1788, with the spruce redcoats and the convicts under the gumtrees – and no Aborigines. Idyllic, even *triumphal* scene of our nation's beginnings – far from the brutal reality of hangdog convicts surveying with dismay their terrifyingly alien new prison, as far from their homeland as it was possible to go. Naturally I absorbed it all uncritically.

With the Second World War breaking out the year I entered Primary School, the fostering of Empire loyalty was accentuated. In the boys' assembly, there was a weekly patriotic ritual: gazing at our national flag (today's design but oddly until 1953 red, when schizophrenically it turned *blue*) we chanted: *"I honour my God, I serve my King, I salute my flag"*, vaguely waving a right arm near our forehead. I never quite got the point of it and no one ever explained

On 1st June 1942, war comes to Sydney, rudely awakening me in the small hours by the chilling wail of air-raid sirens. After all our practice at filing calmly into the covered air-raid trenches dug under our school playground, I feel a surge of excitement: wow! This is the real thing … and promptly go back to sleep. Next morning, we read of the first naval attack ever launched on an Australian city, by a Japanese submarine offshore shelling Bondi – leading to the evacuation to their ancestral Broken Hill of an unknown nine-year-old girl and her mother, one Marjorie McKee of North Bondi. Three mini-subs crewed by two men on a *kamikaze* (suicide) mission had penetrated the boom across Sydney Heads to make their way up (under) the Harbour and attack Garden Island naval base, killing 21 sailors and inflicting damage on naval installations.

Earlier in 1942, the Australian population had been traumatised by a Japanese bombing raid on Darwin, the first aerial attack ever launched on Australian soil. As would come to light only many years later, 1000 or more people were killed including many civilians. There followed some 100 further air strikes on northern Australia, including on Port Hedland and Townsville, crowned by the ignominious rout of the British garrison of Singapore which condemned our 8th Division to the hell of Japanese captivity as slave labourers building the Thailand railway, from which a mere handful of living skeletons would ultimately return. That event would spell the end of Australian reliance on the protection of the British Empire and mark the cultural shift of turning towards America for our national security.

But for a nine-year-old romantic, the incomprehensible horror is balanced by the grandeur of Elgar's *Land of Hope and Glory* sung in Marrickville Town Hall by the 'big girls' on the patriotic feast of Empire Day, 24th May 1942. An anthem from heaven – or the funeral march for an Empire tottering towards its deathbed?

Reconciled!

It would take all of sixty years before experiencing liberation from that hatred of the Japanese so purposively inculcated during our wartime education. As a patriotic Australian, unwittingly I had nurtured it all those years. And with good reason. In the tradition of the Knights of Bushido, hideous cruelties and merciless deaths had indeed been visited upon both the conquered and the captured: slave labourers, Western 'comfort women', work gangs of emaciated and half-starved POWs.

It happened one cold day during a brief stay in Hiroshima to visit a university friend now professor of English: a redemptive moment would embrace me. On the way back to his flat from the city, an old man sitting next to me on the near empty tram suddenly asked, *Was I an American?* When I said Australian, he mentioned the brave Australian soldiers he had fought against in the New Guinea jungles. Next (in clear English, a rare phenomenon in Japan), he asked me *Was I a Christian?* I said I was a Christian pastor, and he replied that he was secretary of the Hiroshima Baptist Church. *We were brothers!* The tram reached its terminus and we both alighted. We walked across to the footpath where, moved by an irresistible impulse – and most likely a very non-Japanese thing to do – I hugged him... For a long moment, we stood there intertwined while sixty years of pent-up hatred of the Japanese leached out of my soul. With a smile, we parted. He crossed the street one way and I the other. At the same instant, we both turned to wave to each other, before I stumbled off in tears. Liberated! *Reconciled by the blood of the Cross.*

Opportunities for creative learning

Back in 1942, towards the close of 4th grade our class had been visited by a roving band of IQ testers from the Education Department's head office, who had us racing through long sheets of simple logical, sequential, numerical and verbal questions to see who could finish first and best. The winners were subsequently nominated to leave the school and undertake 5th and 6th grades in regional *'Opportunity C classes for academically gifted children'.*

But that same year, with fears of a Japanese invasion impending, the sudden death of grandfather Hughan brought my world crashing down around my ears. We moved out of the house into which I had been born, to the bushy southern outskirts of Sydney on Port Hacking where my parents had managed to buy a Spartan 'weekender'.

In the Opportunity C Class at Hurstville catering for the Illawarra line suburbs, besides the usual though accelerated curriculum, we also undertook a range of creative learning experiences favouring the 'project method', researching topics in our specialised library, and visiting community facilities ranging from a Municipal Council meeting to a glass factory, as well as attending matinee performances of light opera and a symphony concert. Despite our boyish cheerfulness it was the depths of the Second World War, with Australian servicemen dying in New Guinea and the Pacific islands. In Europe, during our time in 6A1, the momentous 'D-Day' landing on the beaches of Normandy on 6th June 1944 would usher in the final drama of the war against Nazi Germany.

Wartime austerity measures would prevent any observance of our 'graduation' from primary school, but our teacher was kind enough to buy me out of his own pocket my prize as Dux of the Class of 1943-44, a boys' adventure novel. They had been stimulating years, triggering the development of a measure of self-reliance and self-confidence (partly through the significant daily travel involved). They had vastly expanded my horizons, symbolised by the view out into the Pacific Ocean beyond the Botany Bay heads clearly visible from our top-floor classroom, beckoning me to serious encounter with a world beyond the classroom door. But maybe above all, at a time when the 'civilised' world was tearing itself apart in a frenzy of hatred, they were (unwittingly) preparing me for the venture into 'otherness', to be later embodied in foreign language learning, including the tongue of the erstwhile enemy.

Suburban life in the Forties

Unwittingly, we stood before a watershed triggered by the 2nd World War. Before long a social and technical revolution would sweep away our comfortable old world. In the streets, the millennia-old role of the draught horse for shifting loads was already giving way to the motor engine. Before the advent of supermarkets and the family car, much of our daily food and drink was brought to the door. Our daily bread was delivered from a two-wheeled, horse-drawn baker's cart. Likewise with our milk, poured directly into our 'billy' from taps at the back of a cart. But the ice man would deliver the large block for our 'ice-chest' by a motor-van – for the ordinary household, refrigerators were quite unheard-of. Hence our food purchases daily. And our fruit and vegetables would be bought straight off the back of the fruiterer's lorry. Vendors never came to the door, so you had to listen for their distinctive cries around the same time every day, when a little knot of immediate neighbours would emerge to buy their needs. On weekdays, our mail would be delivered to the letterbox mornings and afternoons by the postman walking his beat, and weekly leaflets mysteriously appearing in our letterbox would inform us of the offerings at the two local cinemas.

Encountering the world of music

At seven, I was enrolled in a violin class held after school in a local hall, and took to the experience eagerly. After about 18 months, I was selected in a small group to participate in the popular weekly *Youth Show* broadcast on the Sydney commercial radio station 2GB. At nine, time to move up – to Mischa Dobrinski, a Polish Jew who taught violin to up-and-coming musicians. He was a small man, brass-bespectacled, with a heavy accent but kindly manner. I can still savour the pungent but heady reek of central European cigars. To a nine-year-old romantic, irresistible – my first enticing hint of Europe.

After a year or so, the maestro had me playing Handel's *Largo*, Schumann's *Träumerei*, Mendelssohn's *Auf Flügeln des Gesanges (On Wings of Song)*, Rubinstein's *Melody in F,* plus *Stephanie Gavotte* and *Czardas*, not to mention Boccherini's challenging *Violin Suite in C*. Already I was falling in love with the melodies, the moods, the colours of a world of music opening before me. The sheer pleasure of making music was being imprinted on my soul. Indeed, I find it virtually impossible to write the story without the inspiration of FM radio now playing classics in the background.

Adventures by tram

By no means the least of my memories of that era was the romance of travelling alone by tram to music lessons in the city at the tender age of nine. Often, we would wait interminably in Broadway for the policeman on point duty to wave us on, after heavy four-wheeled 'drays' full of beer barrels emerged from the brewery, drawn by two huge draught-horses with long hair around their ankles. To serve their thirst, water troughs were placed at the kerbsides near strategic spots around the city and along main roads, often through the bequest of some humanitarian. In the industrial zone near the city, ancient steam lorries were still occasionally to be seen, cumbersomely puffing along on solid rubber tyres.

Before long I was experimenting with alternative routes home via other combinations of tramlines, exploring suburbs unknown. Compared to Melbourne, Sydney trams were born archaic because of their primitive design. In the most ancient type, dubbed 'jumping jacks,' passengers could even sit in the driver's cab. Somewhat less ancient, though of the same impractical design, was the commonest type of tram – universally known as 'toastracks' – with two open-air compartments at each end (and pull-down blinds against pelting rain) and six closed ones in-between. With no central corridor, you couldn't move from the compartment you opted into on boarding.

So how did the 'conductor' collect the fares? He had to be a trained acrobat balancing on a narrow running board flanking the tramcar, set lower than the floor level, and sidling along poking his head into each compartment in turn, plaintively querying *"Fez, please?"* and then pulling individual tickets off their butts in a leather-bound folder with one hand and giving people change, the while hanging on for grim death with the other. Ten years later, one of our fellow students at university who gamely took on a holiday job as a tram conductor was knocked off his perch by a truck in his first week. I was surprised his career lasted so long.

The trams featured a visual destination panel at front and rear incorporating geometric patterns of crosses, squares, circles or panels in contrasting colours for the different regions, while for those who could read, the destination was also written discreetly below. At least you could identify your tram coming from a long way off! At the terminus, you might be lucky enough to catch the driver winding the destination reel backwards, flashing through all the psychedelic designs. Together, the five non-connected Sydney tram networks were said to form the largest system in the world.

'Austerity for the duration'

At the height of the War with Japan in 1942, food was strictly rationed, requiring coupons authorising the purchase of meat, butter, sugar, and tea, and also for clothing and petrol. Every family was issued with coupons that needed to be surrendered to the retailer. Only after the American GI's went home at the end of the War did I get my first taste of chicken, strawberries, and cream. But though it did trigger common allegations of black-marketing, rationing didn't seem to hamper our modest lifestyle. It also led to the frequent appearance on the backs of cars of large, cumbersome 'gas producers' fuelled by briquettes of coal. Rationing would continue until 1950, a full five years after the War ended. In fact, antagonism to this austerity regime (fair and responsible as it still was during the post-War commodity shortages) was to become an important factor in the exasperated election of the long-term Menzies coalition government in 1949, led by the Liberal Party he had newly founded. This occurred in the last week of my school career.

Shopping before supermarkets

At the age of eight or nine, after school I would be despatched 'up the Hill' by Mum to buy things for dinner or for school lunches next day. From the butcher in his navy blue-and-white striped apron, moving around on his freshly laid sawdust, I would buy short loin chops or undercut blade steak, thick beef sausages or mincemeat – butchers never prepared ready-to-cook dishes but blazed away with their terrifying meat cleaver laying into sides of mutton (cheaper than lamb) or beef. Pork was off the menu because of American army tastes. From the 'cake shop' a large jam roll, a square of fruitcake and half a dozen iced cupcakes, perhaps eked out by some pikelets. Then to the 'ham and beef shop' – to pick up thick-sliced corned beef, or occasionally the dearer ham, but more often slices of fatty 'pork fritz' or even the terrible speckled brawn with its cow parts and jellied bits. Finally, to the greengrocers to pick up things overlooked when the old fruit and veg. lorry had lumbered down Challis Ave. In those unsophisticated times, we had never heard of the later innovations: kiwifruit, avocado, broccoli, eggplant or zucchini as well as the more exotic berries. From time to time, I would also pick up from the chemist's some patented medicine in which my parents put great faith, far cheaper than a doctor's visit plus a trip to the Marrickville Friendly Societies' dispensary – or sometimes pay the bill at the 'paper shop' for delivery of the stuffy *Sydney Morning Herald* with its front pages consisting of nothing other than small classified ads – the news didn't start until about page 5!

Other shops 'up the road' included a couple of chain grocery shops (there were several such chains across the country, like Derrin's or Buttle's or Moran & Cato's), a fish shop, a drapery, a haberdashery, a milliner's, an ironmongery, the 'produce store' (for bulk potatoes, pumpkins, grains, sugar), a stamp & comic shop cum small lending library (I doubt that public libraries existed in suburbia), and a 'lolly shop' marketing itself as a trendy new 'Milk 4d Bar'. These had only recently made their appearance, based on a glitzy American model with mirrored walls reflecting a counter where 'milk shakes' were produced by small mixing machines using flavours like vanilla, chocolate, strawberry, banana, lemon *et al.*, overseen by the typically Greek shopkeeper. They cost four pence (4d) – perhaps a whole five cents today!

The age-old era of the specialist trader was still the norm, and the employees prided themselves on providing personal service based on expert knowledge: an older cousin spent his life as a grocer with Derrin's. This meant that, still in the infancy of capitalistic dehumanisation, the word 'supermarket' hadn't yet been coined, let alone 'shopping mall' – and certainly there was no off-street parking – nor chains of franchised fast food outlets (a world without McDonald's!) nor even 'convenience stores'. Indeed, this American synonym for 'shop' was not then in general use: they were all simply 'shops' specified by what they sold.

Of course, in our shopping we used paper bags, cardboard boxes and cane baskets. Plastic only appeared after the war, so many products like flour and sugar and oatmeal came in bulk. 'Takeaways' barely existed except for fish and chips which were wrapped in plain white paper. Pizzas were unheard-of except in Italy. Soft drinks only came in glass bottles, returnable on receiving a penny, and drinking straws were made of paper. Aluminium cans and plastic bottles would only make their appearance in the 1970s, but the notion of buying water in bottles would have been derisory: what's wrong with the tap?

And tea only ever came in china cups. Everyone drank it numerous times a day but not, I might add, made from teabags – also then unknown. In all but the veriest cosmopolitan, blue-ribbon suburbs like Vaucluse with its recently arrived Jewish refugees from Nazism, the coffee shop was unimaginable. In the absence of the coffee habit, across the length and breadth of Australia a Lygon-street precinct could not have existed. Of course, there was no such product as instant coffee. Not until university days would I first get to taste coffee – and at first shied away from its bitterness.

I doubt that there would have been a single restaurant (of any cuisine or none) in our Marrickville-Dulwich Hill area. What was wrong with the dinner table at home? Besides, in the evenings all the shops were shut! And what could 'cuisine' mean: we all simply ate 'good Aussie fare' – was there any other? Curiously, twenty years later, when the concept of eating at restaurants began to take hold, the commonest cuisine would become Chinese (Cantonese, actually). I guess my first restaurant meal ever – well into married life – would have been Chinese.

On the other hand, reflecting dour union struggles, trading hours were rigidly controlled: 9 to 5:30 weekdays plus Saturday mornings with everything closed on Sundays. And, of course, organised sport on Sundays, in all codes and forms, was unthinkable. Sunday was sacrosanct as family day and, at least in the middle-class suburbs, a day for worship, for many both morning and evening. The Old Testament concept of the Jewish Sabbath largely maintained by the Protestant Churches was still a factor, albeit increasingly shorn of religious considerations, but still a useful concept for defensive campaigning by the unions. Even today the fight to preserve penalty rates of pay on Sundays is still being fought, though victory for the employers is looming. But already in my later childhood, the anti-sectarian (read anti-Christian) forces were mobilising: ere long their day would come when we too would 'go cosmopolitan' (in the 1950s still a dirty word). But like their counterparts in Catholic Europe where the 'continental

Sunday' was the norm, with shopping, sports, festivals, entertainment, cinema, etc, the local Catholics were never into the vestigial Protestant Sabbath. We found them 'worldly' (a derogatory term).

Shape of the future

The most visible outcome of the simpler diet of plain fare was people's shapes. Very few were overweight, particularly among men – as is the case in China today, with its no-sugar diet. Gyms and health studios were unknown, unneeded. Through my entire schooling, I cannot recall more than one boy who was overweight and he was cruelly dubbed 'Fatty'. On the other hand, our diet was infinitely healthier: simpler and more wholesome. Chemical additives were unknown. Cows and pigs and chickens ('chooks') roamed free on farms (or in large pens); in that age family farms without much mechanisation were the norm, rather than the industrial-scale food factories of today. And by the way, toilet paper was unknown in our home: what else were out-of-date newspapers useful for? Besides, you couldn't read toilet paper.

Safe streets

From eight to ten, I was roaming freely around Dulwich Hill alone, walking a good kilometre home from Sunday School and church. For haircuts (short back and sides) I used to walk to a little shop where the worldly-wise barber, a great talker, treated me like the sensible young man that I was .... This may sound like irresponsible parenting but at the time parents wouldn't have given safety a thought: there was no fear of public interference with children. Certainly nothing was ever mentioned to me about children being kept off the streets. Whom to fear? Of course, we'd all heard of Hollywood gangsters and crooks, but in the 1940s fear of children being molested on the streets of Sydney cast no shadow over our lives. Perhaps this fact alone encapsulates the extent of the social revolution in today's permissive society (permissive for whom?).

The 1940s media

It would be decades before television would put in an appearance. Apart from music ABC Radio ('on the wireless') brought three news bulletins daily and also projected the insights of experts in many fields. From the early 1940s, I rarely missed the creative *Argonauts' Club* for older children on weekday afternoons, presented by professional actors, artists and musicians, each projecting an amiable persona, educating by amusing and stimulating. There were serial dramatisations of children's books, each day with its own cultural focus: on music, art, literature, writing, music. Those who formally joined the Argonauts' Club were allocated the place of a 'rower' in one of the named boats engaged in Jason's *Search for the Golden Fleece* from ancient Greek mythology. I was 'Arethusa 13'. Rowers who distinguished themselves by the quality or profusion of their literary contributions gained the 'Dragon's Tooth' or the lofty 'Golden Fleece' awards. (Only in 1969 would the *Argonauts' Club* succumb to the allure of television with its deceptive genius for passive spectating). From 1944 Gwen Meredith's midday family serials, *The Lawsons* and later *Blue Hills* (set near Canberra), would establish records for longevity by enduring for thirty years.

But our family didn't limit our listening to the stately ABC: we were also connoisseurs of serials broadcast around dinner-time on weekday evenings by commercial radio stations. *Firstlight Fraser* did exploits behind the enemy lines in Nazi-occupied Europe, *Dad and Dave* immersed us in the joys and struggles of farming in Snake Gully, *Mrs 'obbs* (my favourite, oddly presaging our Broadmeadows experience 'alf a lifetime later) brought to life the streets of Redfern and the bumbling efforts of a (presumably Christian) welfare do-gooder, Mr Bundle, while *The Search for the Golden Boomerang* actually evoked Aboriginal life in the Dreamtime – but safely removed from the tragic actuality of Aboriginal people, then expected to oblige us by soon dying out.

The commercial radio programs would be punctuated by incessant advertisements e.g. the first-ever jingle, *"I love Aeroplane Jelly, Aeroplane Jelly for me"*. The *Amateur Hour* featured competitively selected aspirants singing, playing instruments, doing comedy. Another evening *The Quiz Kids* would test their wits by answering questions submitted from the public. Evening drama programs acted by professionals drew huge listening audiences. As for 'pop music', the term hadn't yet been invented, nor celebrities, nor touring bands, nor live concerts, so all the music came from breakable vinyl records played on the studio gramophone. Occasionally, ragtime and Dixieland jazz would be heard but not yet 'swing music' later played by the Big Bands. Weekly 'Hit Parades' were canvassing the top songs emerging – by then England was mired in a fight to the death with Nazi Germany. I well recall *When the lights go on again all over the world* and *There'll be bluebirds over the white cliffs of Dover* and even the Germans' favourite *Lili Marlene* and during the years of the war against Japan *Johnny got a Zero* [shot down a Japanese Zero fighter plane]. As I write I am humming their well-remembered tunes (unlike contemporary pop songs) all eminently hummable.

At Canterbury High School

Canterbury was one of Sydney's nine academic high schools for boys, based on selective entry on merit. It drew on about 25% of the metropolitan area (socio-culturally the least endowed sector), but had produced more than its share of significant figures in public life: academics, leaders in education, medicine, science, national heroes in cricket and tennis – and later a prime minister, John Howard from Earlwood. At the beginning of the 1945 school year, as we newcomers waited anxiously in the 'playground' I was surprised when my name was the first one called out: for Class 1A, to be mostly made up of Hurstville boys.

The magic of languages

High school would open up an unknown world of learning as well as spurring on earlier interests. In a day when cohesion was highly esteemed, we were proud to wear the Canterbury High uniform of grey suit and shirt with red, blue, gold tie, the school badge embroidered on the breast pocket. The school song was original and creative, its words and music attributed to a former music teacher. We also learnt the traditional German student song in Latin *Gaudeamus igitur, iuvenes dum sumus*[2]. In addition there was a 'war cry' of rhythmical but euphonious gibberish reserved for the annual combined high schools athletics and swimming carnivals at the Sydney Cricket Ground and North Sydney Olympic Pool, when it would be lustily chanted after a victory.

From day 1 the discovery of foreign languages held me captive. I took to them like a duck to the proverbial. Unwittingly I had found the love of my life. Everyone learnt French and Latin, and from second year I also took up German. I seemed to have a head for the limitless storage of words, organised in new frameworks compelling in their elegance. Particularly was this true of Latin, with its rigorous structures of five 'declensions' of nouns and four 'conjugations' of verbs with their endless variations marking case, gender, number, tense, voice and mood – not to speak of the subversive irregular verbs. But really, I never did comprehend how anybody could have spoken that long-dead language at normal speeds when every second word had to be mentally plucked out of its pigeonhole, dusted down and adjusted in multiple ways before tumbling out! Did they have computers for brains?

Over the next five years, we wended our way through the complexities of the Latin words themselves, learning both *'accidence'* (the discrete systems of noun-endings and verb endings) and *'syntax'* (how they all interact to produce meaning), i.e. grammar. It was a sort of linguistic algebra. In addition, in third year we were looking at the actual Latin text set for the public Intermediate Certificate exam: historian Cornelius Nepos' account of two foreign heroes from earlier ages, Epaminondas from Thebes in ancient Greece and Hannibal, Carthaginian military genius who led his army (with elephants!) across the Alps to inflict the most crushing defeat in the Romans' centuries-long history. In fifth year for the Leaving Certificate we studied the thoughtful and elegant treatise by the greatest of Roman writers, Cicero, *On Old Age* (highly relevant to teenage boys! Must look at it again now...).

---

[2] 'So let us rejoice while we are young'. I still recall the four Latin verses.

With the modern languages, as competent as the teachers were, we never saw much evidence that they could actually speak them. So, we were never trained in accurate pronunciation, though probably I had a fairly good ear. I actually enjoyed learning lists of words from the Block Vocabularies, in subject categories (geographical, culinary, etc.). I well remember with a friend cobbling together a sentence from words recently acquired: *'A short-sighted, lame horse-stinger eating whortleberry jam'*[3] – undoubtedly a reliable conversation starter. The only native speaker was a rotund elderly Swiss teacher of German whose English was far from perfect, larded with a thick accent.

But the initial encounter with the structure of the languages, as well as the memorising of vocabulary, would become the merest tip of an iceberg. A whole new world was opening up – initially of linguistics, unfortunately at the time a discipline unfamiliar to the teachers because not taught in Australian universities

But foreign language study (especially of German, taken up only five months after the war ended) was also seditious of the eternal verities embodied in the concept of Empire: *'British and best'*. Of course, *our* language was the norm for the human race... And patently, white men ran the world because they were superior to lesser breeds without the law. Yet within the white race there were also gradations, from upper-class Englishmen (the gentlemen) down through their brash American cousins (discounting the coloureds), to Scandinavians and Dutch, then a big step down to the Gallics, Italians and Hispanics, and lower still to the Greeks, Slavs and Eastern Europeans. Naturally Middle Eastern *wogs* and *gypos* were beneath contempt. As for the Germans, by their political choices they had irredeemably fallen from grace – though destined to be reinstated ere long.

Beyond language – culture

But more: the encounter with the foreign raised the concept of culture – and in wartime Australia spawned the unpatriotic notion that there was more than one worthy culture in the world, let alone the unthinkable theory of cultural relativism. Language study offered a

---

3 Un taon borgne et boiteux, et qui mange de la confiture d'airelle'. We had actually acquired all these useful words!

fleeting glimpse that English was just another language, in fact at the time spoken by less people than many a Chinese or Indian language. It was the time before the worldwide hegemony of English, a time when the language of international diplomacy was still French.

Further, learning the language of a foreign people elevated the concept of peoplehood (today's ethnicity) above nation or economy – an ultimate blasphemy in a fractious world of politically-nurtured nationalisms. Of course, at age thirteen none of this was clear to me but an inchoate scepticism began sneaking into my mind: *what if...?* Could peoplehood be more significant, more human, than nationhood? After all, wasn't French also spoken by Belgians and Swiss and Canadians? And German also by Austrians and Swiss?

It seemed curious that the underlying aspects of linguistics never got a guernsey, such as any inter-relationships existing between the three languages I was learning – and of a possible common origin – or how and when Latin evolved into French, or how Latin was actually pronounced (we were taught the 'German' pronunciation). Again, in Latin we learnt little or nothing about the mentality of the ancient Roman world – rather less than I'd picked up from the Scriptural portrayal of Pontius Pilate and of governors Festus and Felix. Nor virtually anything about the day-to-day life of the Romans. Maybe as a safety measure, the teachers remained fixated on the language textbooks – or were they just plain uninspired?

But away with such retrospective musings! In 1945 I was 12, revelling in school, uncluttered by any dream of a future beyond the next homework assignment. At the first half-yearly exams, I came first in English, (Ancient) History, French and Latin and overall first in the Year. So, the transition to high school had gone smoothly. It was a similar story at the end-of-year exams, which opened up the prospect of choosing German or Classical Greek instead of History from then on. Paying a reluctant farewell to history I opted for the Modern Languages rather than Ancient Greek (which I would later take up in evening classes in Canberra).

Betrayed!

But in my first year at Canterbury a traumatic episode befell me which long had me puzzled. Making for Hurlstone Park station as a class group one afternoon after school, as we passed the small park under reconstruction in the hollow beside Crinan Street, without warning I was set upon by a gang of my fellow Cantabrians. Hoisted up bodily, I was carried across to the lowest point recently filled with deep grey mud transported from the dredging of the nearby Cook's River – and unceremoniously dumped into it! To the accompaniment of great merriment as they ran away. I can't recall how I got home by train dripping in stinking grey mud. Nor who was involved in the prank – though all my continuing friends foreswear any memory of it. But I retained a vestigial sense of betrayal by my classmates, and never did I work out their motivation: obviously dislike, but on the grounds of my demeanour? A smart alec, insufferable? Or too clever (by half)? Certainly, it did nothing for my wobbly self-confidence or capacity for trusting others. But lifelong, it would prove the only episode of violence suffered at anyone's hand.

State aid

After the Intermediate Examination at 15, beyond which most students would leave school, my parents were advised that I had gained a bursary to cover the last two years of study, granting them a modest monthly payment and me an amount for supplementary textbooks (though these could not assist me in learning to *speak* the languages). Besides, at that period of total Anglo-Saxon hegemony there was no one to speak to – native speakers (especially ancient Romans) being thin on the ground – so languages served merely as a window on a wider world.

For the final years of schooling, besides the compulsory subjects, I chose the three languages in which I regularly excelled – and also often in English. At the end of each year, I had mostly come out top student overall.

On the threshold of manhood

But by 5th year a flickering sense of *'life is real, life is earnest'* was creeping into our collective consciousness. We were approaching the age when, four years earlier, young men hardly older than us were killing and being killed in the name of our country. Already the 'cold war' between East and West was warming, with the Korean War brewing and the prospect of reintroduced universal conscription at 18 (as in the final years of the war).

In our coterie two reactions were a growing recognition that, if we were to play our part in the exciting reconstruction of a more peaceful world, we would need good results in the looming Leaving Certificate in order to bring higher study within reach. And also, the broader God question: in such a world did Christian faith have anything to offer?

Late in 4th year I had become aware of a student initiative, the Inter-School Christian Fellowship meeting in a classroom at lunchtime, but I felt torn between a pang to link up with it and loyalty to my erstwhile pagan mates. By then I was aspiring to become a 'real Christian'. It was the period when at Punchbowl Methodist Church I was earnestly groping towards a personal faith – seeking to ground the Sunday faith half forgotten by Monday! Actually in 5th year some of my mates began to attend the meetings sporadically, and later they would all become practising Christians.

It was a time when overseas preachers were again being invited to Australia and local prophets like Alan Walker were emerging, a noted Methodist preacher and social reformer (for example, against the White Australia Policy). A bold initiative was the invitation to the German pastor Martin Niemöller to tour Australia to foster reconciliation between erstwhile enemies. In the First World War, he had been a German U-boat commander but during Hitler's régime a founder of the anti-Nazi *'Confessing Church'*, for which he had spent years in Dachau prison.

Mugged by reality

Late in 4th Year I had decided to attempt three Honours at the Leaving Certificate – at a higher standard assessed through a further exam, offering credit towards university scholarships, though more commonly attempted in maths and science. I opted for the three foreign languages. I had come to see being top student as my birthright rather than a personal achievement. Yet I under-estimated the scope for maths and science students to gain higher (even full marks) for their efforts, inconceivable for linguists.

But the Leaving results amounted to a severe mugging by reality. After five years, in the top class only two scored an A in English! And I was not one of them, though in the Trial Leaving having come near the top of the Year in the subject. For all five years, we had endured the one slothful mentor more preoccupied with writing for a vulgar Sunday paper than imparting to his students a taste for literature and poetry. In fact, we had *never* had a poetry lesson! The sorry deficiency has haunted me ever since: I still have small 'feel' for literature, and was to forfeit its potential for life-education.

Accessing university study

But I gained first class Honours in French, coming fifth in the State rankings, and in German twentieth – though the first fourteen (to judge from their names) were native speakers. In Latin, I gained second class Honours. But a student doing Honours in Maths and Science who had never been top of any Year, by gaining Honours in both these subjects and high marks all round, would become Dux of the School. Pipped at the post!

However, there was another factor: on meeting my counterpart linguists at university the following year, I was astonished to learn that throughout Fifth Year their high schools had offered (gratis) after-school tutoring for Honours students. I had never had five minutes' tutoring in any subject! Had to do it all off my ear!

In retrospect, the uninspired quality of the teaching received in those early post-war years, whether from the time-servers or the traumatised, may also have reflected our country at large. War over, time to relax now, plenty of jobs around, no migration, no cut-throat competition, the world owes us a living. God is in his heaven, Bob Menzies in the Lodge, all's well with the world.

Nevertheless, my exam results did win me a free place for a three-year Arts degree at Sydney University (an 'exhibition') plus the offer of a four-year scholarship for high-school teaching from the State Education department, with a generous monthly allowance. In exchange for this I was obliged to sign up for five years' teaching service. No other way could I have attended university, the first to do so from both sides of my migrating clans. It represented an *entrée* to an entirely unknown world of ideas and to unattainable sectors of society: at the time only 3% of school leavers went to *the* University.

Ironically, the very next year the Commonwealth Scholarship Scheme would be inaugurated: able students could now gain the same benefits without being bonded to an employer! But what working-class kid would have declined the unsolicited offer, not only of a tertiary education but also of a lifetime career? Of course, at barely seventeen I had scant idea of who I was, let alone what I might become. In any case how many people achieve their dreams? In retrospect, I have no regrets about how my lot was cast. Unwitting to me then, a divine Shepherd was leading me into green pastures.

CHAPTER 5:
Long Day's Journey into Light

About the age of five I had been enrolled in the Dulwich Hill Presbyterian Sunday school by parents who had never set foot in church since their wedding day. Perhaps my godly Uncle had encouraged them to enrol me. Memories are unreliable: kind ladies 'teaching'. Boys mucking up. Music and song: *Jesus Wants me for a Sunbeam*. Praying with palms pressed together. Bible stories: *The Good Samaritan*.

Primal flicker of faith

In the absence of a Presbyterian church, our move to Dolan's Bay at 11 had introduced me to the Methodist Church, a small timber building on a bush block. But unlike the Presbyterians, Methodists were not an ethnic church, stemming rather from a revivalist and social reform movement within the 18th century Church of England, and still reflecting that blend of head and heart of John and Charles Wesley's fervent preaching in the fields to miners and day labourers, and also their commitment to the poorest and imprisoned. The leading Australian Methodist was Dr Alan Walker, a latter-day prophet.

At 11, my teacher had invited the four boys in his Sunday School class to a camping weekend in the Royal National Park: the first night I had ever spent away from the family. In the evening sitting around a campfire in the pitch-dark bush – pure romance – we heard the Gospel explained in simple terms, concluding with the first invitation to faith I had ever heard. When invited to respond personally I said 'Yes'. Although not clear at the time, it was the inchoate beginning of a lifelong pilgrimage, but its significance lay in its focus on the interior life of faith rather than the catechetical approach of traditional religion or mere churchgoing. It marked the embrace of the theological camp of experiential religion rather than propositional truths. God is there not only to be believed, but to be known. Whole denominations have taken this distinction as their *point de départ*.

Moulded by church life

In 1946, when I was 13, we had moved from our temporary quarters at Dolan's Bay to the brand new house at Punchbowl built on the land gifted long before by my grandfather.

By then my brother and I had developed a loyalty to the Methodist Church. At Punchbowl, the Sunday School was populous and well organised. We worked our way up the grades, politely listening to untrained but well-meaning housewives and kind gentlemen leading us through the printed syllabus materials, absorbing a good deal of the teachings.

For the next eight years during the crucial developmental period, the church would become the cradle for a growing Christian identity. Then in its heyday, with modern brick buildings and about 200 members, as well as worship it offered the large well-structured Sunday School and a plethora of organisations for men, women, children and youth. In my young adult years, I rarely missed a Sunday service, morning and evening. To belong to such a church community was a holistic, life-shaping experience offering much in all areas of life: spiritual, social, educational – even physical. In Punchbowl Methodist teams I played cricket and soccer in the Sydney-wide church competitions, winning a couple of premiership 'blazers' with embroidered breast pocket. It brought my first real contact with older men, offering a model of Christian manliness.

Christian 'prac work'

Another formative factor was involvement in an optional extra, a 'Christian Endeavour' society, meeting for an hour prior to the Sunday morning service, led by a respected layman. A multi-denominational training organisation for serious-minded young Christians, the CE (motto *'For Christ & the Church'*) had been established in America in the late 19th century by a Congregational minister, and by the early 1900s it commanded public attention across Australia: in 1907, Prime Minister Joseph Cook spoke at a State Conference in Adelaide. It was worldwide, mainly in the Free (non-Anglican) Churches, operating at various age grades: ours was intermediate. But by then its fortunes locally were in decline.

The meetings were virtually conducted by the young members themselves, introducing hymns, doing Bible readings, leading prayers, reading out self-prepared 'papers', all focused on the topic of the day, perhaps 'Thanking God'. My memories of it are congenial. In a people's church like the Methodist perhaps it served the purpose of ensuring transition to the next generation of lay leadership. A serendipitous outcome for me was gradually building up a working knowledge of the Scriptures and something of the history and cultural backgrounds of the ancient Near East.

Among my sharpest memories are of the music that characterised every meeting. We sang the informal songs with all the fervour of new converts seeking to internalise the faith that they projected. A further benefit of CE was to be part of a wider para-church entity balancing the Methodist emphasis with contacts across the Churches. There were district and city-wide 'rallies', sports tournaments, as well as excursions and harbour cruises on public holidays.

Moment of decision

Of ultimate significance, at 16 I went with the CE society to an evangelistic meeting in Sydney Town Hall, conducted by an American Jewish convert in the pre-Billy Graham era, Hyman Appelman. A barrister and academic gifted for evangelism who ministered worldwide, it was his first (maybe only) Australian tour. There was a choir singing fervent songs, soloists, and then the rousing address by the preacher. I can only remember the text of his sermon *"The Spirit and the Bride say 'Come' ... and whosoever will, let him take the water of life freely"* (Revelation 22:17) – fifth last verse of the Bible. When he made the appeal, urging people literally to 'Come' to the front of the huge crowd, I felt impelled to respond – not to him, but to Jesus offering lifelong friendship and eternal salvation. Not that I understood its theological significance (far from it) but I sensed the divine authority under which the evangelist stood and the imperative to allow control of my life to pass to Jesus. *"To all who received him, who believed in his name* [= claims?] *he gave the right to become children of God ... born of God.* It was my first conscious step on the long day's journey into light.

Joys of fellowship

Christian Endeavour continued to influence my growing understanding of the life of faith. Once a month we were encouraged to go to Wesley Youth Fellowship in the city's Methodist headquarters. It was the great 'Saturday night out' event for young people of the Church (Methodists were known for not dancing, smoking or drinking), but never having experienced any of these lures we loved its vibrancy, informality and fervour. We would hear (often remarkable) 'testimonies' of people's everyday encounters with God. There was always an inspirational speaker from horizons broader than the suburban, such as a missionary amongst the Aborigines or working in Tonga. It was my first encounter with the wider Church and this I found exhilarating, affording glimpses of an all-embracing vision: a Kingdom-oriented life.

With good companions and a growing sense of identity, what a privilege it was to be alive at that optimistic and idealistic time, amidst the growing comforts of post-war Australia and safely remote from the tensions brewing between the power blocs of the northern hemisphere.

Internalising ethical living

Initially, it had been through Christian Endeavour that the rudiments of ethical behaviour had first been encountered. Prior to that I had subconsciously followed my mother's (lapsed-Christian) injunctions about respectability – though doubtless honoured as much in the breach as the observance. Personal commitment to a pattern of ethics had never occurred to me nor, I suspect, to most of my school friends. Certainly, this dimension was never hinted at by our teachers in State schools, primary or secondary. Even in our weekly 'Scripture' classes the visiting denominational clergy seemed coy about suggesting ethical principles or morals. A sharp contrast to the rigorous catechism and ethical training in Catholic schools. In retrospect, I fancy this reflected the effete, liberal Protestant theology of the times expressed in 'take it or leave it' attitudes. But shorn of any commitment to experiencing God inwardly through repentance and faith, much Protestant teaching at the time might actually have verged on the sub-Christian, hardly worth carrying into adult life.

From 4th Year at 15 I developed an involvement of sorts in the Inter-School Christian Fellowship. I would marvel at the self-possession and confidence of the two leaders in publicly asserting their faith. But in the absence of students willing to take the reins, in 5th Year I found myself more involved, if rather diffidently. Oddly enough, encountering an old school friend a few years ago, I would be astonished to hear about my 'courageous witness' encouraging him in his subsequent Christian walk.

More significant was it to be invited to take part in Sydney-wide advisory sessions for ISCF leaders in the city. Probably for the first time I was discovering the possibilities of real friendship based on deep, shared interests transcending the patterns of background and temperament.

It would only be later in university circles that the ethical foundations of Christian behaviour would take shape, firmly linked to the authoritative role accorded the Scriptures. By then we were also exposed to the 'holiness' teachings of the original Wesleyan movement, updated by reports of the remarkable east African revival and the heroic commitment of missionary societies such as the Worldwide Evangelisation Crusade: living by Christian morals results from the indwelling Holy Spirit rather than systems of ethics. Of course, for me internalising this would prove to be a lifelong process.

CHAPTER 6:
Embrace of the Alma Mater

In the 1950s, an appealing portrait of Sydney University framed by the Port Jackson figs of Victoria Park could be glimpsed from the tram descending City Road. In the middle distance, cresting the grassy slope, loomed the Gothic Revival façade of the Arts Building, evoking a sense of ordered tranquillity. Founded in 1850 it is Australia's first university.

Orientation Week mid-century

Certainly, it impressed the excited 17 year-old Fresher setting foot for the first time in his new *alma mater* during Orientation Week of 1950, midpoint of the 20th century. As you passed through the Arts Building's wide portal under the clock tower with its Gothic gargoyles and carillon, the first glimpse of the spacious, part-cloistered courtyard with its manicured lawns quickened the pulse.

Around the perimeter of the Quad with its sacrosanct lawns and lone jacaranda were stalls crewed by older students spruiking the virtues of their multifarious societies and canvassing new members: Sydney University Dramatic Society, SU Musical Society, the Speleological Society, the Jewish Students Union, the Labor Club, the Anarchist Society, the Psychological Society (and likewise for every discipline taught), the German *Vereinigung* with its folk-singing group, the *Société Française*, the Newman Society (Catholic), the Student Christian Movement (liberal Protestants), and the Evangelical Union – not to mention the 'Sydney University Union' to which all (male) students belonged by virtue of their enrolment.

With its own suite of buildings, this august institution best marked the transition from school to university, bridging a community of scholarship, staff and students by servicing their diffuse needs like a gentlemen's club. At that time women were excluded, having to settle for the minimalist amenities of the Women's Union at Manning House.

With its range of ivy-covered buildings, the Union boasted some exotic amenities – the Buttery and the Bevery, the outdoor Pleasance, with the Union Theatre offering cinema and opportunities for would-be thespians to strut the boards.

At the Evangelical Union stall, I recognised some other freshers from the ISCF leaders' meetings, and forthwith signed up as a member of SUEU. On the back, the membership card laid out the commitment of *"acknowledging Jesus Christ as my Saviour, my Lord and my God, and accepting the Bible, in the languages originally given, as the Word of God, sufficient for guidance in all matters of faith and life."* As such, it stood in the succession of the Methodist Church, the Christian Endeavour, and of course the ISCF/Scripture Union, as well as historic university counterparts at Oxford and Cambridge. It was the only form of the Christian faith that I had ever encountered. Unwittingly, in linking up with the EU I was tacitly enrolling for the initial training towards my ultimate profession, beyond teaching and community education.

Delight in learning

The NSW Education Department allowed us freedom to choose our own courses, so naturally I opted for French I, German I, and Latin I in first year – and revel in the language study I certainly did! To a romantic soul, a source of endless delight was the classrooms' location in the original 1862 building. The German room was particularly charming, high up in the top storey, its opaque Gothic windows set in leadlight diamonds – and with rows of antique wooden benches bearing the carved names of the illustrious nobodies who had preceded me. I didn't feel worthy of joining the honour roll. Besides, 1950s men no longer carried pen-knives.

The Latin class met in a corner of the cloistered quadrangle building, offering Catholics the chance of developing prowess in the language of the Mass. Some may have become priests and nuns, I imagine. As unbelievable as it sounds today, it represented my first contact with Catholics, objects of my family prejudice. Though there was scant incidence of building Christian relationships across the prickly divide, I did make friends with a fellow-commuter who was also a teacher trainee. Together we picked our laborious way through the cynical Odes of Horace, Juvenal's devastating satires on the vices of his fellows, and Lucretius' riveting treatise on metaphysics. What carried the day for me was the window afforded onto an ancient world, marked by cruelty, greed and ruthlessness, with hints of democracy foiled by treachery. Only in antiquity?

Germanic affinity

A warmly human environment, the German I class was spiced by the presence of several Jewish girls who, but for the prescience of their parents, must have perished in the Holocaust. Understandably, at university they weren't interested in their oppressors' language (mother tongue though it was for them) so that I often scored higher in my translations. But of course, neither did they spend a whole long afternoon in the Fisher Library laboriously cobbling together the foreign text – instead of reading the set novels. We were making the acquaintance of a people and a culture as well as of a language.

Although not yet five years after the War ended, there was no sense of it being unAustralian to study the enemy's language. The links with German language and culture were strong enough to retrigger the normalising of relations in Australia. And before long, German would be heard spoken around the regions of the Snowy Mountains Hydro-electric Scheme, sometimes as a *lingua franca* between workers from opposite sides of the conflict.

But after all, English was a Germanic language with a kindred feel, the language of everyday mediaeval life spiced with learned terms from the Norman conquest. The language of Queen Victoria's household was still German, and our long-reigning Queen Elizabeth II, a great-granddaughter of the Duke of Saxe-Coburg Gotha, married a Battenberg whose uncle had discreetly reversed his name to Mountbatten. Certainly, Nazism was a monstrous aberration which had spawned an appalling and bloody nightmare in which 20 million people had died, but 'Nazi' and 'German' were by no means obverse and reverse of the same coin.

A humanising touch

Unlike in the French department, where the purely literary emphasis was unrelenting, some minimal efforts were made by the German lecturers to engage students in practising the spoken language. At the examinations we had to recite a poem or some other text to a native speaker: once I did the 23rd Psalm *Der Herr ist mein Hirte* and another time a Romantic nature poem.

Kulturgeschichte (cultural history) was presented by a real Baron who looked like a cultural relic himself: tall, thin and aristocratic, with old-world manners and charm, a living examplar of cultural history from pre-Nazi days. He lectured in an elegant German, slow enough for budding linguists to follow, and writing all the esoteric terms on the board. He traced the outlines of German history, from the Germanic tribes doing an Asterix by defeating the Romans in the battle of the Teutoburg Forest – thus forever precluding the eastward expansion of the Roman Empire in northern Europe – to the ill-starred Weimar Republic brought down by Hitler's *putsch*. All perceived through styles of art and architecture: Carolingian, mediaeval, classical, baroque, romantic, rococo, Biedermeier, impressionist, expressionist – but drawing the line at Nazi brutalist.

A secret longing

And what of actually using the language? After four years' school and three years' university study of German I had acquired a wide vocabulary, I knew all the grammar and the strong verbs, I could read most texts (including those in old-fashioned Gothic script, beloved of the Nazis) with a good measure of understanding and even write competent, if stiffly formal German, but I *could not conduct a normal everyday conversation* – unless my partner had the patience of Job. Same story with French. The heavy literary emphasis quite precluded any practical use of the languages for communication. In me this triggered a secret longing to 'make it' as a competent speaker of both languages. It would become a sub-theme of my later life.

For French, it would not be attained until the age of 75, during my lone safari to France when for weeks I spoke no English while staying with hosts connected with an international friendship network. But in the case of German, the goal would be attained a good 45 years earlier during the year of teaching in a State Grammar School in Minden, Westphalia.

Gallic rigour

Though my French studies were longer (from Day 1 at high school) they held scant social relevance. You never heard the language spoken. Ironical when you think of our being sacrificial allies of the French in the Great War, while the Germans were implacable enemies in both wars. But having their own colonies, the French never migrated to Australia.

Yet from the outset I had found French an enticing language, sufficiently different from English in grammar (reflecting its Latin origins) to offer a challenge, but not too seriously, since it shared an immense common vocabulary. Its difficulty lay in grasping the meaning of the *spoken* word, given the breakneck speed with which words tumble out, fusing into an opaque torrent of sound. Yet since there seems to be no other way of understanding a language than by recognising individual words, it requires close concentration to separate them out. As to aping this speed in replying, it called for more practice than I could manage, given the dearth of native speakers.

The professor, an austere figure, would rattle off a literature lecture in French, some of which on a good day we could understand. He had two assistants, one of whom was a real Frenchman, whose role it was to give us a weekly *dictée* to teach us phonetics – and break our spirits! With no conversation classes, French studies assumed a terrible rigour. We would often spend a whole afternoon in 'Fisher', surrounded by massive dictionaries and books of contemporary French usage, wrestling with a translation into the language, perhaps an extract from a recent English novel – a herculean task except for professional book translators. When we got the 'fair copy' it would so far exceed our imagination as to crush our spirits. The challenge was certainly character-forming.

Over the three years we studied periods of literature: the classics (Molière, Corneille, Racine), the romantics (Chateaubriand, Rousseau, Hugo, Dumas), moderns (Balzac, de Maupassant, Verlaine), and contemporaries (Camus, Mauriac, Giraudoux). The trouble was that I had neither the background in literary appreciation (in any language) nor a French reading speed capable of wading through large tomes. In the end, I developed the tricky expedient of reading them in English translation in the NSW Public Library. It sufficed to get me through the exams each year. For shame!

Was it the human quality of the professor and lecturers that made German more appealing? Or something subtler about the two nations and their cultures, conceivably bound up with underlying religious values. The French ethos was very Catholic (of the old school, prior to the *aggiornamento* of the Second Vatican Council of the 1960s), at that time quite alien to me, though less so now in an ecumenical world, while the German spirit, partly born of the Protestant Reformation, seemed more accessible. Not insignificant has been our link with a German Methodist family in Minden now surviving into the third generation. Despite worshipping with the *Eglise Réformée* in Paris in 2006 and also attending a cosmopolitan service in a packed Temple Pentecôtiste, it is still German devotional life that resonates with my spirit. And it has always been a delight to address German-speaking migrants in their own tongue.

New era looming

But the end of an era was impending. In the immediate post-war years, the Labor Government of Ben Chifley, heeding the trauma of near-invasion by the hordes to our north and the resultant cry of *'Populate or perish!'*, had created a Department of Immigration with offices in Australia House in London, to tempt Britons to our sunny shores. It would be the dawning of a new era of immigration that continues to this day in ever-increasing intensity, but now drawing from the whole world – while ruthlessly (and illegally) rejecting those desperate enough to essay the crossing by makeshift boat.

Of course, in those student years I could have had no inkling that the training I was receiving would, in my subsequent life, relate not so much to school teaching as to the broader societal task of nation-building through immigration, with all its latent cultural challenges. This migration was to bring about no less an outcome than the transfiguration of Australian society from colonial to cosmopolitan, and of Australians from self-conscious Anglo-Celts to people confidently reflecting the world of the nations. And in God's good providence I was destined to have a meaningful role in it.

Birth of a dream

Already dreams of travel beckoned: the intensive focus on Europe from eight years' study of its languages, living with Scottish exiles yearning for 'home', plus the urge to flee a rather dysfunctional family. But beyond these idiosyncrasies there was also the ambivalence shared by not a few young professionals in the 1950s, reflecting a distaste for the Menzies-era colonial/conformist society, in all the manifestations of its cloying predictability and physical ugliness, and bent on trying themselves out in a more sophisticated context while drinking at the Elysian fountainhead of European culture.

One golden evening coming home from university I recall something of a tawdry epiphany, as our commuter train was overtaken by an express straight out of *Every Boy's Book of Trains*, steaming off grandly into the westering sun, bound for some exotic destination like Mullumbimby or Murrumburrah. The first twinge of incipient *Reiselust* hit me. At that moment could I sense that in the not too distant future, I would be on the maritime version of that express – and ultimately destined to circle the globe?

But not before indulging my passion to breach the horizon by hitch-hiking to student conferences in Geelong, Strathalbyn (SA) and Indooroopilly (Qld). Once on a stifling day in the heart of the trackless forest of the Victorian alpine region, on a little-used road, I would experience a last-minute rescue from the approach of a terrifying bushfire.

CHAPTER 7: Student Daze

In my first year at university I read a foundational article by an English don on 'the idea of the university'. He traced the historic notion of the university as a community of learning, engaged in the pursuit of the good, the true and the beautiful – exchanging ideas freely, thinking critically but creatively, fostering curiosity, reflecting lucidly but arguing cogently, transforming the self in the interests of producing passionate citizens marked by an appreciation of nature, art and intellectual rigour. And keeping alive the memory of the great wisdom of the past

It was confidently expressed in the elliptical Latin of the university's crest *Sidere mens eadem mutato* ('The same mind under different skies'). But beyond this aspiration is the moulding of the liberally educated professional, whose integrated faculties are brought to the service of the community.

In its mediaeval origins, the focus of scholarship was the study of creation in all its plenitude including humankind and its Creator. Hence theology was the queen of the sciences and the ultimate professional was the theologian, in an integrated universe (hence *universitas*).

Not exactly what we encountered at Sydney in 1950 – but not utterly alien to it either, at least in the Arts Faculty. Of course, in our foreign language studies we simply pursued the 'good and the true and the beautiful' through struggling with the original words of great philosophical and literary figures like Goethe and Schiller, and Pascal and Rousseau.

University tribes

Under the southern cloister of the Quad, a permanent fixture was the cluster of scruffy-looking philosophy students doing the above (minus the theology), but animatedly and noisily. It was the heyday of the terrible John Anderson, scourge of God as philosophy professor, a controversial Scotsman who reputedly set out to destroy the faith of any student believer who crossed his path. Nevertheless, there were some robust philosophy students among the membership of the Evangelical Union. One of the Quad's student politicians would become head of the World Bank, James Wolfensohn, while Sylvia Lawson would become a significant literary figure.

My rather pathetic contribution to exchanging ideas freely and arguing cogently was in debates with members of the SCM (Student Christian Movement), held to be more intellectual but less devout than EU members. Perhaps what linked us EU members (many of us not yet career-oriented) to the great tradition of the European university was taking the claims of theology seriously by asserting the centrality of Christian ideas. In the great tradition of the philosophers of Mars Hill in ancient Athens: *'All the Athenians and the foreigners who lived there spent their time doing nothing but talking about and listening to the latest ideas'* (Acts 17:21), some of us Arts students and demagogues were as engrossed in our pursuit of God as in our studies. In a sense, without knowing it, we were struggling with that ancient university tradition of relating to God as the centre of his integrated universe.

As overblown as such a claim may sound in today's world of pressure-cooker study courses and the primacy of finding a niche in a globalised world, I believe it was true for some of us then. On the one hand in those rosy post-war days there were few external pressures on us. The Education Department had no contact with those of us on teaching scholarships unless we failed a year in the exams, in which case we would be summarily relegated to the dreaded Teachers' College – in the university but not of the university.

On the other hand, the majority of my fellow-students (including some of the Christians) were from the leisured classes or at least people of assured means. Best known were the 'social butterflies' doing physiotherapy, allegedly to entrap a medical student. Of course, we young men were also known to pass the odd insightful quip about the nubile Christian nymphs abounding on every hand - a veritable epiphany after the long drought of school years in single-sex institutions!

World within a world

In the 1950s, the Sydney EU was perhaps the largest and most active of student associations, with a membership of some 500 scattered across the ten faculties. It was led by older ex-servicemen studying under a Commonwealth re-training scheme. They could speak credibly and with authority about their faith tested in their years in the Services. The president in 1950, Dudley Foord, would become a Bishop in the church in South Africa and the following year's leader, Warren Adkins, ex-RAAF with a Bible College diploma, had an amazing grip on the Scriptures and their devotional power.

The EU weekly program was intensive: a daily prayer meeting at 8:30am in the Latin I room; a weekly public outreach meeting one lunch hour attended by a hundred or more students brought along by their Christian friends and featuring an outstanding invited speaker; and Bible Studies for the members led by some of the best Scripture scholars in Sydney. They laid the foundations for my growing and systematic understanding of the Faith.

The weekly public meeting sought to provide a socially engaged apologetic for the historic faith, but slanted to the contemporary post-War West with its rationalistic scepticism, to which the Gospel offered a balance by appealing to both head and heart, meeting deep emotional needs as well as proffering a sound theological edifice. The analogy of a deeply moving symphony comes to mind.

An informal though central function of the EU was to link evangelical students from many denominations, possibly for the only period of their lives which, in the pre-ecumenical era, were destined to be lived out entirely within one denomination, and maybe within one parish (the original meaning of *'parochial'*). I remember students who were Anglicans, Methodists, Baptists, Church of Christ, Salvation Army, Presbyterians, Congregationalists, and Plymouth Brethren. It was the era before the advent of Pentecostalism. But labels were irrelevant. The oneness in Christ within the evangelical (Reformation and Puritan) traditions was tangible, albeit with the wisecracks and witticisms inspired by the labels. On the other hand, we were consciously schooled by the national IVF[4] leadership to be conscious of the historic evangelical distinctives which were seen to be closest to the heart of God (doubtless a card-carrying evangelical).

The EUs were seen as a training ground for future church leaders, and indeed numbers of us (all men, of course) were later ordained to the ministry. I suspect that I was the latest of them all, at the age of 55. But probably I learnt as much about the ways of God from EU members as from the formal teachings. Some of these students, albeit unconsciously, truly incarnated the Gospel and sixty years later we are still in contact with at least 13 of them, some of them lifelong friends. Their influence and ongoing friendships have indelibly marked our lives.

Liberating friendships

Enduring friendships were birthed in the weekly life of the EU and around the Quad, but particularly at the 'house parties' during the university vacations, when some 30 of us would spend a few delightful days in the bushy surrounds of Sydney. For me the liberating experience was to be able to relax in mixed company, across gender and social class, and to sense that I belonged – and even feel I was popular, maybe fun to be around.

In my third year, I was elected to the EU committee of about 10, as Prayer Secretary – ironical in retrospect, since I had little idea of what it implied, other than reminding people and attending lots of prayer meetings. Romantic though, the opportunity of roaming pastorally around the large campus to consult and communicate with members across the ten Faculties. What Arts student would normally experience the horror of a half-dissected human amid the laconic comments of future medicos?

---

[4] The Inter-Varsity Fellowship National Parent Body of the Evangelical Unions in Australian universities, based in Sydney

Global perspective

In September 1952, our committee organised a residential Missionary Conference at Thornleigh at which some leading figures on the world missionary scene outlined their work in Africa, China and the Middle East. The heroism of their purpose-driven lives made a profound impression on us all, particularly that of the most outstanding, Norman Grubb, author and leader of the Worldwide Evangelisation Crusade, whose practical saintliness deriving from his intimacy with God opened new possibilities for the Christian life. Several student participants in the conference experienced it as the pivotal moment of their lives, and went on to serve overseas as missionary doctors, teachers, preachers and Bible translators. One became the world head of a mission network in the south of Sudan, instrumental in forming the Christian character of a nation recently freed from oppression of the Arab/Muslim north. Though for the next six years my own path was prescribed by my teaching scholarship, the ultimate option of full-time service for Christ never quite faded.

A frequent emphasis of the visiting Bible scholars at EU meetings was the theme of God having a perfect plan for every life, to be progressively revealed through our daily walk with Christ as we opted for God-oriented choices. Seek that purpose! Obviously in those days of preparation for our professional careers this focus was very strategic. But we also heard the admonition that *'the cares of this world and the deceitfulness of riches'*, as Jesus himself had warned, had the capacity to bring many people undone in their faith. The universal appeal of greed. In later life, we had the sad experience of witnessing the truth of this gloomy prognostication in the lives of some of our erstwhile colleagues. This challenge I have never forgotten and at several points along my way have been admonished to take it to heart, with due regard for the power of the dual snare.

But how different the experience of a close friend from those days, Warwick Davies, who early forsook civil engineering to become a Methodist minister and whom we visited in hospital some years afterwards where he was dying of an incurable illness. He described how he had been pronounced clinically dead (though not brain dead).

To my obvious question of *"What's it like to be dead, mate?"* he replied with verve, *"It's great! I was approaching these magnificent gates into a glorious garden but as I was about to enter they began to close. I longed to go on but felt myself being drawn back. Now I'm looking forward to going on into that beautiful place"*. Not long afterwards he did.

Prophetic moment: first contact with Chinese

At the prompting of the national leadership of the Evangelical Unions, a number of us responded to the missionary challenge of befriending the first south-east Asian students coming to the university under the government's new Colombo Plan – future élites literally on our doorstep. I began a lifelong friendship with a science student from Indonesia, Oh Wie Tat who, though not a Christian, readily joined in with some of the EU activities, including participating in the vacation house parties.

Years afterwards I was to attend his wedding with an Australian-born Chinese in Sydney's St Mary's Cathedral. We remain good friends. He and I share a common (though actually very uncommon) mania for grammar and foreign languages. With a doctorate in science, he speaks his provincial Chinese mother-tongue, plus Mandarin, Indonesian, Dutch, English, also German and French and – Turkish!

Mid-century Mission

Our student days coincided with the great 'Mission to the University' of 1951, an ambitious SUEU project jointly planned with the IVF headquarters, focusing on a week of lunch-hour public meetings in the University's largest Lecture Theatre, where the Missioner, Dr Rev. Howard Guinness from the UK spoke on the Gospel passionately and compellingly, as also at an amazing array of 'subsidiary meetings' for the various faculties and subject areas, designed for members to bring along friends to hear the Gospel explained and reasoned about.

The Mission proved a memorable week or more, marked by a number of public conversions, including of a self-proclaimed agnostic who later became a professor of theology on the staff of the United Faculty of Theology in Melbourne when I was studying there in the 1980s.

Howard Guinness, godly scion of the Irish whisky family, was a medico turned student evangelist: the Australian EU's had originated from his preaching tour in the 1930s. In the 1950s, he moved permanently to Australia to become rector of St Barnabas' Anglican church on Broadway, closest church to the university, and an honorary chaplain to students. I saw him as a sort of latter-day Jesus of the Western imagination, tall and straight, with dark hair and piercing blue eyes, and of a commanding presence that I had never encountered, before or since, dispensing authoritative biblical truth in his clipped Oxford accent. *(Jesus was like that, wasn't he?)*

Encountering Anglicanism

One Sunday evening each month we would attend a 'University Service' in his remarkably shabby inner-city church. They were the first Church of England services I had ever attended. Though fumbling with the printed liturgy of the venerable *Book of Common Prayer* (1662), I found it an appealing variation from the trite 'hymn sandwich' of Methodist worship. As something of a linguist, I marvelled at the dignity of the language in the *Magnificat* and the fervent prayer of Simeon *("Now lettest thou thy servant depart in peace, for mine eyes have seen thy salvation...")*, the mellifluous Collect (prayer of the day), the imperious Creed and the richness of the Benediction. On the other hand, it had never occurred to me before that hymns were still being written. After all, the *Methodist Hymnal* was a closed canon. I was entranced by the power and simplicity of a modern text set to the Londonderry Air *('Danny Boy')*:

> *"I cannot tell why he whom angels worship*
> *should set his love upon the sons of men ....*
> *...*
> *But this I know, all flesh shall see his glory,*
> *and he shall reap the harvest he has sown,*
> *and some glad day, his sun will shine in splendour*
> *when he, the saviour, saviour of the world is known.*

CHAPTER 8: Joining the Real World

Marjorie McKee and I had met during our first year at university. We had a good deal in common: Welsh/Scottish extraction and working-class origins, both 18. Diminutive, with fair wavy hair and inner glow, she was full of *joie de vivre*. Both involved in the EU, we spent a lot of time in groups of mutual friends – having lunch on the front lawns (the Union Refectory was for the wealthier), endlessly chattering about study and life. Though both doing Arts, we had no subjects in common. She was doing English, History, Psychology and Geology, and after graduating, went on to a post-graduate Diploma in Social Work while after language studies I was exiled to the Teachers' College to do a Diploma in Education.

It was the year when the mantra *Life is real, life is earnest* began to seep into our consciousness. Now on the verge of attaining our majority, it was time to address the novel idea of actually earning a living. I focused on acquiring the skills of teaching languages and Marjorie on the insights of social work. To my surprise my practice teaching sessions at Sydney Boys' High School were to gain me one of the few A grades awarded to my cohort of teacher trainees in any subject that year, and Marjorie's study results scaled even loftier heights.

Because our lives were so parallel and our paths crossed so often there was no need to conduct a romance by 'going out together' – spending money we didn't have on creating 'occasions'. Maturing individually, we were also growing together as our lives took on more and more common content. She was also elected to the SUEU committee, while the national leadership of the Evangelical Unions appointed me as chair of the Sydney Teachers' College EU committee, an error of judgment since I was not leadership material. My feeble efforts met with little success, though I blundered through. At the end of the year I was appointed graduate assistant at Muswellbrook High School.

Military glory

But not before being conscripted for three months' training for military service in 1954 (with the 'Cold War' brewing), already deferred for years because of my student status. By then, being four years older than my fellow conscripts, I quite enjoyed the *camaraderie* that traditionally makes military life bearable. Indeed, stationed at Ingleburn south of Liverpool, life was *almost* enjoyable because my platoon of 25 or so were all university students. Providentially (?) – since I was in the process of contemplating Christian pacifism – I got to avoid the last of the three months of training through breaking an ankle in that most heroic of military struggles, the inter-battalion cricket match, when the raised edge of the concrete wicket precipitated me into the ground while bowling the game's opening over – and into the nearby army hospital! I would finish the training period limping around as an Amenities Officer with the Christian chaplaincy organisation that humanised camp life, to the derision and envy of my mates. In each of the following three years as I moved to Muswellbrook, Wagga Wagga and Queanbeyan high schools I would complete several weeks in the bush doing military manoeuvres with three different but equally heroic regiments.

The joys of teaching

My five years of teaching French and Latin bore out the initial promise, conferring the joys of sharing my new-found language insights and identifying with the students. After one year, out of the blue transferred to Wagga Wagga High School I landed on my feet teaching French and Latin in the A classes to some very talented young people, several of whom would later become nationally known figures.

On Marjorie's graduation, at the end of 1955 we both opted to move to Canberra, where she took up her appointment as *the* social worker for the whole population of the national capital of some 35,000 people. Since there were no modern language teaching vacancies in the Canberra schools, I was appointed to Queanbeyan High School where I taught French (and later Latin) for four years. Initially we resided in spartan hostels for single public servants near Civic Centre, and on 15th

December 1956 the knot was tied in Sydney at Penshurst Methodist Church. We became the first residents of an apartment within a new complex close to Civic Centre and Reid Methodist Church.

The world lay at our feet!

CHAPTER 9: Launch of an Odyssey

Some three years later, having honourably discharged my five-year bond with the NSW Education Department, the old dream of overseas travel would resurface. During the later years I had also undertaken further language studies in the evening at Canberra University College, then a branch of Melbourne University, with advanced Latin, two years of Classical Greek, and one of Italian. My vision was to plumb the life as well as the languages of those exotic lands, with the aim of becoming fully equipped to teach Classics as well as the two modern languages. Through the good offices of my Greek professor, an English gentleman, I was offered a position in modern languages at the King's School, Ely, not far from Cambridge.

Shipboard life

In July 1959, we joined the excited band of would-be expatriates on the good (though tiny) ship *Fairsky* which brought Italian migrants to Australia on its outward voyages. Soon the brilliant tangle of multi-coloured streamers linking the ship to the shore would be cruelly torn – symbolising the wrenching asunder of the light hearts of the departing adventurers and the heavy hearts of parents and family left behind. *Farewell*, Australia! *Hello*, world!

The next six weeks were to become a heady brew of excitement, flashy entertainment, experiencing the exotic – and ultimately boredom. We literally ate our way to Europe. The world's a big place with a lot of remarkably similar sea to watch, punctuated by the odd leaping shoal of flying fish. But the tropical nights on deck were magical, warm and moist and salty, with the fluorescent waves sliding past to leave a broadening wake of foam astern under the blazing stars.

Some like me would hover alone by the rail, awestruck, unwilling to break the spell and pluck ourselves away to re-enter the tawdry human world indoors, in the air-conditioned lounge-bar with its supercharged, alcohol-fired jollity and its Neapolitan rhythms. And wondering if we were doing the right thing by deserting our family and our country.

While I had never said it to Marjorie, in my heart I pictured myself not as a pleasure-seeker doing 'the overseas trip' but as a serious emigrant likely to spend many years – if not the rest of my life – in Europe. My whole Eurocentric focus demanded it. The stultifying Australia of the 1950s offered little competition! Already, the best and bravest were getting out, later to become a veritable 'generation of expatriates' like Germaine Greer, Clive James and Rolf Harris, disillusioned with their boringly predictable homeland where the fusty Liberals looked like reigning forever – while asleep at the wheel.

First contact with the foreign was disturbing. In Colombo, it was the raw challenge of entering a non-Christian holy place: an ornate temple with a massive, gold-clad squatting Buddha and saffron-garbed monks bowing at the reeking offerings of incense and fruit. In my head, I had no categories to file it under, other than the familiar Old Testament denunciations of idolatry. Coming from an Australia at a time when the only traces of non-Christian worship would have been the few Jewish synagogues, an old Afghan mosque in Adelaide, and a neglected Chinese josshouse in Melbourne (none of which I had ever seen), it brought me face-to-face with the issues posed by the reality of a world of many faiths.

Far out in the Indian Ocean we fell foul of a tropical monsoon with a Force 8 gale. Patrons for the elegant continental meals shrank to a few cast-iron-stomached or super-greedy, albeit looking a little pasty around the gills. I was among them. The diminutive *Fairsky* gave a very fair imitation of gyrating like a corkscrew, not only rolling (sideways) but also pitching (fore and aft) – the dual causes of seasickness.

All homage then to our gutsy ancestors migrating south on slow and fragile sailing ships. Actually, many migrated direct to Davy Jones' locker, including those on the ship out of Liverpool before my maternal grandmother's, as family legend has it.

European landfall

After a brief pause at Aden, sun-baked and shabby, then up the Red Sea to the Suez Canal – punctuated by a coach-trip to Cairo to marvel at the priceless treasures of Egyptology – we made our European landfall at Naples. We took the opportunity to check out the archaeological site of ancient Pompeii – the first ever practical application of my Latin. A few days later, from the ship nearing the dock at Southampton, we gained our first impression of England. We had arrived in a Toytown of Lego blocks.

It was like beginning life all over again. We had come, not as tourists doing the standard European tour, but as 'British subjects' from overseas bent on succeeding in our professional migration. In the few weeks before term started, we 'did' London, entranced by the picture postcard familiarity of it all: the world's most powerful hub of commerce, power and influence, steeped in history. With the perfectly cast stage characters. Bobbies, Beefeaters, bowler-hatted bankers, elegant *dames* with peaches-and-cream complexion, jaunty Cockney street vendors, tarts and spivs, all set against the backdrop of red double-decker buses and black taxis and entrances to the London Underground. *London!*

CHAPTER 10: "Hullo, Cobber"

In good time for the start of the school year we reached Ely by the British Rail express *The Fenman*. We found it a unique 'city', 170km north of London, England's smallest. For the last few miles we had watched the Cathedral looming ever larger against the billiard-table horizon. Originally a small island in a region of marshes (the Fens) abounding in eels, it had been the last refuge for Hereward the Wake's resistance against the Norman Conquest. In the 7th century an abbey had been founded on the island by Saxon princess Etheldreda and the Cathedral was built from the 12th century. In the 17th century, the Fens had been drained through new canals flowing *above* the rich agricultural lands.

The King's School lays contested claim to King Edward the Confessor (c.1020) being its first 'old boy' – making it probably England's oldest *Public* (i.e. private) *School*. Yet we couldn't identify anything remotely like a school, nor locate any sign. Nevertheless, all around us was the School, charming and discreet, in heavy disguise.

Puzzled, we reported in at the Headmaster's House, to be ushered into the study of a classical 1930s figure, a tall, dignified, pink-faced, silver-haired gentleman, ramrod straight, who greeted us in a cutting, almost satirical Oxford accent. (Did we respond *"G'daaay"?*)

Well disguised, the school was scattered among mediaeval monastic buildings fraternally propping each other up beside the Cathedral. Entrance was by way of The Porta, a large, ancient gatehouse to the Abbey. Of playgrounds, there were none!

But across the street was a 15th century stone cottage destined to become our family home. Soon we were installed at 5 Silver Street – a quaint winding alley straight off a chocolate-box – in an utterly captivating stone cottage with foot-thick walls, tiny windows and front door giving right onto the street – and up a perilously broken-edged spiral stone staircase to the bedroom with its dormer windows and alarmingly undulating floors. Downstairs was the living room with open fire and the kitchen, with an ancient bread oven set within the huge chimney wall. Outside was a pocket handkerchief garden. The house had been near derelict until laboriously restored by the Cambridgeshire Cottage Improvement Trust: we were the first beneficiaries. With the birth of Sara-Jane Elise we had become a family and Marjorie had taken on a challenging new dimension of her caring profession.

Encountering a new educational culture

Our first year in Ely saw us clambering up a precipitous learning curve. At virtually every encounter a social or linguistic pitfall lurked, made all the trickier by our appearing to be plausible young Brits. But apart from being sundered by the same language, we had limited common discourse with our peers, little shared experience, no awareness of the times that had shaped them, especially the War. And they had little interest in us. In fact (a broad generalisation), early on I concluded that the *higher* people rated themselves on the social scale, the *less friendly* were they towards others, particularly colonials. While of course such experience awaits anyone migrating to a new society, the fact was that I had come to teach others, and was expected to model behaviour appropriate to a school conscious of its place in the rigidly class-structured society. It raised the scary prospect of being unmasked as a charlatan or worse, a despicable *arriviste*.

But my apprehension about being inadequately prepared for teaching in such an august institution faded as I discovered that, despite their MAs from 'Oxbridge', all the masters had only a first degree in arts, science or divinity. Moreover, only about three of the staff had any formal teacher training, since the 'inspired amateur' was considered more appropriate to a Public School. But I discovered that two of the younger masters, who became my friends, had a *grammar school* background (élite 'state' schools) plus a Dip Ed – suppressed in the school prospectus!

Colonial apprehensions

But we were ready learners, and game as Ned Kelly. Early on I overcame the dread of turning out to be an incompetent language teacher. How dare an Australian from the wrong side of the globe pretend to be competent in the language and culture of a country a mere 40 km offshore? Let alone of the powerful enemy nation that some of my fellow-teachers had only recently been fighting!

But these fears soon turned out to be unfounded. The saving grace was the English (and particularly the educated classes') proneness to disdain foreign peoples and their languages. A little racial superiority goes a long way: in 1959, they were heirs of an Empire populated by lesser breeds outside the law. It was non-U to take other tongues seriously: *let them learn ours!* And whereas I had shrunk from the prospect of teaching French to rich kids whose families probably spent every summer on the Riviera, I soon learnt that most had never set foot outside England – indeed some barely beyond their own county! So there was little interest in, let alone any feel for foreign languages and cultures – *"The wogs begin at Calais"*, you know.

On the other hand, I came to appreciate that we had been well schooled in modern languages at Sydney University, and especially in approaching French pronunciation through phonetics, rather than simply relying on our mimicking ability. I taught French and German to Year 10 students, sitting for the 'O' level of the General Certificate of Education (GCE) and also to smaller groups at 'A' level (Advanced) leading to university entry. But I judged my classes to be below the ability level of the top classes at Wagga High School. For me a vainglorious innovation: in the classroom, we wore our academic gown every day – though beware of the doorknobs conspiring to rip the gown apart to the merriment of the students!

What of the students?

The chief criterion for entry to the School was not intelligence nor performance but the ability to pay. Strictly speaking, KSE was an *East Anglian* boarding-school with a 'day-boy' component, totally composed of comfortably-off descendants of the original South Saxons. We gathered, however, that East Anglia is considered as something of a rural backwater. Car ownership was rare, even by masters at the school. Our next-door neighbours had never been to London!

But as befits their breeding as sons of gentlefolk, the boys were universally respectful, even of a colonial. However, Christian names were universally shunned. I hardly knew any. My nickname Cobber was good-natured, as an honorific in Australia. Mostly my Australian-ness became irrelevant as my accent faded *(if a language teacher can't work on his accent, who can?).*

Patterns of school life

Being a boarding school, to me the weekly routine was novel. Mondays, Wednesdays and Fridays we had a full day of lessons, with a longish break after lunch, resuming from three until five-thirty – in winter pitch dark. But on Tuesdays, Thursdays and Saturdays teaching was only during the mornings with 'games' in the afternoon – never termed 'sport' *(too 'state')*. The first XV played *ad hoc* inter-school rugby fixtures arranged by invitations from the 'masters' (never 'teachers') to 'worthy' schools in the region. An organised competition would have seemed vulgar, and soccer was only for the lower orders. Every master was expected to take an interest in games. Being cricket master, I had no duties in winter. Groups headed off with designated masters to the School's hockey fields, tennis courts, athletics track, the boatshed on the river Ouse for rowing, or for cross-country running. [Today the School has its own golf course.]

Living conditions for boarders

KSE was divided into four 'Houses', three of them literal buildings and the fourth a virtual concept, the body of day-boys ('Oppidans'). The two oldest Houses were part of the original monastic precinct, quaintly mediaeval, though cheerless and uncomfortable. I would become associated with School House as associate master. Its dormitories with undulating bare floorboards each accommodated 24 boys. It is now claimed to be the oldest continually occupied dwelling in Europe! On midwinter nights, the boys reported snowflakes swirling about *inside*. Certainly, it was acquiring an alarming lean towards the narrow street outside, then frequented by double-decker buses.

Ely's magnificent Cathedral

The School is overshadowed by Ely Cathedral, since 1109 seat of a bishopric covering Cambridge and surrounding areas. Begun by the Normans soon after the Conquest, it is in Romanesque style (with round-topped arches) supplemented by a central section rebuilt in 1322 in Gothic style to replace the collapsed central tower. This 'Octagon Tower' is the glory of the cathedral, and one of the boldest feats of early English architecture: the wide octagonal space opened up by the fall was bridged by the vertical construction in stone, crowned by an interwork of massive lead-sheathed oaken beams supporting the Lantern Tower. Thanks to the Cathedral Choir School (the junior section of the King's School) the Cathedral often features in the BBC Christmas broadcasts.

But the King's School Chapel is a stunner. It is the Lady Chapel of the Cathedral and is the largest and most ancient school chapel in Britain, beside the chancel, but built later in Perpendicular Gothic, conveying an extraordinary sense of light and space. Its entire walls are decorated with niches where life-sized carved figures stand – every one of them decapitated or defaced by Oliver Cromwell who lived in Ely.

Every school day began with a service of Morning Prayer attended by the entire school and led by the School Chaplain. But the Anglo-Catholic worship style was new and alien to me, so my random attendance was more out of duty than desire. Once in the common room I overheard an offhand remark passed by the School Chaplain: *"Thank God, we've almost overcome the Reformation".*

Instead, we chose to go way downmarket, worshipping on Sundays with the Plymouth Brethren in a tasteless little chapel in Littleport, the next Fen village. After all, we were not Anglicans nor ever would be – *ahem* ... Two of the families would become our closest English friends, to this day.

An Australian critique

Towards the end of my first year, I was invited to write a piece for *The Elean* magazine about my antipodean impressions of the School. Outlining my childhood dreams and patriotic wartime aspirations, I went on to sketch some initial impressions of the School: the charm of its mediaeval buildings, and the more advanced level of senior studies, reflecting differences in curriculum and teaching style, and concluded,

The essential freedom of an independent school has been a revelation after experiencing the government-run education system of the Australian States. However, the danger is that this freedom may become a freedom to resist change and to conform more rigidly to what may well prove to be no longer valid traditions for a modern democracy. To some extent the independent school tends to become a refuge for those dedicated to the preservation of the status quo in all spheres of life.

I never did comprehend why no one, student or master, ever commented on my views!

Life-changing epiphany 'on the road to Damascus'

In my second year at the School, I was shocked at the departure overnight of the senior history master – a mature, warm and charming man popular with everyone. It emerged later that he had been encouraging his 'A Level' history students (aged 18) to take part in the annual Aldermaston nuclear disarmament march – surely a heinous crime in a Christian school where the Prince of Peace is proclaimed in its chapel services.

It produced the shock wave that swept me into political consciousness. Until then I had instinctively followed my mother's dictum that *nice people vote conservative* (or whatever the reactionary party is named). In England, I began to perceive that many even nicer and cleverer people supported the Left, that they held deep convictions about fairness and equality (the biblical term 'righteousness', reflecting the very nature of God). Incredible as it may sound, it had never occurred to me that politics could have an ethical dimension. Let alone a Christian sanction! I had seen it merely as an inter-play of interest groups. The epiphany was that for Christians, the Bible's vision of the Kingdom of God becomes the model for political imagination, and all the activity that follows must move society and the world a fraction nearer its embrace. It would herald a passionate and lifelong identification with the biblical stance for a follower of Christ: political radicalism balanced by social conservatism.

Perhaps it was this brutal episode that brought home to me the unbridgeable chasm between the school's ethos and progressive, democratic politics. It also alienated me from most of my colleagues (with a couple of exceptions of younger and more open masters), and left me with a sense that I could never 'make it' to become one of them, shaped as they were by generations of the 'born to rule' mentality. Naïve that I could ever have imagined otherwise!

Cricketing fortunes

Our first summer of 1960 brought the characteristically English sound of willow smiting leather. I would be master-in-charge of cricket, a key role in projecting the School's image. It was of cardinal interest to the Head, famed as he was for his three passions: Classics, Cricket and Christianity – in that order.

The challenge was to train up the best dozen players in the School and arrange games by gentlemen's agreements with 'public schools' within motor-coach distance. Though not a bad bowler – from age 16 to my current 28 having knocked back many a stump – I was scarcely a student of the game, having never been coached.

But the first summer went off well enough, thanks to the hang-over of good vibes from the coaching of the previous master – although in that previous summer the School XI had only notched *four wins* out of 16 matches.

Of the 12 matches we won more than we lost, with several honourable draws. Better than the previous year. There was even talk of a cricketing renaissance! In the school's magazine, *The Elean*, the cricket section (as ever) ran to no less than eight pages, including my two-page report outlining our fortunes, commending the heroes and encouraging the others.

But that was the high-water mark. With the departure of the best players the following two seasons would see less talent on hand. As the golden summers ran their course, the team limped on from draw to defeat, with the odd win.

In retrospect, it seems extraordinary that the Head never remonstrated with me but was ever the true English gentleman, loyal to his underlings. Perhaps he also recognised, as I did only too well, that a silk purse is not easily made from a sow's ear, of which there was no lack. On the other hand, I assume my language teaching efforts were appreciated, and since in my own mind I had never aspired to be a cricket coach, I didn't take it overly to heart. But it did mean that after three summers of declining success on the cricket field I sensed it was prudent to stand aside – or move on.

By then I had participated in two summer schools for 'foreign teachers' sponsored by the West German Government, and was in correspondence with the authorities of several of the German States and the French Ministry of National Education. A more enticing alternative future was beckoning from beyond the flat horizon.

In search of Britain

During our three summer vacations, on our own wheels we had virtually explored the entire British Isles, deepening our feel for the people and the cultural factors that had shaped the nation, as well as feasting our eyes on the lush beauties of creation so different from our austere antipodean version. In particular, we were bent on exploring our own roots in the Celtic lands, staying with my last surviving Scottish cousins in Dalbeattie and later meeting William Heughan, a world-renowned bass opera singer and actor who had visited Australia and met my mother, his cousin, during his concert tour in the 1920s.

Through those years the perspectives gleaned from BBC radio (as yet no TV) and the urbane *Observer* on Sundays had conferred an awareness of the texture of British society: the weight of history, the fading glory of Empire, the tensions of continuity and evolution, the range of linguistic usage and regional dialects – and the rigidity of the class structure. But of course, this is to speak in terms of breadth rather than depth. In a country teetering on the cusp of transformation, in our rarified environment, our daily lives were safely sheltered from the social and political challenges brewing just beyond the Fenland horizon.

CHAPTER 11: Migrating to Germany

The brief exposure to German life through two summer schools, both of which ended in a (gratis) flight behind the 'Iron Curtain' to Berlin and back for propaganda purposes, had whetted my appetite. I found myself musing, was this why I had been born a linguist? Why I had so eagerly grasped the opportunities offered at school, and had then acquiesced in being bonded to an employer for nine years? Did it all now set the life task of proving to myself that I could make a success in an unknown society, functioning in a language and culture different from those I had chanced to be born into? If so, it was now posing an enticing, character-probing challenge which I dared not shrink from. But how to go about earthing this romantic but grandiose dream, silly as it may have sounded with its overtones of rebirth? Stemming as I did from such ill-assorted parents, maybe the lifelong search for my own identity was finally yielding some dividends?

An important-looking letter arrived from Düsseldorf, capital of the State of North Rhine-Westphalia. The Education & Culture Ministry was offering me inclusion in a UK/West German teacher exchange program (I rated as a Brit.). I accepted with alacrity and found myself posted to the *Staatliches Altsprachliches Gymnasium* (State Classics Grammar School) in Minden in Westphalia. I could live in my exchange partner's house and take over his school responsibilities without needing to arrange for him to take my place at the King's School Ely – he would be posted elsewhere in England. It would go into effect in the new school year (September till June, 1962-63). The dream was morphing into reality!

We were farewelled at Ely railway station by a few friends from Chapel in a bitter-sweet moment: would we ever meet again in this life? Yet our hearts surged with anticipation of our overseas emigration. Was this *"Farewell to Old England forever"?* … though not yet *"bound for Botany Bay"?*

A migrant family arrives

The overseas component was the night voyage across the North Sea by the Harwich/Hoek van Holland ferry, continuing next morning by train through the severe brick townscapes of the Netherlands and on into Germany, with half-timbered, gabled farmhouses nestling among the rolling hills followed by the Westphalian towns and industrial zones. And finally, through the Porta Westfalica where the river Weser breaks through onto the North German Plain. First town Minden. Journey's end.

Like all European cities, Minden was an ancient place. Like all German cities, largely destroyed but tastefully rebuilt after the Second World War. In 1962, a modest-sized city of some 65,000 when we added to its population, Minden offers that classical European townscape of an *Altstadt* (central core of historic buildings within the original walls), preserved under heritage orders, now ringed by parkland and boulevards on the site of the walls, and beyond that the modern urban environment

Minden boasts a goodly number of surviving mediaeval buildings: several large Lutheran churches, the restored Rathaus (City Hall) on the Market Square, the Museum, and large numbers of half-timbered, gabled houses in orange and black, some cutely askew. Great camera fodder. Most of the significant buildings were destroyed in the Allied air raids, but are now faithfully restored. As everywhere over the 65 years they have mellowed to blend in seamlessly with the original ones.

In the surrounding areas, there had been concentration camps supplying slave-labour to munitions factories concealed in tunnels under the mountain range near the Porta Westfalica. In a British air raid in 1944, the long aqueduct carrying the *Mittelland Kanal* across the river Weser on the edge of town had been bombed and many factory workers below were drowned as the canal disgorged its waters. Too wet for a scene from hell.

Then near war's end in March 1945 came the devastating raid on the city, like all the late raids on German cities and towns (especially Dresden) designed not so much to destroy strategic targets as to break the civilians' spirit and drive them into an uprising against Hitler. But as much as Hitler was feared and loathed, this underrated the German spirit. So, the innocents were hideously slaughtered in their tens of thousands.

To an Australian raised in wartime, at first it was exciting to be *'behind the enemy's lines'*. But the enemy turned out to be just as charming in manners, just as valiant in hardship, and just as petty in frailties as we brave victors.

Unheralded and unsung

As with the universal migrant experience, no one met us on arrival. I guess we took a taxi across town to Karlsbader Weg 13, which became our home on the departure shortly afterwards of my exchange partner and his wife, an older couple. Their modern terrace home of three storeys plus an attic was tastefully furnished and well equipped. There was a good-sized, sunny garden behind, great for our two-year-old. In every respect, a dramatic contrast with our quaint mediaeval English living quarters.

In the study was a veritable wall of books, including triumphalist accounts of the Nazi invasions of the surrounding countries: *"Our Heroic Campaign in Poland"*, etc. Some staff members suspected my exchange partner of Nazi sympathies: indeed, many of the older teachers had been subjected post-war to the formal 'denazification' process.

A daunting challenge

Scouting around the town, I identified the location of the school, a solid Prussian-looking building of brick and masonry, circa 1920. On the first day of the new school year, I reported in to the *Direktor*, Herr Hennlich, and was courteously received and briefed about my exchange partner's duties. To my alarm I sensed that no concessions were to be made to my foreignness: it was to be a genuine exchange between two professionals – equals, not an apprenticeship arrangement. I had to give as good as I got.

My misgivings proved to be only too real. It amounted to the time-honoured learning device of being thrown in at the deep end without a life jacket. I spluttered and flailed about but ultimately managed to somehow stay afloat. But the goal of confidently using German as the sole means of communication was not easily attained. I was embarrassed to recognise how many common terms I had never learnt that typify everyday life in a school. It called for both will and wit – and boundless energy. At times, I would feel sick and tired of the unequal struggle and long to be done with it all, but on other days it would amount to sheer exhilaration.

But of nights I used to have recurrent dreams of conversations where I was consciously constructing perfect German sentences, and would wake up wondering whether in fact I did have that ability, except for the factors of nervousness or shame. At least it would generate a compassion for the NESB (non-English-speaking background) migrants who, back in Australia, would in later years become my bread and butter.

In the first few weeks, to my mortification, an *Elternsprechtag* (= 'parent speak day') came along. Naïvely, I assumed no one would want to find out from me how little *Johann* was getting on in *Englisch*, since I had only just met him and his mates *'Thomas, Richard and Heinrich'* (Tom, Dick and Harry) not to speak of their girlfriends, *Lisel, Brigitte, and Angelika*. How wrong could you be! The parents were queuing up at the classroom door, to get a close-up of the antipodean freak, and hear his bumbling *Deutsch*. Not many kangaroos around Westphalia!

Early Reformation grammar school

The school was almost 450 years old: a significant Minden institution. Founded by the Town Council in 1530 soon after the Reformation to teach the new doctrines, its curriculum consisted of (Lutheran) Religion, Latin, Greek, Hebrew and Singing. It soon became known for teaching the strictest Lutheranism in NW Germany. In the following centuries, it suffered many vicissitudes reflecting the wars of religion and the Seven Years War. In 1759 during the Seven Years War a decisive victory was gained over the French by Prussian and British forces in the *Battle of Minden*. Though its curriculum had broadened over the centuries, the classical languages had always remained prominent.

Only in the last few years have German schools forsaken the time-honoured but ridiculous practice of having classes only in the mornings. In my time in Minden such a change would have seemed unthinkable. Lessons took place from 8am to 1pm, with two short breaks when students munched their *'zweites Frühstück'* (second breakfast) of black bread with cheese and Wurst (sausage products) and fruit – it was before the fast food industry was invented when people on the whole were slim and healthy. Driving to school during the winter term I used to marvel at the crowds of kids standing at the traffic lights in the dark (and sometimes in the snow) on their way to school at 7:45am. For some seniors, there was even an extra lesson at 7am, *die nullte Stunde* (the noughth (!) period)

Though for me it all amounted to a daunting challenge, especially in the first term, it was also a stimulating break from the English school model that we have inherited in Australia. There was virtually no sport, except for PE (gymnastics). The grade rankings worked backwards, from the Latin-named Sexta (Sixth) aged 13, through Quinta, Quarta, Tertia, Secunda to Prima, aged 18. There was even an Oberprima, of students older than we were at university entry, where teaching was mostly in the form of seminars.

There were no major exams, but assessment was done throughout the year by having students do a number of *Arbeiten* (Assignments) in class. I would constantly be asked by anxious students, "Are we doing an *Arbeit* today? - as though these were customarily sprung upon them unawares. It kept them on their toes.

Classroom life

In class the students were polite, restrained and often quite charming. The Direct Method was used in the English classes, whereby the language being learned is used the whole time, in order to simulate something of real-world language interaction. But I found most of the students, especially in the younger grades, weren't really up to this so I would resort to German for explaining unknown words and phrases in the prescribed textbooks. Otherwise it became stiffly doctrinaire, with some risking being left behind. Oddly enough, at Queanbeyan I had experimented with this mode of teaching but with little success. Maybe just a slight difference in cultural values and ability levels...?

Early in the term, an embarrassing if amusing episode occurred when unaccountably a dog wandered into the classroom. Jocularly I addressed it, asking what it wanted – but my linguistic ineptitude brought the house down. At once I realised I had blundered into using the formal pronoun for 'you' reserved for *polite* communication with *(human)* strangers. It must have come across as though I had addressed it as *'Your Dogginess'!*

I was impressed to learn of educational guidelines providing that, at all levels, a number of days per term would be allocated to class outings beyond the local community. I found myself leading (?) a coach trip of my 16-year-old co-eds to the Hermann Denkmal (monument) on a summit in the Teutoburg Forest. A larger than life-size Hermann stands in armour and helmet, sword upraised, gazing eastwards in triumph over the lands that he saved for all time from Roman imperialism, ensuring that Germanic tongues would never be blended with Latin.

Deep Christian roots

However, at *Himmelfahrt Christi* (Ascensiontide, after Easter) I recall an indelible episode in my Prima class of 17/18 year-olds, practically all boys who, as I walked into the classroom, spontaneously burst into song in an impromptu Ascensiontide hymn *Macht hoch die Tür, das Tor macht weit/ Es kommt der Herr der Herrlichkeit.* I couldn't believe it: the young men of a State high school spontaneously testifying to the Christian faith, in a hymn celebrating the Risen and Ascended Christ, the words of which they knew by heart! Perhaps unwittingly, they were living out the original rationale for the foundation of their school 433 years earlier. With their booming male voices, they made such an impression on me that, although I have never heard the hymn-tune before or since, I remember it note-perfect to this day. I have since hunted it up in hymnbooks, to find it was written by a German, Georg Weissel, during the Reformation period in the 16th century. Its English translation runs *'Lift up your heads, you mighty gates/Behold, the King of glory waits'* (from Psalm 24).

It was one of several indications during our time in Minden that in Germany, despite the dreadful traumas of the 20th century – with crushing defeats in two world wars, soaring inflation and unemployment, and then the Depression leading to the nightmare of Nazism, with its legacy of a nation divided down the middle – the Christian heritage was more alive and out in the public realm than in peaceful, secular Australia. How unthinkable in an Australian high school for a teacher to be honoured by a hymn! We would probably view it as weird or naïve – if charming. I found it moving.

Likewise, in November came the surprise of a national public holiday, 'Buß und Bettag' *('Repentance & Prayer Day')*, ironically akin to the Jewish Day of Atonement. Originally observed from post-Reformation times in Protestant provinces, in the late 19th century it had become general, calling for both personal and national repentance for wrongs. Appropriate music by Bach and other classical composers was broadcast throughout the day on North German Radio and prayer services were held in the churches. It seemed to be calling forth a national sentiment comparable to what is now being intentionally contrived by Australian governments on Anzac Day, but from a sane Christian motive rather than bowing to the war gods. And what a divergent attitude to militarism: Christian repentance rather than an inverted triumphalism even in defeat (Gallipoli). And what a contrast to the Japanese, from whom the Chinese still wait for an apology for atrocities such as the Rape of Nanking committed 65 years ago. In 1963 at least, the Gospel roots ran down deeply into the North German psyche.

Attaining a life goal

Towards the end of the exchange year, the headmaster suggested I might also take over some of the classes of a deceased English teacher at the Girls' Grammar School. It was a surprising development, but by then I was hitting my straps and beginning to enjoy the advanced role of *Studienrat* ('study advisor'), inheriting my partner's formal title. For a few delightful weeks, I had a foot in two worlds of study, with handsome and hardworking senior *Schüler* and beautiful blond

Schülerinnen. I also met a young *Sprachassistent* from England and was surprised to notice his German was more hesitant than mine had been. Since by then we had a car, he asked me to enquire at the lost property office at the edge of town about a cap he had left on a bus. When I explained his loss to the counter clerk he shouted the request to an assistant in a back room, who asked: was the Brit there? In memorable words came the reply *"Nein, nicht der Engländer, der Deutsche!"* Lifelong mission accomplished.

After critiquing to the publisher a reading passage on Australia in one of the prescribed English textbooks – as being out-of-touch with Australian realities – I was invited to submit an article on life in the Outback. The outcome was the publication of my story in the next edition of the widely used textbook.

Bitter-sweet moment of insight

At the end of the school year my teaching contract closed with a poignant exchange. When I called in at the *Direktorin's* office to thank her for the opportunity of being at the girls' school and to say good-bye, the principal seemed shocked that I was leaving. When I explained the situation, she indicated there was a permanent job there for the asking, teaching English at the *Mädchenlyzeum*. I was stunned. Now you tell me!

Left to myself I would gladly have settled for it there and then, but the fact was that we had agreed to return to Australia at the end of the exchange year. For one thing Marjorie's mother's health was in decline, and I was receiving increasingly pathetic letters from my mother about staying overseas so long. But I was crestfallen: it was gratifying to have achieved my life-goal of going to Europe, living in Germany, and making my way in the world. In retrospect, I wonder whether I would not have stayed on for years, arguably for the rest of my life, content to be a reverse migrant.

By comparison with Europe, and especially with Germany, Australia at that time held scant appeal, seemingly unexciting, conventional, conservative, provincial, predictable, stagnant, as well as blighted by 'the great Australian ugliness' exposed in 1960 by Robin

Boyd – and just plain boring! For all of this I felt little loyalty, let alone identification, rather I was beginning to feel a citizen of the world.

Besides, something strange was going on in my head – or was it my heart? Somehow, I had come alive in a way that I had never experienced in my Australian setting. It was as if I had started adult life all over again, on a new plane. I had given myself permission to disclose myself, to express myself more freely and without my customary hesitancy and constraint, and to actually begin revelling in life.

Maybe it was linguistic: when you learn an alternative speech code for relating to your social environment as an adult, rather than by slowly assimilating words and ideas as you blunder through childhood, it somehow seems liberating to the spirit, and more artistic, to have this new instrument at your command, and to have escaped from the prison of the past. Perhaps it's at the heart of bilingualism – a double existence conferring a new ground for confidence. As Charlemagne, first Emperor of the Holy Roman Empire mused, *"To have another language is to possess a second soul."*

CHAPTER 12: Minden Days

What pre-eminently humanised our life in Germany was joining a local community of faith. Early on we had noticed a domestic-looking two-storey building with a sign proclaiming it as the worship centre of the *Evangelische Gemeinschaft* (Protestant Fellowship). I suggested we try it out especially as on our first Sunday, at the Lutheran Marienkirche we had had a similar experience to our Anglican worship in Ely. In both cases superb music – organ and choir – in an architectural masterpiece but little 'feel' for what we expect of worship, nor any human contact. It might have been a concert attendance.

The contrast with the little community on the Königstraße could hardly have been starker: we were warmly welcomed publicly and privately, and on the spot decided to throw our lot in with them. On my later visits to Germany I would discover that they had erected a more conventional church building and had formally linked up with the *Methodistenkirche Deutschlands*. Implausibly, by then they actually had a German-speaking Englishwoman as minister!

Their patterns of worship were familiar. At first it was something of a linguistic challenge to pick up the dated vocabulary of devotion, preaching and praying, though the style was familiar enough. Sara-Jane was greatly fussed over, and we were invited for the ritual Sunday afternoon coffee to a number of homes. To them I guess we were a fairly exotic breed. Indeed, we soon learnt that, on the whole, Australia was quite unknown except for its kangaroos. What was particularly unknown was that we had fought against the Germans in two world wars. For our part, to perceive the wartime and post-war sufferings of our brothers and sisters in Christ at 'our' hands was a powerful lesson in developing Gospel perspectives on peace building and universal brotherhood.

Gathered into a German family

On our first Sunday, we met a warm-hearted older man, Helmut Gressler, who invited us around for *Nachmittagskaffee* with his family – an epic moment for us all. The warmth and love of their friendship was to lend a special quality to our year in Minden and has spanned the decades until today, now into the third generation. A 'late homecomer' in the 1950s from a Russian slave labour camp, deprived of the chance of higher education, he wrote poetry in a copperplate script and was a considerable Bible scholar. He seemed to have appointed his task for the year as caring for our family. He became our cultural interpreter on community values and everyday life.

Sunday afternoons were often spent together with his small family in their nearby flat. He gave me a whole album of commemorative stamps, including many from the Nazi era featuring Adolf Hitler (of whom he was no supporter). At two, Sarah-Jane was a great hit. The evening meal would always consist of the regulation *kalte Platte* of rye bread, cheeses, ham, and various types of *Wurst*. Of course, we must never drink coffee after four o'clock. German order ruled! Now Marjorie's three years of high-school German came into their own, unencumbered by mere grammatical constraints, but touching to the monolingual family. Evenings would always end with the heartfelt farewell *'Kommt gut nach Hause!'* as we faced the rigours of our two-minute drive to Karlsbader Weg all of two blocks away.

Soon we had bought a newish Opel Karawan station wagon and, at their request, we all drove to the Baltic coast to the tiny port where his wife's family had landed after their refugee ship from East Prussia was sunk in the last days of the war. Nearby we drove to the border with the so-called 'German Democratic Republic' backed by Soviet Russia – actually at the northernmost tip of the Iron Curtain which sundered Europe into two armed camps during the 45 years of the Cold War. Gazing into the forbidden territory of the 'other Germany' Helmut wept openly: all his family and friends were trapped in Leipzig, where he had never gone home from the war and never expected to see them again.

On the brink of nuclear holocaust

In the early months of our stay, in October 1962, a threatening episode had brought home to us the harsh realities of the Cold War. Minden was only about 160km from the Iron Curtain. If the Cold War had turned hot, we would immediately have been exposed to Russian invasion and nuclear retaliation. Since the war years, security had been maintained by the 'balance of terror' between the two nuclear arsenals ensuring MAD ('mutually assured destruction').

But without warning this was set at risk when Communist Cuba pulled off a deal with Russia to have nuclear missiles stationed there. This was designed to deter imminent American invasion, by ringing Fidel Castro's island with nuclear missile sites targeted on the USA. It led to mutual threats to unleash a nuclear holocaust: a fleet of Russian ships bound for Cuba was already on the high seas carrying the missiles. The Armed Forces of both camps were put on red alert, as Presidents John Kennedy and Nikita Khrushchev held threatening, then pleading phone calls to each other, with the military chiefs on both sides urging war. With the leaders' fingers poised over the nuclear triggers, the world held its breath, teetering on the brink. Throughout Saturday 27th October (later recognised as *'the most dangerous day in history'*) we were glued to the radio, tuned to the BBC, as the hours ticked down to doomsday. Then came the blessed word: the Russian ships were turning back! Thank God! Our lives had been given back to us all.

Winter wonderland

Another memorable time had been the winter of 1962-63, severest for the best part of a hundred years. The port of Hamburg and the Thames in London were frozen hard, and the German Army held tank manœuvres on the Weser river ice. At first encounter the cold was actually frightening, as though we were in a freezing chamber. Although well rugged up: capped, be-scarfed and be-gloved, you still couldn't stand the burning cold of your ears.

Then came the snow, stately, thick, silent. The outside world was hushed. Soon our back garden was knee deep, and every bare branch was silhouetted in dazzling white, with the conifers sagging under their frigid load. Truly it was a wonderland, the like of which we had never experienced in our three English winters. In the garden, we hastily built a celebratory snowman tricked out with buttons, pipe, scarf, and gloves, lest the snow should melt before we could capture him on film. In his glistening glory, there he stood undaunted for two months. When two Australian guests turned up for Christmas our childish glee knew no bounds. From our cellar, we unearthed a wooden toboggan and off we all trooped to the *Mittelland Kanal* to slide along the ice.

As the weeks of freezing weather continued, I became familiar with driving conditions to the point of finding it all rather exhilarating. Until the day came when moving along slowly behind a truck making coal deliveries, I had to brake a little harder than usual. The Opel slid ever so gracefully along the icy surface, quite beyond the power of any braking to impede, to come to a gentle meeting with the truck's tailgate. Fortunately, smashed headlamps and mangled grille were covered by our insurance. *"Pride goes before destruction, and a haughty spirit before a prang." (Proverbs 16:18)*

Later I heard of an adult evening class starting where you could learn Russian. We decided to build on the rudiments of Russian we had been acquiring at the Ely Evening Institute, based on a BBC radio program. Learning Russian via German seemed an attractive *tour de force*.

A maritime view of the countryside

My parting shot in Minden was to persuade the inland shipping company by the Weser to let me take a ride on a barge on the Mittelland Kanal. I had always been fascinated by the intensive river and canal traffic, especially on the Rhine where at every turn the long, low ships are to be seen – either the luxurious glassed-in tourist boats or else powerful cargo barges, sometimes with a second one in tow, surging upstream or pouring downstream, carrying coal or building materials or containers. They say that one such barge carries as much freight as a dozen goods trains.

So I was allowed to board a ship as it headed westwards over the aqueduct towards the Ruhr industrial area. We powered through the countryside, past modern farmhouses and ancient half-timbered barns, beside wheat fields and dairy herds, under road bridges, the powerful diesels throbbing away at the stern, beneath the low deckhouse where the steersman stood by the wheel. Sometimes the broad funnel with radio aerial would need to be folded down to fit under a tight bridge. Viewed from inboard, the great bulk of the cargo is carried below the waterline, with very little freeboard when fully laden – no waves on the inland waterways! I had the run of the ship but my efforts to make contact with the two or three crew members came to nought for want of a common language. Taciturn as they were, they seemed to understand my comments. But I couldn't be sure whether they were replying in Dutch or Plattdeutsch.

After a lazy summer's afternoon, it was time to disembark. But there are no quays beside the canals and they have sloping sides, so that in open waters a heavily laden ship cannot come close to the bank. The simple but rather alarming expedient is to drape your body over a long *Schlagbaum* (wooden boom), bent at your middle, head on one side, feet on the other, bag hanging from your arm, and get swung out at right angles until you're over the land, and then drop off. With an incomprehensible shout they were away again, leaving me to find my landlegs – and work out where I was.

CHAPTER 13: Dicing with Death

What is it about travel that is so alluring? To earth the imagination? To confirm or challenge beliefs long held from childhood? But also, to see for *yourself*, to listen, to interact – just to be there.

Having booked our passages back to Australia we planned an extensive camping tour of the Continent in Ossie the Opel. But first I would take a lone train trip to Moscow, leader of the Second World, more than 2,000km due east of Minden, while Marjorie and Sara-Jane moved in with our German friends.

Initial impression was how huge was the European sector of the Soviet Union, let alone the lands that stretched off across the width of Asia to the Sea of Japan half a world away. But how empty! And how poor! Weathered *dachas* in wood, unpainted, miserable farmsteads, peasants in baggy trousers with black-scarfed women, horses drawing heavy wooden carts along unpaved roads.

In the cross-hairs of the Cold War

In Moscow, our assembled party fell into the hands of Intourist, the official travel agency which retained our passports for the duration and daily guided our steps. First to Red Square, bordered by the walls of the Kremlin, the veriest heart of the 'Evil Empire', the Most Dangerous Spot on Earth: how many inter-continental ballistic missiles with radio-active warheads were trained onto us at that moment? But at another level, the historic and beautiful buildings around Red Square made it a tourist's delight. Beyond the cobbled expanse of the Square rose the stunning complexity of the former St Basil's Cathedral – closed to business – but alluring under its exotic clutch of multi-coloured onion domes. *Inside* the Kremlin walls rose several other church towers, all crowned by the Cross of the Prince of Peace, in gold.

But apart from a few highlights the week remains something of a blur in my memory: the very dead, embalmed body of Lenin in its mausoleum; the near-empty GUM department store, but also the splendid infrastructure of a Metro system running through stations like art galleries in marble – fares optional. World class concert and ballet tickets for a song. The Gallery of Peasant Art with its idealised paintings of pretty farm girls loading hay and heroic teams of steel workers sweating before blast furnaces topped by belching smokestacks. The workers' paradise – mercifully minus our banal Western advertising.

My final day was indeed spent in paradise, allowed to travel alone by overnight train to Leningrad (St Petersburg), walking all day long in mild summer weather among the architectural glories and cultural treasures of a city today rated a Unesco World Heritage site, the 'Venice of the North'. The flight back to Moscow was enlivened by a cackling chook's head protruding from a peasant woman's chaff bag. The people's aerial bus – fares optional?

Farewell – but not forever

Near the end of September 1963, we bade our sad farewells to dear Minden friends and colleagues, and to our adoptive city. Not for the last occasion: several times have I been back since. Initially our planned route would take us northward across the Baltic to Sweden and Norway from where our ancestors in Scotland had stemmed, then south to Denmark whose early Jutes were forebears of the King's School boys. Peaceful, modern yet harmonious democratic communities.

For us benignly brainwashed Aussies, Continental Europe was an unexplored treasure trove of history and culture. It fairly exploded on you at every hand. Breaking out of the colonial mould, to engage in a liberating encounter with wider Western culture was an enticing prospect, rendering trite the long-inculcated notions of *'British and Best'*. It seemed our school history teachers had no concept of culture or language, while our language teachers had no communicable grasp of history. No wonder they turned out ignorant, uncritical young people happy to settle for next Saturday's vital sport fixtures.

Linguistic border crawl

I opted for exploring the linguistic faultline through western Europe separating Germanic from Gallic speakers. For a boy from a monolingual island continent, why have I always been fascinated with borders – those markers of beginnings and ends, arbiters of different worlds (land and water, sea and sky, mortality and eternity?) Are the markers real? Or only what they demarcate? And are they true? The real world seems full of muted greys, so that the hard-edged descriptors tend to grow fuzzy under the magnifying glass.

We had crossed into *the Netherlands* (= Lowlands) and checked out whether Germans (like me!) could understand Dutch and vice versa. To me it sounded like a very Low German of the canal boat fraternity, but some communication was possible, at least once in conversing with a primary-age schoolboy. Next door in bilingual Belgium we tried out our German on the Flemish speakers (Belgian word for Dutch!) with less success.

Somewhere near Liège in Wallonia (the French-speaking part of Belgium) we crossed the invisible linguistic faultline to enter Gallic territory – or was it so invisible? We had often observed that the 'Germanic' communities (whether in Germany, Scandinavia or Holland) presented orderly streetscapes, with well-painted houses, window-boxes and flowers, but now the unfamiliar 'Gallic' streetscapes came into view with shabbier or unpainted houses, maybe the odd pile of bricks or sand in front, and a general air of *laissez-faire* indifference. Or was it admirable freedom from external regimentation? The prized Gallic *liberté?*

Next, into the Duchy of Luxembourg, one of the smallest but most successful countries in Europe, long uniting peoples of Germanic and Gallic origins, with three languages in use including *Letzebürgisch* (a local tongue). *Egalité* – but what price the subtle internal borders? Then southwards along the linguistic faultline to the political football of Alsace-Lorraine (German *Elsass-Lothringen*) alternating between forming part of Germany or France. Movable borders. Straddling the faultline, people were speaking both languages and, while today it is under French administration, most of the place names are still German (but with a cute French pronunciation!).

We found a charming region of forests and gentle mountains (the Vosges), and the *Protestant* city of Mulhouse (in France!). Strasbourg/ Straßburg with its superb pink-stone cathedral is now the seat of the

European parliament and, bridging the old Franco-German divide, becomes a symbol of reconciliation. Borders transcended. Common humanity wins out. *Fraternité* at last, bravo!

Alpine rapture

Triggered by our childhood holidays at Katoomba, my lifelong love affair with mountains would bring both rapture and terror. In the Alps the first sight of the famous north face of the Eiger, a forbidding wall of black ice-flecked rock, crowned by a tapering snow-clad peak rising to double the height of Kosciuszko, literally took my breath away. Throwing myself down in a lush alpine meadow to scan the grandiose peak rearing starkly above me at once I fell captive to the power of the vista. At first imperceptible: an uncanny sensation was creeping over my soul, as though I was no longer in my body but being ushered into a world of gloriously heightened sensibility. It was as if I had never truly lived until that moment of blinding clarity. Ineffable, intoxicating – an out-of-body experience where time had no meaning. Literally *enraptured!*

How long I lay there gazing heavenwards – 'lost in wonder, love and praise' – I have no idea. I was out of this world, in a heaven sublime, utterly indescribable, being drawn into the infinitude of a Creator revealing himself through the majesty of his creation.

Divine deliverance from death

But in the French Alps to the east of Grenoble I would encounter the first of the two witting brushes with death in my longish story. Lured by the grandiose alpine landforms and glaciated peaks we make for the highest mountain in Europe, the majestic Mont Blanc As we reach the higher levels of the ranges we come upon a glacier in a deep valley far below the road. Having never been close to a glacier, I am determined to record it on my camera for posterity. So, leaving the family in Ossie I clamber down to pick up the best angle for a dramatic shot. On the steep snow-patched slope (perhaps approaching 45°), I come upon a bare strip where myriad stones form a broad band of scree. But no sooner do I set foot on them than the whole mountainside begins to slip away under my feet, the hail of stones clattering far below onto the face of the glacier. With them I am sliding off into the abyss!

In utter panic I fall full-length, face down onto the scree, arms outstretched and legs akimbo, desperately clutching at nothing, crying out to God to have mercy, as the slide continues closer to the point where the vertical drop can only mean a glacial death. (The horror flashes through my mind of my embalmed body emerging from the glacier in a thousand years' time.)

Instinctively, as the pace of my slide quickens, I am clutching wildly at the earth for something solid to grasp onto. But the whole world is sliding away.... Gradually the movement slows and slows until, after an eternity, it stops altogether, leaving me panting spread-eagled amidst a field of scree, hardly daring to breathe lest I set it all off again. If anything, solid ground looms nearer to my right and I am edging in that direction, at every move dislodging a hail of looser stones to go crashing away beneath me. It seems forever as I inch my way to *terra firma*, staring into the depths that I have cheated of their prey.

"But as for me, I came so close to the edge of the cliff! My feet were slipping and I was almost gone"[5]. Mercifully, God has intervened. I recall his promise: *"He will give his angels charge over you and hold you in their hands, lest you dash your foot against a stone."*[6]
I never do get that photo but what I do get, in lieu of sympathy, is a well-deserved earful on rejoining those I feared never to see again in this world. I had lost all track of time.

To gai Paris

But to resume our southbound family odyssey: as the glorious days of autumn hold sway, we eagerly point Ossie westwards. *Voilà...* Paris! Capital of the World. Elegant, enticing, bewitching, *romantique* Paris! So familiar from literature yet utterly unknown, as we drive around, mouths agape: the Arc de Triomphe and the Champs-Elyseés, Le Louvre, La Place de la Concorde, Notre-Dame Cathedral, the Seine with its many *Ponts*, the Left Bank, the Latin Quarter, Les Invalides,

---

[5] Psalm 73: 2, The Living Bible, 1971.

[6] Psalm 91: 11-12, also quoted by Jesus in his temptations in the wilderness.

the Eiffel Tower, Montmartre. Elegant streetscapes, charming outdoor cafés. Wow! The power of it at first sight!

That afternoon we come to roost in the Latin Quarter, just off the *Boul' Mich* (Boulevard St Michel) so beloved of students from the Sorbonne, philosophically sipping coffee and Sartre at the sidewalk cafes. But alas! Reluctant victims to our tight and dwindling budget, we fall victim to the 'salubrious' Sphinx-Hôtel, with its romantic peeling walls, dank and mouldering shower, and aroma of damp rot – and from 4 a.m. utterly permeable to the roar of inner city Paris. The dream turns sour. But it is cheap and we've far to go. Can't camp by the Seine.

Roman Gaul

With a new lease on life, I turn Ossie southwards, down the Rhône valley into Provence. At Nîmes we inspect the well-preserved Roman amphitheatre and near Arles gaze in disbelief at the engineering marvel of the Pont du Gard, the intact three-tier Roman aqueduct spanning a rocky valley.

Even in the twenty-first *century, across so much of western Europe the Roman influence* is only *just* below the *surface*, not to *mention* its *linguistic patrimony* embodied in the *French language* and therefore *forming* half of our English *vocabulary*. (Note our debt to the *Latin* words above!)

Then along the Mediterranean coast: the Côte d'Azur and the Italian Riviera to Genoa. We admire the splendid art cities of the Renaissance, finally to set up our tent in the camping-ground on one of the Seven Hills of Rome. But, of course, there are several Romes: the magnificent ruins of the capital of the ancient world; the political hub of a dynamic if erratic nation; the city of fashion and style, of rogues and cheats battening onto tourists; and the Vatican City – the world's smallest country with the widest outreach and the grandest basilica, focal point of the Catholic world.

For the erstwhile Latin teacher, the first stop has to be the *Forum Romanum* – the extensive zone of classical remains in the heart of the modern city. Though much rebuilt by early emperors, it still offers the imagination wings as you picture its triumphal arches, victory columns, basilicas (originally law courts, some later converted into the earliest churches), baths, and marble-paved open spaces where the populace once gathered for political, religious and social occasions. Above all, the many temples whose gods preserved the city.

More starkly than any other ancient site, the Colosseum nearby evokes the bloodlust at the heart of Roman 'civilisation'. Indifferent to suffering, the Empire was mired in blood. Yet it was to be tamed by the 'gentle Jesus, meek and mild', the Jewish prophet hailed as universal Prince of Peace. St Peter is said to have lived in Rome as leader of the Christian community of Romans and Jews, and ended in martyrdom under the megalomaniac Nero – believed crucified upside down because he claimed to be unworthy of the death his Master died. There also St Paul would spend the last two years of his life, under house arrest on the charge of treason against the Emperor, to whom he had appealed under his right as a Roman citizen. Tradition has it that he was beheaded – Roman *citizens* were exempt from crucifixion.

Certain it is that in 313 AD Christian persecution was halted by decree of the Emperor Constantine, opening the way for Christianity to become the official religion of the Roman Empire – and for the 'unholy alliance' of Church and State to develop into the mediaeval Papacy with all its sins.

CHAPTER 14:
Journey to the End of the Earth

The *T/N Galileo Galilei* was an Italian work of art. Far larger than the *Fairsky* and a newly built luxury liner, in her rakish beauty she cut a dazzling white figure against the blue of the Mediterranean. Her economy class was stylish and extensive. As with all southbound ships in that era, there were many emigrants on board, virtually all Italians but well-heeled. At Naples and Messina in Sicily we picked up more.

At Messina, with the family's blessing, I sloped off along the quayside, to fall in with a secondary school and a teacher near the gate. The Italian language I had been using for the past few weeks availed to get me into the building and even into a classroom, where I was presented with the textbook used for teaching Latin to Italians – akin to teaching Australians Anglo-Saxon.

World's longest ocean voyage

To my surprise there were no more ports of call. Setting a diagonal course for Fremantle, we struck out across the Indian Ocean, untroubled by storms and monsoons. For the next three weeks, the only land we were to see was the desolate dun-coloured island of Socotra, part of the Republic of Yemen.

For the southbound voyage (the ship's complement *not* being mainly twenty-somethings trying out their wings on an overseas escapade), shipboard life was rather more staid than on the *Fairsky*. Apart from dining and sleeping, most of our time was spent caring for Sara-Jane. Every morning checking how many kilometres we had covered in the past 24 hours at an unvarying 30 knots[7], I was struck again by the vastness of the world. If air travel shrinks the globe for the wealthy, the rest of humanity still suffers from the tyranny of distance.

---

[7] About 50km/h

Momentous news mid-ocean

Out of the blue on 22nd November 1963 in the middle of the Indian Ocean, the PA system announced that John Kennedy, President of the USA, had been assassinated. The collective gasp was audible. Not only was the entire ship's company devastated: the tidings instantly circled the globe, leaving in their wake a trail of anger and despair. He was the youngest President to die in office. And at the height of the Cold War, he took with him the hopes of the world.

Australia revisited - as an alien

A week later we docked at Fremantle: our first visit to Western Australia. My immediate impressions of our homeland were rather unfavourable: on the deck, outside the air-conditioned staterooms, it was stiflingly hot with no hint of a breeze. My spirits sagged. I had forgotten how much I dreaded and shunned the heat. But where could you go to escape it? And then the view from the ship was so ... *unaesthetic!* Great formless wharf sheds, backed by nondescript-looking low buildings. Everything was so w i d e. Whatever had happened to the vertical dimension? Let alone the balanced proportions of port buildings set in tight townscapes that we had grown accustomed to in Europe? It required a re-calibrating of the visual senses.

Then I noticed the people thronging the wharf and scanning the ship's rails for familiar faces. They all looked so ... *casual!* A crowd of extras hired for a mass scene in a new film about the Wild West. Oh, this is the wild west! Men in shorts and thongs (not that I knew the word – nor even the article then, they had arrived during our absence). Men without style or taste, bellowing names from the depths of their beer-bellies. And the older women, with tanned-leather faces, hair in a mess, shrieking like banshees. Welcome home! *Oh, oh, this is what home looks like?* And then the dawning horror: doubtless they're all lovely people. It's you who have changed! You're the odd man out, become an alien in your own land.

Later, bemused at a billboard about a *surfie*, I would be shocked at young men walking around city streets barefoot. Salutary, to be seeing it all through immigrants' eyes, until the spell wore off. For instance, in the earliest days home after five years' absence, on a trip to my brother Max's place near Gosford, I would experience my first encounter with 'the bush' as truly alienating. I was shocked at the elongated wilfulness of the gumtrees, rebels all, twisted and gnarled, growing every which way except vertically. Why? And where was their foliage? They seemed all limbs – and many of them dead and bare! They struck me as starved ...anguished ... tortured! – and the whole landscape as chaotic. Not to mention the perpetual autumn of their falling leaves. And the colour scheme! A mournful greenish/grey? Wasn't nature *green?*

But down on *terra firma* at last it wasn't so bad. We were kindly welcomed by two brothers I'd met on the Moscow trip: we'd been the only Australians. Somehow, they had brought their car right onto the Fremantle wharf. But I needed to ask what sort it was: it turned out to be a Holden. I recognised it as a cousin of Ossie the Opel with the same wrap-around windscreen.

Nosing our way through the chaotic and distracted crowds on the wharf, we swung out into the main road. Instantly a surge of panic came over me: we were courting disaster, with head-on traffic rushing at us on the wrong side of the road! Relax, Jim, you're home again...

A shocking homecoming

A week later the *Galileo* was bisecting Sydney Heads to thread her careful way up-harbour between pleasure craft and commuter ferries. Rounding Bradley's Head would bring into focus the famous vista of city skyline and the Harbour Bridge. Instantly I fell prey to the half-forgotten but recurrent nightmare from our European years, of sailing under Sydney Harbour Bridge with sinking heart yet always jerked back into consciousness, reassured it was only a dream. But then a moment later would rise the dawning dread that one day it would have to be no dream.

Yet even my wildest dreams could not have prepared us for the actual nightmare unfolding. Marjorie's mother had been unwell in recent weeks, though the seriousness of her undiagnosed heart condition was unknown, even to her husband and her sister, matron of

CHAPTER 14: Journey to the End of the Earth

Canterbury District Hospital. Only in mail received at Fremantle was there any intimation that a significant health condition had developed.

As soon as the *Galileo* docked, we were greeted by three of our four parents. It had been decided that Marjorie's mother would be better off waiting at home than coping with the jostling crowds, heat and excitement of welcoming us home and meeting her new granddaughter. While I remained to collect our baggage and be taken out to my parents' place, Marjorie's father drove her and Sara-Jane to the Beverly Hills home where we expected to stay for the next few weeks.

After spending some time with my parents, I was driven over to Beverly Hills, to encounter the appalling news that the dear lady who had so anticipated seeing her only daughter again and meeting her overseas-born granddaughter, had died from a massive heart attack half an hour after their arrival home!

The next few weeks must forever remain a blur – of shock, grief, remorse. We had been away nigh on five years. Why did we stay so long? And why weren't we told about Marjorie's mother's real condition? Or was it even known to be so serious? The mind ceaselessly churned and turned, trying to grapple with the power and cruelty of the death she died.

Marjorie, already pregnant with a baby to be born within three months, was battling to cope with her own grief while tending a bereft father and a distracted little girl, not to mention a disoriented husband. United by grief we moved in together.

CHAPTER 15: Striking Root

Back to work – but where? The schools had broken up for the summer vacation, not to reopen for six weeks. So what do we live on? Driven by necessity I applied for Unemployment Benefit and was ruled eligible. After a meaningless Christmas and a joyless New Year, I visited the head office of the Education Department to seek a school placement.

I was treated with great courtesy and was at once offered a position of 'graduate assistant' in modern languages at Sydney Boys High School, the premier public school of NSW... or else the position of Subject Master at the newish Narwee Boys High School, within brisk walking distance. But ambition rather than proximity decreed the choice. *Carpe diem* ('Seize the moment'): career building implies making good use of every stepping stone. Returning from five years' professional experience in Europe, including teaching in a German *Gymnasium*, conferred extra bargaining power in the marketplace, at least while it all remained fresh and authentic. I would be the youngest subject master for languages in the NSW teaching service.

So the opening of the 1964 school year saw me and some 500 schoolboys trouping into the newish complex at Narwee, the station beyond Beverly Hills. I was granted use of a specific classroom as the 'Languages Centre', and enthusiastically decked it out with an array of travel posters, a large wall map of France, tourism brochures, road maps, travel tickets and sundry other *Realien* brought back from Europe. My languages staff consisted of two young women, also new to the school that year – a recent Sydney graduate and a young exchange teacher from England. We all launched into our work with gusto.

In the school, there was an Inter-School Christian Fellowship, shepherded by Brian Booth, Test cricket opener and active Christian. But I have to confess that the weekly assembly in the Hall appealed to my ungodly vanity, as the Principal, his Deputy, and the Subject Masters got to parade in, wearing their academic hoods and gowns, to sit up on the stage before the assembled school.

L'embarras du choix[8]

But no sooner were we launched into the grand new teaching adventure than a rocket landed from outer left field, in the form of a Federal Government letter offering the position of Senior Education Officer in the Commonwealth Office of Education, at North Sydney pending relocation to the national capital in Canberra.

The post carried the salary of a NSW high school deputy principal, but the appeal was rather that the project was an innovative one of preparing a set of French-teaching textbooks for schools, based on the 'Australian Situational Method' used in public English classes for migrants with no one common language. I had given no further thought to the application mailed from Paris months earlier in response to a press clipping advertising the vacancy, sent over by my mother. (I've always suspected it was the Paris postmark that swung the deal!) But this now squarely set *le chat parmi les pigeons* (as the French probably don't say). I had a week or so to respond.

I had now arrived squarely before the first of the three great crossroads of my working life: to leave teaching; to leave Canberra; and to stay in Melbourne – all of them associated with significant changes of career and, viewed in retrospect, as all offered and endorsed and blessed by the Lord.

On the one hand, it seemed absurd to contemplate leaving my post so soon, as an ingrate. Naturally I had assumed my life would be in teaching: that was my identity honed out over ten satisfying years. Besides, I was enjoying the new challenge and had every hope of success. What would I be if no longer a teacher?

On the other hand, the NSW educational bureaucracy was known as very 'user-unfriendly', resulting in low morale and little loyalty. For instance, on completion of my five-year bond and resigning to go overseas, their standardised acknowledgment letter had expressed neither appreciation nor regret but ended with a threat over possible undischarged obligations. Positive staff relations!

By contrast the federal public service stood in higher esteem, but it didn't run any schools (even in Canberra, where the NSW Education

---
[8] 'embarrassment of the choice'

Department then staffed them). So the naked challenge loomed, who are you? Akin to other strategic life-altering decisions: what you stand for, whom you marry, where you settle, what faith you live by? Yet what a bitter-sweet moment it was just then, facing major choices in a household of grief and with the advent of new life coming closer by the day, bringing wider responsibilities. Certainly, it gave me pause for sober thought.

But in the end my (long suspected but untested) gambler's instinct won the day. Only decades later would I do the temperament and personality tests that established my extreme propensity (even exhilaration) for living on the edge with the provisional, rather than craving certainty – keeping the options open till the nth hour. The years in Europe offered good scope for this odd preference – as dysfunctional as it can prove in a marriage and with a family. But at the age of 31 and in a teacher shortage, my conclusion was, *"Oh well, if it doesn't work out, you can always go back to teaching"*.

But I never needed to, since I never forsook the profession of educator, but merely swapped locations, in sequence: from school to text book preparation, to educating adults about cultural diversity, to edifying Christian congregations, to lecturing in theological institutions, and finally to promoting cross-cultural ministry. Maybe the instinct for adventure, with all its attendant uncertainties, always won the day. Maybe the horizon always looked more alluring.

Prevenient grace

As harsh as this judgment may sound, it should be matched by one further factor: the surprising role of God's grace which, 'seeing the end from the beginning' constantly yet imperceptibly edges us on in the direction of God's purposes, while encouraging us progressively to own them as ours. The story line is about a lifelong partnership unfolding with God, featuring my bumbling progress along a tortuous path, with many a relapse, but also his patient shepherding towards a higher purpose. As the passage from the book of Proverbs, learnt in Sydney University EU put it (in its Shakespearean English):

"Trust in the Lord with all thy heart, lean not on thine own understanding, in all thy ways acknowledge him, and he shall direct thy paths." (Proverbs 3: 4-5)

It has to be not only learnt but experienced.

So, I have experienced the several changes of scene as proving right and good. As Edith Piaf sang, *"Je ne regrette rien"* [nothing]. Or almost. At least occupational changes keep the brain from atrophying. Certainly, they unlocked more coherent personal growth – and triggered greater contribution to the community – than would have come about through lifelong rootedness in one safe setting. However, the open question remains the degree to which the shifting scene imposed undue burdens on my closest and dearest companions on the journey.

Home sweet home?

Our first son Christopher soon put in an appearance, bringing the grieving grandfather a new focus for living. During my longer workdays, now travelling to North Sydney, he became the soul of kindness and support. Marjorie and I became members of Beverly Hills Methodist Church, where we also received loving support.

But alas, before long the domestic idyll began to tarnish. Across a veritable chasm of values and outlooks, father-in-law and I made little attempt at mutual accommodation. My insensitivity was legendary and his scorn unconcealed. Moreover, his patience with Sara-Jane and a new baby was wearing thinner. The household was becoming unworkable, but despite saving most of my enhanced salary we had little prospect of buying our own home.

To his everlasting credit, he made a huge contribution to our deposit on a house of our own, and on a fat bank loan we bought a pre-war dwelling not far from North Sydney, near the head of a bushy valley still clothed with pristine woodland – I suspect the closest untouched natural bush to the GPO.

Like good *arrivistes* we had now 'made it', owning (with the Bank) valuable property on Sydney's lower North Shore, across the harbour from the generations of our migrant ancestors. Yet it amounted to a modest compromise between vanity and honest ambition, being relatively close to my employment. The house, in double brick and red-tiled, had a well-established garden where we planted some trees that flourish to this day. For the first time since our marriage nine years earlier, like the brave Australians that we were, we now embraced the proper suburban lifestyle. Good job, decent house, nice garden, reliable car, friendly neighbours, kid at school – was there anything more to life?

Yes. We transferred our church membership to a charming old Methodist chapel of hewn stone at South Chatswood. There in 1965 Sara-Jane was enrolled at Sunday School, and on weekdays at Lane Cove Primary School. It was during this period that I won the prize in the church's coloured slide competition. Fortuitously I had managed to capture the utter pathos of war in a photo taken in the rebuilt ruins of Coventry Cathedral: a great bell permanently lying where it fell in shattered shards of metal on the night of the wartime bombing, its joyous appeals to Christian worshippers forever silenced by the triumph of the strident gods of war.

Web of family relationships

As an only child, Marjorie continued her caring concern for her father, with whom we exchanged regular visits, driving his old Holden now handed down to us. With a little girl and a baby and a household to manage, she was a good candidate for the 'virtuous wife' of Proverbs whose price was above rubies. Besides, she was preparing for the birth of a third baby.

In 1966 Nicholas saw the light of day in King George V Hospital near the university, like all our babies, strong and lusty. Marjorie's father kindly moved in to provide intensive assistance. I felt overwhelmed with gratitude to God for his gift of three (later to be four) beautiful children. Sara-Jane proffered great 'practical' help with the new arrivals. In those days before television pre-empted everything, with the older two we looked at picture books and made up stories, listened to children's songs, 'worked' together gardening They were soaking up new knowledge like sponges.

We resumed contact with several friends from SUEU days, married and living in the area. Domestic life was robust but satisfying, we found our existence full of meaning and purpose. The world was still young. *Deo gratias!*

CHAPTER 16: Stirrings of Dissent

It was the days of the Vietnam War (1962-75) bitterly contested in a nation disinclined to believe the aristocrat Menzies' claim that we had to support *'our great and powerful ally'* the USA, by paying the insurance premium in young Australian lives. At the people's level, this raised the prospect of seeing your young men conscripted[9] for National Service in somebody else's shooting war with the high risk of being killed or maimed for life – and certainly traumatised. To top it off came the Government's outrageous decision that selection for such a fate would be on the basis of a 'lucky' draw of marbles from a barrel to nominate which birthday dates would provide the conscripts for the blood sacrifice. Throughout our already long and manic military history never before had conscription been invoked to produce soldiers in peacetime, let alone by a blood lottery of birthdays. Even during the bloodbath of the First World War, two national referenda had had to be held to seek public acceptance of conscription. Though the young nation was deeply cleft by them, both failed to pass. But this time the nation was not even asked for an opinion.

A war that divided the nation

We saw the Vietnam War as based simply on the American 'stop the southward creep of Communism' phobia, publicly invoking the absurd mantra *"Fight now or in your own backyard"* to which the apt reply had to be "No thanks, I'll do neither". To this day it ranks as the most galvanising political action I recall in my adult life. People were simply passionate, on both sides of the divide, and prepared to act out their convictions. I recall the case of 18 year-old triplets from a Methodist Church on Sydney's North Shore who famously opted for gaol rather than accept being conscripted into the ranks.

---

[9] That is, compulsorily recruiting young men into the army without right of refusal, termed being 'called up'.

Anti-war protest

Nation-wide spontaneous protests erupted, in time maturing into the *'moratorium movement'* convened by Dr Jim Cairns, Federal Labor MP from South Melbourne on the left of the Party, with the simple catchcry *"Stop the War"*. Soon it was resonating across Australia, drawing hundreds of thousands of marchers onto the streets of the major cities, but along the way dividing Christians and Churches into the two camps: of reluctant (but dogged) supporters of the war, and Kingdom-focused pacifists quoting Jesus' word to Peter, *"Put away your sword. Those who take up the sword will perish by the sword"*.

Politically, the nub of the issue was of course whose word could you believe: the 'creeping cold war' theorists or the hard-headed realists who saw no prospect of Australia being endangered, let alone invaded? Rather, in SE Asia it was a natural and justifiable uprising against colonialism playing out, not the Soviets marshalling their puppets for an invasion of the Great Southland.

What soon became a remarkable feature of the anti-war movement was the presence of mums and dads and whole families on the streets, not just the leftist opportunists of the media's projection. (It goes without saying that, to a man, the nation's media supported the Liberal Government's tired rhetoric about abstract strategic considerations and obligations to the USA under the ANZUS Treaty.)

"Red rats! Red rats!"

So, as a family we marched, as much out of Christian concern as for political reasons. Besides, it was fun! But not for baby Nicholas, diminutive recipient of conservatives' activism, as we marched in company with thousands down William Street towards King's Cross. As Mum and Dad guided an eight-year-old Sara-Jane through the noisy crowd and led four-year-old Christopher by the hand, while pushing the two-year-old along in his stroller, a utility truck of warmongers drove up beside us, manning a stirrup pump spraying red paint over the marchers at close quarters, the while bellowing "Red rats! Red rats!" We were all 'liberally' sprayed by the Cold War propaganda machine. Besides, what's wrong with rats?

But history would triumph over the fairytales. At the end of 1972, on the election of the first Labor Government in 23 years, Prime Minister Gough Whitlam's first action would be to immediately withdraw the Australian military force from the unpopular Vietnam War, and during the following two years the military might of the Americans would be humbled as they found themselves losing the fight, not against an army but a people, whose disciplined Communist leaders knew exactly what they wanted and how best to attain it (with Red China's moral and practical support). The Western invaders' resolve to hang onto the south of the country faltered and in the end, with the fall of the southern capital Saigon in 1975, they would pull out in disarray while the local business and community leaders fled the country.

It would be the first war that America had ever lost, and also the first time that an Australian involvement was on the losing side. However, one positive outcome was that the new Prime Minister in 1976, Malcolm Fraser – doubtless identifying with the fleeing élites – would boldly offer refuge in Australia to 15,000 Vietnamese from the Malaysian camps, a policy that became bipartisan, ensuring their successful resettlement. The old 'Yellow Peril' phobia had not won the day – though 20 years later John Howard would shamelessly reverse the liberalism to ensure his re-election, on the apron strings of Pauline Hanson, dis-endorsed Liberal candidate and founder of the illiberal One Nation Party.

It would be the best part of fifty years before the nation's leadership, as well as public opinion, would acknowledge that the Vietnam War policy had been a perverse blunder. By then the bulk of the ignored and embittered survivors had slumped into a self-destructive despair, reflected by their woeful medical and mental-health ailments.

"Lest we forget".

What?

CHAPTER 17: *'Let's Speak French'*

The Language Teaching Section of the Commonwealth Office of Education was the plaything of a larger-than-life linguistics guru, the late Neile Osman, with his profound knowledge of French and flair as a teacher. He had talked the COE leadership into applying the 'Australian Situational Method' to the teaching of French as the first foreign language offered in Australian schools. As I now knew from my recent overseas experience, the level of our achievement was embarrassingly low compared with Continental countries. His conviction was that a new approach would liberate teachers and classes from the baggage of the past and usher in a new day in language learning.

So the set of textbooks to be prepared represented not so much the end goal as the validation of a new teaching methodology with the potential to bring about wide-ranging pedagogical reform. Under the title of *Let's Speak French* the series had already been launched, comprising a first-level Teacher's Book and a Students' Book, prepared by Neile himself. He believed they confirmed the potential of the innovative methodology.

To prepare material for the next stage of the experimental project, designed for Years 8 to 10, three 'experts' had been recruited (myself from Paris!) as successful and innovative teachers with a penchant for creative writing. (How they established this in my case is beyond my comprehension.) With our tangible *esprit de corps*, we were dismissed by our colleagues as boffins. I felt proud of the title.

Background to the project

After the early post-war years, efforts were now being made to improve outcomes in the Government's free English classes offered to migrants nationwide. It was obviously impractical to rely on English for teaching our language to monolingual migrants from a wide range of different language-backgrounds, all in the one class.

Enter the Situational Method whereby learners responded to carefully staged and sequenced real-life contexts using tangible objects *('situations')* to learn an appropriate English usage (a 'pattern'), then practised by varying the vocabulary and followed by group repetition to acquire a recognisable pronunciation. If done with flair it could be not only effective but fun. It brought real communication. Of course, the challenge of making a success of a new life in an English-speaking country also provided a powerful incentive.

Until 1966 the Language Teaching Section's only role had been to prepare materials for teaching English (and citizenship) to European migrants, including through radio programs. Neile Osman's vision was to capture the best elements of this *'situational'* method and ally them to new approaches in modern language teaching overseas via the new *audio-lingual or aural-oral* method. From this his plan was to create course materials for teaching French or other languages in Australian schools.

Employing this new pedagogy, over three years our team would draft and publish the second and third level texts of *Let's Speak French*. (But for me one misgiving lingers – most adolescent boys don't like parroting sentences in chorus: girls' stuff!)

In time, under Neile Osman's overall responsibility, I became virtually editor of the Students' Books. For the first time in my life I was being paid to write, to be creative – even though at first my role had been mainly the dreary task of preparing grammatical exercises based on the new material presented in each lesson. But I tried to make the French material sound authentic and even a bit off-beat. Later I was given the more creative task of drafting little human episodes in French by way of introducing and practising some new grammatical point or idiom, e.g. the French mining engineer lost in the Cambodian jungle or the teenager crashing his father's new Peugeot while he was away on business. For *couleur locale* I drew heavily on my recent experience of French lifestyle, place names and tourist spots.

Joy of creative endeavour

I found this the greatest work setting of my employment history. Creative and free-spirited, we all just clicked: I could hardly wait for weekends to pass to get back together on Monday mornings! We stimulated each other, jocularly critiqued each other's efforts, finding way-out humour in many situations evoked in the texts. At times, our laughter would become so uproarious as to bring Neile into our room, hinting that it could be viewed as inappropriate by other Sections for us to be heard enjoying our work quite so much!

Certainly, it put to rest the fears I brought to my change of career that, after ten years' experience of teaching hours, the nine to five drudgery of the working day might prove appalling, not to mention the loss of the nine weeks' vacations. I couldn't have been more wrong! In fact, I would often be disappointed when it was time to go home, even musing "And they actually *pay* me for coming here every day...!" It was pure joy to have found a calling that fitted my soul so well, like a key fits a lock, liberating interest and gifting and passion. As Confucius famously said, "Give a man work he enjoys and he'll never *work* again".

Imaginative writing (in French)

Part Three was more genuinely French in content and flavour than its somewhat awkward predecessors, and at my suggestion it sported endpapers of nicely illustrated maps of France. I also got to choose the cover design, of a speeding electric loco beside the river Rhône in Provence, copied by our artist from one of my travel posters.

Of course, all the French had to be verified by the native-speaking *Assistant* at Sydney University but mostly I managed to hit the jackpot. He also ensured the books' genuinely French cultural flavour. Each new lesson was well illustrated by our artist, whom we briefed in detail to ensure no contradiction between text and illustration.

Ahead of their time?

Under an arrangement unthinkable today in the age of privatisation, the flyleaf proclaimed *'Produced by the Commonwealth Office of Education*

Sydney, on the authority of the Government of the Commonwealth of Australia'. They were published by Angus & Robertson, the largest Australian firm.

However, this did not ensure their commercial success. I suspect the books weren't glossy enough for the late 60s, not being on art paper but only in black & white, with no colour photos. Probably they looked a bit cheapskate, even amateurish.

Authoring a French reader

In 1966 when Neile Osman announced a supplementary deal with the publishers to add a set of short beginners' readers to the *Let's Speak French* series, he invited me to write one, at elementary level. Evoking the adventure games we played in the bush near Port Hacking when I was the age of our projected readers, plus evoking the D-Day landing on the Normandy beaches in 1944 which launched the liberation of France, I dashed off *Le Jour J* [D-Day], an exciting (?) 32 pp. story in very basic French about a group of boys and girls who re-enact the D-Day landing, by canoes, on the southern bushy shore of Port Hacking in the National Park south of Sydney, only to stumble on some undiscovered Aboriginal rock art, which they decide to keep secret. My exotic contribution to world literature – and racially sensitive too!

It was the first 'book' I had ever written, published under my name and later I received a few royalty cheques. Curiously, it was somewhat prophetic of my later concern for Aboriginal people – of whom then I had never met any nor (like most white Australians of my generation), knew anything significant about.

Our 'do it yourself' initiative

But Neile Osman was abashed to be told that the Commonwealth Office of Education did not envisage the need to complete its investment in the textbook project – 'creeping socialism'? The point had been made. It would not be pursued for Years 11 and 12. So he pulled off a private deal with Angus & Robertson's, whereby he and I would devise the books in our own time. He would work on the linguistics: sequencing the grammar and usage to be taught, and then devising how to present it in a situational way (in the Teacher's Book), while I would prepare the reading material and linguistic exercises for the Students' Book. The third member of our trio would be the new *Assistant français* at Sydney University, a charming Gallic character responsible for the authenticity of the French and for general advice. In a Foreword to the Teacher's Book he would note (in English) *"the contribution of James Houston's versatile imagination and talent as a writer of prose passages"*.

Moonlighting to meet a fierce challenge

While continuing my daytime work I now accepted the gruelling challenge of working at home by night on *Let's Speak French, Part Four*, in order to keep pace with Neile's feverish progress. But unlike him I was a family man with home responsibilities. Obsessed with proving the authorities wrong, he now became something of a slave driver. In fact, the publishers had a sword dangling over our heads by a slender thread.

For something like eighteen months we kept up the fierce rhythm, with my turning up every few days with a new, hopefully ingenious solution for encapsulating his teaching points into some readable prose in good French. I would often consult with Michel at dead of night, visiting him at home to establish some obscure point. In a sense, it was an exhilarating life style, with its recurrent deadlines, though scarcely conducive to family life. With the three children Marjorie must have carried a heavy load, particularly at weekends while I sequestered myself in the study, inspired by its graphic black & white wallpaper of Parisian streetscapes.

Not that I had dollar signs before my eyes: I doubt that it ever occurred to me that there might be money in the deal. Rather it was all about the joy of creating French that might be read, studied and learnt from by generations of future students like those I use to teach. If it could also be amusing or whimsical or charming, so much the better. Frankly, I must acknowledge there was some kudos in it: to be publicly writing French for someone in Australia to study is a fairly way-out enterprise, but that's what I was trained to do at university, and I loved it.

The 60 prose passages are much longer than in the two previous books, and far more sophisticated, aimed at 17-18 year-olds. Some reflect the temper of the times: the rejection of established authority that had begun with the student riots at the Sorbonne in the 60s, to sweep the world. Others take a whimsical, imaginative tone, playing up to our stereotypes of the French. Others reflect French technology from the birth of the automobile to the world's first tidal power station. Some evoke great French writers, comparing their high, literary style with the racy prose of today. A plethora of issues figure in the pieces, from both historic and contemporary perspectives: among them, a report on an attitudinal survey of young people, newspaper coverage of a drug bust, a family tree, the history of mail services since the Romans, the French social security system, daily life in the 17th century, reforms in schooling in France, and an offbeat encounter with a cynical enemy of Zacchaeus, rogue tax collector in the Gospels. In all they amount to some 100 pages of readable French.

How were they perceived by their student users at the time? Popular or loathed? Weirdly, I never met any since the books' publication had followed my definitive departure from classrooms and textbooks. Nor can I remember receiving any royalty cheques from the publishers.

As I re-read them now nearly 50 years later, I am rather astonished at their range of interests. Certainly, they come across as more human than any textbook I had ever used with senior classes in Australia or England for teaching French or German. Ironically, in their actuality they seem to compare well with the English texts we used in German schools.

Australians telling Brits how to speak French!

But the textbooks didn't sink without a trace: a few years later Neile informed me that they were being reprinted under licence by Frederick Warne & Co., London for use in UK schools. But since there was already a series of textbooks called *Let's Speak French* in the UK, they had been retitled *Prenons la Parole* [Let's Get Talking]. I have some of these course books, presented to me by the English firm, with the same colour and my cover designs, and an acknowledgment that they were reprinted, with permission, from the Australian originals.

It represented a welcome repudiation of our 'colonial cringe': for once the cultural flow was reversed. So, in all their fading glory, 50 years later the course books still decorate my bookshelves, gathering dust, and evoking Dreamtime memories. Did it all really happen?

Assessing outcomes

The textbook project was to prove a pivotal point in the life of the family. It got me to exchange chalk for pen, and small groups of young people for the community of adults. It got me into the different world of the civil service, with expanded horizons and broader career paths. It severed us from our Sydney setting and led on to life in the national capital, an altogether larger playing field with wider resources affording glimpses of new dreams and visions. It enhanced the legacy of our years spent in Europe assessing the relativity of cultures and enabling us to view Australia from a broader perspective. It got me into writing, exploring a world of imagination and reflection. It triggered unknown abilities and gifts. Not least it added significantly to the resource base of the family.

But what impact did the publicly-funded innovative French course make on the language teaching scene in Britain and Australia? Who knows? In my latest years with the Language Teaching Section, I was talked into preparing a series of ten evening lectures with copious illustrative material on *Let's Speak German*, which I presented for the In-Service Education branch of the NSW Education Department as an evening course for a group of German-teaching enthusiasts. Maybe its approach was too radical, solely reflecting the one-man band of Neile Osman's apprentice.

Soon afterwards I left the Language Teaching Section. The caravan had moved on. Not many years after, I would be one of a handful gathered in a nondescript funeral parlour in Canberra to mourn Neile Osman's premature passing. He was a pioneer educator, bequeathing a creative language-teaching methodology as a legacy. But it grieved and puzzled me that he departed literally unhonoured and unsung.

CHAPTER 18: A Proper Bureaucrat

What do you do when the linguistic dream at the Commonwealth Office of Education comes to an end, and there are 'no more worlds to conquer'? Conceivably return to the classroom? But the Scripture suggests: *"Whoever puts his hand to the plough, and then turns back, is not worthy of the Kingdom of God"*. No, onward and upward! You just trust God and scan the horizon for the next cloud of promise arising.

Unesco functionary

It turned out to be a vacancy in the Commonwealth Office of Education's Unesco Section, not a promotion (though upstairs). Each Member State of Unesco had set up a government body to implement the agenda laid down and accepted at the world level by the United Nations Educational, Scientific and Cultural Organisation, established at the end of the Second World War initially to "build the defences of peace in the minds of men"[10] (sexism appropriate). Australia had set up a secretariat with the requisite specialist national advisory bodies in education, science, and the arts. Each had an executive officer. I found myself the one for education, the key discipline.

I was now a 'proper' public servant, with the role of facilitating the Australian Unesco Education Committee's obligation to earth the vision emanating from Unesco headquarters in Paris. From the outset, Australia had had a hand in defining the world agenda, and we needed to play our part in advancing it by bringing together a dozen or so of the most creative spirits on the national education scene as an advisory committee, speaking to whoever would listen. State Education Departments were represented, as were university faculties of education, research bodies, private and Church schools, teachers' unions, together with a few towering figures in their own right. A tricky beast to manage.

---

[10] The Preamble to the Unesco Constitution: "Since wars begin in the minds of men, it is in the minds of men that the defences of peace must be constructed."

In the next three years, I scaled a precipitous learning curve on being secretary of a corporate body (agendas, minutes, editor of reports, convenor of meetings, travel clerk, organiser of conferences, consulting with stakeholders, handling prima donnas, ensuring concerted action, proffering compromise, etc.). Useful for learning the art of the possible and the need for close attention to detail, while not losing the bigger picture. I loved the challenge of it. For the first time, my boss was a woman – and a hard-headed one at that!

Organising national seminars

The distinctive features of those years were three national seminars that it fell to my lot to convene: in Sydney on 'Education for International Understanding', in Melbourne on 'Social Science for the Secondary School', and in Canberra on 'Planning in Australian Education'. Each produced a report, each one weightier and more significant – books which it was my job to get published. The custom was for Unesco HQ in Paris, in consultation with our local secretariat, to arrange for a world authority as keynote speaker on the topic. To my delight, two were French-speaking: a Belgian lady for 'Education for International Understanding' and a French technocrat for 'Planning in Australian Education', addressing some of the major cutting-edge issues in education: negotiating cold-war tensions, grappling with the unprecedented explosion of social knowledge, and maximising value for money in the provision of public education. The hope was that the bringing together of some of our best minds in a residential setting, over a week or more, might provoke in-depth exploration of new options and generate a creative ferment. Impatience for radical reform was in the air.

Oops!

The choice of eminent expert for the Social Science seminar led to my unwittingly creating a stuff-up of epic proportions. Checking in *Who's Who* on the American we agreed upon, I entered into trans-Pacific negotiations, providing airline tickets and introductory papers. At the seminar in Melbourne the guy appeared bemused by the topic, yet bravely battled on, until it dawned on me: I had brought the wrong academic sociologist by the same name. This one's research thesis was on the changing patterns of barber shops in the USA! Somehow, he managed to sit through the two weeks of proceedings without being humiliated but was not invited to speak. Back in Sydney I made a clean breast of it but my boss Gladys astonished me *by suggesting we keep it as our own sordid little secret.* The truly humane culture of Unesco...

Drafted to the National Capital

In 1968, the Commonwealth Office of Education was upgraded by the Liberal Gorton Government to become the Department of Education & Science, slated for imminent relocation to Canberra. One of the factors for joining the COE had been its projected move to the national capital within the next few years. It was optional to stay – but evident that a career path in the Commonwealth Public Service inevitably led to Canberra. Besides, after our cool European years I was eager to turn my back on the humid Sydney summers.

A frosty epiphany

So, one frosty morning during the Educational Planning seminar I drove off from the ANU's Ursula College in the Commonwealth car that went with the secretary's job, heading up the newly named 'Belconnen Way' over the saddle of Black Mountain. Beyond the crest I noticed on the horizon to the left a rather striking conical hill, its lower ridge tapering down to the point where, in the middle distance, a cluster of new housing was mushrooming. Drawn towards the rim of hills by the hope that it might afford a view down the Molonglo valley, I found a point of entry near a new suburb sign 'COOK'.

Closer to the rocky ridge a magnificent gumtree filled the foreground and beyond it, on the far horizon, was painted the blue line of the Brindabellas. Just where I'd pulled up, a rough track clambered up a mossy boulder-strewn patch of grassy hillside towards a makeshift shed with a sign *'FOR SALE'* and a phone number. There were some excavations, with great mossy rocks dislodged from their ancient sockets, and a few brick piers emerging from the hillside. I clambered upwards and as I gained higher ground, the splendour of the outlook caught my breath.

Splendid 'site for a village'

It seemed the whole winter-lush Molonglo Valley lay at my feet, with a gravel road winding down through the pastures to Coppins Crossing. To the west the view was framed by the highest points of the blue Brindabellas, often snow-capped in winter. I mused that the block might just represent a liminal zone between countryside and suburbia, combining the spirit of both worlds. Maybe we could have the last house in Canberra! The rear boundaries of the block formed a bend in the outer edge of the suburb, which moved down onto the flat land of a working sheep-station with homestead, shearing-shed, and an early settlers' slab hut. My imagination took wings: this is where I want to live!

CHAPTER 19: Citizens of No Mean City

We had sold our house at Lane Cove to the first caller who inspected it. He was an academic historian and a Christian, and we liked him. Conceivably we might have got a higher price, but it seemed fair and enabled us to go in much deeper with our new house. It was being built by two Finnish brothers-in-law, both Christians, with the lounge-dining room rejoicing in the grand view to two horizons.

To create a garden was no mean challenge, since the block was strewn with basalt boulders thrown out from the ancient volcano of nearby Mt Painter. The main gardening tool proved to be our crowbar! Gratefully claiming our new householder's (gratis) allocation of trees and shrubs, we planted the boundaries with a great array of European trees starring an authentic German Christmas tree.

Providential blessings

About this time our family was completed by the advent of our third son, David. Two of our children had enrolled at Cook Primary School on its opening day. Sometimes working away carving out the front garden from among the rocks, I would pause to acknowledge the amazing grace of the God who had so lavishly blessed us with loving family, beautiful new home, a meaningful existence and challenging work. I was in my element, in love with the place and its spectacular setting. What had we done to deserve this? It was *"all of grace, lest any man should boast"* (Ephesians 2:9). And it was to get better.

For the next 16 years 26 Moss Street, Cook was to be our home. The family would be raised in that idyllic setting, with a hillside at the back door designed for wild west games. In the earlier years Marjorie was home carer, only resuming her career in social work after David started school.

CHAPTER 19: Citizens of No Mean City   125

Dreams of community development

Aside from the family and work focus, I was acquiring an interest in the notion of community development. We were residents of a brand new suburb made up mostly of recent arrivals from Sydney, Melbourne or overseas. We were generally of comparable years and occupational orientation, with young families aspiring to create new networks. If we were to get to know each other, together we might be able to enrich our quality of life and shape a more human community.

'Cook's Endeavour'

It was 1970, the 200th anniversary of Captain James Cook's epic journey of discovery along Australia's east coast and we were living in a suburb named after him. The obvious response was to launch a community magazine named *'Cook's Endeavour'*, with a historic engraving of the ship on the cover and Cook's signature below. The initiative began by approaching local businesses to sponsor a page. It worked.

The first issue's editorial explained the vision for such a publication, and then featured some parish-pump news items, interviews with interesting newcomers, plants to grow in starting a new garden, etc. We had a production team and a distribution team, while I took responsibility for writing or commissioning the content. It came out more or less quarterly.

To my surprise *Cook's Endeavour* became known further afield. The National Library requested copies for their local collection. Elsewhere in Canberra, we picked up comments commending the admirable spirit of the Cook community. Then in response to my editorial appealing to the locals to mark the Cook Bi-Centenary, a public community meeting at the school agreed upon erecting on the lower slopes of Mt Painter a vertical sundial evoking Cook's splendid navigational skills, and seeking gazettal of the mountainside as parkland. And this not so much for historic reasons as to provide a focus for community identification.

The story made headlines in the *Canberra Times* and conferred on Cook the accolade of the first Canberra suburb to spawn a citizens' campaign to enhance its own community development. I would like to think that *Cook's Endeavour* may have made some contribution to the formation of 'social capital' locally – that intangible though priceless sense of public wellbeing within a community created by face-to-face contacts, goodwill and shared concerns. In the early 1970s optimism was still around, especially in a brand-new community not yet spoiled by dysfunctionality. People had more time for each other, were less hassled by the struggle to become ever more affluent and, despite the common sneer in the metropolises that Canberra was a city without a soul and class-ridden by Public Service grades, we experienced it as an open, welcoming society.

Soon on a hillside overlooking the suburb the Captain Cook commemorative monument was duly erected on land gazetted as parkland and dedicated in a festive community barbecue by the Whitlam Government's Minister for the Interior, Kep Enderby, our local MP. The community had raised virtually the entire costs of the project. And there it stands to this day in its irrelevant glory, the only tangible fruit of *Cook's Endeavour* apart from the holdings in the National Library, and the historic drawing of the *Endeavour* with Cook's signature above my desk.

As I became increasingly caught up in travelling interstate the illustrious publication died the death. By then it was becoming sadly evident that the anomie of Australian society in the turbulent perplexities of the early 1970s was not to be countered by such slim local 'endeavours', despite the trendy mantra of *'Think globally, act locally'*.

CHAPTER 20: A Nation Transformed

In 1969 those members of the Commonwealth Office of Education who had opted for transfer to Canberra found themselves smaller fish in a larger pond. In the national capital we soon learnt that, for the ambitious, leap-frogging from Department to Department was the name of the game. Essential to keep a weather eye on job vacancies notified in the *Commonwealth Gazette*.

Before long I noticed an interesting vacancy advertised by the Immigration Department involving a slight decrease in salary and status – anathema to the rules of the game! But recalling my interest back in Germany in the phenomenon of immigration, it revived the old appeal. My application for the post of 'National Groups Officer' at once proved successful. It was a newly created position focusing on issues posed by the social outcomes of the mass migration programs during the previous twenty years: a fascinating cocktail worth committing one's working life to. Unwittingly, I had found my true *métier*. Or rather in God's good providence it had found me.

Human flotsam and jetsam of war

By 1969, mass immigration was already a notable Australian success story. Arthur Calwell's bold decision in 1947, as Australia's first Minister for Immigration, to offer a new life in Australia to Displaced Persons (DPs) washing helplessly around Europe in the post-war maelstrom, had triggered the first officially sponsored movement of non-English-speakers into this country. An innovative initiative – historic, almost revolutionary. Australia would never be the same afterwards.

Who were these DPs? People trapped outside their homeland through deportation as Nazi slave labourers, or refugees fleeing from the advancing Red Army, or survivors from the death camps and liberated prisoners of war, or simply victims of circumstances – by 1946 up to two million people unable or unwilling to return to their now communist homelands: Poles, Latvians, Estonians, Lithuanians, Ukrainians, Czechs, Slovaks, Hungarians, Serbs, Croats, Macedonians. At war's end, they had fetched up on both sides of the *'Iron Curtain'*.

"Populate or perish!"

Meanwhile in Australia, in the aftermath of the threatened Japanese invasion, the catchcry had become *'Populate or perish!'*. Of course, the instinctive focus was on the British Isles and the need to reinforce our British identity as a remote part of the Empire: "We must fill this country or lose it" (Arthur Calwell, first Immigration minister).

So the post-war Chifley Labor Government, after due processes of community consultation and public education, and with the backing of both the trade unions and big business, had made a commitment in 1947 to boost the national population from its seven and a half million by an annual target increase of 2%, to be made up of 1% by natural increase and 1% by immigration. Apart from the DP component, the migrants were to come from the British Isles (@ ten pounds per family) and from northern Europe.

But time was of the essence, with the recognition that once the European nations had restored their economies, emigration would be discouraged because of local workforce expansion needs. On the other hand, to many war-weary Europeans despairing of the prospects of permanent security, a new start in a peaceful if unknown country on the other side of the globe was not without its attractions.

So in their hundreds of thousands the migrant hopefuls had poured in: by 1952 some 700,000 of them, including 170,000 DPs facilitated by the International Refugee Organisation which paid the $20 shipping fare for each one. Initially the 'beautiful Balts' – men and women from Lithuania, Latvia and Estonia – were chosen for their fair hair and blue eyes.

In exchange for free passage and assistance on arrival, DPs were contracted to work for the government for two years. The visionary Snowy Mountains hydro-electric project would absorb large numbers harmoniously, including many recent wartime enemies. Later I was to meet *lawyers* and *medicos* drafted into the bush to cut railway sleepers!

Of course, it had amounted to the government taking a calculated risk, that the post-war labour shortage would prove so pressing as to outweigh the past legacy of public hostility towards foreign workers and aliens. But there was no precedent for such an aspiration by governments.

On the contrary, past experience reflected the opposite. Despite the hideous conflict recently culminating in the revelation of the Holocaust, an opinion poll of the time rated *Germans* above DPs! By the early 1940s the percentage of overseas-born people in Australia had fallen to the lowest ever – and nearly all of them were *'New Chums'* from Britain.

Enlisting the civil society

In 1950, the Labor Government had taken the creative initiative of setting up Good Neighbour Councils as umbrella groups to enlist the civil society (the churches, service clubs, community agencies) in the task of generating public support for the resettlement of migrants, while reassuring the public that they too would in time become dinkum Aussies through the process of assimilation to their neighbours. By the early 1970s nearly a thousand community agencies and thousands of volunteers across Australia were involved in providing information and direct assistance to migrants (mostly from non-English-speaking countries): holding seminars on welfare entitlement and the recognition of qualifications and, in later years, art exhibitions and other events celebrating ethnic talents. Some 70 staff were employed to co-ordinate the work of the volunteers, supervised nationally by one senior officer of my grade in the Immigration Department.

But during these post-war years the Good Neighbour Councils had stubbornly discountenanced any meaningful participation by the migrants themselves, stoutly supporting the conservative governments' paternalistic line which *excluded non-Anglo* migrants from offering any input to settlement policy.

'White Australia'

At Federation, we had inherited a chequered colonial record of coping with ethnic diversity. Racial tensions triggered by the presence of Chinese gold-diggers in NSW had simmered for years before boiling over in 1861 in the Lambing Flat racial riots and massacre at Young. Victorian legislation refused them direct entry to that Colony, necessitating heroic overland treks to Ballarat and Bendigo from the tiny seaside village of Robe in South Australia (landed by the original 'people smugglers'?). It also led to the restriction of immigration from China by the NSW legislature.

Scarcely surprising then that the first legislation passed by the Commonwealth Parliament in 1901 had been the *Immigration (Restriction) Act* mandating a 'White Australia'. It led to the wholesale repatriation (mostly to the wrong islands!) of the Kanakas working as quasi-slave labourers in the Queensland sugar-cane fields. So for the next 70 years 'White Australia' would remain one of the underpinnings of Australians' self-understanding. We were, and would remain, a country of white men *(sic)* under the Southern Cross. The alternative was to be overrun by the coloured hordes to the north who would destroy the hard-won gains of earlier generations of British settlers. Both a glance at the world atlas and the memory of the world war put that issue into stark relief.

So was I a *racist?* Certainly not! Well ... er.., maybe we *all* were! But the term was never used in everyday speech. We were simply *Australians* – but there weren't many of us in our whole southern continent. Did that matter? Not until after the war that shook us to our foundations: now we knew there were simply not enough of us to go round. OK, immigration could fix that – but not enough Brits were opting in. Would we be safe here while the world surged all around us, and especially closer to our untenanted northern shores?

But what of the original Australians?

Of course, all this had to be set over against an even darker Australian reality: from the beginnings of European 'settlement' the low-level war of invasion on the moving frontier had generated the desirability of an ethnic cleansing of the 'native peoples', resident in the land for the past 60,000 years. Did they have any inherent human rights? The question never cropped up. But since they had no 'culture' they would not even qualify. They were more akin to the fauna, and that was sadly prone to 'die out' as other species were introduced. Later, borne along by popular sentiment, colonial legislators had upheld the dispersal and marginalisation of the country's Aborigines, creating perennial targets for rejection and scorn. Who remembers the racism of the *'Mine tinkit Pelaco'* ad of a gibbering black man incongruously wearing a white gentleman's shirt?

Was racism caught – or taught? Could this unsavoury if unconscious legacy of xenophobia really be challenged in the second half of the 20th century on the entry of 170,000 DPs?

Unwittingly, this very challenge would become the essence of my work with the Department of Immigration from 1969 to 1974 and then with the Community Relations Office until 1983. But the way in which this key question would ultimately come to be viewed was at that stage unimaginable.

In retrospect, I was arguably the first Public Servant ever to be employed by any government in Australia to grapple with this issue of the community's latent if unconscious racism (even though my Immigration Department bosses at the time never saw it to be an issue).

Responding to post-war labour shortages

With the defeat in 1949 of the wartime Chifley Labor Government, Robert Menzies had formed a Liberal/Country Party coalition destined to last under a succession of leaders for 23 years until Gough Whitlam's Labor victory in 1972. For economic reasons Menzies had continued Calwell's vision of expanding a 'British civilisation under the Southern Cross', but already by 1951 it was becoming clear that the targets set for the percentage of Britons in the annual intakes could not be sustained.

As the Displaced Persons scheme had wound down, with labour shortages now hampering post-war expansion, the Government had initiated a 'Bring Out a Briton' campaign, and also negotiated Assisted Migration Agreements with a number of European governments: Netherlands, Belgium, West Germany, Austria, Italy, Malta, Yugoslavia (a composite Balkan country stretching inland along the Adriatic coast), Spain, Greece and ultimately Lebanon (only involving Christians) and Turkey. As conditions in post-war western Europe had progressively improved, the spotlight had to shift transversely ever south and east, from prosperity to relative poverty.

Assimilation ever the policy

Although the Migration Agreements made mention of the cultural rights of the migrants, no concrete action on this had ever been forthcoming in Australia. It was solely window-dressing. Indeed, on the contrary, every effort was made to 'assimilate' the newcomers (implying discounting their own cultures), beginning with shipboard English lessons that included material on the Australian way of life and ongoing evening classes in the major cities, as well as on ABC Radio, in the hope that migrants would learn to speak *'the King's English'* – a forlorn hope, given that locally-born Australians had never looked like attaining such a lofty goal!

Alternatives to assimilation?

By 1969, the assimilation doctrine was sounding increasingly unconvincing. After all, migrants had not come here individually as 'guest workers' (as in western Europe) who could never aspire to citizenship rights, but as equal partners in building the future nation through family migration. By then forward thinkers were starting to question the glib assumptions of assimilation. As early as 1956 the ABC Chairman, Sir Richard Boyer, had been publicly musing at a Citizenship Convention, *"We have been thinking that the newcomers are on trial. It is we who are now on trial"*.

On the one hand migrants, flooding in by their tens of thousands from a score of Continental nations, languages and cultures, were putting down roots into the Australian soil and beginning to dream dreams. They were mostly young, energetic, highly motivated and hard-working. They were seeing the fruits of their labours, buying simple houses in depressed inner-city areas, and sponsoring family members to join them.

Indeed, the distinguishing feature of our model of immigration was the emphasis on *the family*. In many cases the children were gaining an education unthinkable for workers' children in the homelands. Every second Greek migrant wanted his son to become a brain surgeon! But few if any aspired to ape the Anglo-Saxon lifestyles, attitudes and values they perceived around them. Rather they found personal meaning in the association with compatriots, sometimes as close-knit as having come through 'chain migration' from the same Italian village or Greek island. All this and heaven too!

On the other hand, every year they had been heavily outnumbered by UK migrants, always the largest component of the program. Two-thirds of these came on assisted passages, the famous 'ten pound Poms', and many were housed initially in Migrant Hostels. But when during a recession in the 1960s local unemployment had risen sharply, British tabloids sensationalised the misery of migrants taken in by the Australian propaganda of sunny beaches and neat brick-veneer houses with roses over the garden gate. Many UK migrants were bailing out disillusioned, giving rise to the 'whingeing Pom' syndrome, which led to a Government enquiry.

Throughout this period, assimilation had remained the ruling ideology. It was seen as a one-way street whereby migrants abandoned their irrelevant past, to settle for getting a job, reuniting their family, buying their first home, learning the language and living happily ever after as 'New Australians', the official term for 'non-British' newcomers. In return, locally-born Australians were reassured that their own much-vaunted way of life would not be disturbed. The familiar institutions would not need to be changed: the schools, the health service, the law, trade unions (all modelled on British patterns). It was up to the migrants to adapt and become 'honorary Brits'.

Sectional anti-migrant sentiment

But, of course, there was another and uglier side to the immigration 'success' story. Too often the misgiving was voiced that the New Australians were 'taking over' the inner suburbs and forming 'ghettos' (a ludicrous claim if the meaning and historical associations of the word were understood). Other jaundiced voices chimed in, analysing the merits (few) and failings (legion) of the *poms, dagoes, eyeties, Balts, reffos, wogs, wops, yids, chinks, chows, slanties et al.* In the late 1940s a fruitshop at Punchbowl where we lived, referring to its Italian business rival opposite, unspeakably proclaimed over its doorway, 'Shop Here before the *Day Goes'*. Likewise, the welcoming cry, *'Go back to where ya came from!'* all too often rang around the ridges. Open-hearted Australian hospitality?

Nevertheless by 1969, at least in the capitals and larger industrial cities, immigration had become normalised as a continuing feature of Australian life and most citizens of Anglo-Saxon extraction were in strong support of the steady stream of new arrivals from the UK and other European countries, plus the novel phenomenon of tiny numbers of Eurasians arriving from British Empire countries like India, Ceylon (after independence to be re-styled Sri Lanka) and Mauritius. There was still no major movement of Indians, Chinese or South-East Asians. For both economic and security reasons, it was by then broadly accepted that we needed an expanded population, and the transfer of skills and varied life styles was being hailed as beneficial – *in the cities!* The earlier phobia about ghetto formation had been largely overcome, and it was conceded that migrants would naturally gravitate into groups and formations reflecting their backgrounds and interests.

But country towns often presented a different picture, since rural industries (except perhaps in the tropics) were traditionally unattractive to newcomers. Their low-wage structure and isolation from the great population centres left them more or less untouched by the new phenomenon irrevocably changing life in the cities – in most people's view for the better. Although the great bulk of southern European migrants came from rural villages their life style was poles apart from life in our country towns, and the lure of steady work in city factories paying higher wage rates proved irresistible. Long and painful had been the experience of their compatriots in the north Queensland sugarcane-fields before their *third* generation had become comfortably off – and broadly accepted.

Indicative of the gulf between urban and rural experience of life was the formation in 1962 of the Australian League of Rights, originating in South Australia's Eyre Peninsula and the New England region of NSW. In addition to its main thrust as a right-wing, anti-political movement espousing capitalism, social credit and the monarchy, it was also unashamedly anti-Semitic and opposed to non-British migration. In this sense, it foreshadowed Pauline Hanson's One Nation Party. But that was still 30 years away, and well beyond a watershed marking the irreversible transformation of Australia through worldwide immigration.

Stirrings of community activism

By the late 60s, the incipient murmurings of self-appointed migrant spokesmen were turning into more significant rumblings, emanating largely from migrant trade union leaders reflecting the considerable body of shared experience on the factory floor. In particular a number of politically radical Greek and Italian spokesmen were emerging on the public stage, similarly demanding that their views be given official consideration. But they had no voice at the annual Citizenship Convention, a talk shop for the Establishment where no one rocked any boats. Neither did they figure in the carefully chosen membership of the two advisory bodies which the Immigration Department used for window dressing: the Immigration Planning Council (largely economists) and the Immigration Advisory Council (largely Humanities academics). The grassroots went unnoticed – though their subterranean networks were steadily evolving.

Walter Lippmann, who had arrived in Melbourne from Germany in 1938 and later became leader of the Australian Jewish Welfare Society, was to become the first migrant member of the Immigration Advisory Council. He and a number of academic sociologists backed by the Ecumenical Migration Centre in Melbourne, plus ACOSS representatives[11], were also strongly advocating the recognition of cultural differences in partnership with migrant organisations. Professor Jerzy Zubrzycki from the ANU in Canberra had become a confidant of the Permanent Head of the Immigration Department, Sir Peter Heydon. He and the *doyenne* of Australian immigration sociology, Professor Jean Martin from La Trobe University, would meet in his office from time to time at close of day to discuss trends in immigration.

However, his Department did not operate in a vacuum. Its existence had been decreed by a bold decision of a Labor Government in 1945, maintained by the conservative Menzies Government beyond 1949.

---

[11] Australian Council of Social Service, roof body of the welfare professions

Thus, from the outset it enjoyed bipartisan support, a vital factor in the hesitant public acceptance of the immigration program. But as is customary in a liberal democracy, competing groups engaged in a tug-of-war. Employers wanted cheap labour. Trade unions were concerned about newcomers undercutting wage rates. The public were often uninvolved or sceptical.

In the early decades, academic interest was slight and economically oriented, but by the late 60s the new breed of sociologists were beginning to examine the human costs and outcomes, drawing on the experience of grassroots welfare workers, leading to something of an informal alliance destined to exert a powerful influence on migration policy once alternative visions of the future began to come into focus. What was still lacking was any input from the migrants themselves, or from any elements within the Immigration Department who might be interested in change.

There was now a need for an over-arching concept for building the culturally diverse Australian nation of the future – still on the principle of the fair go, to be proven by offering equal access to education, health, welfare, and legal systems (while providing translators and interpreters). It opened up the prospects of a permanent cultural pluralism, matching the diversification with the ongoing transformation of our social institutions.

Bureaucrats shunning the new social realities

But reasoned debate had no place: almost no one in the Department had a university degree. Assimilation had been such a simple goal to pursue, and had clearly enjoyed the broad support of the Anglo-Saxon populace. On the other hand, what did 'integration' mean in practice? What would happen differently? So on the early death of Sir Peter Heydon, the Department's leaders began to grope about in the policy no-man's land between the proven program of assimilation ('one size fits all') and the nascent dream of 'integration' – whatever that meant!

Though the Department's Assimilation Branch had been renamed the Integration Branch in 1964 in recognition of the changing trajectory on offer to migrants, it is doubtful whether it had amounted to more than semantics. On the other hand, what would 'integration' mean in practice? What would happen differently?

I was soon to discover that, beyond the Integration Branch, there was barely an officer able – or willing – to make the mental readjustment. Certainly the senior leaders of the Department whom I would later encounter seemed to be unreconstructed assimilationists, jealously guarding the future national unity of an Anglo-Saxon Australia increasingly under siege, with its nostalgic concepts of mateship, a fair go, self-reliance, plus 'the national interest'. But who could define 'the Australian way of life'– let alone inculcate it – threatened as it was by every new shipful or planeload of migrants arriving from ever-widening backgrounds, bringing their 'cultures' with them? Moreover, specifically catering for migrant needs had hitherto been deemed non-egalitarian.

The nub of the problem was that we could never lure enough Anglo-Saxons here: indeed, in the mid-sixties there was an actual outflow of the disgruntled back to Britain. For the ageing leaders of the Department, appointed when the Department was launched in the late 1940s to co-ordinate migration from Britain, it had always been a quantitative business: *"a migrant is a migrant is a migrant"*. Even after many years, you could not characterise 'the migrant opinion' on anything. They no more shared a collective opinion than a carriageful of train commuters.

The actuality was that, from Day One – powerless and inarticulate – migrants would be cast into survival mode. Their experience after disembarking from ship or plane became an issue for other Departments – social welfare, health, education – properly equipped for such tasks. But was that actually the case? It begs the fundamental issue of understanding language and culture: even if people were all archetypal 'migrants'. Who in these Departments could understand their cultural expectations, let alone speak their 25 languages? Or should the Department that brought them here have accepted some specialised responsibility for their subsequent wellbeing?[12]

---

[12] In future years, it would in fact be tasked with such wider responsibilities, as reflected in a later name 'Immigration, Local Government and Ethnic Affairs'.

Already, over twenty-five years their combined impact had rendered Australia one of the most *quantitatively* diverse nations in human history. But what did this mean for our self-understanding? As an outcome of earlier British colonialism the current situation had never been envisaged, planned or devised: it had simply come about as an unforeseen by-product of the post-war immigration program.

So what did the situation now imply *qualitatively?* Could a modern nation cohere in the face of such structural diversity? Or continue to be a nation which prized freedom and equality? Was there some limit to the endless diluting of the intent of the founding fathers? If not, what might be the overall concept that could emerge to hold it all together harmoniously?

Public service conservatism

To senior officialdom the challenge stemmed from their sheer ignorance of the newcomers' views and sensibilities about anything – how could these be heard, politically voiceless as migrants were? While migration studies were beginning to become a focus of sociology and demography, who knew anything about *grassroots* migrant opinion beyond the few articulate (and largely leftist) self-appointed spokesmen? But, of course, the leaders of the Department were not seeking out migrant voices to dialogue with.

So my task as the National Groups Officer would be to foster nationwide a balanced and wide-ranging input from the migrants themselves about their emerging prospects, and ensure that this would be taken into account in the planning of future services ... no mean challenge! And certainly, until then the most demanding, if exhilarating task ever laid upon me.

CHAPTER 21: Taking the Ethnic Pulse

If the father of the new brainchild had been the Head of the Department, the midwife was the Gorton Government's Minister for Immigration, Billy Snedden. Persuaded by Sir Peter Heydon, in a speech prepared within the Department and delivered in Kogarah, Sydney in 1969 the Minister had announced an initiative designed to build relationships between his Department and Australia's migrant communities. A specialist officer would be appointed to undertake this policy development, with the designation of 'National Groups Officer'.

But, of course, public servants have a natural investment in upholding the status quo and have no mandate to become innovative. This was to become a serious issue for me on joining the Immigration Department in 1970. My prior work in the Public Service, both in Sydney and in Canberra – not to speak of life in the teaching profession – had always been, and perforce, creative. Students had to be motivated, textbooks had to be drafted, Unesco seminars had to be organised on behalf of professional interest groups. Now I belonged to a Department that created nothing, but uncritically administered government policy. That is of course what public servants do. But really, I had never been a proper 'public servant' – nor would I ever become one!

Blissfully unaware of this at the beginning, before long it would loom as an area of risky shoals to be negotiated, but only after I started developing my own convictions about what government policy might become. And really, under the benign eye of Sir Peter a former diplomat, that's what I had been appointed to contribute to. But as it soon transpired, he had little support from his most senior officers for this creative initiative, and before long he was invalided out of the service, to die relatively young. Indeed, when it became clear what I was on about they would oppose the thrust of my work. And what was my dream? A typically romantic vision? Or something capable of being earthed in the developing Australian reality? And who would be involved in bringing it about? With the Department leader's untimely death, the senior officers would grope about in the policy no-man's land between the proven program of assimilation ('one size fits all') and the nascent dream (not of 'integration' – a meaningless term) but of *cultural pluralism*.

A quizzical welcome

Turning up for duty with my new Department on my first day I had discovered I would be part of the Welfare Section, my boss a social worker, located within the Integration Branch. It was the only part of the Department concerned with what happened to migrants after they got off the ships – or later the planes. I had been taken to meet Sir Peter Heydon, an urbane, distinguished-looking man of impeccable manners. Later I was to discover he was also an elder of the Presbyterian Church, imbued with the Christian vision of humanity and social justice. To me he stressed that the creation of my new position reflected the abandonment of assimilation as the desired outcome of our immigration program and a new turning towards the migrants themselves, in order to forge a positive partnership full of promise for the future.

Departmental scepticism

First morning on the job, enquiring how I should start, I had encountered the bland reply, *"Search me. That's your job!"* Thanks for the encouragement! On the other hand, I had been given a blank cheque to spend, a rare situation indeed for a middle-ranking officer. Go where you will, speak to whom you wish.

Enquiries soon brought to light that the Department had very little knowledge of the number or whereabouts of the migrant organisations to which it might conceivably relate. If any local officers had gathered such information in the course of their duties, it was held in the Branch Offices in each State capital. For instance, the senior social worker in Melbourne, himself a former Dutch migrant, reputedly had a list. Obviously, what was needed was first-hand data gathered in the field. But what sort of data? Simply the existence of an organisation and its ethnic identity? Its location? Its purposes? Its membership? What about its programs, resources, its leaders – its *potential?* And how well disposed it might be towards relating to a federal government department? But what are we talking about here: the Greek Orthodox Archdiocese of Australia or the Polish Rats of Tobruk Association of Hobart?

My dream – too grandiose?

I put forward the suggestion of attempting a nationwide survey of migrant organisations – the *what?* and the *where?* and the *why?*. I was referred to the statistics unit, skilled in social research projects, and especially random sampling techniques. But my proposal was not about head-counting but qualitative research, if possible to locate every migrant organisation in the Commonwealth, and then go and talk to its leaders, exercising my professional judgment and encouraging them to partner with the Department in building a better country for us all. A grandiose project? No doubt. Some of my colleagues were sceptical: surely such a plan is going beyond what government departments do in discharging their statutory role of administering government policy? What if it unleashed demands the government could not meet? Certainly, it seemed beyond supervising from Canberra. After all I did have a blank cheque book – but not for dispensing government goodies.

A few weeks later, a pilot project in the Canberra-Queanbeyan region was approved and set to go, combining my draft research questionnaire with impromptu discussions. This would set some limits to open-ended interviews. The 104 questions covered the basic identifiers of the organisation: name, national group, address, number of members, leaders, purpose, property, resources, program, activities, etc., all designed for processing by the new-fangled computers. The discussions would explore the leaders' attitudes and their own evaluation of their achievements, assess motivation and hopes for the future, with or without government assistance. And garner any suggestions about taking part in a new co-operative role with the government in nation-building.

Launching the nationwide survey

Scouring the Canberra regional telephone directory, and also spotting numerous migrant clubs and associations scattered through the city and suburbs, as well as enquiring among many colleagues from migrant backgrounds – and being assured many more organisations would come to light from the early contacts established – it was soon *'all systems go'*, as the space exploration jargon of the day had it.

How shall I forget meeting with the organisation chosen for the initial visit, the Macedonian Orthodox Church in Queanbeyan? There was a certain poetic justice in opening the nationwide campaign in Queanbeyan, a decade earlier the scene of my labours wearing a different hat before leaving on a mission to broaden my understanding of European cultures. Also as a Christian I rated highly the prospect of tapping into a co-operative spirit by contact with a church, with its serious purpose and its service orientation, and I meant to try out this theory early on.

So one week night I met with half a dozen men representing the church, together with the (non-English-speaking) priest. Because of their limited English, it was uphill explaining my purpose in the face of their general suspicion of my motives, identifying me more likely as a security agent than a genuine learner. Nevertheless, in a longish session the atmosphere gradually thawed out, and we ended up accepting each other's credentials, mine as a fellow-Christian as well as an official. The questionnaire was hurriedly done at the end and I realised at once the difficulty of making the questions wide-ranging enough to be meaningful to the huge range of organisational types likely to be encountered

After several months' work around Canberra and Queanbeyan (mostly in the evenings, when organisation leaders were available) I had completed 75 questionnaires, reflecting 32 ethnic backgrounds ranging from American to Ukrainian and including Swiss, Jewish and Slovenian – a broader outcome than anyone had anticipated. Suddenly an Australia-wide survey looked like scaling Mt Everest!

Yet I couldn't work on it full-time because any issue raised by or about 'national group' organisations from anywhere in Australia landed on my desk, and this kept me hopping. But I had been allocated a graduate trainee for a short stint as an assistant who had helped in the design of the questionnaire.

Handling the data

Of course I should have taken the completed questionnaires to the Research Unit to analyse the data by creating a customised computer program which might have been used progressively State by State to build up a national picture. But I was sceptical of what computers could do, and indeed ultimately the project proved quite beyond the wit of the Department's sole 'computer expert', so that the thousands of hours of laborious data-gathering Australia-wide would never be turned to much account!

But in the early 1970s the absence of 'hard' data from an ethnic-organisational perspective was hardly a problem, given that what was also gathered for the first time was a qualitative analysis of migrant leaders' insights, experiences, attitudes and aspirations (how is goodwill *'computable'?*) – and that from coast to coast.

With the agreement of each interviewee, and after establishing my credentials and purpose, I always took detailed notes of points made in our discussion. Later, as the survey progressed around Australia, after each stage (perhaps three weeks' work) I would submit to my bosses a field report which included case studies of significant organisations encountered and new insights gained. I don't know what they made of it all. The senior officers, honest tradesmen that they were, were simply not on that analytical wavelength and some seemed to view it as a personal indulgence on my part. One contented himself with the comment that my reports used too many adjectives!

Looking back, I doubt that anything was passed on to Sir Peter, patron of the project. But I came to feel that an accurate reading of migrant opinion would be an indispensable factor in developing community relations for the future – and perhaps the ultimate evidence of the success of Australia's bold post-war experiment in nation building beyond our British comfort zone.

But, of course, in those early days such societal-level considerations were hardly imaginable: my simple task was to track down organisations and pick their leaders' brains. It was a quite untilled field of social research, despite the presence in our community of people speaking a hundred languages, amounting to some 15% (about one person in six) of the whole population.

Incidentally, English-speaking migrant organisations were also targeted, including those set up by Scottish (now perceived as my own national group), Irish, Welsh, American, Canadian and South African migrants. *Inter alia*, an analysis of their attitudes towards non-English-speaking migrants could prove an interesting by-product: we hardly needed to import fresh reservoirs of racial prejudice!

How fascinating it would have been to include a question or two about migrants' understanding of, and attitudes towards the First Australians. But in such remote retrospect that might have been too clever by half!

Let's not overlook the fact that in 1970 the White Australia Policy was still alive and twitching, though its days were numbered. The chorus of would-be reforming voices was still off stage, rather than at concert pitch. Hence our subsequently published *Directories of National Groups* for all States and the ACT make little mention of migrants from Asia subsequently destined to transform the immigration scene.

CHAPTER 22: Courting Ethnic Allies

Armed with the insights gained from our regional survey I decided that the Premier State should be targeted first. By then Jan Reksten, originally from Norway, had become my colleague for the nationwide research project. More importantly he would become a lifelong friend. Not only did he bring a non-Anglo approach to the task but was also a Sydney University modern languages graduate. So we were congenial company and together we soldiered on for months, on and off – in Sydney, Newcastle and the Illawarra – interspersed with lengthy periods back in Canberra. After all, I had a family to consider as well as other tasks in the Department to attend to.

Over the next three years Marjorie would emerge as the unsung hero of the Australia-wide survey. I hardly dare contemplate what my frequent absences must have cost her as she coped with the sole parenting of four children aged from ten to one. While I mostly came home for the weekend from Sydney, this became impractical as we moved further afield, and I shudder to think how she coped with my three-week absences. It was not compensated by the lift in our family budget through my working so many hours of higher-paid overtime (interstate we worked every evening and often at weekends too) and also saved on my accommodation allowance. The Travel Clerk had informed me that it was no concern of the Department where I stayed outside Canberra whether at the Hilton or the Houstons'. So, in Sydney I would stay with my Dad, by then a widower.

Cordial yokefellows

Jan Reksten and I had decided that, from the outset each should go his separate way: seeking out contacts, following through with interviews, completing questionnaires and making notes. Flying in from Canberra, we would head for the Commonwealth garage at Waterloo to pick up two self-drive cars for our visiting program. Beyond the Sydney campaign, we used to book rooms in the same motel, sharing meals, swapping the moments of humour, pathos and challenge that we encountered. Really it was a sort of working holiday, full of human interest and appeal – but they paid us (very well) for it! We reckoned we had the best jobs in the Immigration Department.

Amazing range of organisations encountered

Soon we discovered the receding horizon syndrome: the more organisations we encountered the more (perhaps of the same ethnic group) would come to light. Could the survey ever be finished? For instance, to meet with the committee of a Greek 'Brotherhood' (migrants from the same district or island), was to learn of perhaps 60 other Brotherhoods e.g. the Castellorizian Brotherhood (established in Sydney as early as 1924). Ultimately the NSW Directory would list no less than 13 pages of Greek Brotherhoods!

Over several months in Sydney in 1970 we interviewed leaders of specialist organisations of 61 different ethnic backgrounds, including the Ukrainian Artists Association, Latvian Credit Union, *l'Association des Anciens Combattants Français*, Ecuador Sports Club, Irish Musicians Club, Druse Community of NSW, Club Filipino, Welsh Society of Sydney, Basque Society, Peruvian Community Association *et al.*

Some of these turned out to be major social clubs with extensive premises and one-armed bandits providing an assured income, some of them sponsoring sporting teams in top-level competitions: Marconi Club, Pan-Hellenic Sporting Club, German Concordia Club.

But we also discovered that several of the larger national groups had their over-arching 'umbrella' body covering a plethora of both generalised and specialised organisations: Hungarian Council of NSW (with 13 affiliates), Maltese Community Council of NSW, NSW Jewish Board of Deputies (representing 38 organisations), Federation of Netherlands Societies in NSW. These greatly facilitated our work, since they could speak for very large numbers of migrants and had a capacity to deliver on agreements made.

One of my first meetings in Sydney proved a memorable Saturday afternoon spent with the Ukrainian Council in their own HQ building at Lidcombe. They claimed to be able to speak for the whole Ukrainian community in Sydney, spanning the Catholic/Orthodox divide. For me it was a blooding for what was to come over the next three years: facing an initial reception sceptical of the government's motives and wary of being taken in by sweet talk, but becoming increasingly cordial, and in the end positively helpful in planning my further (Ukrainian) contacts. On this occasion, I infringed Public Service regulations by accepting the personal gift of a traditionally embroidered table mat. Maybe I should have lodged it officially with my Department but by then I knew all too well that someone else would purloin it. I reckoned that over a long Saturday afternoon, I had well and truly earned it.

Religious smorgasbord

As a Christian, of absorbing interest to me were the religious bodies, a veritable ecumenical fruit salad: the Newcastle Hebrew Congregation, the Islamic Society of NSW, but mainly the 'national' churches: the Coptic Orthodox Church of Egypt, the Armenian Apostolic Church (est. 301AD!), the Holy Apostolic Church of the East (Assyrian Iraqis) – which before the advent of Islam had spread the faith across Asia as far as China – the Greek Orthodox Archdiocese, the Russian Orthodox Church (but actually two rival networks, the official Church under the Patriarch of Moscow and another based in Chicago, shunning the Moscow brigade as *"Communist dupes betraying the true Church")*, the Serbian Orthodox Diocese (with two similar competing networks), the Romanian Orthodox Church *("the priest is a spy")*, the Antiochian Orthodox Church (Lebanese), the Ukrainian Orthodox Church, the Macedonian Orthodox Church, the Byelorussian Orthodox Church (not recognised by the Russians). As may perhaps be detected, I revelled in the Byzantine flavour of it all – an exotic world within a world! But amply justified because of the Churches' unique capacity for reaching wide swathes of their ethnic communities, while speaking with authority to a Department foreshadowing a partnership for the common good.

Not to mention the Roman Catholic migrant parishes: Italian (many), Maltese, Spanish-speaking, German, Dutch, Polish, Hungarian, Ukrainian, Croatian, Slovak, Portuguese, Lithuanian, and the Maronite and Melkite Catholic churches (sub-denominations really, both with their own buildings) from Lebanon.

And then the Protestant versions: German Lutheran congregations, Estonian Lutheran Church, Finnish Lutheran Church, Dutch Reformed churches and their Association of Parent-Controlled Christian Schools, Chinese Presbyterian Church, Italian Pentecostal Church, Finnish Pentecostal Church, Greek Nazarene Church, French and Polish Seventh Day Adventist Churches, Norwegian Seamen's Church.

Did I go overboard *(just slightly!)* on the religious bodies? Probably. It was my particular area of interest and I brought some understanding to it. On the other hand, my surmise was amply justified that most churches did in fact play a significant role in the resettlement, wellbeing and social support of migrants, often being the most crucial and enduring focal points of community life. Again, it must be remembered that in the 70s, for people of all cultures, church life was far more vibrant than today, as well as the source of personal identity, social connection and practical assistance. My strong impression was that higher proportions of migrants from continental Europe attended church than did Britons or Australians.

In NSW centres of heavy industry

Some months after our Sydney survey was done and dusted – though really you could never make such a claim – we flew direct from Canberra to Newcastle, for me something of a homecoming because previously base and workplace for generations of Houstons. But this time our quarry was the variegated migrant communities drawn to the jobs in heavy industry: the BHP Steelworks, Lysaghts galvanised iron works, the lead and zinc smelter, coalmining and exporting. Unsurprisingly, many of the local organisations mirrored their Sydney counterparts.

Evangelists of Government goodwill, we roamed city and suburb, brandishing questionnaires and bearing hope. And not only in Newcastle: our focus was the Hunter Region, including towns like Maitland and Morpeth further upriver. I even seized the opportunity to seek migrant contacts in Greta, my father's original stamping-ground which had hosted a post-war Migrant Hostel. Sure enough, there was a Greta Polish Ex-Servicemen's Association and also a Ukrainian Catholic community. In the Newcastle region, we made contact with 43 organisations reflecting 23 ethnic backgrounds.

The NSW survey concluded with a brief visit to the Illawarra coast in the Bulli/ Wollongong/ Port Kembla/ Dapto area, a beautiful strip of narrow coastline, urbanised and industrialised, backed by a sheer mountain escarpment. The BHP steelworks had long been a mecca for incoming migrants. In its shadow, the Cringila Primary School told the story with its child migrant component of 85%, and a fantastic range of languages spoken in the playground. In all we identified 41 migrant organisations from 21 ethnic backgrounds.

One State down, five to go

Phew! Where to next? We opted for Queensland, or more specifically, Brisbane. After our experience of Newcastle and Wollongong, in the interests of getting the survey in the State capitals finished, we gave up any thought of visiting provincial centres. We had to keep a wary eye on our bosses, spoiling for 'a quick fix' and prone to hint that we were off junketing, or big-noting ourselves, or raising expectations unrealistically high. For our part, we considered the humanistic project intrinsically worthwhile, not only for our Department but for the future of our country –or was this a bit over the top?

Queensland exceptionalism

If this dilemma was emerging in the metropolis of Sydney, it was off the radar in Brisbane. Since the 1920s, migrants in Queensland had learnt to keep their heads down: Italians on the Innisfail sugar-cane fields, Albanian tobacco-growers at Mareeba, Finnish carpenters in the Mt Isa mines, Russian Old Believers at Yarwun – not to speak of their exploited predecessors, the Kanakas, victims of the colonial 'blackbirders'. If one size didn't exactly fit all, in Queensland it was the only size on offer in those days.

Not that Queenslanders weren't hospitable to strangers. They saw themselves (and still rightly do) as the archetypal bestowers of hospitality. But the fact was they did not see these new 'foreigners' as having any claim on their kindness. *"They keep to themselves, so let them look after themselves."*

No one could ever explain to us why newcomers excluded from mainstream society by every impenetrable barrier: language, culture, social class, inexperience, prejudice, should be expected to *assimilate*, presumably one by one, shunning each other's company in case they were accused of forming 'ghettoes'! Yet that expectation still seems alive and well in rural pockets across the nation, as Pauline Hanson's One Nation Party has legitimated.

In October 1970, Jan and I sallied forth again, stepping into an oven of humidity. Picking up our Commonwealth cars we checked into a holiday flat on the River at West End, in the South Brisbane migrant belt.

Our research project led us into contact with the customary range of European and Middle Eastern organisations plus some others: Scottish (8), Albanian, Indonesian and Polynesian. In all 119 organisations from 35 backgrounds – a quite restricted range compared to the southern States. But unlike their Sydney counterparts, many seemed defensive. They appeared to have internalised the role for migrant organisations hung on them by the paternalistic Good Neighbour Council – of assisting in the assimilation of the migrating generation, rather than offering a precious haven for the enjoyment and maintenance of cultural identity and a bridge to the homeland (like my Dumfries and Galloway Society – essentially a type of Greek Brotherhood).

Many migrants' apparent reluctance to assert (maybe even to perceive) such a role had led them to keep their heads down, like the earlier generations of migrants. Nevertheless, the progress they would make over the next few years as multiculturalism began to be articulated would see them play an active role in reshaping community relations in the new Australia.

Next stop Adelaide

A few weeks later, questionnaires lodged and reports to our bosses written, we set about planning the next campaign. The lot fell upon

Adelaide. To avoid another prolonged absence from the family I decided to have the mountain come to Mohammad: I would take the whole family for a South Australian holiday and do the survey on weekdays during the January 1971 school vacation! Sarah-Jane was ten, Christopher six, Nicholas four and David one. The travelling menagerie opted for two overnight train journeys, with a day between in Melbourne. In Adelaide, we would stay with old university friends, with whom we had exchanged visits when we were all living in England in the 60s. Their children were of comparable age to ours. It was a pleasant break and they did lots of holiday things together.

Power of the Adelaide Establishment

As though asserting 'ownership' of the National Groups Survey in SA, some months earlier the Good Neighbour Council had invited me to be the speaker at their AGM, and I had flown over for one evening's meeting. In the traditionally blue ribbon conservative State of that period, the paternalistic GNC held undisputed sway in matters of migrant 'assimilation'. So, the elderly Knights and Dames among the audience assumed I would be their agent in locating and recruiting new migrant members for their organisation. They were full of advice to me on how to make contact with 'their' members. Without spurning their offer, I tried to point out the approaches we had pioneered in the NSW survey for locating many smaller and previously unknown communities of more recent arrivals. But they doubted that such new organisations existed in 'their' Adelaide. So, for appearance's sake I agreed to work in partnership with them, initially using the lists of their member organisations.

In the event, we encountered 115 organisations from 62 backgrounds, plus listing another 46 organisations affiliated with umbrella groups – a vastly expanded list. Among the backgrounds, in addition to all the usual ones, we discovered Belgian, Japanese, Malay, Swedish, Thai and Vietnamese organisations. We also identified the oldest city mosque in Australia, in Little Gilbert St, established in 1888 by Afghan (probably today's Pakistani) cameleers. A feature of the lists was the large number of UK organisations resulting from Liberal

Premier Thomas Playford's 1950s initiative of establishing automotive industries and the satellite city of Elizabeth. Among these were the John Bull Association, the Northamptonshire Club, and the Society of Yorkshiremen. But probably the Cornish Association reflected the migration of the 19th century copper and tin miners.

Unpremeditated, in Adelaide I made my *début* on the media scene. From somewhere an ABC radio reporter thrust a microphone in my face to ask what the two Canberra officials were doing in Adelaide. I explained our activity and its rationale, and felt reasonably reassured that I had been able *"to give a reason for the faith that was in me"*. Back in Canberra, the head of the Integration Branch sneered about my being 'a limelighter': didn't I know the Department employed specialist officers responsible for communicating with the media? And who could speak about anything the Department did? I deferred, musing how much they could know about our field experiences in Adelaide.

Up-country research in SA

Nothing loth, we made an executive decision to check the scene in SA's second city, Whyalla, with a population at the time of some 30,000 and with steel mills and shipbuilding. In the late 1940s some of the DPs had been directed there and large numbers of migrants had arrived since. It was the Port Kembla of South Australia. Sure enough, the eight largest ethnic communities had established clubs and societies: Scots, Croatians, Dutch, Germans, Greeks, Italians, Poles & Spaniards. While I flew there from Adelaide, Jan Reksten drove northwards to check out the German settlers of the Barossa Valley and include centres like Port Augusta and Port Pirie, with their Germans and Greeks, but also the ubiquitous Caledonian (Scottish) Societies. The SA Directory subsequently published listed 35 organisations from 8 ethnic backgrounds in provincial areas.

The most exotic organisations reported were the Greek Orthodox Church and Community of Thevenard (on the Nullabor Plain) and a similar one at Coober Pedy, an underground church – but not in the Chinese tradition!

CHAPTER 22: Courting Ethnic Allies   153

Top level encouragement

About this time, back in Canberra, Sir Peter Heydon had invited me to appear during a meeting of the most senior Immigration officials from around Australia, to lead a short segment on the National Groups Survey. I had reported on our research approach and the range of responses encountered. I recall one exchange of comments on whether the Jews were a national group or a religious group (I reckoned both), after I had reported that, *"to the Greeks I became a Greek, to the Jews I became a Jew"*. Not knowing then of his Christian profession, I was surprised that Sir Peter so manifestly warmed to the Scriptural quote. I sensed then that we were on the right track, although the second level of top officials seemed unimpressed, then as later.

To a lush south sea island

Ten months' later we rounded off 1971 with a Christmas trip to the Holiday Isle. Tasmania has the longest migration history of any State, dating from the arrival of a unique Aboriginal community of Tasmanoids more than 35,000 years ago! After 1804 their world came to a tragic end with the advent of a penal colony of convicts and soldiers, followed by a slow movement of free settlers after the Napoleonic Wars and the gold rush. By its miniature scale it never became a drawcard for mass migration, so that by then when one in three Australians were overseas-born Tasmania counted only one in ten.

But the post-war migrant flow did lap Tasmanian shores, when DPs were directed to work on the building of the hydro-electric dams in the central mountains, and subsequently many took root in the cities with their families. Early on they were joined by Dutch and German free settlers, plus Italians, Greeks and Yugoslavs. In 1947 nearly 800 Polish ex-servicemen had arrived in uniform, including many former Polish 'Rats of Tobruk'[13], their association one of the most remarkable organisations ever to cross our path. Of course, the non-English-background migrants were always greatly outnumbered by 'the ten pound Poms'.

---

[13]Tobruk, name of a town in Libya, became a household word in 1941 when the besieged Australian (and Allied) forces survived repeated assaults by the Germans under General Rommel, who sneered at the defenders as the 'rats' of Tobruk. It would become a badge of honour.

Doubtless the more European climate appealed to many newcomers, and the townspeople sensed no threat but offered grateful hospitality. Certainly, folk arts were often on display, indicative of the confidence of the national groups. A unique discovery was the string of Dutch Reformed churches, often with their 'parent-controlled' Christian school, along the Bass Strait coast and in Hobart and Launceston. Burnie and Devonport also offered an array of associations, while in its ethnic diversity Launceston was a slightly lesser replay of Hobart.

Infected by the seasonal spirit, we had no compunction in responding to the attractions of the Holiday Isle. For our work in Hobart we had booked into a cabin and Jan, being a Norwegian mountain man, insisted one weekend we should climb Mt Wellington by a frontal assault. Scree permitting, we mastered the challenge. Dutifully, we sent a postcard to our colleagues in the Integration Branch in Canberra imaginatively spelling out our activities: *"yachting on the Derwent, horse riding in the Mt Field national park, walking the Cradle Mountain trail, visiting the convict ruins of Port Arthur"*, etc. On our return to base our immediate boss took me aside in a fatherly moment to point out that, although we all do these sorts of things during our interstate duties, we should really be more circumspect about advertising them. After all, the card was sent without an envelope. *Come in, spinner!*

In all we visited some 40 organisations of 17 backgrounds, dispersed around the island – a signficantly more decentralised pattern than in the major States.

In Australia's ethnic heartland

After a protracted spell back in the office and living it up at home with the family, we ran out of excuses for not getting back into the field. The most significant State beckoned. Taking our courage in four hands we began thumbing through lists assembled from various quarters of 'national group associations' (the term still hadn't died) in the Garden State of Victoria. Their number and scope was daunting.

Small wonder that, with word of the survey now getting around, in several of the larger migrant communities there were stirrings towards more creative alternatives to assimilation as the desired outcome of immigration. In the inner Melbourne suburbs, where many migrants were doing it tough – long hours, low pay, work injuries (especially women with repetitive strain injury), overcrowded housing, lack of English – frontline welfare and education professionals, making common cause with migrant workers' spokesmen, were now advocating for more radical action. In our reading of Sir Peter Heydon's vision, we felt bound to listen to these views, as well as seeking partners for dialogue and assessing the communities' capacity for collaboration. Besides, in the stultifying climate of our society in the early 70s, this was creating an opening for change: the surge of discontent in America and Europe in the 60s was tardily reaching our shores. The old structures of power and authority were on notice.

But at the level of our field research such lofty considerations had to take a back seat. As with the Sydney survey, we needed several protracted visits to Melbourne to make much headway. Jan Reksten recorded that we undertook 'search-and-encourage' campaigns in March, April, May, and twice in June 1971. For me, it would mark the beginnings of a love affair with Melbourne that continues to this day. But criss-crossing it by Commonwealth car I had to work hard at 'getting' the layout of the entire broad metropolis. For the first time, we opted to stay in Departmental accommodation, at the Maribyrnong Migrant Hostel in the inner west, though apart from breakfast we drew the line at eating there. Partially rebuilt, it offered some of the residents a good standard of self-contained flats.

Identifying with the migrant experience

With our diaries rapidly filling we spent long days and evenings meeting community leaders, appreciating their cultures, distilling their experience and eliciting their judgment, as well as completing the boring questionnaires so highly valued by our bosses. Often, they would prove a positive embarrassment, trivialising the human interaction and debasing the currency. But our files back in Canberra were fattening with rafts of useful insights carefully recorded from our discussions.

Within the one ethnic community, at times complementary but also adversarial viewpoints would emerge, reflecting diverse religious, political and class perceptions, as well as the moment they left their homeland and the reason why. Hungarians especially come to mind, the great watershed being the 1956 uprising against the Communist puppet government, cf. the famous defection of 45 Hungarian athletes at the Melbourne Olympics.

Perhaps the most salient fact to emerge from our discussions was the gulf between the received wisdom of our Departmental leaders and the actuality of the migrant experience, for instance in the 'push' and 'pull' factors motivating emigration (awful European climate, competitive life with no prospect of improvement, tired old hatreds) over against the appeal of Australia (sunny climes, land of opportunity, mateship and the fair go). Both were of course simplistic generalisations, not at all nuanced – and both equally wide of the mark.

Naturally, migrants engaged in the inevitably desperate struggle to find a footing still maintained their identity, cultural loyalty and perceptions of the world. How could they not? When Marjorie and I disembarked at Southampton 12 years earlier we had not automatically transmogrified into Britons. Jan and I were becoming increasingly critical, indeed sceptical, about Departmental attitudes as out of touch with the grassroots 'consumers' – and indeed naïve. In particular the myriad differentiations we were identifying often challenged the official stereotypes, e.g. what price a *Latvian* leftist – or a *Greek* brain surgeon? So, what had this to say about Departmental expectations of the future outcomes of mass migration? Was assimilation still a thinkable goal?

As we began tuning in to contrary voices, whether of progressive migrant 'politicians' or from engaged professionals, we found our loyalties coming under strain. Perhaps this was unavoidable once you fluttered down from the ivory tower (still *fibro*, actually) overlooking Lake Burley Griffin. By definition we were go-betweens. But we could not be mere departmental ciphers. The evidence was pushing us to change sides. After all, we were nearing the end of an era. The new order established at war's end – now visibly ageing – was expiring. In Australia, it would take all of 23 years before the barely audible voices from the grassroots were to penetrate the political static in Canberra and help elect a reformist government.

'Good morning, ASIO'

On his untimely death at 58, Sir Peter Heydon had been replaced as Permanent Head by his 2iC, Bob Armstrong, one of the old post-war bureaucrats. My immediate boss was becoming alarmed at the security implications of so much frank material secluded in our hundreds of files on individual migrant organisations. He decreed that they be not only locked into the filing cabinets, but that a great iron bar be pushed down through all the drawer handles and padlocked every evening before going home. I suspect his fear was not from nefarious agents but of ASIO who could well find it rich pickings. Sometimes on arriving at my office I would amuse myself by telling the spook at the other end of the phone line that it was time to trigger the listening device.

Getting at the naked truth

I soon had a chance to cool down, visiting a representative of the Finnish Lutheran Congregation of Melbourne. As we worked through the questionnaire together he was most forthcoming, and we got on like a house on fire. Indeed, after a while he suggested we take a sauna bath, in his specially equipped outhouse. I thought, why not? So, I descended gingerly into the scalding water and suffered till I could take it no more, then leapt for rescue under his shower. As the afternoon wore on I got used to the alternating parboiling/chilling process, and we actually completed the questionnaire sitting naked in the sauna (though we refrained from beating ourselves with birch twigs afterwards, from lack of snow to roll in). A practical exposure to Finnish cultural values – and what devotion to duty! Perhaps it rates a place in the Guinness Book of Records: the first public official to complete a work brief stark naked.

Historic link with China

As in Sydney, old-established Chinese organisations were significant, the most venerable founded during the gold rush of the 1850s. Thus, they are the oldest national group organisations in Australia. Indeed, it has been claimed that in the mid-19th century Chinese was the second language of the colonies. But it was arguably not Mandarin, the 'common language' but Cantonese, a minority language of the south-east barely comprehensible elsewhere. The Sze Yup Society (variously See Yap) has been providing charitable services since 1854, and in 1856 had built a joss house for Chinese from the 'Four Districts' near Canton (today's Guangzhou, third city of China) – currently under restoration. Even older, the Kong Chew Society from that region dates from 1853, today focusing on young people's social and sporting activities, including martial arts and an Australian Rules team: Jackie Chan playing for Collingwood?

We were delighted to encounter the Chinese custom of only relating to visitors over a restaurant meal, and became denizens of Little Bourke St (Chinatown). Such occasions were often quite formal with florid speeches of welcome and appreciation, interspersed by interminable courses. If it *was* a junket we were on, its flavour was Chinese!

Whose side am I on now?

But at the time, of greater significance were contacts being made with welfare agencies committed to the wellbeing of migrant workers, both men and women: Co.As.It and FILEF (Italian welfare groups), the Australian Greek Welfare Society, and the Australian Jewish Welfare and Relief Society, all of them led by significant figures in the coming struggle. By now mass migration was leaving something of a trail of human debris in its wake, apart from the many disillusioned returnees. Moreover, some of the community leaders were well enough aware of the Australian realities – and competent in English – to the point of becoming formidable campaigners. Clearly, migrants' welfare problems were not being handled by the services available for the general public, and "the needs on the ground were horrendous". [14] Who could deny the justice of their cause? Whose side was I on now? But really, there could be no question: whose side would Jesus be on? Administrators of the status quo? Or strugglers with the poor? And on

---

[14] Interview with Rev. David Cox, reported in Mark Lopez, *The Origins of Multiculturalism in Australian Politics, 1945-1975*, Melbourne University Press, p. 538..

what grounds could the migrant aspirations be discounted? Outdated assimilationist theory?

As new bedfellows, I had now come into contact with two unique Christian agencies: the Ecumenical Migration Centre (EMC) and the Fitzroy Ecumenical Centre, with its specialised Centre for Urban Research and Action (CURA). At the time, I saw myself as on my own journey of discovery but later it dawned on me that, because of my role, I was being assiduously cultivated and landed by some canny anglers. (What was it that Jesus said about becoming *'fishers of men'?*) The EMC had two outstanding leaders, David Cox and Alan Matheson, the former a Presbyterian minister and later Professor of Social Work at La Trobe University and the latter a former Churches of Christ pastor. Years later I would be approached about becoming director of the EMC and travelled to Melbourne for an interview but it didn't seem right to either party. At the time of the National Groups Survey my main impression of migrant workers had been more about their desire to maintain their cultural values and transmit these to their children, rather than their campaigning about 'ethnic rights' as espoused by the EMC and CURA.

Calling it a day

By the end of June 1972, we agreed to terminate the Melbourne survey as virtually inexhaustible, in the interests of completing the national picture and drawing ultimate conclusions from the masses of data now in our files. The Victorian Directory subsequently published ran to 167 pages, listing 300 organisations covering 53 national groups, including for the first time Bulgarians, and with a further listing of 23 multifarious organisations visited in Victoria's second city of Geelong. As we closed the book on Melbourne after so many months of discovery and mellowing transformation, I wonder whether I had any inkling that one day I'd be back – for good?

Go west, young men

Our survey in Australia's largest State turned out to be something of a rest cure. We went west in about September 1972. Everywhere the migrant presence was reassuring, and we soon took up our beat around the inner suburbs and in Fremantle, meeting the sorts of organisations identified across the nation.

However, we came upon four national groups never before identified: Burmese, Rhodesian (from today's Zimbabwe), South African, and ... Icelandic! Among the UK groups there was a Manx Society. In all we visited 103 organisations, covering 37 national groups.

At the end of the survey, flying back east, I was shocked at how soon the gleaming salt claypans made their appearance, some even surrounded by growing crops. Then without warning came the end of the world as we crossed the stark perpendicular cliffs of the Nullarbor Plain to be over the Southern Ocean, making a bee-line for Melbourne. No coastal plain, no beach, no shoreline. No liminal zone. Either earth or sea. Maybe like the transition to eternal life?

The last word must be one of tribute to the unsung hero of the historic survey who, for three years and more, had held the fort through thick and thin, too frequently caring unassisted for four lively children. All my gratitude and heartfelt appreciation!

Implications of the research findings

By 1972, Australia-wide, the national groups survey had identified 1,350 of the organisations created by migrants, speaking countless tongues and drawn from over 100 lands/regions of the globe. Doubtless there were many more organisations not specifically detected or visited – now clearly revealed as an impossible (and maybe meaningless?) task.

Vainly looking to the novice computer staff to devise a program for analysing the mass of quantitative date collected Commonwealth-wide over three years, it was becoming clear that, beyond the death of Sir Peter Heydon, the top brass saw little value in the protracted exercise.

CHAPTER 23: An Evolutionary Ferment

In the circles I moved in (with the possible exception of our church) the election on 2 December 1972 of the first Labor Government in 23 years triggered unimaginably euphoric scenes. In the highly charged political atmosphere of Canberra, in those days when the world was young, we had a naïve faith in the potential of the political/administrative system to deliver the Golden Age. Besides, Gough Whitlam was our hero.

Opening to the Left

For the nation, it ushered in a sort of renaissance, tinged with romance but anchored in solid realities. The ALP's election slogan admirably captured the mood, "It's time". Time to break with an anachronistic past, discredited – yet an unconscionable time a-dying. Time to declare for *aggiornamento*, renewal, vision, optimism. In a word, regime change that might lead to the reconfiguring of the Australian community: towards greater social justice, equality of opportunity, and readier access to community services. Not least for migrants.

For a public servant in such a strongly community-oriented role as mine, the new opening to the left was to bring about profound changes of fortune, unlocking undreamt-of opportunities

Without waiting for the election results to be finalised, the duumvirate (two-man government) of Gough Whitlam and his deputy Lance Barnard had set a cracking pace for implementing election promises not requiring legislation: bringing the troops home from Vietnam, releasing conscientious objectors, recognising the People's Republic of China, banning racially discriminatory sporting visits, *announcing the intention to ratify the International Convention against All Forms of Racial Discrimination.*

In his speech at the opening of the new Parliament (drafted by the Prime Minister), the Governor-General outlined the Government's reform priorities, including changes to the education and social security systems, universal health insurance, Aboriginal land rights, the elimination of racism, and the improvement of welfare services for migrants.[15]

---

[15] "The welfare of migrants will receive the closest attention ... A higher priority will be given to retaining migrants than to recruiting them". (Hansard, 27th February 1973)

Prime Ministerial antipathy

However, for the top-level officers of the Immigration Department the Prime Minister harboured a personal dislike. He regarded them as custodians of racially biased policies and saw the Department as an anachronistic obstacle to social progress. Long accustomed to 'guiding' their minister to implement their views without question, these officers now found themselves required to carry out a program they did not believe in, indeed resented. Public *servants?*

Listen to the migrant voices!

How could the results of the three-year National Groups Survey now be utilised within the new political framework? In the light of the ethical principles I had been taught earlier about how the Public Service is the administrative arm of the Government of the day and bound to carry out its directives, I mused about where my duty lay. Should an officer at my middling level just ignore these ethical considerations and simply do as the boss decrees? But what if the boss's directions were contrary to what you knew government policy to be – and who couldn't know this, given that the media were in a constant frenzy of reporting the implications of the changing of the guard?

Before long in the Integration Branch there were the first hints of a new climate breaking in, where personal political orientations were becoming apparent. During our lunch-time walks around the leafy streets of Turner, my immediate superiors were now openly declaring for the new Government – hardly a radical thing to do, given the ethics of the Service, but brave because it was challenging the past era of Departmental philosophy apparently set in concrete, and backed by the expectation that the new Labor Government was somehow an aberration that would soon go away – so in the meantime didn't need to be obeyed.

The obvious solution was to let the migrant voices speak. During our Survey, we had listened to leaders of organisations from over 100 ethnic backgrounds nationwide, as well as identifying the existence of many others, and of course more were being established all the time. It was a lively scene, and undoubtedly from now on, their voice would be an element in our community and national conversation. Along the way our horizons had expanded and our convictions deepened about the vision of a new egalitarian, multi-ethnic democracy as Australia's future. How else to realise it if not through the new people's government?

But how could the migrant leaders' views, mediated by our conclusions, be heard if the channels of communication were not open? In the new era of impending change, could the nationwide survey legitimate the coming of age of the newly added ethnic sector as a partner in shaping the future nation? Our immediate boss who, we assumed, had long had to defend the interminable survey against the higher critics, saw the urgent need to be the processing of the data that we had so laboriously garnered. This could indicate the practicality of recruiting the national groups in making welfare services more broadly accessible.

Actually, over the next few years the Whitlam Government was to develop a holistic scheme for earthing welfare services and stimulating community development *across the whole community*, named the Australian Assistance Plan, though before long the incoming government of Malcolm Fraser would strangle it at birth.

Beaten by the technical 'experts'

But sadly, the quantitative data gathered during our survey was never to be turned to account, because its complexity defied the incipient 'expertise' of the Department's early computer programmers.

More significant to my mind was the mountain of files now held on all the organisations visited, which as well as the completed questionnaire contained a handwritten record of the discussion with the leader(s), and personal observations of matters of significance. Pondering how best to distil this vast range of qualitative material into broad conclusions about the character and potential of Australia's migrant organisations and the views of their leaders, I came up with the idea of drafting an analytical, forward-looking book. During the Melbourne survey, near the end of the nationwide project, I had visited Professor Jean Martin, Professor of Sociology at La Trobe University, to discuss my findings, and a year later had spoken at length with Professor Jerzy (George) Zubrzycki, Professor of Sociology at the ANU and a great advocate for humanistic integration policies, when we had drafted out the chapter headings and structure of the proposed work, which might amount to a *'people's charter for multiculturalism'*. He offered to act as my mentor in the writing project.

Beaten by the bureaucrats

There had never been a wide-ranging study of migrant organisations, neither nationwide nor global across the range of ethnicities. Nor of migrant leaders' views. Who else but governments would have the resources to undertake such a broad research task? My hope was to draw on the evidence gathered of leaders' attitudes and values and then on this basis put forward the vision of a pluralist society based on mutual respect and legitimacy[16].

But it seemed impossible to contemplate writing a major work while attending to the daily round of duties arising from or about migrant organisations, so I sought permission for a year's leave, to be attached to the ANU. The proposal survived the Branch head's scrutiny until it came across the Divisional head's desk. I was summoned to his office. He was furious. He summarily dismissed the idea as mere grandstanding on my part. He is quoted in Mark Lopez's study of the development of multiculturalism as observing that "Houston was not my favourite officer. I think he spun that job out endlessly, on national groups"[17].

> *Immigration Department and assimilationism (the past) 1*
> *Houston and cultural pluralism (the future) 0*

Not just a voice crying in the wilderness

But if that was the view in the Department, in the community I was by no means an isolated voice. By now there was a concerted move by what Mark Lopez terms (using later terminology) the *'proto-*

---

[16] The terms 'ethnic' and 'multiculturalism' had not yet entered the national discourse, let alone the popular vocabulary. Terms like 'national groups' or 'migrant organisations' ensured that no implications could be drawn about society as a whole.
[17] Lopez, op.cit, p. 121

multiculturalists' in the general society, particularly in Victoria where all the issues were more glaring, to ditch both assimilation and its effete cousin, integration. My top boss must have been well aware of this. But being essentially a loyal son of Empire, presumably he saw no value in speculations about an alternative future.

So who were these innovators? Walter Lippmann had become the first migrant member appointed to the old-established Immigration Advisory Council (IAC). And this 23 years after the Department had been set up to facilitate post-war immigration! He used the forum to promote a whole new deal for migrants and was very supportive of the National Groups Survey, to the point of defending its continuation when it was jeopardised by opposition from the top officials. Rather he proposed that a sub-committee should be created to assist my work, and with Professor Zubrzycki's support the IAC Sub-Committee on National Groups was set up.

Lopez observes: "This manoeuvring was successful. Houston, supported and guided by the sub-committee, was incorporated into the network of multiculturalists." [in the outside community]

A creative new coterie emerging

This informal network had been gathering strength since the mid-60s, comprising a number of forward-thinking academics in the social sciences, and Christian community activists in Melbourne closely identified with migrant welfare issues: Rev. Brian Howe (a Methodist minister and later Deputy Prime Minister in the Hawke Labor Government), Rev. Arthur Faulkner, Rev. David Cox and Alan Matheson. A further newly emergent component were the leaders of several migrant welfare agencies in Melbourne (Greek, Italian and Jewish) visited during our survey.

It is instructive to note that this ferment of new thinking was limited to Melbourne, and that Christians were in the forefront. All these voices opposed the continuation of the previous Government's policy of 'integrating' migrants into the existing social fabric, implying that it was the migrants who had to do all the adapting while the Australian institutions soldiered on unchallenged and unchanged.

This amounted to a policy of what I termed *'adaptive assimilationism'*, with the pressure always on the newcomers to identify which elements of society they had to adapt to. Join the British Empire! But as more and more non-British migrants arrived from an ever-widening range of countries with no experience of the British Empire, it became more and more blurred: just who was this mythical model to be imitated as 'the typical Aussie'?

The academics were calling for a new social contract for all, whereby pluralism would replace the Anglo-Saxon monism: let all the flowers bloom! Of course, all the flowers needed tending equally. Yet this was not how it had been working. One of the community activists observed, "The needs were horrendous ...but the government was not putting any money into dealing with the issues of immigrants."[18]

Official responses inadequate

The official neglect of the human dimension of migration was now assuming crisis proportions. In fact, during the 1960s no less than one in three Italian migrants returned to Italy homesick or disillusioned. In many cases the brutal change of lifestyle of rural workers transplanted to process work in factories – and especially their wives – proved impossible to negotiate. In any case, many of these had anticipated their Australian episode to be merely a *'guestworker'* experience no different from the thousands of their compatriots who had gone to Germany for a few years to make money quickly, leaving wives and families behind, but with no thought of settling into the alien society. Such a mentality challenged the official assimilationist position which assumed that all could make that interior journey as they had made the external one. But the harsh reality of the steady loss of 'non-British' migrants returning home was never addressed by the top bureaucrats, as being too threatening. Quite understandable, given how reluctant the authorities had been years earlier to address the embarrassing failure of so many 'ten pound Poms' to make a success of their migration, returning home disillusioned. Our national pride was at stake.

---

[18]Rev.David Cox, op.cit, p. 54

On the other hand, the campaigners saw the need to encourage newcomers to imagine a real future for themselves in an open, evolving society where they too might find a place in the sun. What could be done to earth this vision? Whatever the measures might be, they needed to be proffered in a language migrants could understand. But even more than that, migrants needed to glimpse how their cultural world (the only world they knew) might become respected and positively articulated with the majority culture of the new land. To expect migrant workers (sometimes illiterates or speakers of regional dialects) to be able to thrive to the point of adopting the folk ways of their Australian counterparts was no more realistic than imagining, for instance, that Queensland stockmen transplanted to Calabria – resisting the temptation to hang out with each other in 'Aussie ghettos' – might within a few years pick up the lingo and join the local sub-culture. Get real!

Academic pioneers

The first academic to speak out publicly had been Professor Jean Martin who many years earlier had identified *assimilationism* as mainly responsible for migrant welfare problems, since it devalued their cultures and led to isolation imposing an intolerable burden. On the contrary, she praised the formation of national groups then developing, valuing them as a means of preserving cultural traditions and a safety zone for migrant newcomers.

Later, with David Cox, Walter Lippmann and Alan Matheson joining the coterie, the informal group began to make headway in enunciating alternatives, though stoutly resisted by the Good Neighbour Councils and of course the Integration Branch leadership with their settled imperialistic views. But in community and public circles there was now a modest clamour which other academics began to join in: Ronald Taft and Laki Jayasuriya in Perth, JJ Smolicz in Adelaide, James Jupp in Canberra and Andrew Jakubowicz in Sydney.

Joining the 'alliance'

At that stage, of course, I had no brief to do the rounds of the academics but later found opportunities to meet them all, sometimes at conferences or when they visited the Department, and to absorb their views. During and after the Melbourne survey, I had met a number of the key ethnic activists: Dr Spiro Moraitis, George Papadopoulos, George Zangalis in the splintered Greek community, and Giovanni Sgro among the Italians. They began to ply me with their speeches and reports.

Then in 1972, in order to push the debate beyond migrant welfare to ideology, Walter Lippmann had proposed a bold initiative: a national seminar of fifty selected academics and experts sponsored by the Immigration Advisory Council (IAC) to examine ways of implementing a culturally plural Australia. Among those nominated were Al Grassby, then member for Griffith in the NSW Parliament, Bob Hawke from the ACTU, and my immediate boss and myself from the Department. Ironically, it would never meet because Gough Whitlam upset the apple-cart by being elected Prime Minister!

Al Grassby arrives on the scene

From Day One, Whitlam's new Immigration Minister, Al Grassby, now MP for Riverina, plunged into a veritable frenzy of activity, some of it ill-directed or calculated to build his own image as the new dynamo on the block. Overnight he became a 'media tart'. He never paced himself, was perennially running late and leaving early for his next appointment. He declined no one's request and accepted everyone's invitation. For the Department, he was an absentee-landlord – an enigma, a nightmare - but was soon recognised as being easy to 'snow' (an old Public Service art wondrously articulated in the BBC comedy series *Yes, Minister*).

Yet when he tabled in Parliament a Progress Report from the IAC, he failed to note its ideological novelty of proposing to shift the Department's emphasis away from migrant welfare towards managing cultural pluralism. To the proto-multiculturalists it was now becoming clear that it would require more than a single Council report to make real progress.

As yet the outcomes and conclusions of the National Groups Survey had not been released. Presumably, no one had bothered to tell the new Minister of the survey conducted by his Department over the past three years which might have provided the indispensable points of contact. The Integration Branch leaders (mere managers) just weren't interested in fostering new initiatives.

But early in 1973, they did agree to a suggestion from Walter Lippmann that the IAC should set up a committee to examine *anti-migrant discrimination* in Australia, to be chaired by Lippmann.

In the first weeks of the Whitlam Government, probably as a means of sidelining the two existing Immigration Councils, Al Grassby had unilaterally announced a set of six State 'Task Forces' with the purpose of identifying the most serious migrant problems and making recommendations for action. Each State Task Force was to be chaired by a capital city Labor MP and consisted of Immigration Department officers and Good Neighbour Council representative – no mention of migrant representatives, let alone the proto-multiculturalists!

But in the case of NSW Grassby used his prerogative to appoint a personal contact, Andrew Jakubowicz – his patronage system swinging into action. Outraged, the Melbourne coterie lobbied hard and gained seats for three ethnic activists and the redoubtable Alan Matheson, who promptly consulted the proto-multicultural community, so that between them they *de facto* controlled the Victoria Task Force. It was the first official opening in Australian history for such elements to influence government policy.

Al Grassby's main initiatives in reform were the first move towards creating publically funded ethnic broadcasting, and the removal of any vestiges of White Australia from the migrant selection criteria. It was in Manila, during his tour of the south-east Asian countries to explain the new migration regime, that he spoke the immortal words, *"The White Australia Policy is dead. Give me a shovel and I'll bury it".*

Moving on to North America he held discussions with his Canadian counterpart, who explained their new national model of *'multiculturalism'* – but it did not appeal to him. Rather he preferred his own 'family of the nation' doctrine, homespun, woolly and ill-defined, focusing on national unity (but how?) in the face of the ever-brooding spectre of racism. An inveterate speech-maker, he wrote his own journalistic material full of catchy phrases, but his doctrine found favour neither with the assimilationists nor with the proto-multiculturalists, and eventually it passed into history. A better option was looming.

CHAPTER 24:
A Multicultural Society for the Future

So what was it that the reformers envisaged as the ideology for providing migrant settlement, education and welfare services, and for building broader community relations?

Enter the term 'multiculturalism'

For the first time, in 1974 the term *'multicultural'* was to emerge – not yet as a Government initiative but as a recurrent emphasis in the reports produced by some of the State Task Forces. Also at that time, I first came across the term 'multiculturalism' as a Canadian policy option. I was fascinated: a federal government of a British Dominion declaring that the national policy should envisage not only the two 'founding cultures' of Canada as equally worthy of respect (English and French) but also and equally the newer migrant cultures. The document itself was printed in English at one end and (turning it back to front and upside down) at the other end in French. So, in Québec, French-speaking Canadians were reading about honouring the *Ukrainian* culture (strong in the Winnipeg area) – in French! Hmm...

What might multiculturalism imply?

But what did the word purport to convey? It had two meanings: *first*, the social situation characterised by the presence of many ethnic cultures as a simple, observable fact. In this sense, it might be claimed that, prior to European settlement, Australia displayed a multiculturalism based on some six hundred Aboriginal languages, with wide cultural and even racial divergences. But *secondly*, and far more significantly, it came to describe an ideological concept not only about how people of diverse cultures might live side by side in harmony but how the total society might be organised. This is what the Canadian model implied, dismissed by my departmental leaders as merely a ploy to defuse tensions simmering across Canada between the English and French-

speaking charter communities. Be that as it may, in Australia from the earliest days of the pluralist dreaming, the term came to evoke four different though complementary approaches.[19]
- cultural pluralism
- structural pluralism
- welfare multiculturalism
- ethnic rights

From the outset, the major divergence was between 'life-styles' and 'life-chances', which also evoked the old political battleground between right and left. For instance, the (Greek) left sneered at the charming ethnic folkdances performed by people excluded from equal opportunities, while the (Ukrainian) right feared the leftists were merely building new alliances for the class war. Doubtless there was some truth in both claims – yet neither encapsulated the whole story.

The early emphasis of the academics (Zubrzycki and also Lippmann) was on *cultural* pluralism but others (Jupp and Jakubowicz) advocated a more *structural* approach (tackling inequalities through access to political power). Naturally the community activists' perspective from the grassroots (Cox) focused on more equal access to services: schooling, health and welfare, while the ethnic rights advocates (Matheson, Des Storer) stressed that such access should be based on the *recognition of rights for all* rather than an option for some.

What about the views of the migrants?

Over this early period there was no broad movement or even ideological aspirations emanating from the ethnic groups themselves. Rather, small groups or élites carried the campaign, through their eager co-operation, particularly the Melbourne ethnic activists. Indeed, opinion polls of the day registered lack of interest and widespread resentment on the part of the general population towards the new ideas. But with the tabling of the State Task Force reports in Parliament, the Minister's sources of policy advice were now considerably broadened beyond his Departmental advisors. Starting from the desire merely to

---

[19] I am indebted to Mark Lopez, op.cit, p. 5.

CHAPTER 24: A Multicultural Society for the Future 173

James meets Marjorie, Sydney University

James at 6 with brother Max 4

Punchbowl Methodist Church, Sydney

Graduation, Sydney University, 1954

Wedding Day, Penshurst, Sydney, 15th December, 1956

In front of home in Minden, West Germany, with Opel Karawan 1963

CHAPTER 24: A Multicultural Society for the Future

Off on family camping holiday, 1973

With Al Grassby, Commissioner for Community Relations, 1978

Australian teacher at the King's School Ely, Cambridgeshire, UK, 1960

Canberra public servant, 1974

With Archbishop David Penman on Ordination to Anglican ministry, St Paul's Cathedral, Melbourne, 1987

Award of Medal of the Order of Australia by Governor of Victoria, Sir James Gobbo, 2001

Young family near The Porta, gatehouse to Cathedral Close, Ely 1962

In the living room, Minden

improve the situation in migrant welfare, Grassby had become more and more open to the influences exerted by the multiculturalists. During 1973 their vision began to be earthed as the inchoate basis for government policy consideration. Unwittingly I would become deeply involved.

Opportunity beckons: write a speech for the Minister

Stung by Opposition attacks in Parliament about being vague on policy detail, Grassby responded by starting to give more substantial speeches. On 3 August 1973, he was scheduled to present a paper on the Government's policy on *'Foreign Languages in the New Australia'* at the State conference of the Modern Language Teachers' Association in Brisbane.

Interviewed by Dr Mark Lopez 21 years later, Al Grassby recalled that "It was my private secretary who found an officer considered suitable to draft the speech: Jim Houston, the National Groups Officer in the Integration Branch. Houston's multiculturalist views did not figure in the equation of his selection; he was chosen because of his previous experience as a teacher of foreign languages."[20]

In my speech (the first I had even written for a Minister) my reasons why migrant languages needed to be taught included:
- enabling all students to understand how richly diverse our society is;
- the intrinsic worth of exposing students to horizons broader than the school's;
- expressing our friendship, guidance and support in times of stress by using a migrant's own language as the vehicle of our communication; and most compelling, our concern for the human dignity of those who choose to take their place among us.

Mark Lopez's analysis continues:[21]
"The speech Houston drafted reflected cultural pluralist ideas about the development of the 'linguistic resources' brought to

---

[20] Lopez, op.cit., p 243
[21] Lopez, op.cit., p. 243

Australia by migrants, and drew on his knowledge of the ideas of Zubrzycki, Lippmann, Martin, Smolicz and others. Houston was careful to express these ideas in language that would not provoke his superiors to veto the speech before it was submitted to the Minister. Houston recalled that the speech provoked no ripples of criticism in the Department and was appreciated by Grassby: 'This speech went over well. This was because I had produced it by the deadline, more than the content. There is nothing much in it.' Houston, who had not previously been asked to draft a policy speech, had now earned the respect of his superiors in the Department as someone capable of producing a speech on time that would appeal to the Minister.

" .... Houston became embittered against his superiors by their vetoing of his proposal to produce a book on the pattern and structure of ethnic group organisations in Australia, based on his field research: 'I had begun to be deliberately seditious in the Department on behalf of the ethnic fraternity.' But his superiors did not know about his resolution".

Genesis of historic speech defining multiculturalism

Some weeks later, when Minister Grassby received an invitation to be keynote speaker at a major symposium convened by the Cairnmillar Institute in Melbourne, the request was also referred to my desk. The theme was to be *'The nature of Australia in the year 2000'*.

Lopez writes:

"The speech had to be prepared at short notice, and Houston had proven his ability to meet a tight deadline. Houston had resolved that Andy Watson [Divisional Head] would not have his way ideologically within the Department, and he seized this opportunity to write an explicitly multiculturalist speech for the Minister. The strength of his resolve was measured by his apprehended risk of being 'cashiered' as a consequence."

I had about a day and a half to produce the speech, using a new-fangled hand-held dictaphone and progressively lodging the mini-tapes with the 'typing pool', following up with a spate of corrections of the inevitable errors. (A classic: the first time I dictated the new term 'ethnic' it came back to me as *'efnic'*.) I tried to imagine the Al Grassby whom I had never seen in the flesh flamboyantly rolling my metaphors off his tongue. By then we all knew much of what he was on about from the daily press clippings about immigration news, circulated for information among the more senior officers, including reports on his speeches.

But beyond that, of course, I had a head full of many-accented ethnic voices throughout Australia sharing their critiques and dreams and aspirations. I wanted to do them justice. But also I had to be true to my new allies (mainly in Melbourne) whose views I had boldly embraced, alone among all my colleagues. By now I hardly belonged to the fossilised Immigration Department – though I considered myself a loyal public servant honourably serving the Government.

A dramatic night alone in the office

But by close of day it was clear that time was not on my side. The brief but intense Canberra peak hour had already passed by the time of my brisk 10-minute drive home to Cook for a cursory family dinner, and then back down the hill to a darkened and deserted Northbourne House in Turner, clutching the keys to the building. Alone at night in the nerve centre of the Integration Branch! The stakes were high: I sensed the night would be a long one, but it could re-orient government policy – and, of course, make or break my career. *"O Lord, give me strength and wit now. I look to you."*

For three years, I had had a unique exposure to the temper of ethnic leadership Australia-wide. I was familiar with the range of their aspirations for the future of this country. On the one hand, I wanted to acknowledge the worth of all the patterns of multiculturalism I had been imbibing: cultural pluralism (essentially a new deal for migrants) and ethnic rights – but it also had to respect the sensitivities of the majority community – while still encapsulating a practicable vision for an Australian future. Beyond all that, it had to get past the Branch and Division heads or it would never make it to the Minister's office across the Lake in Parliament House. A trapeze-artist's act!

Mark Lopez again:[22]

> "To write the speech Houston drew on his comprehensive collection of ideological material covering all the streams of multicultural thought. It was a collection of multicultural concepts, arguments and policies, combined with additional material reflecting some values and concerns of the Whitlam Government and its Immigration Minister, expressed in a fashion to facilitate the speech by-passing the bureaucratic checkpoints and being appreciated by the Minister. The multicultural ideas were predominantly cultural pluralist ideas, in particular those compatible with the ethnic rights position, plus some elements of ethnic structural pluralism."

I had decided to call the speech '*A Multi-Cultural Society for the Future*'. It would be the first time the term had been used in an official government policy statement. It sought to outline how our society might be developed according to a grand new design based on equal opportunity for all, '*a goal which no right-thinking person could dispute*' and a social democratic norm proclaimed by all political parties. I considered that these values were rationally and morally unchallengeable, in line with the values incorporated into the UN International Covenant on Civil & Political Rights signed by Australia immediately after Whitlam came to power, and which guarantees freedom of social and cultural expression for all residents of countries ratifying it.

Seeking nocturnal counsel

Late at night, I felt the need to check out some of my proposals with Des Storer[23], whose conceptual approach I admired, and whom I had met when he had come from Melbourne on a delegation with Rev Brian Howe to see the senior officers – but had been shunted off to see me! That night we talked long on the phone, exploring how to balance out idealism and pragmatism, and ensuring that the values propounded were not incompatible with the Labor Party's policy stance. By then I

---

[22]Lopez, op.cit, p. 244.

[23]The supreme irony was that, some 30 years later, he himself would become one of the top mandarins of the Immigration Department.

was shivering, but only from the August cold, since the heating in the office block had been turned off once the staff had gone home.

Next morning the speech was typed out and sent up the line and, to my amazement, was taken over the Lake to the Minister's Office – unaltered! Maybe it was not read, though this would seem out of character for the two dogged defenders of the assimilationist faith long unimpressed with my views. Twenty years later, Watson was to tell Mark Lopez that he couldn't recall the speech. Yet it had turned out to be epoch-making! The only conclusion can be that (as an answer to prayer?) he had scales before his eyes.

Text of the speech

The speech begins,

> "Any contemplation of the character which our urban society might assume by the year 2000 must naturally begin with a hard look at our present society and the potential forces of change already discernible. Any other approach to futurology would be day-dreaming".

After a brief analysis of the diversity of our urban society and the waves of immigration underlying this from the beginning – nor overlooking the ancient Aboriginal presence – I drew attention to the need for balance between maintaining the cultures and building social justice for all.

In a key passage on social justice for migrant communities, it continues,

> "A society dare not, in the long term, devalue the presence of one in four of its members. Is one out of every four to be permanently denied the dignity of self-expression and self-determination – should he so desire – as taken for granted by the other three? We do not need to be gifted with a vivid imagination to picture the explosive pressures – or else naked repression – that would inevitably become the consequences of devaluing or ignoring ethnic communities till the year 2000".

The speech further contends,

> "Our prime task at this point in our history must be to encourage practical forms of social interaction in our community. This implies the creation of a *truly just society* in which all components can enjoy freedom to make their own distinctive contribution to the family of the nation. In the interest of Australians in the year 2000, we need to appreciate, embrace and preserve all those diverse elements which find a place in the nation today. This involves the most fundamental issues of human rights such as those enshrined in the U.N. International Covenant on Civil and Political Rights".

After exploring these issues and their implications, the concluding words:

> "The social and cultural rights of migrant Australians are just as compelling as the rights of other Australians. The full realisation of these rights would lead to reduced conflicts and tensions between the groups that are weaving an ever more complex fabric for Australian society as we hurry towards the turn of the century".

All of 40 years later, the vision of the *'truly just society'* still tarries – now impeded by other factors but perhaps as elusive as ever!

Al Grassby travelled to Melbourne and gave the speech at the Cairnmillar Institute in Camberwell, set up in 1961 by Rev. Dr Francis Macnab to provide psychological treatment services and training. Appropriate setting for the public launch of a vision for shaping an eirenic community in an evolving nation.

Historical evaluation of the speech

I never heard any comment about its reception on the day, but Mark Lopez continues:[24]

> "Due to Houston's initiative the Minister, Al Grassby, was presented with a multicultural manifesto as a basis for migrant settlement, welfare and socio-cultural policy. When he delivered the speech on 11th August 1973 he had effectively given

---

[24] Lopez, op. cit., p.249

CHAPTER 24: A Multicultural Society for the Future   183

multiculturalism official endorsement... Houston's initiative had forced Grassby to end his prevarication about ideology, and in delivering the speech Grassby became the first Minister for Immigration to endorse multiculturalism.

This event constitutes the turning-point in the multiculturalists' campaign to have their ideology accepted as the basis of government policy.

Yet at the time it was delivered the speech had no impact in the public arena, doubtless because all the Minister's policy speeches had press releases accompanying them – except this one. This must also be seen as inexplicable, in that the Immigration Department had a whole Information Section with professional journalists crafting press releases in order to attract the attention of the news media. Why had Watson (the highest authority needed to give the nod) not referred the speech to this Section but presumably despatched it straight to the Minister's Private Secretary at Parliament House?

Consequently, the leading broadsheet daily newspapers, *The Age, The Sydney Morning Herald* and *The Australian*, without a press release to guide them, did not report the speech and overlooked the emergence of multiculturalism in public policy. The convoluted origin of *A Multi-Cultural Society for the Future* also helps to explain the virtually inconspicuous nature of the emergence of multiculturalism. This curious inconspicuousness was reinforced by the lack of any discernible change in the ideological content of Grassby's press releases in the following weeks – and that he did not accompany such an important document with a Ministerial Statement in Parliament".

It goes without saying that from my superiors there was no comment, let alone any commendation. A deafening silence. Surprise: I was never asked to prepare another speech in that Department. But material prepared shortly afterwards by the regular departmental speechwriter (why had he not been given the brief to prepare the speech?) indicated a drift back to the integrationist line, reaffirming our traditional links with Britain!

But how could I have known at the time, caught up in the daily whirl of the Whitlam Government's emerging policy initiatives, that the speech would prove to be the founding document, the basic charter for our future national policy of multiculturalism?[25]

Certainly, in retrospect, history seems to have near-unanimously accorded it that accolade. Subsequently its importance was widely recognised in the historical literature, although even Jean Martin and several later Marxist critical theorists of multiculturalism would assume it was written by Al Grassby himself.

Meeting Al Grassby

What he did do though was to summon me to Parliament House, to his ministerial suite, an unheard-of occurrence for a middling public servant. I went with trepidation: had Watson made a formal complaint of insubordination? But it was to become the strategic moment marking the start of an exciting era – indeed, the rest of my life! To be precise, nearly a decade of working closely with Al Grassby, though in another setting. Certainly, no other Anglo-Australian could have had such a grasp of the thinking and dreaming of the country's ethnic leadership. It amounted to the first tangible outcome of the National Groups Survey. Initially it meant having a friend at court, which conferred a sense of security within an alienated Department.

But neither did it mean that, from then on Grassby single-mindedly pursued a multicultural course – though he was firmly on his way to joining the multiculturalist camp. But it did mean that the version of multiculturalism spelt out in my speech (cultural pluralism) moved ahead of the other models vying for official acceptance. And since no other official statement of multiculturalism was produced under the Whitlam Government, this became the official version. It has gained the accolade of history.

---

[25] It would be subsequently published as 'Immigration Reference Paper, A Multicultural Society for the Future, speech presented by the Hon A. J. Grassby, MHR Melbourne, 11 August 1973', by the Australian Government Publishing Service, Canberra, 1973, 15pp.

CHAPTER 24: A Multicultural Society for the Future   185

Verdict of history

All of thirty-two years later, in the Melbourne *Age* of 27 April 2005, Joe Ludwig MHR, Labor Opposition spokesman on multicultural affairs during the Howard regime, would write a feature article on the editorial page under the heading *Grassby's Baby stands Test of Time.*

"Grassby's short reference paper *A Multicultural Society for the Future*, changed the way our nation thought about itself. The 'father of multiculturalism' postulated what his progeny might look like when born. His vision was of such great impact that 32 years on we are still debating it. In short, the idea was to introduce a range of policies to assist migrants to call Australia home without abandoning their own cultural heritage. A society able to sustain growth and change without disintegration is a society based on equal opportunity for all, the striving for which has traditionally led to some of the deepest conflicts within societies. He boldly looked ahead to 2000 and laid the cornerstone for a just society where all could make their own contribution.

The new direction of his paper meant that we would recognise that "the social and cultural rights of migrants were as compelling as the rights of all other Australians". His concept was grounded in a huge amount of common sense and a love of this country. He knew "the full realisation of these rights would lead to reduced conflicts and tensions between groups in our communities who are weaving an ever more complex fabric for Australian society".

Grassby's big idea has never been a favourite of the small-minded. It has been attacked often enough even by misguided critics like the historian, Geoffrey Blainey, and by our Prime Minister, John Howard, who labelled it "a confusing, even aimless concept". I believe he has not mentioned the Word in Parliament since 1988. His Government has sought to belittle Grassby's contribution. It may be able to cut him out of its official history.

But the message of Al Grassby is enduring. It is a message about a just and fair society for all. As Grassby's baby, our multiculturalism has stood the test of time. In the conclusion to his historic paper that started it, he said "My personal ambition is that Australians of all backgrounds will be proud before the world to say – in whatever accents – *'I am an Australian'*.

I think you got there, Al"

By 2015 no less than one Australian in two is either overseas-born or has one or both parents born overseas (for instance, all four of our grandchildren), and all the evidence is that people of non-British extraction are no less enthusiastic about being Australian. In 2015 a polling agency reported that 86% of the population warmly endorsed multiculturalism. Indeed, Liberal Prime Minister Malcolm Turnbull has claimed that *"Multicultural respect is the foundation of our nation"*. Certainly, as we are now frequently reminded, we are the world's finest example of a functioning pluralistic society.

This is a large claim but I think it bears critical analysis. Many other pluralistic countries (for example India, South Africa, Brazil, the USA and perhaps even the UK) are less functional than ours, perhaps because they lack an overall conceptual framework: they just 'happened'. But Australia consciously chose to 'go multicultural' from the conviction that our vast land needed populating and there were not enough of the original British stock to provide the growth. Enter our Australian conceptual framework: a grand over-arching scenario for developing our future within a defensible, reasoned policy that has gained wide, almost total acceptance, and which has clearly worked in practice. It involves a deal: incoming settlers – in response to the respect accorded to their culture – must respect the national framework. So, the operational challenge is to convey this deal to them, especially to those harbouring a private if inchoate vision of a future not acceptable to the nation e.g. some Islamists resenting our celebration of Christmas or demanding that all meat must be *'halal'*. The common good is not so lightly to be held to ransom.

Multicultural policy adopted by Shadow Minister

But back in 1974, if the ALP had been slow and half-hearted about endorsing the new policy direction and in developing measures to give it some teeth, Malcolm Fraser had no such misgivings. Though viewed in the Liberal Party as a leading conservative, he was in fact philosophically opposed to racism and sympathetic to the migrants' struggle to gain a footing while retaining an affection for their homeland – as indeed he regarded his own Scottish ancestry. Named the Opposition's shadow minister for Labour & Immigration a few days before Grassby gave the speech, in one of his first parliamentary speeches, Fraser attested to his appreciation of cultural pluralism and his acceptance of migrants maintaining their old links and associations, thus adding to the richness and breadth of our national culture. Early in 1974, he drafted a new immigration policy for his party, profoundly influenced by his lengthy discussions with the Greek multiculturalists in Melbourne. He had also written to Minister Grassby requesting his principal policy statements, and promptly received three key documents, the first of which was *A Multi-Cultural Society for the Future*.

The immigration policy which Fraser took into the double dissolution election of 1974 represents the first public adoption of multiculturalism as official policy by a major party. But he had had to drop a call for government funding for migrant welfare associations, as he had promised to the Greeks in Melbourne. His policy document 'recognised the need to overcome the complex problems confronting migrants living in the multi-cultural society of today's Australia', and made commitments to achieve 'equality of opportunity, the elimination of discrimination, and an appreciation of the growing richness and diversity of our way of life'. There followed a pledge to set up a special bureau within the Immigration Department responsible for migrant welfare, staffed by experts who would interact directly with migrant organisations. Another fruit of the National Groups Survey?

Although Labor retained power in that election, eighteen months later Fraser's immigration policy was to be fully adopted by his new coalition government elected beyond the Whitlam Government's dismissal on 11 November 1975. True to his word, an Ethnic Affairs Division would be set up within the reconstituted Department of Immigration & Ethnic Affairs. For the first time, multiculturalism would be instituted on an administrative basis – in the very bastion of the sceptical!

Even more strategically, a new bipartisanship was emerging, without which the new infant could never have survived. Almost certainly, at that time an open vote within either major party would have produced a negative outcome, as surely as a national plebiscite would have done. This emphasises the key role of leadership with conviction, apparently gone missing from contemporary politics (2016). It also ensured that the future progress of multiculturalism would not be dependent on the electoral fortunes of either major party. The rare beast of bipartisanship, even within Parliament!

Fraser cites the *'MultiCultural Society'* speech

In a parliamentary debate on immigration in March 1974, while still in opposition, Fraser had accused Grassby of policy confusion and inconsistency, citing speeches including *A Multi-Cultural Society for the Future* and others written by the official departmental speechwriter (colonialist to the backbone) This was the first mention of multiculturalism in Hansard, the Parliamentary record. But he did not criticise the ideological content of the Cairnmillar speech, which he named as 'essentially hopeful'. So, in a real sense multiculturalism can claim two political fathers. Ironically it might have been Fraser who pushed Grassby into perceiving the implications of the speech. Some time after he gave it, Minister Grassby had belatedly issued a press release promoting *A Multi-Cultural Society for the Future* now published as an official government document in the series *'Immigration Reference Papers'*. The series also included my previous *'Foreign Languages in Australia'* speech for Grassby.

Significantly, once again the country's three major broadsheet newspapers ignored the press release. Given due Press mention, it could have resulted in the public launching of multiculturalism. Their silence reflects the popular disinterest in this ideology at that time, but in turn highlights the remarkable (providential?) character of its political advent.

However, during this tumultuous period of the first ALP Government for 23 years, and with Gough Whitlam's towering profile, the media were fully preoccupied with the radical advances being made in other areas of public policy. The old barriers were being swept aside. Well do I remember how exciting the ABC evening news broadcasts became on the day of a Cabinet meeting: each week a major new policy. Australia was being reshaped before our eyes and a new society was emerging. A radical new thought: politics was all about the public good! But, of course, the boardrooms were full of foreboding, and the vested interests were already itching for redress. All too soon their day would come.

Vainly promoting multiculturalism as election issue

Meanwhile, beavering away in the Department one day not long before the 1974 double-dissolution election I happened upon a report from the USA about federal government funding for ethnic community arts programs. Wow! Why not here? At least we had a handle on what ethnic community bodies existed Australia-wide. And I had laid the groundwork for establishing a new co-operative relationship which augured well. My imagination took wings, and ere long I had a splendid program surging through my mind (and oozing out onto paper) of grants available to worthy organisations within a strict framework of accountability. The storm cloud overhead was the old guard upstairs.... Or was it? Dare I act alone? Wasn't I a good public servant dutifully serving the elected government through advising my Minister, who had indicated I might work with him? The rationalisations were welling up around me like a foam bath.... *Act I would!*

By the end of the next day, the plan with its ethnic rights flavour was complete, eligibility criteria designated, and name bestowed: the *Australian Ethnic Heritage Program*. I had had to type it out at home myself (two-fingered) for fear of it coming to notice within the

Department. But how to get it to the Minister? Bypassing not only the gatekeepers in the Department but also his private secretary in Parliament House (a departmental officer)? My covering note to Minister Grassby accompanying the draft program explained both its intrinsic worth and the timeliness of announcing it during an election campaign expected to be tightly contested. Indeed, as he was to write subsequently,[26] he went to the poll reluctantly, fearing the worst. (How right he was!)

As I suggested, the program could be expected to appeal strongly to all ethnic groups, whether of the left or the right, in their struggle to maintain their cultural values and traditions, while not offending the great bulk of non-migrant Australians. It amounted to a distillation of the consensus of the ethnic opinion that I had gathered and internalised through the National Groups Study. It would be seen as evidence of the Government's seriousness about translating the multiculturalism policy into actual programs on the ground.

Unheralded, on my way home on that dark autumn evening I dropped in for the first time on Al Grassby in his Canberra home base in Aranda, next suburb to Cook, to share my proposal. On the spot, he bought it 100%. Next night the full, detailed document was discreetly dropped into his letterbox.

The very next day he took it up swiftly and energetically, though I've often wondered where he said he'd got it from. Maybe that he had dreamt it up himself? We'll never know. But he had hundreds of copies printed off, presumably in his Parliament House office unbeknown to the Department, with a covering letter he wrote himself, introducing it to ethnic organisation leaders Australia-wide. While flying to Brisbane for an election rally, he signed that letter by hand hundreds of times, and the Program became the main feature of his election campaign launch.

Mark Lopez concludes:

> "Houston, having by-passed the Departmental hierarchy, was less inhibited about what he covered in the *Ethnic Heritage Program* than he was for *A Multi-Cultural Society for the Future*. He included ethnic rights policies related to the employment of 'migrant rights' workers' to increase the awareness by

---

[26] A.J. Grassby, 'The Morning After', Judicator Publications, Canberra, 1979, p 85

migrants of government services relevant to their problems; proposals for incorporating pluralist values into the system of delivering welfare services; and cultural pluralist proposals for measures to further the development of ethnic cultures. ... [Grassby's] adoption of a multicultural policy package without question or hesitation signified the completion of his ideological transformation, and confirmed that he had indeed moved into the multiculturalist camp. Having adopted the *Ethnic Heritage Program*, he had a reform agenda to complement the multiculturalist ideology he had adopted in August 1973; but he had only hurriedly incorporated the Program into an election speech, so the measures had not been initiated within the Department to implement the policies in it. The package had no status within the Department and was therefore likely to disappear with Grassby if he lost his seat"[27].

A few days later the Whitlam Government's Minister for Social Security, Bill Hayden (later to become Governor-General of Australia), announced a Welfare Rights Program in a campaign speech in Melbourne. The two Programs announced by the Ministers differed in that Hayden's Department had already taken practical steps for the implementation of the program on being returned to office. Subsequently Grassby stated that he had wanted the Ethnic Heritage Program to be implemented in order to serve as a manifestation of his legacy in the immigration portfolio[28].

Exit Al Grassby from Parliament

There were two serious casualties of the Whitlam Government's success in the 1974 double dissolution election: the Minister for Immigration and his Department! A local blatantly racist campaign and a dwindling of the ALP's rural support base saw Al Grassby lose his Riverina seat by 792 votes to the Country Party. The bones of contention were his flamboyant style, a racist resentment at his popularity with the large Italian community, and his abolition of the White Australia Policy.

---

[27] Lopez, op.cit., p. 266
[28] A.J. Grassby, 'Credo for a Nation', pp.13, Immigration Reference Paper, Australian Government Publishing Service, Canberra 1974

Of course, the rural Riverina was a naturally conservative seat but Grassby took the defeat hard, writing a book about the racist campaign waged against him, including by one Nicholas White-Australia Maina, who had adopted his compound middle name by deed poll. A farewell rally that Grassby convened at the Sydney Opera House saw a *crowd of two thousand* turn out, mainly from the ethnic communities. But my judgment is that his departure from the day-to-day political fray in Parliament and the cloying duties of the Immigration ministry released him into the general community in a new role, which he was to play with great flair, destined to capture even more hearts.

Exit the Immigration Department!

Initially in the Department of Immigration the senior officers were jubilant at Grassby's defeat. As one remarked, "Anybody who replaces him has to be better". But not only was their Minister not replaced, neither was their Department! As Whitlam told Mark Lopez in an interview in 1995, *"Its time was up"*. Besides, it would cease to be a target for racists, and arguably no one else wanted the portfolio. The re-elected Government distributed the abolished Immigration Department's functions among other specialist Departments where more targeted attention could be given to the areas of need: Labour, Social Security, Education, and Media. Whitlam saw no need for a special department to administer multiculturalism: better to make this focus mainstream to all departments. Clyde Cameron, tough-minded trade unionist, took over the migration program, now tailored to meeting labour market needs, within his new Department of Labour & Immigration. On the other hand, migrant welfare services (including my Integration Branch) would now go to the Department of Social Security.

The leadership clique of the former Department were devastated. The Permanent Head, Bob Armstrong retired; my immediate boss Ted Charles with his unit on English-language teaching for migrants was relocated to the Department of Education, a fish out of water, himself a non-educationist; Andy Watson was shattered, reliably reported as being traumatised by the split, with a leg on either side of a widening divide. The old guard, together since the Department's inception at the end of the war, regarded themselves not as mere public servants but as specialist immigration officers (my own designation was Immigration Officer, Grade 8). In diaspora, the old boys' club would maintain regular contact through private meetings, even machinating with the Opposition's new spokesman on immigration, Michael McKellar (an unreconstructed assimilationist and later Minister for Immigration under Fraser), against the day of a future return to their kingdom.

Mark Lopez writes

> "The progress of multiculturalism in public policy between 1972 and 1974 had been largely a consequence of the influence achieved by multiculturalists in the Department's advisory system. Now Zubrzycki and Lippmann lost their influence.
>
> In addition, Jim Houston's influence had largely depended on his rapport with Grassby. With Grassby no longer Minister, Houston no longer had this influence.
>
> The future of the Integration Branch, to which Houston belonged, was also uncertain at the time when he was nearing the data-processing of his National Groups Survey"[29].

Outcomes of the National Groups Survey

In point of fact we never completed the quantitative analysis of the National Groups Survey. In a Department rife with rumours and contemplating the imminent end of the world, things were at an impasse: the computer analysis of the data still hung in the balance while the IT 'experts' blundered about in unexplored territory. Moreover, despite completing four years' field research nationwide and gaining the support of the country's premier academics in the discipline, I had been deprived of the opportunity of making a distinctive contribution to our understanding of the ethnic scene by producing a book detailing my qualitative analysis, while also offering a blueprint for the multicultural society of the future. Should another door open to me it would be time to depart.

---

[29]Lopez, op. cit., p.344

However, the historic survey was to prove fruitful: in 1975, after I had left Immigration, the quantitative data we had gathered formed the substance of a set of reference books, *National Groups in Australia – A Directory* published separately for each State and the ACT by the Department of Social Security. Based wholly on our Survey, they offered detailed entries on the great majority of the organisations we contacted, covering addresses, leadership, and services provided. They amounted to a detailed national compendium listing specialist allies for workers in the civil society to collaborate with.

For me it was a proud moment to be present (though unacknowledged) in the Sydney Town Hall when the seven Directories were launched by the Prime Minister, Gough Whitlam, appropriately in a crowded meeting that also saw the launch of the Ethnic Communities Council of NSW, after Victoria's the second in Australia. In later years the reconstituted Department of Immigration & Ethnic Affairs was to publish at least six updated editions, as single volumes covering the whole country. I have the 1989 volume, *Directory of Ethnic Community Organisations in Australia*, running to 413 pages. By then the organisations came from 137 different ethnic backgrounds, including interesting new entries like Hmong, Kurdish, Ogadan and Romany. Its cover design features a recurrent pattern naming 85 of the ethnic groups[30], slanted discreetly in diagonal bands, from Afghans to Zimbabweans.

The Foreword by the Minister observes:
> "The Directory reflects the cultural diversity of the Australian community. It also demonstrates the importance of ethnic community organisations in acting as a focal point for the social, cultural, welfare, religious and educational activities of their communities. It will be a great help to those providing services to, or working with ethnic communities, including governments, academics and private organisations. A broader purpose is to facilitate communication and interchange between people of all cultural backgrounds in our community, thus enhancing mutual understanding and tolerance."

---

[30] By 2017 the figures would expand to 270 ancestries and 140 languages

CHAPTER 24: A Multicultural Society for the Future

Also prepared in 1975, but after I had left my old position, was a sketchy report on the character and significance of the National Groups Survey written in the Department of Social Security but to my knowledge never published.

However, preoccupied with new tasks of speech writing and preparing material for the Immigration Advisory Council's *Committee on Community Relations Final Report* in mid-1974, for the moment I had lost heart. Moreover, my good colleague on the Survey, Jan Reksten, had moved off to prepare for appointment to a post overseas. It was all too uncertain and, with the demise of the *Ethnic Heritage Program*, I felt disillusioned over my aborted sally into direct political action.

But despite the abolition of the Immigration Advisory Council, its Committee on Community Relations was saved by Walter Lippmann's Jewish connections within the ALP. Its Final Report, largely written by Professor Laki Jayasuriya, provided a historic document espousing the ideology of cultural pluralism and including a section *'A Philosophy of Community Relations'* destined to be influential in shaping the future work of Al Grassby – and me.

But though unbeknown to me at the time, that dream was still over the horizon.

CHAPTER 25:
"A Name to Conjure With!"

About June 1974, in my unsettled frame of mind, my eye fell on a vacancy advertised in the *Commonwealth Gazette* for a position within the newly created Schools Commission. This was one of Gough Whitlam's boldest initiatives, his solution to the running sore of 'State aid for private schools' that had deeply divided Australia since Menzies' later years as Coalition Prime Minister.

In 1964, out of the blue Menzies had made grants to Catholic schools Australia-wide for secondary-level science laboratories and later also for libraries (and was duly re-elected). I remember that many of us, products of the State school system, were shocked at the unilateral decision, at one stroke reversing a hundred years of established practice all over the country.

But by 1972, the ALP felt obliged to drop its traditional opposition to funding Catholic schools, since there was even some prospect of the system collapsing under the rapid expansion of pupil numbers through immigration from Catholic countries, far eclipsing its capacity to provide the requisite financial resources. It was shaping up for a crisis. But it had always been considered that the States were responsible for the funding of education at all levels.

Labor took a more egalitarian course by committing to a 'needs-based' allocation of the funds, implying an end to funding the wealthier 'schools with pools'. Hence a massive injection of funds was envisaged for government and non-government schools alike, on the basis of need (predictably triggering outcries of discrimination *against the rich!*). Of course, this implied knowing authoritatively which schools were the neediest.

To examine and determine the needs of all schools in Australia – primary and secondary, State and private – and to recommend appropriate grants, as well as setting minimum standards for schools that fell below the line, was obviously a daunting educational challenge.

But it reflected the new Government's vision of working towards reducing inequality in Australian society, and the schools' capacity for either alleviating it – or perpetuating it. The mooted reforms struck a chord with the great majority of the Australian public.

Breaking the old mould

Acting urgently on this, within its first weeks in office, the Government had set up the Karmel Committee of eminent educators and representatives of the many nationwide interest groups in the field, to report in six months. Finally after lengthy parliamentary wrangling (since the Government lacked a Senate majority) from 1 January 1975 the Schools Commission was established under the leadership of Professor Ken McKinnon, previously head of the colonial education system in Papua-New Guinea, and with a budget of $660 million to be disbursed, two thirds to government schools and one third to non-government schools (a sixfold increase on the former Coalition Government's spending on schools), according to a complex formula devised on the basis of schools' needs.

In addition to the huge programs of recurrent funding for running costs and school buildings, there were five other programs: for Disadvantaged Schools, Special Education (for disabled children), Innovations in Education, Teacher Development, and Primary School Libraries. Schools below the minimum standards (mostly in poor Catholic parishes) were to be funded to reach the general standard by 1980. Conversely, aid to the richest private schools was to be phased out, starting immediately.

Predictably this led to a veritable frenzy of opposition, which ultimately prevailed through the hostile Senate. But since the Government had an undeniable mandate to implement the education policy it had put to the electorate, the remainder of the visionary reforms passed into law. They represented blueprints for the most radical revision of schooling in our history, backed by a huge increase in funding – and that from the Federal Government with its taxing powers for raising funds. For that period, the funds allocated to the Schools Commission seemed mind-blowing – astronomical! A senior teacher of my acquaintance enthused: "Ah! The Schools Commission – *a name to conjure with!*"

Farewell to Immigration Department

The position I saw advertised was for Director of the Disadvantaged Schools Program, at Class 10 level. I had been at Class 8 level for something like five years, which might be taken to imply a lack of ambition and initiative, though the reality was that I enjoyed my professional role in Immigration and had not yet really completed the huge task of surveying and reporting on Australia's ethnic organisations, so was loth to run away. But in the event, the Department ran away from me! I was interviewed and duly selected. Farewell Immigration! My new air-conditioned office would be on the 12th floor of the new 20-storey MLC Tower built in the heart of the Woden Valley office and shopping complex, with sweeping panoramic views to the mountains.

An appealing bribe

When I announced to my superiors that I had been promoted to the Schools Commission, they seemed shocked. The next day I was offered an appointment (but not on promotion) to an overseas post, in Stockholm, Sweden. I knew of course that this was why many people joined the Immigration Department – overseas appointments, perks, bring home a Mercedes. And Scandinavia was the top of the tree. I was seriously tempted. But, of course, it didn't feel right. Providential moves don't come that way. I was being patronised, bought off. After 24 hours, I turned it down. Wisely, because after a few months the person sent instead of me found his position abolished and was relocated to Australia House in London. Been there, done that.

In a tailor-made position

Schools Commission, here I come. But alas! An appeal against my appointment by a better qualified Brit was upheld – a decision I couldn't disagree with. But instead, a far more appropriate new position was offered to me, as the field researcher in Migrant & Multicultural Education, at Class 9 level. If I had been invited to design an ideal position for myself I could scarcely have done better! This time, in God's good Providence, a door had opened before me.

The task was, by June 1975, to recommend what the Schools Commission's policy should become in a new and hitherto under-resourced domain – the education of migrant children – on the basis of a wide-ranging consultation within the ethnic communities. (But who could have known them better than I?) And what a strategic – not to say humanitarian – privilege: to be responsible for devising the national policy for educating the children of migrants across Australia, to be implemented over the next three years (1976-78), and with the requisite funding guaranteed by the Commonwealth! Subject of course to professional constraints: my evidence would have to convince one of Australia's leading academic educationists, who in turn would need to persuade the full Commission to approve the funding measures we recommended and then allocate the funding nationwide.

In God's purposes, was this the practical outcome of our years of visiting ethnic communities around Australia? And enduring the cynicism of the troglodytes at the top of the Immigration Department? To be able to bless the newcomers through ensuring that their children at least need not be disadvantaged from having crossed the world to join us? Maybe at last a brand new day was dawning.

The first phase was to study all the recent education reports, from State Education Departments and academia, and report on these to the fulltime Commissioner with whom I would work, Dr Jean Blackburn, a distinguished and humane educationist from Melbourne University and destined to become the inaugural Chancellor of the University of Canberra. Beyond that, in my self-confidence I reckon I could have devised the policy single-handedly, so familiar was I with the aspirations and claims from the ethnic grassroots, particularly in Melbourne. But these had to be experienced in face-to-face situations by the Commissioner herself.

Generating hope among ethnic parents

So we decided to concentrate on Sydney and Melbourne, twin microcosms of ethnic Australia, and I arranged many encounters with the leaders of organisations previously identified during my Survey. Of course, the meetings were conducted by Mrs Blackburn, while I recorded significant points by hand, a facility developed years earlier with Unesco Committees, instead of relying on recording technology dependent on typistes' familiarity with the material. Mostly we concentrated on inner-city or outer migrant-belt suburbs, covering the full range of ethnic groups but particularly newer ones like the Vietnamese starting to arrive as refugees after the American defeat. They represented the first ethnic community to arrive from Asia since the Chinese in the Gold Rush days – and the initial beneficiaries of the recent burial of the White Australia Policy.

All our encounters were positive, indeed full of hope – after all, we were capitalising on Labor's popularity among the migrant communities being so carefully cultivated by Al Grassby. Really it was a delightful task, generating hope and enthusiasm among people who had often been treated as second-rate since their arrival in this country. Although mainly poorly educated themselves, they had towering aspirations for their children, many of whom were performing amazingly well, later to make the transition to middle-class professionals. My best memory is of a tumultuous meeting in Melbourne, in a crowded West Sunshine café, where competing ethnic speakers were literally leaping onto the tables to get their points across. Well might they, since these were the very suburbs where the schools were least able to cope with the ethnic presence. A book on Melbourne schools published at the time, *The Myth of Equality*, had said it all.

In the next few months my task was to distil these aspirations into policy initiatives, based on an essay expounding who the migrants were, what were the needs of their children and their communities, and how sensitively framed educational measures might bridge the gap from their current reality. It went through several versions, becoming ever more defined and refined, since it was to end up as a brief chapter of eight pages in a massive 300-page document: the Schools Commission's program for earthing (and paying for) its vision over the next three years. Beyond Jean Blackburn it had to be approved by several bureaucrats up to the level of Professor McKinnon with his background of indigenous and cross-cultural education.

Drafting the national policy for migrant children

But there could be no debate about my first sentence: *"Australia is a multicultural society"* – established by the statistics from the chalkface and the demonstrated desire of the parents to raise their children *biculturally*, since "assimilationist policies do not dissolve cultural differences". And this without prejudice to the over-riding need (and desire) to produce young people proficient in English and able to compete on the labour market with native speakers. No ghettoes for modern Australia, the bane of many other lands of migration.

As established by the federal Department of Education's parallel *Inquiry into Schools of High Migrant Density*, migrant(s') children across the country were (naturally) performing below the level of the locally-born. Hence by its founding Act, the Schools Commission was committed to addressing such disadvantage. This in turn required action to gauge the efficacy of the existing Federal Government support, made available under the long-standing Child Migrant Education Program until recently administered by the Immigration Department. Australia-wide we established that only one migrant child in three was receiving adequate attention.

We therefore recommended greatly increased funding for teaching English to newcomers in special classes, but also for integrating migrant children into the mainstream through a strategy of assistance across the whole curriculum, with ESL specialists collaborating with the regular class teachers. Beyond that there was need for all schools to reflect the multicultural reality of our society, in curriculum, staffing, organisation and in the library. Not only would this undergird the self-esteem of migrant children but also enrich all students by the sharing of diverse cultural heritages. Further, where there were large numbers of pupils of a specific language background, there was need for experimentation with bilingual approaches. Finally, teacher development programs were called for, to sensitise teaching and liaison personnel and interpreters to issues arising from the students' cultural backgrounds.

For such new programs, generous extra funds were required. Our proposals recommended that $47 million be allocated over the triennium 1976-78 to schools throughout Australia, both government and non-government. But the Commission's recommended overall funding of $2 billion for schools in the coming triennium was rejected by the Whitlam Government because of its developing financial woes, to be replaced by a one-year report for 1976 alone, focusing on building costs and running costs, and deferring the other five creative programs. Certainly, the Senate would not have passed it at that time. But since the Migrant & Multicultural Program was part of the recurrent funding program it survived and in succeeding years, it would be largely implemented by the Fraser Government.

Schools Commission's achievements in migrant education

Mark Lopez evaluates what was nevertheless achieved in those few crucial years[31]:

> "The Minister for Education, Kim Beazley [father of the later Leader of the Opposition of the same name] was broadly interested in the kinds of policies advocated by the multiculturalists... The multiculturalists saw opportunities to influence policies when Beazley established several new enquiries. Jim Houston was the first to capitalise on this. He left the Department of Labour & Immigration shortly before his Survey of National Groups was presented, to begin working for the Schools Commission. He also became a member of the [Department of Education's] Steering Committee for the Inquiry into Schools of High Migrant Density. .... Meanwhile Houston worked to orientate the Schools Commission towards adopting multiculturalism as part of its education policy proposals, by arranging for the Commissioner, Jean Blackburn, to visit the Australian Greek Welfare Society to discuss migrant education. .... [Moreover] the multiculturalists' efforts proved to have been successful when the Schools Commission

---

[31]Lopez, op. cit., p.354

presented its *Report for the Triennium 1976-78* in May 1975. Its Chapter 8, 'The Education of Migrant Children', written by Jim Houston, began with the forthright declaration of Australia as a multicultural society and presented an unequivocal endorsement of multiculturalism as an approach to education. .... The Report also included a manoeuvre to transfer the control of funding to the Schools Commission from the existing Child Migrant Education Program [headed incidentally by Ted Charles!] which reflected integrationist values, perhaps as a precursor to the abolition of that Program. The *Report for the Triennium 1976-78* represented the long sought-after breakthrough for the multiculturalists in education policy, which they were quick to consolidate. Houston drafted a speech for the Minister for Education, Kim Beazley, delivered on 28th May 1975 at the Banquet-Symposium of the Greek Society of Letters, which included an endorsement of the Schools Commission Report and its 'vision of multicultural education'".

Of course, at the time, the Schools Commission's Triennial Report only had the status of an advisory document.

"The gallant hand-written thank-you note that Beazley sent Houston for drafting the speech suggests that he was happy to endorse the report and also multi-culturalism. The report of the Steering Committee for the Inquiry into Schools of High Migrant Density further confirmed the multicultural trend established by the Schools Commission Report. Jim Houston, a member of the Steering Committee, had a considerable influence over the contents of its report, echoing the contents and recommendations of the Schools Commission's Report; it also began with the similar assertion: 'This report is predicated on the fact that Australia is now a multi-cultural society'. During 1975, the multiculturalists had achieved a shift in the ideological content of advice to the Government on migrant education, and an endorsement from the Minister for Education. Their breakthrough in this area resembled their breakthrough in Immigration in 1973-74"[32].

---

[32]ibid., p.399-401

A strategic invitation

With some sense of 'mission accomplished' at the Schools Commission (and not being a professional educationist at heart, still less an educational accountant), I was delighted to receive a note from Al Grassby about that time, inviting me to join the staff of his Community Relations Office as soon as it was created, on the anticipated passage of the *Racial Discrimination Act*. Again, it seemed so providential and perfect in its timing that I needed no second bidding.

The only cloud on the horizon, though a heavy lowering one, reflected the current political climate. The Whitlam Government was making heavy weather of it, under increasing pressure from the Coalition-oriented media, and with the Senate turning increasingly unco-operative. Many of my colleagues had a sense of impending doom (whatever their own political colour), since it was clear that the Schools Commission with its expensive crusading zeal would have its wings clipped by the financial straiteners, if not be altogether abolished. Of course, this fate also confronted Al Grassby and his mooted Community Relations Office.

But as history sadly laments, beyond the dismissal of Gough Whitlam, the incoming Coalition Government of Malcom Fraser would indeed dispense with the expertise of the Schools Commission and its carefully drafted consultative plans for reforming the national education scene in the dimensions of quality and equity.

In memoriam

Incredibly, it would take no less than *forty* years – a whole generation – before another Labor Government would commit to a further attempt at a comprehensive evaluation of schooling needs of the whole population, introducing the Gonski Plan in 2013 (this time produced by a businessman not an educator) as a blueprint for seeking equal outcomes of schooling irrespective of type of school, location, or parental resources. Tragically, again it would founder on the inability of wealthy parents and their political sponsors to countenance the needs of less favoured children, while clamouring for the wealthiest schools to gain a quite disproportionate share of the resources available.

Regretfully, I have been unable to trace in contemporary media any awareness of the previous valiant attempt by the Schools Commission to address the same issues, while taking a more professional, broader-based and pedagogically sound approach. Such is the close horizon of the media, custodians of the public memory! It is now claimed that, alone in the world, Australia subsidises the *most élite* private schools! But with no vision for the establishment of a Schools Commission-type co-ordinating agency across the country, by 2016 the Gonski Plan appeared to have met with the same fate at the hands of a similar Coalition Government, au fait with the price of everything but the value of nothing! And *they* sneer about *Labor* dredging up the old class warfare shibboleths!

In 1974, with this climax impending, I took the family for a holiday at Terrigal, on the NSW Central Coast. I have clear memories of sitting on the beach poring anxiously over the political pages of the *Sydney Morning Herald's* reporting of the double-dissolution election campaign, with our three boys playing happily on the sand nearby and an adolescent Sarah-Jane at 14 asserting her independence by opting to sit at the other end of the beach, alone. I felt just as alone, oppressed by a sense of impending doom. Was that my future teetering on the crest of the next wave inexorably curling in towards the beach?

CHAPTER 26:
Fostering a Fairer Australia

With its mandate renewed by victory in the mid-term double dissolution election, the Whitlam Government resumed its heroic reconfiguring of the nation in pursuit of the equitable, caring, and humanised society. The recent tentative espousal of multiculturalism had garnered broad support from the 'migrant vote' for this unfolding vision of Australia. But the flamboyant pin-up boy who embodied the dream had perished in the fray.

Needing to retain Al Grassby for his magic touch with migrants, Whitlam appointed him 'Special Consultant on Community Relations', pending his Government's enactment of racial discrimination legislation. During its first term, the proposed legislation had languished in Parliament. Grassby was now able to influence its redrafting, providing for a Commissioner for Community Relations able to exercise legal and educative powers for the combat of racial discrimination within the multicultural society – a historic step forward and one unlikely to be reversed.

One lunchtime early in 1975 while still working with the Schools Commission I had driven over to the Parliamentary Triangle to meet with Al Grassby. He had invited me over for a briefing about planning for the future Community Relations Office, and indicated that he would like me to be his principal assistant, on the grounds of our earlier collaboration on immigration matters and the *Ethnic Heritage Program*. I pretended not to be ravished with joy. Could it be for real?

Traumatic start to earthing a dream

So, late in the 1975 winter, having made my contribution to the Schools Commission's optimistic triennial planning, I bade farewell to my colleagues to join George in setting up shop in the granite and marble monstrosity of the Administrative Building just across the lawns from the old Parliament House. An eminently accessible spot for our short walk into history on the fateful November afternoon of Remembrance Day.

CHAPTER 26: Fostering a Fairer Australia

But beyond the Dismissal Grassby was not to be axed as Commissioner for Community Relations. Instead our unit would be consigned to irrelevancy and ignored. But not totally. The saving grace was that there were some liberal elements within the Fraser Government – it seems including Malcolm himself – who endorsed the need for a *Racial Discrimination Act* and appreciated its origins and the obligation to set up an agency to administer it.

Sadly, to the people for whom it might just have brought a new beginning, the Aborigines, our Office and the Act remained largely unknown. They didn't follow the media, and why should they hold any belief that Canberra could actually affect their situation for good? The real tragedy was that, now that there was a legal instrument backing equal rights and equal treatment, there were insufficient human and financial resources – or the sheer willpower – to make it work. Small wonder that the prevailing mood of my professional life through the next seven years was one of disappointment and frustration, at times bordering on bitterness.

This was the case when it first became clear what cast-iron bounds were set around the functioning of the Office. We could expect no additions to our minute staffing complement. Even to survive in our roles we needed Grassby but equally he needed us: George for his administration of the Office and handling all the complaints of discrimination that soon began to pour in from Aboriginal and ethnic communities nationwide, while I tried to follow up on the glib promises Grassby offered to all who besought him, and in between wrote papers for him to present at conferences and monitored the stream of documents appearing on multicultural developments, but also attended to the daily correspondence, often from well-wishers offering bright ideas.

Reporting directly to the people

At the end of the first year came the challenge of preparing the first of seven mandatory Annual Reports to Parliament by the Commissioner for Community Relations.

Our report would turn out to be a blockbuster, omitting nothing of the spate of frenzied activity by the Commissioner and his four trusty henchpersons Commonwealth-wide: two of them in Sydney and Melbourne, with George and me in Canberra. What a ludicrous travesty was our commitment to change the temper of an indifferent though largely racist nation, by attending to the anguished complaints of the losers while challenging the attitudes of the public. I could hardly decide whether it was a sick joke or a ridiculous charade. Or maybe just a bad dream ...

Each of us drafted our report on our own bailiwick but the result would have shamed a tin of dogfood. Grassby's journalistic slickness, George's sober account of his case-handling, and my purple prose, compelling in its lucidity, about our achievements on the community education front *(joke!)*. None of it read like a government report: restrained, objective, factual. I offered to act as editor, on the basis of my earlier experience in the Public Service, and was duly confirmed editor for the seven-year stint.

With the first report, after literally weeks of frantic labour – writing and arguing and re-editing, in the office and at home, with a deadline hanging over me – at last the job was done and sent off to the Government Printer. All 200 pages of it. I felt like a man let out of gaol, only more exhausted.

That evening, as I drove home in the dark, the ABC radio brought the Largo movement from J S Bach's *Double Violin Concerto in D minor*. I began to cry. Pulling over to the bushy roadside of Belconnen Way I simply sat there, blubbering and exhausted, as the intertwining melodies outdid each other in anointing my spirit with heavenly balm. To this day I never hear them without again re-living those gentle waves of peace lapping ever higher on the shingly seashore of my soul.

How were the Annual Reports received?

Over the seven years the parliamentary reports traced the temper of community relations, illustrated by accounts of cases reported from all over the country, balanced by encouraging indications of progress. But it was clear that the Fraser Government, for all its liberal elements, was not serious about building community harmony and combating racism – as the International Convention on Racial Discrimination required of all Member States. But neither was it going to disband the Office because of the likely electoral fallout. By then we had acquired a pronounced nuisance value: like a good watchdog, respected but lean because half starved.

In our first year of 1976 we had been surprised at the ubiquity of the discrimination reported Australia-wide – previously unrecognised because not encountered by the media, nor experienced by the élites, nor even by the middle class, hence traditionally unremarked and unreported. Who of us had ever been refused service in a shop because of our skin colour? Or had the chagrin of seeing our daughter's basketball team refused access to the Council's courts because it was 'not Caucasian'. Or resented what the school textbooks said about our culture? Or been sacked because of our ethnic group's reputation? In 1979 alone, a total of 903 cases of this type had been investigated, lodged Australia-wide by people from 105 backgrounds (but predominantly Aboriginal). It revealed a world of daily tension and distress unknown to most of us in the land of Oz, so well renowned for its openness and commitment to the fair go.

Handling racial discrimination complaints

The daily staple of the Office - the complaints - arrived with every mail, either referred to Grassby for advice or tackled by George. They would be referred in writing to the alleged offender (the respondent) and many would be resolved by clearing up misunderstandings or by an apology. But in an angry dispute, or with the respondent refusing to co-operate, the *Racial Discrimination Act* provided for a compulsory conciliation procedure and, if this failed, the issue of a Certificate opening the way to a Court hearing – but on the initiative of the complainant, not the Office. Hence almost no complaint ever ran the whole gamut, clearly too daunting for a rural Aborigine or a newly arrived migrant.

Once during a visit to Townsville for educational purposes, I found myself handling the only complaint I ever had to conciliate, lodged by an Aboriginal against a recalcitrant hospital worker, requiring my convening a compulsory conference between the two parties, since I was on the spot. How galling to discover that the respondent was a migrant! – from Uruguay. To my relief she agreed to back down so that the case was resolved amicably.

But apart from that episode, I had no involvement in casework at all. During the seven years of the Office's existence, over 5100 cases were conciliated upon, about a quarter of them involving government departments and public agencies. It demonstrated how entrenched racist attitudes were across the community. Could these attitudes ever be changed by somehow re-educating the community about the rights of all Australians irrespective of their race or ethnic origin?

Primacy of public education

From the outset, the Commissioner had laid down the priorities of his Office as firstly, *education of the community*, then the provision of public information, and thirdly casework. It was clear that historic community attitudes towards people outside the Anglo-Celtic mainstream needed to be tackled, and that merely handling the flood of complaints would amount to stationing an ambulance at the foot of the cliff rather than building a fence at the top. His own tireless efforts, travelling incessantly around the States, were directed towards promoting the benefits of community harmony.

Inauguration of ethnic radio

His first great breakthrough came with the establishment of public ethnic radio, initially with an experimental station in Sydney and Melbourne broadcasting in 40 languages, which became the embryo of the SBS (Special Broadcasting Service) in radio and TV, seeking to close the communication gap with two million residents cut off from mainstream sources of information. The other side of the coin was encouraging federal government agencies to recognise the rights of all their clients to information in their own language. These initiatives were designed to empower 'ethnic' Australians, and thus contribute to their sense of wellbeing in a new society.

Building community alliances

But given the absurd paucity of the resources available to the Office, it was essential from the outset to build alliances with other community groups sharing our vision. They included educational bodies at all levels Australia-wide; the Churches; and ethnic and Aboriginal community leaders. As Assistant Commissioner for Education and Research, these agencies now became my natural constituency. It brought many invitations to participate in conferences and seminars, sometimes as a speaker, as at the annual NSW Synod meeting of the Uniting Church (UCA), and as an observer attending that Church's triennial National Assembly in Adelaide. It also involved acting as a catalyst on committees: the Council of the Canberra College of TAFE, the Multicultural Education Committee of the ACT Schools Authority, and the Board for Social Responsibility of the UCA in NSW. In the Public Service, I represented the Office on an Inter-Departmental Committee. Always and everywhere patiently sowing the good seed or preparing the ground for it, since our Office had no real powers other than moral suasion.

But this passing parade could never address the structural issues needing to be tackled head-on. The education system itself and specific areas of community life awaited attention.

Widespread community ferment

At that time, the ferment in educational circles was palpable everywhere: change was in the air, with the injection of Commonwealth funds opening up new perspectives. Among these, a key one was the growing vogue for 'multicultural education' in which I had been involved in several States during my Schools Commission days. Now in the Community Relations Office, with its mandate to stimulate community education in the spirit of the *Racial Discrimination Act* and the International Convention against Racial Discrimination, it seemed a far-seeing initiative to involve the schools, imbuing future citizens with a sympathetic understanding of cultural differences. Fortunately, much was afoot all over the country in university faculties of education, the new Colleges of Advanced Education, and the teacher training institutions.

Animating education conferences across Australia

The special contribution our Office could make to a series of broadly representative community conferences on multicultural education convened by local activists in several States, was to offer liaison with the ethnic communities that we knew so well. Given our slender resources, it seemed best to encourage the 'converts' to get together in their State capitals to make plans for a nationwide advance. With typical energy Al Grassby took up this cause.

Over the next few months, working with local enthusiasts, he and I initiated action leading to the convening in several States of two-day conferences canvassing the prospects for multicultural education, in collaboration with the ethnic communities. In three of these historic initiatives, in Brisbane, Perth and Hobart I was involved as animator or resource person. There were also conferences in Sydney and Melbourne. The broad aim of all the conferences – moving beyond the earlier struggle of a fair go for migrants – was how to educate all young Australians to live justly and with understanding in a multicultural society.

Before me I have the *Proceedings of the First Queensland Conference on Languages and Cultures in the Australian Community* held at Mt Gravatt College of Advanced Education in 1977, in the organisation of which I had closely collaborated. Following Al Grassby as the keynote speaker, papers were presented by leading Queensland educators, and then workshops met on such issues as:

- language and culture needs in the community
- improving the school environment.
- changing attitudes among teachers
- training multicultural teachers
- bilingual programs
- ethnic language schools
- adult migrants learning English
- an Aboriginal view of Australian history
- English for Aborigines

It was a similar outcome from the multicultural education conference we had convened in Perth, with variations reflecting local conditions such as the new Asian presence (now including Burmese) but also the special educational needs of Aboriginal people.

ACT Conference on multicultural education

Our campaigning for *'cultural equality within a cohesive society'* as the watchword for our future culminated in 1978 in a local conference focusing on the ACT under the title *Our Multicultural Capital* (with its deliberate *double entendre*).

To our surprise we discovered that no less than 20% of Canberra's school population had an 'ethnic' background, a figure second only to Victoria where so much had been done to recognise their special needs, whereas locally little attention had been paid to them. Scarcely surprising that the conference drew together parents and teachers and other community workers from no less than 91 organisations, speaking 52 languages – our multicultural 'capital'! Over two days the participants produced a blueprint for government, the professions and civil society groups to enrich and diversify our city[33]. An immediate outcome was the creation of the Ethnic Communities Council of the ACT, an essential co-ordinating agency in line with the pattern then developing in the States.

Fostering an ACT ginger group

A further outcome was the convening of an ongoing 'Canberra Multicultural Task Force' whose several specialist sections (focusing on schools, health, community services, the law, the media) would each seek to earth the 'vision splendid' of *developing a multicultural capital for a multicultural nation.*

I represented the Community Relations Office and acted as secretary of the Task Force. Later in 1978, in company with three kindred multicultural agencies, the Task Force convened a one-day Workshop on *'The Prospects for Multiculturalism in the ACT'*,

---

[33]Published as 'Our Multicultural Capital: Community Conference Report', Don Phillips & Jim Houston (eds.), Canberra College of Advanced Education, 1978, 130pp.

specifically examining what the Fraser Government's much trumpeted Galbally Report[34] had to offer Canberra.

Under the Fraser Government this national Report and Program had been tabled in Parliament in ten community languages (a 'first'), as the most comprehensive initiative in government assistance for migrants ever taken, with the aim of ensuring equal rights and access to services with other Australians. It introduced a raft of creative new programs and services, including funding ethno-specific agencies (my earlier abortive initiative), setting up Migrant Resource Centres throughout Australia, creating the Australian Institute of Multicultural Affairs (AIMA) and, perhaps most significantly, officially defining multiculturalism. In all, it was a heartening public manifestation of a new bipartisanship – indispensable to the future success of multiculturalism.

Moreover, the Galbally Report's candour was truly historic in recognising the inadequacy of past services to migrants, proposing real community consultation, and calling for a new sensitivity on the part of Government service providers – in short proposing a new partnership between government and the community in *positively reconfiguring Australia as a multicultural nation*.

But the Workshop concluded that the lack of mention of the ACT, and the failure of the Department of Immigration to suggest any consultation with ACT residents as was being done in the States, together with the absence of funding support for the ACT Schools Authority or local health initiatives, meant that "the ACT would be the only part of Australia excluded from the undoubted benefits offered the nation through the Galbally Report". Subsequently, I was editor of the published report of this strategic Workshop[35].

Rectifying a local education oversight

Subsequently our Office was much involved in the ACT Schools Authority's tardy recognition of the need to develop a policy on

---

[34]'Review of Post-arrival Programs and Services for Migrants' (The Galbally Report), Australian Government Publishing Service, Canberra, 1978
[35]'Galbally Report in the ACT and the Prospects for Multiculturalism: Report & Resolutions of the Community Workshop, Canberra 1978'

multicultural education. An Advisory Committee was set up of which I was a member. A survey I conducted identified 21 Canberra ethnic communities offering Saturday morning childrens classes in their own language and culture, including in Finnish, Slovenian, Arabic and Sikh. The surprise was to find that the classes were in the hands of skilled and experienced people – though mostly not pedagogues – using sophisticated textbooks, sometimes supplied by the home country's government. On the whole, a picture of resourcefulness and dedication in transmitting language and culture with loving attention to the next generation of young Canberrans.

It was evidence that ethnic consciousness was on the rise in Australia, as indeed throughout the world, doubtless a response to the contradictory pressures of mass conformity and individualism. It was recognised that the maintenance of a child's family identity offered a firm base for later negotiating the pressures of adjusting to two cultures. It also asserted the primacy of human values within what was sometimes seen as a Philistine environment.

Historic national congress on multiculturalism

At the dawn of the new decade, the series of State conferences culminated in a historic national congress, *Australian Society in the Multicultural Eighties*. With over 500 participants, the nation came to us in Canberra to assess the prospects for multiculturalism right across our national life. It seemed that for too long the campaigning had been carried on the backs of schoolchildren, as it were. If it was to emerge out of the classroom and into the marketplace, it was time to start drawing up agendas for areas such our national identity, population policy, politics, the health services, social welfare, migrant women, the media, religion, the law, law enforcement, prejudice & discrimination. If multiculturalism was indeed rooted in the demographic imperatives and not merely in the sentimental aspirations of idealists, how could it be made normative for the movers and shakers of our land to permanently factor in the new challenge? Hence the strategic target audience for the congress: senior 'unconverted' decision-makers.

Since the *Racial Discrimination Act* also posed the educational challenge of addressing the issues of cultural and racial diversity – defending the victims and tackling the impediments – our Office had originally proposed the event, convened an exploratory gathering of representatives from government departments and authorities in Canberra and the civil society to develop the range of topics, drawing in the ethnic bodies – before 'outsourcing' the conduct of the whole project to a commercial firm of conference organisers who staged the complex event at the ANU with great pizazz.

It proved to be quite the most ambitious and comprehensive conference ever attempted on such a theme in Australia, with delegates drawn from a great range of occupational categories nationwide navigating their way through a complex array of congress strands and workshops.

They had previously received a document giving abstracts of all 76 papers to be delivered by nationally recognised experts, covering every area of national life – social, cultural, and economic. In the event the quality of the workshop discussions was striking: well-informed, humane, future-oriented.

At the time, some of us even had concerns that, unless a new level of human sensitivity could be fostered in Australia, the issues might become polemical or even explosive before the 80s were out, given the heightening racial passions in many lands. Yet the fact that by 2016 there has been relatively little communal tension in Australia speaks volumes for the wisdom of our policy makers in those formative years of striving to build a multicultural consensus.

Subsequently 27 of the papers presented were published as a major sociology textbook.[36]

Challenging racist school textbooks

In the 1980s, the rising tide of ethnic consciousness across Australia was contributing to the emergence of a society impatient at the perpetuation of past indignity and crippling discrimination towards minorities. But if the First Australians could not find an honoured

---

[36] 'Australian Multicultural Society: Identity, Communication and Decision Making', Don Phillips and Jim Houston (eds), Drummond Books, Blackburn. Vic 1984, 206pp.

place in multicultural Australia, all the rhetoric must ring hollow. So, the time was opportune for a rethinking of the basis of race relations, and for school textbooks to report this to the next generation.

In his annual parliamentary report, Al Grassby had set the goals for appropriate educational approaches in a multiracial and multicultural society:

> "The schoolrooms of the nation are in many ways the best barometers of community relations. If children are being actively encouraged to relate on a human plane to all their fellow students, there will be little risk that they will grow up to inflict discriminatory treatment."

As a community education initiative, he asked me to draw public attention to the often slanderous nature of school textbooks' treatment of Aboriginal people and their culture. *Let's End the Slander* was to be the first book for which I had been solely responsible: researching the data, gathering slanderous material, developing the argument, writing the text, arranging for a cover design featuring Aboriginal art motifs, and shepherding the production through the Australian Government Publishing Service (AGPS). In the Acknowledgments, I dedicated the book "To the many friends I have made among ethnic and Aboriginal circles in the past ten years. I have enjoyed working with them *to end the slander*."[37]

My analysis was based on the examination of a cross-section of school texts which the Community Relations Office had gathered from around Australia. On the back cover, the book poses the question:

> "Why do so many white Australians have a poor opinion of the Aborigines? Is it largely because of cruel myths and racial slanders that have endured through six generations of Australian life? Is the school – wittingly or unwittingly – to blame?
>
> Does it perpetuate through textbooks and teaching materials the outdated and prejudiced views of earlier generations?
>
> This book analyses the reality of racial prejudice in Australian school-books often associated with distorted history and ethnocentric smugness. Such materials have no part in educating

---

[37] Commissioner for Community Relations, Let's End the Slander: Combating Racial Prejudice in School Textbooks, AGPS, Canberra, 1979, 124pp.

young Australians for living in one of the world's most dynamic multicultural societies".

Many of the textbooks that came to hand taught damaging untruths and slanders:

> 'Mentally the Aborigines stand very low on the scale of humanity.'
>
> 'People who live together in tribes like the early Aborigines are called primitive people.'
>
> 'The Abo's, as they are often called, were and in some areas still are among the most primitive people on earth.'

Such texts are marred by a racial prejudice arising from culpable ignorance, in turn reflecting the uglier realities of hatred and fear dating back to the colonial period of conquest and near-genocide. Only in the past few years had a new perception of Aboriginal origins based on data from prehistory, archaeology and anthropology rendered untenable the tired old stereotype about the inability of *'Stone Age survivors'* to live in the modern world. It was this earlier understanding that had made any thought of a Treaty unrealistic which might have established ongoing rights to land and culture, as in New Zealand in 1840. Rather, the colonial task was simply to develop the land in the name of progress, implying what has since been described as our duty *'to smooth the pillow of a dying race'*. But it is now established fact that all the world's inhabitants (including the Chinese, despite the Maoist doctrine claiming their superior origin in *homo sinensis*) have come from *homo sapiens*.

Of course, in earlier decades of the 20th century the dire prospect of ultimate genocide had appeared to be a sad inevitability, as indeed earlier suffered by the Tasmanian Aborigines. However, in many cases, as at the (Anglican) Roper River Mission in east Arnhem Land, now Ngukurr, history has recorded that it was Church mission initiatives that had actually averted the extermination envisaged by the early 20th century cattle industry[38].

---

[38] Recorded in detail in Murray Seiffert's comprehensive biography 'Gumbuli of Ngukurr: Aboriginal Elder in Arnhem Land', Acorn Press, Melbourne 2012, 414pp, (Christian Book of the Year for 2012).

CHAPTER 26: Fostering a Fairer Australia

In 1979, shortly before my book appeared, I had presented a paper at the 49th annual congress of the Australian and New Zealand Association for the Advancement of Science (ANZAAS), held at the University of Auckland, on *Combating Racial Prejudice in Teaching Materials*. A 36pp précis of the book was also included as a chapter in *Multicultural Education: Issues and Innovations*, part of a new series of pedagogical studies published in W.A. in 1981.

Remarkably, the egregious historic material presented in the book seemed seldom to have been challenged either by indigenous organisations or by educationists. This seems explicable from the voluntary apartheid of the period: the average white schoolchild in the big cities had probably never seen an Aborigine, nor had the average adult ever met one, including me. As a public servant, I was *paid* to shake hands with the first Aborigine I had ever met!

Now at last the contrasting reality is coming to be perceived (at least in the non-commercial media and in the major metropolises) that the country was not 'settled' as much as invaded and the inhabitants dispersed and conquered. A widespread recognition of such realities would seem to be a precursor to the moves now widely afoot (and especially within the Churches) towards reconciliation and restitution, and for this new perception to be recognised in our nation's Constitution.

CHAPTER 27:
"The Most Racist Town in Australia?"

The strident claim by a news-stand for a Sydney tabloid was of course idle: how could such a ranking be determined in 1977 – given the potential competition for such an egregious award? It referred to an article recounting how the sergeant in charge of the Ceduna police (though a local son) had been 'relocated' to Adelaide because of his notoriously harsh and violent treatment of the area's indigenous people. In response, a petition of protest had garnered the signature of virtually every adult resident of the town. However, the State Labor Government of Don Dunstan, committed to reforms in Aboriginal affairs and the abolition of the White Australia Policy, rejected the petition out of hand and sent the sergeant off for retraining. Ceduna was up in arms. Aborigines don't win against the legal system!

Ceduna is the last hurrah of South Australia before the Nullarbor Plain starts in earnest. It is a pleasant enough little place, a tuna and oyster fishing port wedged between a sandy coastline and semi-desert at the far west of the Eyre Peninsula. Hot and dry in summer, cool and damp in winter, it is essentially a marginal sort of place. And not only geographically. It is a white outpost in an Aboriginal land.

Mission Incognito

Al Grassby asked me to visit the town incognito to assess the race relations climate and recommend what the Community Relations Office might do in a positive way to encourage the greater recognition of Aboriginal rights guaranteed under the *Racial Discrimination Act*. He agreed to my request for a colleague to join me in tackling the secret service assignment and sanctioned the involvement of Brian, an American ANU student of social sciences, a humane young man able to bring an outsider's perspective – and a friend of Kevin Rudd, both known to me from the O'Connor Uniting Church.

In September 1977, we flew to Adelaide and drove a Commonwealth car to Ceduna where we booked into a motel. At Grassby's suggestion, our policy was to lie low while getting a feel for the place, perhaps locating potential allies and making what discreet contacts we could with the Aboriginal community. To me (naïvely) this implied contacting clergy first. With my affinity for Germans I headed for the Lutheran manse and explained our mission frankly to the German-named pastor. He looked glum. Recently ordained in later life, it was his first parish and he'd only been there a few months. Of course, as a Sydney man he was shocked at his parishioners' attitudes to the Blacks, but he wasn't going to be run out of his first parish by taking a stand. Naïvely, I was shocked.

The local Aboriginal story

From the Anglican vicar and the Uniting Church minister, both of whom had their fingers on the pulse, there was a more positive reception. They knew many of the town Aborigines and explained that some were Displaced Persons, Pitjantjatjaras moved off their lands 150km to the north for the British atomic weapons trials at Maralinga in the early 1950s. They had been relocated to a Lutheran Mission, Yalata, 200km west of the town, from where many had drifted in to Ceduna. He suggested that we should consider visiting the Mission.

We were given a church document assessing the work of the early Lutheran mission:

> "Let us remember that the first people courageous enough to reach out to the Aboriginal people and to fill the social, psychological and spiritual vacuum created by the loss of their own culture and nomadic way of life, were the Christian missionaries of early pioneering days. Stout-hearted men, full of faith and compassion, they nurtured and succoured where others drove out and killed, protected where others plundered and misused, and in place of the superstition and fear of a non-existent spirit world, taught a religion which, although new to the Aborigines, was understood and accepted by some, as the missionaries themselves gave a living example of the religion they confessed.
>
> It was also customary for the Lutheran missionaries to learn to speak the Aboriginal languages."

Relating to town Aborigines

But first we had work to do in Ceduna, particularly in contacting the town Aborigines. We were well received by a number of well-known figures, and were passed on from one family to another, hearing the same old stories of hatred, scorn and rejection of them by the white community – and for all their race. While I engaged with the speakers, Brian noted down much of what he heard. Some 35 years later it still makes depressing reading.

Only a few Aborigines had jobs, working for the Area Council on the roads. As we were to experience later almost everywhere in rural Australia, none were employed in private businesses, but some worked as aides in schools or kindergartens. In fact, the Area School had a good remedial program for Aboriginal children, with some humane and committed teachers. But Aboriginal health was abysmal, there were no health facilities provided for them, and service in white clinics was often refused e.g. by the ambulance service. The death rate was high and TB was rife, with few older than 60. But the major health problem was alcoholism. So many stories were told of drunkenness and the terrible toll of violence on family and community life.

While we were at Ceduna, a well and unfavourably known Aboriginal drunk was run over and killed by a Council truck on a main street. For the best part of an hour his body lay where he fell, with the seagulls picking at his brains. Later the patch of blood and guts was sanded and swept clean, like a dog run over. It offered a bad image for tourism, a major industry. Not to speak of observers from Canberra.

Aboriginal resentment was mostly directed at the police and the legal system which weighed so heavily upon them. Police were all too prone to violence, with breaches of home privacy leading to frequent arrests and short-term imprisonment for trivial misdemeanours, almost invariably handled punitively by the untrained JPs locally cast as magistrates. Hence a procession of bleary-eyed blacks shuffled through the 'kangaroo court' to the police station, in and out of the cells, again and again in a dismal rhythm. The cells were said to be filthy, with lice in the blankets. In breach of the *Racial Discrimination Act*, publicans and shopkeepers, sporting clubs and children's playgrounds imposed their own bans on Aboriginal use. Discrimination was a way of life, widely resented, but present at every turn. A fully-fledged Australian apartheid.

In particular, the out-of-town blacks were hated and feared. Still in touch with their ancient roots, the cleft between them and a media-driven modernity loomed as unbridgeable. Shortly before our visit, presumably about the time the police sergeant was cashiered, the daily *Adelaide Advertiser* (Murdoch-owned) ran an inflammatory and irresponsible front-page article on 'Black power in Ceduna', utterly dreamed up from the new phenomenon of a growing Aboriginal consciousness spurring the people on to create self-images other than the stereotypical drunk. What a failure of imagination, and how malicious, to lock Aborigines into the alternative image of either drunks or terrorists!

Aboriginal Christians

The message was coming across loud and clear. But we soon discovered another side to the story. Christian Aborigines were among those playing a part in reviving the fortunes of their people, sometimes in collaboration with other agents of goodwill working for a new day, including relative newcomers to the town from ethnic backgrounds. A Latin American livewire, with her friends from many countries, as well as Aborigines and the leaders of the town's schools, had organised a highly successful community festival a few weeks earlier, *'Ceduna 2000'*, striving to build a community 'that cares and shares' in the years remaining to the millennium. It had gained the support of many town businesses, social and sporting clubs, and featured a parade of floats, a multicultural concert and international food tasting. For their trouble, the ethnic organisers were urged in a letter to the *West Coast Sentinel* to "return to their own countries and sort out the problems there, before they buy into another country's affairs". The classical racism blindly directed towards all out-groups.

However, National Aboriginal Week, on the theme *'Open up your heart'*, had brought hope to many. Launched on the former Koonibba Lutheran Mission a little way out of town in a church service led by

Aborigines, it included displays of artefacts at Yalata and a fashion parade, school presentations and dance groups at Ceduna Aboriginal Community Centre, culminating in a service in the town's Lutheran Church with special singing by an Aboriginal choir, which went on to sing in all the town's churches. It seemed to come down to a contest between the old Ceduna and a new Ceduna struggling to be born.

Police attitudes

After several days of discreet observation and discussions, I arranged a call at the Police Station. We were politely if coldly received by the Acting Sergeant, his body language eloquently evincing the traditional scorn for Canberra and its fraternity of bleeding hearts. Ceduna was the centre of the universe and its people good honest burghers. The Blacks only got what they deserved. They were a blight on the town. They wouldn't get off their butts, they got 'sit down money', they couldn't hold their grog. As he unburdened himself, my eye fell upon an old file box on the shelf behind him, marked 'NATIVE MEETINGS'. 'Nuff said.

'Australia's version of apartheid'?

As a comment picked up a few times put it, *"The most practical solution would be to shepherd the Aborigines to an offshore island and bomb them".* I still have the Inward Cablegram (not just a photocopy) sent to Canberra from the Australian High Commission in Cape Town, South Africa, marked for referral to the Prime Minister (Malcolm Fraser), the Foreign Minister, the Department of the Prime Minister & Cabinet, and the Commissioner for Community Relations, reproducing the editorial in *The Citizen* (Johannesburg daily) of 5th January 1978, from which the suggestion above is taken. It continues

> "As we have pointed out before, Australia treats its Aborigines abominably and, having killed off most of them and maltreated the survivors, is hardly in a position to point a finger at [apartheid] South Africa. Confirmation of the sad lot of the Aborigines comes from an Australian Government investigation. The Community Relations Bureau *[sic]* received

a complaint from Australia's only Aboriginal senator that he was refused bar service in a Queensland hotel because he was a 'Darky'. In a report, the Bureau says that relations between the white community and the 110,000 Aborigines in Australia are a cause for grave concern.

In the almost total absence of factual knowledge about Aborigines, their culture and their rights, there is a danger that a de facto apartheid will prevail, under which Aborigines are permanently excluded from the general community.

What do you say about that, Mr Fraser?

After lecturing at Queensland University for four years, one of our own Witwatersrand University professors came to the conclusion that "white Australians are certainly the most racist people I have ever come into contact with. In almost all respects the Aborigines are worse off than the black people in South Africa."

Elsewhere the professor is quoted as alleging that, "Aborigines are the slum dwellers, prostitutes and criminals on the fringes of the urban areas. Alcoholism and drug abuse is staggering. I have known black women who have been raped by police while in gaol. Formal complaints by Aborigines about the treatment meted out to them seldom get anywhere: the police are never at fault."

The report from the Community Relations 'Bureau' cited above was prepared on the race relations situation in South Australia generally by Lorna Lippmann, our Melbourne colleague in the Community Relations Office and academic expert on Aboriginal issues, after visiting areas of the State and compiling her experiences.

On the other hand, the report that I subsequently wrote for Commissioner Grassby on returning from Ceduna was never released, *because deemed to verge on the unbelievable* and hence likely to be counter-productive to our mission.

Too heinous an outrage for public report!

Since the worst situation that I encountered in the district was so distressing, I wrote it up as a separate report from which even Al Grassby shied away in horror. It was based on a long evening's discussion I had at the home of Bob, a PMG worker [Postmaster-General's Department, forerunner of Telstra], who had written up his long awareness of the abuse of Aboriginal women at Smoky Bay, 40 km south-east of Ceduna. But he had never known what to do with it for fear of repercussions on his employment and even his personal safety. He was a humane man, from a metropolitan city, deeply troubled in his conscience, and on hearing of our visit determined to bring it to our notice, come what may.

His handwritten account recorded that, every summer in living memory, an Aboriginal 'tribal' group would move to the coastal fringe of their lands for a traditional time of feasting on the oysters for which the area is justly famous. It was still happening in 1977. Local graziers were still clearing the scrub along the coast for new sheep runs, and every summer would engage Aboriginal workers for the job, paying in sugar, flour and 'baccy – and in grog. On hot nights, after hours of drinking by both parties, now much the worse for wear, the station hands would come down to the dunes where the Blacks camped and brutally have their way with the Aboriginal women. It was the highlight of their year, delicately termed *'gin-jockeying'*. Bob's complaints to the graziers and threats of exposure to the authorities were laughed out of court. Locally it was an open secret. (Did the police also know? And do nothing? And what would the Johannesburg *Citizen* have made of that?)

It amounted to a contemporary flashback to colonial times when the land was being tamed – and cleared *(sic)*. A living part of Australian settlement history still being played out, evoking earlier atrocities akin to the one also reported to us while in Ceduna: of the earliest settlers pushing a whole Aboriginal clan off the top of one of the mighty cliffs along the Great Australian Bight. Now as late as the 1970s, the children born of the ongoing mass rapes of Smoky Bay were still joining the 'stolen generations'? It seemed incredible.

Yet these Aboriginal women had been Australian citizens and electors of the Commonwealth and State parliaments for a decade, since the Constitutional Amendment following the referendum of 1967. Moreover from 1975 Australia had guaranteed to the world that action would be taken to ensure that they enjoyed equal rights with the rest of the population. *The right to be pack-raped without redress?*

So the barriers excluding them from the enjoyment of their civil rights were not legal but attitudinal and (unlike the women!) apparently impregnable. In the absence of legal powers by the Office to pursue such blatant cases of racism, local community attitudes and concomitant actions demeaned a whole race, and ensured their continuing status en bloc as despised outsiders on their own land. After all, the Eyre Peninsula of SA was one of the heartlands of the neo-Fascist Australian League of Rights. In the eyes of the many Cedunas around our country, the crime of the Blacks was to have survived.

Personal misgivings

Over the years of exposure to remote country-town mentality I developed a rough-and-ready rule of thumb that, the more murderous the early settlement of an area had been, the more silent are today's townsfolk about it – but the more deeply rooted are the subconscious animosities and prejudices. Hence while there can be reason for hope of a new day dawning in our metropolises as they become more multicultural, with shrinking proportions of people exposed to the settlement story (and more people of colour about), the rural areas still wait for deeply held subconscious attitudes to fade. Until this day comes, for many perceptive overseas tourists our image as a country must remain deeply flawed.

Visit to Yalata Mission on the Nullarbor Plain

After making arrangements for a visit to Aboriginal lands, Brian and I drove out to Yalata Mission and spent two days there. In the 1950s the Menzies Government had requested the Lutheran Church to open a new mission closer to the coast for the tribal people about to be dispossessed from their lands by the British atomic bomb trials. We learnt that other Pitjantjajaras from an earlier Mission at Ooldea, on the Trans-Continental railway south of Maralinga, where the redoubtable Daisy Bates had lived among the Aborigines for many years till 1935, had also been moved to Yalata.

But since the official end of the assimilation policy in 1975 under Whitlam, the old days of the missions *protecting* (i.e. paternalistically controlling) the Aborigines were gone, replaced by attempts to generate self-governing communities where former church workers became advisors (though invariably still *de facto* managers). Ignorant and ill-equipped as we were, we had no way of judging the situation at Yalata. Although in the past few years I had met many town Blacks in NSW and Queensland, already several generations removed from their tribal roots and languages, Yalata was my first encounter with 'bush Blacks' still leading a traditional life on their own lands, speaking only their own language and practising their spirituality, including occasional corroborees deep in the bush, despite the thin overlay of Christian teaching.

Of course, there were real Christians among them, but we detected no signs of an Aboriginal-led church emerging, as in the remote northern Mission communities like Elcho Island and Ngkurr. Frankly I felt overawed at the face-to-face encounter. The gap in our understanding of each other was an unbridgeable chasm. Particularly was I unnerved by the lengthy silences: while we somehow feel impelled to speak they are quite content simply to sit and 'be'.

Yet Yalata appeared a purposive enough scene, with reasonable facilities: shop, workshops, offices and a school where the children were taught by whites assisted by four indigenous teacher aides. Only the youngest pupils received any teaching in Pitjantjajara language but the high staff turnover meant that no white teachers knew any language, though some longer-serving community workers seemed able to communicate. But we saw scant evidence of any commitment to training in work skills, even such a task as driving the school bus, let alone health or nutrition advisors who spoke the language.

We learnt that there were about 400 people, mainly from four family groups living on the extensive lands comprising the Reserve, located in two camps: the 'big camp' of family *wiltjas* made of branches and other bush materials, some 10 km away, and the group living around the community buildings, many of them employed by the Mission, and rather more sophisticated. A meagre income was derived from an 'artefact industry' making didjeridoos and carved birds, etc. and others received unemployment benefits. Alcohol was on sale at the shop but strictly rationed, and we saw no evident drunkenness. A health sister visited twice a week from Ceduna but there were many chronic problems, including lack of hygiene, since at the 'big camp' there was no washing or laundry facilities and only one tap! Doubtless sound diet was also a problem but they seemed to have little English and we had no way of accessing information.

Interpreting the Racial Discrimination Act

Of course, no one (black or white) had heard of the *Racial Discrimination Act* but I felt obligated to explain its implications. A daunting challenge! The advisors convened a meeting with the community leadership at which I tried to communicate some simple concepts (Christian concepts, actually) about the government now saying that all people had equal rights and deserved to be treated with equal esteem. I did not dare address what happened if they weren't. My feeble words were translated by the advisors into the Pitjantjatjara language – at least there was only one Aboriginal language in use at Yalata, unlike on all the settlements in Queensland or the NT where in the early days people from several language groups were taken for *'protection' against genocide by the settlers*, with a debased form of English as the only common language, in later times developing into an acknowledged Kriol.

Going bush

More meaningful was our request to encounter some bush lore. A couple of young fellers took us a way into the semi-desert foraging for food, and showed us how to grab big stumpy-tailed lizards, which they taught us were *yalda* – origin of the Mission's name? Staying overnight in the visitors' guest house, on that evening we had long discussions with the church workers about how the new Government policies might affect everyday life at Yalata. The manager came across to us as a fine man, respected by the residents who had dealings with him, but we suspected that under the new policies, so far not much had actually changed: the atmosphere was certainly paternalistic, despite official policies of attaining self-management through an elected Community Council. Perhaps it was still early days, and introducing more humanitarian Australia-wide policies represented a grandiose project hard enough to imagine, let alone implement locally.

Can the Racial Discrimination Act avail?

So what future did the Community Relations Office envisage as desirable and attainable? Certainly, a future – unlike the unspoken conviction of the full-blooded racist that, since Aborigines were manifestly and inevitably a dying race destined to be bred into oblivion by white genetic dominance, they deserved no special consideration. The original frontier view was even starker: the country had to be cleared of them in order to become productive for the settlers, as a higher (and greedier!) order of humanity. Of course, for many rural people at the time, such ideas were inchoate rather than openly expressed or argued, but deeply rooted and emotionally held.

The guiding principles for a better future would have to include the values inherent in the *Racial Discrimination Act* (derived from the International Covenant against All Forms of Racial Discrimination – and actually consistent with Christian understandings): equality of respect and equality of human rights, backed by special compensatory measures for minority groups, specifically deemed not to infringe the Act. In Australia, these would clearly cover special programs in health, education & training, backed by access to language learning, housing, and especially the development of employment opportunities. All of these areas continue to be intractable since the Whitlam Government took over responsibility for Aboriginal affairs from the States in 1973 – despite vast amounts of funding made available by subsequent federal governments.

The over-arching philosophy would have to be to maximise individual freedom to opt in or opt out, rather than coercion. But this implies real involvement of Aboriginal people themselves in the process of creating the programs, i.e. real consultations before the decisions in principle are taken. I doubt that this has ever been done honestly by any government. It betrays the underlying attitudes of a patronising paternalism, which really knows all the answers beforehand but goes through the motions of consulting, usually with too little time or too little range of opinions tapped. Even the Rudd/Gillard Labor Governments showed little evidence of real consultation. The NT Intervention, blatantly launched by the Howard Government for political advantage, and then continued with minor changes by the Labor Governments, is a case in point. The fact that, to make it possible, the *Racial Discrimination Act* has had to be suspended in part (contrary to the International Convention!), says it all.

But back in 1977, on the morning we drove away from Yalata, we felt quite over-awed at the magnitude of the task they were committed to in that desolate place. For the several Christian workers, Christ's command had been truly heeded: with the massive cliffs of the Great Australian Bight not so far away, they had literally gone 'to the ends of the earth'.[39]

Epilogue

By a delightful irony, 20 years later, our son David with his sensitivity to Aboriginal people and their ways, would report a memorable response at the Yalata community school to his travelling roadshow *Talking Drums*, with its rhythms and comedy routines. But the head teacher's dismissive comments on his Aboriginal pupils still rankle. So the sad old white ambivalence lingers on, with the young generation as ever the slender hope of a more humane future.

But further, all of 37 years later the Anglican minister encountered in Ceduna would turn up as an invited speaker at a Melbourne parish where I was working. He recognised me as his erstwhile visitor!

---

[39] In the words of the Risen Christ's 'Great Commission' in Acts 1:28

I was pleased to hear that, after the time of our visit, the Ceduna scene had improved, with Aboriginal leadership initiatives and the formation of a town committee on community relations in which he had been involved. The epithet 'most racist town' was no longer valid!

"O God of every nation, of every race and land,
redeem your whole creation with your almighty hand;
where hate and fear divide us, and bitter threats are hurled
in love and mercy guide us, and heal our strife-torn world."[40]

---

[40]Verse of a hymn by William Watkins Reid, Jr., from 'Together in Song: Australian Hymn Book', no. 621

CHAPTER 28: Monitoring Rural Racism

In the early years of the Community Relations Office an extensive field trip had been undertaken through the west of NSW and almost the length of Queensland to Cairns and beyond by the two Assistant Commissioners along with Joe, an indigenous officer of the Department of Aboriginal Affairs as our mentor. It was to prove a powerful learning experience. Through Joe, George and I began to glimpse the reality of what it means to live as an Aborigine in rural and remote areas where racial discrimination is pervasive. In the words of an Aboriginal woman subsequently used as the title of an Office publication on racial prejudice, *"You live and breathe it from the day you're born"*.

Challenge of rural attitudes

Taking turns at driving the Commonwealth car, we headed from Canberra through the central west of NSW to Dubbo where we made contact with the Aboriginal Legal Service. Then on to Narrabri and Moree, in those days infamous for their *de facto* apartheid identified by Charles Perkins' 'Freedom Riders' of 1965. It was there that the immortal remark was addressed to me by the owner of a pastrycook's: "You can't expect us to employ Abo's. Nobody would buy anything touched by a black hand".

Nothing daunted, we visited the mineral spring baths, cinema, hotels, and clubs with the message that their treatment of the Aborigines was now in breach of the law of the land.

It wasn't taken very seriously. In the absence of proper funding for the Office there was no possibility of publicising the behavioural changes called for – and required under the Act: no radio announcements, no TV commercials, no local newspaper ads, no posters. And of course, no Federal Government support. So how could rural people know about such a profound legal challenge to their long-established attitudes and lifestyle? Really you couldn't blame them.

But it didn't say much for Australians' broadmindedness or hospitality towards 'the strangers within our gates', including the near-total unconcern of the local Churches. Indeed, more often than not the topic would raise the ire of the local gatekeepers: *"How dare Canberra tell us how to behave in our own town! What would they know about our lives here?"* What was undoubtedly true was the yawning gap identified between the country-town mentality and the outlook of middle-class, educated city-dwellers. Both parties more or less unchallenged locally – and to all intents and purposes indifferent to the other's existence.

> *If you're white, you're all right.*
> *If you're black, stand back.*
> *–Aboriginal informant*

"I love her far horizons…"

Beyond the Queensland border, and bypassing Brisbane, the distances began to appal me. I had never realised that from Brisbane to Cairns is as far as from Melbourne to Brisbane!

We ticked off the landmarks: Gympie, Maryborough, Gladstone, Rockhampton, shattering my illusion that the Queensland coast was an unbroken tropical paradise – actually mostly drab and in sections even bordering on semi-arid – until Mackay where paradise finally set in. Across the mighty Burdekin River (varying from the volume of the Yangtse to a fickle trickle) and on to Townsville (paradise lost again, thanks to the successive strips of the Wet and Dry Tropics found along the Queensland coast). Joe and I headed for an Aboriginal family where we stayed.

'Black armband' view of settlement history

At James Cook University, I had a long discussion with Henry Reynolds, academic historian whose research was tackling the traditional understanding of our history of ignoring the stark truth, conveniently expunged from our national consciousness, that *"Australia wasn't settled, she was raped"*. We struck up a cordial entente that would lead to ongoing contact with our Office. During the political 'Culture Wars' of the 1990s (*'Black Armband'* vs *'White Blindfold'* postures) his work would be dismissed by Prime Minister Howard. But significantly, twenty years later, the Anglican Archbishop of Melbourne would publicly contend at the 2015 Diocesan Synod that "There is an ongoing issue over the failure of our nation to remember the 30,000 Aboriginal people who died defending their land in the frontier wars that accompanied European settlement of Australia. I look forward to the day when we can make a proper recognition of their heroism and love for this land by a suitable commemoration ... leading the way with a memorial in this very Cathedral." This could prove an apt counter-balance to our growing national obsession with keeping alive the overseas wars in which our Diggers fought.

From Townsville to Cairns was pure delight: the tourist industry's Queensland. The wet tropics. Sugar cane, pineapples, bananas, heat, humidity, pesky insects. It's got it all. A few years later, as one of the Stolen Generations, Joe was to discover that he had a twin sister living in Darwin! They had been separated 50 years before and raised in government institutions in different States. A sorry tale: two of the Stolen Children.

Racial discrimination in the Outback?

The Commissioner displayed little interest in the casework as long as it got done. To be sure, this factor provided something of a shield for the unit, justifying its existence while not threatening any established interests. But the Commissioner's agenda, which I amply shared, was to bring about change, drawing on progressive visions of human rights and social reform, empowering minorities, and challenging the locus of power. In the political climate of the time this implied something of a subversive orientation vis-à-vis the Establishment *("our side was losing").*

I have a copy of an internal memorandum I addressed to the Commissioner in February 1977, to draw attention to the need for the Office to *publicly identify issues of structural discrimination* that locked minorities (particularly Aborigines) into second-class status.

Aboriginal communities in the remote Outback posed a particular challenge: they had not – and doubtless never would – produce cases of alleged discrimination of the type handled by the Office in respect to town dwellers. I suggested the Commissioner might use the media to target and expose unacceptable aspects of the life experience of more remote Aborigines.

It could make the *Racial Discrimination Act* a more potent champion of change, while also generating wider support from people of goodwill across the land. I cited the Queensland Premier Bjelke-Petersen's recent veto of a commercial land sale to Cape York Aborigines, as a blatant infringement of the *Racial Discrimination Act*.

In the event, the Commissioner (maybe rightly) decided against such radical frontal action, although a few years later the Aurukun people would succeed in having the High Court of Australia overrule the Queensland Premier's veto, opening the way for the Act to be subsequently invoked in the Mabo case, revolutionising Australian legal history and leading on to Aboriginal land rights legislation – closing 200 years of ignominy. In the end, the Act would prove to be far more than the paper tiger so often dismissed by the wiseheads. Arguably the most powerful Act in our national history!

CHAPTER 29: A Tale of Two Towns

Beyond the national congress *Australia in the Multicultural 80's* and in order to pursue the rural focus in greater depth, in 1980 the Commissioner proposed that, along with the newly appointed Librarian/Resource Officer, Sylvia, I should conduct a whole-town field research project in Kempsey, NSW and Rockhampton, Qld.

A little earlier George had somehow wangled permission from the Public Service Board to engage a librarian to consolidate and extend our burgeoning collection of strategic documentation (often donated by enthusiasts in the community) as well as the field reports, papers and speeches we were producing apace, and Sylvia immediately proved a great asset with her enthusiasm and well-ordered approach.

Taking the pulse in Kempsey

At the time, we found Kempsey a rather unprepossessing town in a hard-pressed dairying area. We hired two cars, Sylvia insisting on a Mini-Moke. The plan was to carry out a more transparent version of the Ceduna campaign, starting again with the sizeable Aboriginal community. But this time we actively sought to make our mission known. We visited the ABC regional radio station, contacted school leadership, local police, clergy of all the churches, and found particularly congenial companions among the Sisters of Mother Teresa's order, the Missionaries of Charity, based in a dilapidated house, doing grassroots community development work among the town's Aborigines. We visited Aboriginal homes, attended the church funeral of an indigenous elder, I was guest speaker at a Lions Club dinner, we spoke to an after-school teachers' meeting, and sought to encourage schools to address the issue of 'attitudinal discrimination' which all too often robbed Black students from attaining their full potential.

In a town producing more than its share of discrimination cases, we were aiming to raise the profile of the *Racial Discrimination Act*. By appealing to decision-makers we hoped to move from band-aiding to addressing underlying causes. But we found little for our comfort.

History still casts a long shadow over the town and the Macleay Valley. At an after-church meeting, over supper, an elderly white Australian confided to me that his grandfather used to speak of the days when hunting parties would gather *after church some Sundays* "and they weren't hunting kangaroos!" (nudge, nudge, wink, wink). He added that his grandfather used to mention the Aboriginal heads sometimes stuck on fence posts along the river valley back in the 1840s in the days when the country was being taken up for dairying.

The facts of massacre still cry out: "The wind-stench of burning bodies hangs heavy upon the nation's conscience and in the clouds."[41] Peter Gebhardt goes on to quote from an editorial in the *Melbourne Argus* as early as 1856,

> "The white man takes possession of the land as a matter of course. He alters water- courses, drives off game, fences, clears and cultivates, tears open the very bowels of the earth and walks away with uncounted wealth, while the original occupant of the soil not only looks helplessly on but sinks, contaminated by the new vices and wasted by imported diseases, into premature extermination.
>
> And we – a Christian people, God-fearing, magnanimous, intelligent – stand quietly by and do not feel the disgrace and sin of such a position."

More than 150 years later, the Greens MP for the federal seat of Melbourne, Dr Adam Bandt, referring to the day when the Australian Parliament took a first step towards recognising Indigenous Australians in the Constitution by passing the Aboriginal and Torres Strait Islander People's Recognition Bill 2012, would observe in the House of Representatives (13th February 2013):

> "Australia remains the only Commonwealth Country without a treaty with its Indigenous inhabitants. We have never properly acknowledged that Indigenous Australians never ceded sovereignty. We have never properly acknowledged that what we call 'settlement' was accompanied by violence, at times and in places extremely brutal. Until we acknowledge this, and until we acknowledge it in the form of a treaty, these wounds at the heart of our country are going to continue to fester."

---

[41] Peter Gebhardt, Victorian County Court judge, writing in the 'Melbourne Age', for Australia Day 2013

My personal troublesome memory, from the last of several campaign visits we made to the town over a few months, is of the final remark made to me on air at the end of a half-hour talkback show that I led on local ABC Radio on our last morning in town. The final caller identified herself as a recently arrived Victorian retiree, saying that she had listened with growing alarm at the remarks being passed by almost all the previous callers, and just wanted to mention that she had now decided she couldn't continue to live in a town with such racist fellow-citizens. She was moving back to Melbourne.

Taking the pulse in Rockhampton

Several times we punctuated our Kempsey campaign with visits to the beef capital of Queensland, the major city located on the lower Fitzroy River, on the cusp of the tropics, and the hub of the vast Central Queensland region. From first arrival, I noted the hungry-looking natural environment, featuring tall rank grass drying out in the hot sun – though of course great for cattle. Indeed, in proud testimony to the major industry, there stands at the city's northern gateway the Big Bullock in bronze. We found Rockhampton a 'civilised' place, boasting botanical gardens, riverside walks, an art gallery and the Capricornia Institute of Advanced Education (now Central Queensland University which features a number of outlying campuses, including one in the heart of Melbourne!). It is also the centre for both an Anglican and a Catholic Diocese, each with its mini-Gothic cathedral.

Anglican Chaplain for Aborigines

This collaboration was to become crucial to the trajectory of our project. From the outset, we were taken in as house guests by Canon John Warby, a popular identity long active as Anglican Chaplain (*read* friend) to the widely scattered Aboriginal community of the Capricornia region. On his sideboard, he kept a diver's helmet, a huge brass and glass contraption, in witness to God's calling him from 'out of the depths' as a young pearl diver on Thursday Island. Appointed pastoral assistant on the Lockhart River Mission on Cape York Peninsula, as a young man he worked both in 'hands on' and spiritual roles, enjoying wide respect and affection in the Aboriginal community. After later study in Brisbane he was ordained priest in the Rockhampton Diocese.

An important focus of his work was the Woorabinda Aboriginal Reserve 200km inland from Rocky. At the time of our visits, the apparently indestructible Bjelke-Petersen Government, resisting the transfer of Aboriginal Affairs responsibilities to the Federal Government, still maintained the outdated practice of 'protecting' (i.e. controlling) Aborigines in prison-like conditions on State-run 'Reserves' where their forebears had been gathered from many language groups[42] and confined since colonial days, with missionary collaboration, and minimal contact with the settler society. The three major Reserves were Cherbourg in the south of the State, Woorabinda in the central Queensland region, and Palm Island in the north (also used as an Aboriginal prison island for the whole State). It represented a form of apartheid antedating the South African policy.

Tensions with 'go-it-alone' Queensland

In this climate, our project was not without its tensions, evident in our relations with State officials. They had been instructed from Brisbane only to engage with Commonwealth officials when a representative of the State Aboriginal Affairs Department was present. But John Warby's name opened every door, so universally was he esteemed for his bluff humour and genuine Christian street cred. He allowed me to accompany him (incognito) through a long day's drive on one of his regular visits to Woorabinda. The drive was a delight: he was a marvellous raconteur.

Though the atmosphere at the Reserve township seemed sullen, he told me it had improved over the last few years, reflecting policy concessions made by the State Government, though still upholding their determination to go it alone in Aboriginal affairs in defiance of the Commonwealth's assuming responsibility nationwide in 1967. Before the Queensland Supreme Court, the State Government had claimed that

---

[42]For instance, the anthropologist Norman Tindale recorded in 1938 people from 44 language groups being brought to Palm Island from all over Queensland. Hence their only means of intercommunication was by rudimentary English, facilitating their oppression.

the *Racial Discrimination Act* was invalid because unconstitutional. It had also condemned the Community Relations Office, in company with other august bodies like the World Council of Churches, Amnesty International, Queensland church leaders and Aboriginal leaders for meddling (sic) in their affairs. Correspondence by our Office with the State Government was routinely ignored, and directions to attend compulsory conferences as part of complaint settlement procedures were not complied with. Hence, we risked being caught up in an ugly inter-governmental conflict, dogged by the risk of being hung out to dry by our own Commonwealth Coalition Government (philosophically inclined towards alignment with Queensland) for stirring up communal tensions. Community *Relations?*

The Commonwealth race legislation triumphs

On the other hand, we had the law on our side, since the State was manifestly part of the Commonwealth. In fact, a Queensland Court challenge to the constitutionality of the *Racial Discrimination Act* would subsequently be thrown out and the Act upheld. When the Bjelke-Petersen National Party government would likewise be thrown out in the 1987 election in the wake of major corruption scandals, the reforming Labor government would make wholesale changes to the legal situation of Queensland's Aboriginal population, including passage of anti-discrimination legislation. Woorabinda Reserve would be vested in a local Council. But the challenge of building respect, let alone goodwill, towards the indigenous people of the State would remain daunting. History continued to cast a long shadow.

But back in 1980-81 Queensland was an impregnable Country Party fiefdom (with a change of name to National Party after 1982) based on a glaring gerrymander favouring rural electorates, whose votes were vastly inflated in value (hence the familiar sneer *'One sheep, one vote'*). In the absence of an Upper House (a situation unique in Australia) the Premier was literally a law unto himself, and his notorious paternalistic attitudes kept the State's Aborigines in virtual serfdom, endorsed by the great bulk of the white population, perennially convinced that their interests were under siege by the Blacks. My earlier theory from Ceduna upheld?

Again and again, we were told, at many levels of local society, how much public money was squandered in handouts and other special favours from Canberra. Addressing a Lions Club meeting I experienced a bruising encounter. Of course, Canberra-bashing was the local blood sport. Fortunately, to balance the equation, Sylvia and I would often be regaled by Fr John with his wry anecdotes reflecting the parochial mentality of his fellow-Queenslanders, the more extreme of whom – forever suspecting some new conspiracy against their interests being hatched in 'the South' – barely seemed to identify as Australians at all.

Support from local allies

In the 1980s our Office had set up in Queensland, as elsewhere, Consultative Committees on Community Relations made up of community volunteers concerned for the wellbeing of the entire local society, the lessening of inter-racial tensions, and assisting in the conciliation of complaints under the Act. They had no legal powers but mostly acted in collaboration with staff of the Office, spearheaded by George. Throughout the country there was seldom any lack of humane (and often Christian) souls imbued with such convictions. One such Committee was established in Rockhampton.

Strategic challenge of re-educating clergy

Apart from his passion for his Aboriginal flock, Fr John sensed a special calling (enthusiastically promoted by his Bishop) to re-educate his clergy colleagues across the Diocese about the grassroots implications of God's love for his whole creation, and his 'preferential option for the downtrodden'. He was widely known around the Diocese for conducting study days on Aboriginal issues. Hearing of my background as a community relations educator and as a Christian, he enlisted me forthwith as an apprentice. He was the very model of a modern Anglican priest, and an inspiration. From him I was to learn much to stand me in good stead for my subsequent calling.

Under his guidance, Sylvia and I planned our programs, making contact with the regional education authorities, administrators and school inspectors – who needed no convincing – and subsequently visiting several schools for useful staff discussions focusing on countering discriminatory attitudes towards Aboriginal pupils. As at Kempsey Sylvia drew attention to current educational materials available in the race relations field. My visit to the Anglican Bishop, George Hearn, also opened several doors. I was also interviewed on Central Queensland ABC radio, and spent some productive time exploring the potential of the Capricornia Institute of Advanced Education for promoting inter-racial programs.

Documentary support for clergy on the road

This led to plans being made for me to be based at the Institute in future visits to Rockhampton, while preparing supplementary educative materials for John Warby's use in his clergy education initiative. His project was based on utilising the most modern communication technology then available, the new-fangled audiotape with tape player, for clergy of all denominations to listen to while driving their cars around the far-flung reaches of their rural parishes, to be followed up by a residential program in the diocesan conference centre on the Capricorn coast near Yepoon. He had named the project '*RECOCAP – Regional Ecumenical Course with Clergy & Aboriginal People*'. The genius of the program was the interaction between the two races during its preparation, sharing the task as equals. Aborigines as *equals?* In the Queensland of 1981 ... revolutionary! By then he had recorded the taped material, featuring story-telling and interviews with Aborigines, local inter-racial news items, and lecture materials from academics. But he needed documentation in print to systematise, support and flesh out the content of the audiotapes. This was what he asked me to prepare.

Writing the three RECOCAP units

Returning from Canberra to John Warby's home alone, but setting up a working base in the Capricornia Institute of Advanced Education, over about three concentrated weeks of work in 1981 I wrote 172 pages of educational material for the RECOCAP Project, organised in three sequential 'Units', enlivened by Aboriginal artwork, to back the aural messages on the tapes. The frequent cross-references to the tapes are designed to unite the written and spoken word. At the end of each section are exercises for the clergy hearers and readers to complete, targeting both cognitive and affective reactions.

UNIT 1 – The historical perspective on Central Queensland. This provides an oversight of the culture, spirituality, ritual life, social organisation, diet, arts and crafts of the Darambal people of Capricornia, followed by a survey of the frontier warfare of the 1860s, including the raids on isolated cattle stations and the resultant mass slaughter of entire communities, including by the Native Police.

After surviving countless æons of time, little more than fifty years from the founding of Rockhampton the Darambal Aborigines had almost disappeared from the face of the earth.

In the end about a dozen survivors were rounded up and railed out to distant Reserves in cattle wagons – presaging Hitler's Final Solution? None were ever impounded in their own territory. With the loss of their homeland they lost their spirit and virtually the will to live.

Unit 1 closes with an appeal to today's clergy to make up their minds on these issues, aware that we will surely have a fight on our hands with someone in the parish. We should recall that many of the earliest Europeans in Australia were disturbed and insecure people. And there are still unresolved issues in our Australian consciousness: as Christian clergy, how shall we approach these issues?

Many believe the time is overdue to create a moral basis for such re-evaluation, for invoking our theological and ethical framework, for putting to rights the unfinished business of the past through acts of peace-making, reconciliation and mutual forgiveness. The Crucified One comes to us today to make peace, to end the war within by helping us become more human, to come to terms with the destructiveness in our history, and to release us into creativity.

UNIT 2 – Re-thinking our dismissive attitudes

This raises the nagging question: why have relations between Aborigines and white Australians been so bad for 200 years? There is a need to consider the Aboriginal world view, how they still relate to each other – and to us and our institutions, including our Churches.

What is culture? Not so much the fine arts as the ideas and values that hold everything together, defined as 'what remains when we have *forgotten* everything we ever *learnt'*. The problem is we view our own culture as the norm and all others as alien or inferior. So the indigenes present a mass of deficits: no clothes, no houses, no agriculture, no livestock, no boundaries, no leaders, no law, no religion: *no brains?*

'Utterly different but not inferior' has been too hard a call.

Certainly, the leaders of the First Fleet confronted the most exacting cultural dilemma ever encountered by Europeans settling the New World. The conclusion they reached was elegant in its simplicity but devastating to both parties: the land was conceived as *terra nullius* ('the land of no one'). The occupants did not count as human! Was ever any other nation predicated on such a grand lie? By the 1870s the Aboriginal people appeared to be doomed.

Some philanthropists spoke of *'smoothing the pillow of a dying race'*.

But why were Aboriginal Missions less successful than the Pacific Island missions?

Arguably because the dispersal of the clans from their lands and way of life led to alienated fringe dwelling, but also because the profusion of languages and their complexity deterred missionaries from presenting the Gospel in comprehensible tongues – a terrible dereliction.

The readings then cover ongoing issues like the spiritual significance of land, and the legal definition of who is an Aborigine (often bitterly disputed in outback towns).

The Unit closes with many practical suggestions on making contacts and being of service.

UNIT 3 – Current issues in Aboriginal affairs

This begins with a protracted analogy of the invasion of Australia by purple people from outer space who, over the course of the years and applying uncannily similar treatment to the earlier European settlers, have reduced the white Australian population to a demoralised, disinherited, alcoholic, broken remnant!

The range of Central Queensland Aboriginal situations is outlined: Woorabinda, river-bank camps, stockmen, workers with Aboriginal organisations, those living in the community in Housing Commission houses, and the 'drop-outs'. In all, some 5,000 people.

There follows an attempt to address the objections commonly made in rural Australia that our claims are exaggerated, the statistics skewed, the motivation merely political, or that nothing will change – so 'too bad'! And anyway, since Aborigines don't attend Anglican churches, it's not a concern for their clergy.

The policies on Aboriginal Affairs of the Federal and State Departments are laid out dispassionately. The statistics of Aboriginal disadvantage – soberly presented – are quite stunning. There are still tremendous challenges to be faced. Of particular concern are tensions between the federal and state Departments over basic policy orientation: *guided development* vs *self-determination*. The Aboriginal leadership is united in opposition to the Queensland policies.

The RECOCAP series closes with an appeal to clergy to become familiar with their local scene and its needs by offering supportive contact with local Aboriginal people, and discusses new ways in which the churches could become more understanding and hence more helpful to Aborigines. All the Units are moderate in tone, positive, and theologically oriented towards building common ground in the great cause of Christian justice and liberation.

After the RECOCAP print material had been circulating for some time among the clergy of the Diocese (and other Churches too, I suspect), Canon Warby convened a study conference. I remember enjoying the fellowship of the clergy (at that time all men) for a couple of days, for me a new experience of mixing with ministry professionals. I was struck both by their earnestness and their *bonhomie*. It may even have planted a seed in my mind about a possible alternative future to the one I was still committed to in Canberra ... though how long was that going to last?

Deadly conflict on the moving frontier

> *Pity him, stranger, thus cut off in his early youth whilst in the discharge of his duty and in obedience to that earliest of God's commandments, "Go forth and subdue the earth".*

On a tombstone in Rockhampton Cemetery for a young settler speared by the Blacks in 1868 but omitting to mention, as history records, that the settler had 'put a bullet' into his antagonist.

Racial conflict was a fundamental dimension in the economic struggle of settlers to 'subdue the earth', whether directed against Aborigines, South Sea Islanders (Kanakas), or Chinese on the Palmer River goldfields. The colonial history of Queensland is perhaps the bloodiest of any State, because the indigenous people were not so passive – and too numerous to meet the fate of the Tasmanians. A district newspaper had reported in the 1850s that *"While ever we jointly occupy the country, we remain in a state of actual warfare"*. To be sure, Central Queensland's pioneer warfare included infamous murders by tribesmen of settlers at Mt Larcom Station in 1855, at Hornet Bank in 1857, and at Cullin-la-ringo in 1861. The 35 settler deaths were avenged by unknown hundreds of Blacks being killed. From contemporary newspaper reports, while Aborigines had 'massacred' the settlers, the Europeans merely 'dispersed the natives'. In 1855, W.H.Wiseman, Crown Lands Commissioner, actually a humane man, had recorded that "Destiny proclaims the certainty of the future triumph of the white race and the final extirpation of the Aborigines". Living together in mutual respect seemed inconceivable!

A cynical Queensland expedient

A peculiarly Queensland expedient had been the raising of a Native Police Force to control the frontier, with Aborigines brought in from remote parts unable to speak local languages. They soon became feared for running riot with their firearms, ruthlessly shooting other Aborigines, at times entire communities of men, women and children, and occasionally turning on their white benefactors.

Such 'racial memories' seem indelibly marked on the psyche of many Queenslanders even today, possibly because of the lack of much human contact between the races over the years (thanks to the policy of detention on the Reserves) and the long maintenance of punitive powers against the Aborigines, seen even in the 21st century in the treatment of Palm Island 'natives' e.g. *the 'Tall Man' saga*. (Was it actually a crime to be black in Queensland?) To this day, the Aboriginal deaths in custody statistics continue to echo the dismal story.

'Constrained by the love of Christ'

But there is also another story told in the regions. Despite the popular myth that missionaries weakened Aboriginal culture, thus contributing to their exploitation, many of the missions were founded by faithful white Christians who had left home, privilege, wealth and status to become one with the indigenous people. Words matching message, they shared in the life of the people, imparting their insights and skills while respecting personhood, culture and often languages laboriously learnt over decades. Some were even incorporated into kinship systems, humbled to be called family. In some cases, in the far north, in the first decades of the 20th century, the missions had proved the last bulwark against the threatening genocide at the hands of overseas-owned cattle empires such as Vesteys.

At least on the NE Arnhem Land coast where the spiritual awakening of the 1970s had its birth among Aboriginal communities, we must conceive that God's Spirit was at work, with scriptural revelations in mother tongues penetrating the existing spirituality of a people very much in touch with the mystical world. Fresh images of God continue to be birthed, including among strong women owning a God who is neither male nor white, a God who has been present among them from the Dreamtine though obscured by exogenous cultural perceptions inimical to their own. The New Testament makes clear that God treats everyone on the same basis: "Whoever worships him and does what is right is acceptable to him, no matter what race they belong to."[43] As Aboriginal people come to see themselves as beloved by God and valued for who they are – a unique part of creation – they can be empowered to stand tall and begin to deal with the appalling personal and communal situations confronting them today – triggering the Howard Government's military intervention in 2007, lamentably maintained in amended form by the Rudd Labor Government.

Far to go – yet signs of hope

Back in Canberra after several visits to both towns, mentally and physically drained, with Commissioner Grassby we evaluated the two-town project and I wrote a detailed report for publication. It was clear that Aborigines in the Kempsey and Rockhampton areas had little expectation that anything could change in their relations with the white community, reflecting the internalisation of their assigned status, nurtured over generations. However, we identified a significant nucleus, especially in Rockhampton, of potential change agents, in strategic professional roles, eager for change and social progress. Conversely, many others in the white society found it difficult to take our case seriously: were we perhaps being merely mischievous in suggesting that the universally accepted social norms needed to change?

Wouldn't it be a revolutionary act to get a white man of power and affluence – say, a popular publican, or the president of the Lions Club, or a town Councillor – to say a simple *"I'm sorry"* to a Black man he'd treated unfairly, dismissively, or stripped of his dignity and human rights? How to convince people that long-established social norms were now legally unacceptable – and that there were reserve powers waiting in the wings to be invoked?

---

[43] Acts 10:34-35

But this wasn't the deep south of the USA, nor was there a Civil Rights Movement afoot. There was no sign of an Aboriginal Martin Luther King nor even of a Rosa Parks in the offing (though neither were there vicious activist groups like the Ku Klux Klan prepared to go beyond the pale). Sadly, there didn't need to be in Australia: *the Aborigines had long since got the message.*

The sorry reality was that in our country the legal forces seeking an end to racial discrimination amounted to a bunch of naïve white amateurs dismissed as 'do-gooders' – as though 'do-badders' would be preferable – citing legislation that had little public purchase, largely ignored by the governing Parties and the media, flotsam left on the beach by the receding tide, the legacy of a Party now re-consigned to the wilderness where maybe it did belong – for another 23 years? Was the answer only ever more community education? But how long might that take to have any effect – one generation, two ...?

A future for the Community Relations Office?

And then there was the new cloud looming on the horizon: how long could we in the Community Relations Office assume that we would survive, on the expiry of Commissioner Grassby's seven-year contract at the end of 1982? He had been tolerated, even humoured, because to strike him and his Office down could be seen as petty, vindictive, childish. But once the bough that he clung to was withered ...? How strong was the civil society: the human rights activists, lawyers, teachers, academics, church leaders? Could they simply be bypassed, marginalised while the real business of government proceeded untroubled? There's no money in social upheaval! At the personal level, my future looked bleak.

On the other hand, around the world there was evidence of the stirring of a human conscience, of a strong and rising tide for human rights. There were increasing migration streams, more insistent calls for recognition of minorities, and irksome Christians from the Pope down demanding that the human factor should not be made subservient to the interests of big business.

Among the local outcomes of these movements was the creation by

State Labor Governments of Ethnic Affairs Commissions and/or anti-discrimination bodies in SA, NSW and Victoria, and the emergence of a State and national network of Ethnic Communities Councils, voicing migrants' aspirations for cultural recognition. And ironically, whereas in the late 1970s Malcolm Fraser was seen by the Left as the very incarnation of the Devil, over the next 20 years he was to be progressively rehabilitated and rise in public esteem (outside his own Liberal Party) for his principled stand on behalf of Aborigines and asylum seekers and Other Good Causes.

A new day dawning?

I suppose the main outcome of the published report on the *Tale of Two Towns* was producing a snapshot of the anti-Aboriginal prejudice and discrimination barring the way to equality, and marring the face of our nation in the early 80s. Yet a generation later human rights and anti-discrimination philosophies would be ineradicably rooted among better-educated Australians in the urban centres, especially younger people, espoused by the arts community, the mainline Churches, and in the media.

But, of course, the indigenous people themselves have contributed vastly to their new standing, with many of them now well-educated and playing strategic roles as doctors, lawyers, teachers, academics, nurses, artists, dramatists, sportsmen, community workers – and Christian pastors – in shaping a new Australia, though the old is far from gone.

And what of the remoter rural towns, the Australia of the bush? We had little data. Arguably the more remote the town and the more frequent the daily contact with the local indigenous people, the less race relations have improved. But I doubt that legal sanctions have played much of a part. As Grassby was wont to say, attitudes can only be changed by exposure to better ideas, through informal contacts and education programs. And these must now as ever be the driver of change.

CHAPTER 30: Ebb Tide

Change was in the air. The last sands in the hourglass were trickling away as the Fraser Government debated the merits of retaining the Community Relations Office beyond the statutory seven-year term of Commissioner Grassby, due to end in October 1982.

A puny champion?

While the previous years had amassed evidence a-plenty that the *Racial Discrimination Act* could prove a champion – albeit often seen as a puny one – for combating racial discrimination against *non-Anglo*-Australians, its achievements were principally in the realm of demonstrating the reality of racism, objectively measured by the incessant flow of cases alleging real harm inflicted. This made it clear that if Australia were to develop as a robust multicultural society, the bounds would need to be drawn around anti-social denigration and harm.

But, of course, the case-by-case approach could go on for ever without definitively reshaping public opinion towards opposing racism. A broad re-sensitising of the community through school curricula, educational practice, media emphases and professional development would require a solid moral commitment matched by public funding, but this had always been lacking. In the straitened economic climate of the early 1980s, it looked more unlikely than ever. Yet the embarrassment for the Government was that it seemed unthinkable to abolish the Office in a period of growing ethnic activism, partly resulting from the Fraser Government's own highly financed program of multicultural development stimulated by the Galbally *'Review of Migrant Programs & Services'*.

A new legal framework

Fortunately for the Government, a new framework was emerging, drawing on a much older and broader UN sanction than racial discrimination: the *Universal Declaration of Human Rights*. This had been adopted in the first Assembly of the United Nations Organisation in 1948, under the presidency of Australia's Dr H. V. Evatt. Many countries had subsequently enacted laws to recognise the Declaration as binding. In Australia in the late 1970s this was under discussion within the Fraser Government, and was finally formalised with the setting up of a Human Rights & Equal Opportunities Commission in 1981 as a watchdog, which also took over responsibility for the administration of the *Racial Discrimination Act* and the Community Relations Office.

Newly empowered – though clueless

But until the expiry of Al Grassby's term of office a few months later, for want of staff experienced in the field of racial discrimination, the newly fledged Human Rights Commission had to permit our Office to function virtually untouched. Of course there were tensions between the two groups: on the one hand the properly empowered, legalistic new body based in Sydney but which lacked experience, expert staff, or community credibility and on the other the vestigial remains of a Labor Government dream with real runs on the board for community activism, supported by an actual nationwide constituency of ethnic and Aboriginal groups, and determined to go down to the wire in the struggle to keep its well-articulated, communicable vision alive

Doomed – though working frenetically

As a true romantic, I rather revelled in the death-defying challenge, doomed as we recognised ourselves to be. If we had always worked hard and with little administrative support, now we grew positively manic, the closer the end drew nigh. Our final independent Annual Report to Parliament, for 1980-81, tells the story. Publications: 19, including my published report *A Tale of Two Towns*, several published field reports by Lorna Lippmann on anti-Aboriginal racism in widely scattered regions of Australia, my article in *St Mark's Review of Theology*, Canberra, on "Religion in a Multicultural Society" and Grassby's own challenge to the Government, *The Future of Community Relations*.

He is recorded as having given no less than 179 public addresses, TV and radio interviews in eight States/Territories, plus submissions to public enquiries, including one on *"Prior Ownership of the Australian Continent by the Aboriginal People"*.

Our previous Annual Report, the largest ever, had listed 26 publications including my book *Let's End the Slander* and our 'blacklist', *Organisations Propagating Racial Prejudice in Australia*. Three of my articles had been published in Christian journals: "Educating for justice and human rights" in the *Journal of Christian Education*, "The Aboriginal situation and the Church" in *St Mark's Review of Theology*, and "Christians in multicultural Australia" in *Zadok Centre News*. I had given keynote addresses at the "National Consultation on Racism" of the Australian Council of Churches, and at the Uniting Church in Australia's national consultation on "Multiculturalism as a challenge of the 80s".

My world comes crashing down

But when applications were invited for setting up the new Commission I applied for the equivalent of my old post as a matter of course. I assembled what I considered a formidable record of achievements, never doubting that the transition would be a formality. The interview with the interim Chair and a henchman or two went well enough. I was cordially received and encouraged to expound my philosophy of community relations and a practical program for its implementation.

The outcome was indeed a formality, but it came in the form of a bald Public Service communication informing me of my non-appointment. George was to meet the same fate. Despite our naïve expectations, no quarter was given. A journalist from the Attorney-General's Department had been appointed in my position, in order to give the fledgling Commission a higher media profile. Reporting on the new appointment, the *Canberra Times* of 30 May 1982 wrote

> "Among the applicants was Mr Jim Houston from Al Grassby's Office... The new appointment recognises that first and foremost the new Commission has a public relations problem: after its first five months, it has no profile on the street at all, nor a strategy

for reaching out to the masses, or having the masses reach out to it. The fear is that the Commission, stacked with lawyers, will adopt a legalistic, jurisdictional approach. Already odious comparisons with the work of Mr Grassby's Office are being made, particularly among migrant organisations. By contrast the more sociological approach of Grassby's Office focuses on attacking the problems of racism from many directions – education, publicity, and sometimes sanctions."

A supreme irony

In the Interview Report on my subsequent hearing before the Public Service Appeals Committee, among the evaluative comments made on me were:

"Highly committed in the field of racial discrimination, experienced in public education, pleasant, assured, very articulate. Slightly defensive and a little cynical. But sincere and very dedicated: his degree of dedication could be a disadvantage (*sic!*). May be more suited to appointment as a Commissioner than to the staff of the Human Rights Commission."

Damned with faint praise! It was a political fix, of course. But at the foot of the letter advising of my non-appointment to the Human Rights Commission I had scrawled in later years *"Thank God I didn't get the job – how different my life would have been after 1983!"*

Belated vindication

All of 34 years later, at the age of 84, the record would be put right, on receiving an invitation from the Australian Human Rights Commission to be the opening speaker at a commemoration of the 40th Anniversary of the proclamation of the *Racial Discrimination Act* in 1975. A little earlier, at a Melbourne function I had met the Commissioner for Racial Discrimination, Dr Tim Soutphommasane. Subsequently I was invited to Sydney, all expenses paid, to a high-profile occasion which included the Attorney-General in the Rudd & Gillard governments, the Social Security Minister from the Fraser Government, current politicians from both sides, and of course being seated next to the President of the AHRC, Prof. Gillian Triggs.

She was then under siege by Prime Minister Abbott and his colleagues for her report on the inhumane conditions faced by children in the detention centre on Manus Island, while stoutly resisting government demands for her resignation from her statutory office as chief defender of the human rights defined in the International Conventions that she was pledged to uphold. I was able to (dispassionately) present my explication of the climate within which the original Community Relations Office had been obliged to operate in the face of government resentment and obstruction, and of our heroic efforts to cope with near-starvation rations while working like Trojans within the prevailing climate of (largely unchallenged) racism across the country – and especially in remoter areas. It was a great tonic to have the opportunity of publicly recalling the past, and of being so warmly received. A grand occasion: vindicated at last!

Pivotal moment: a dire medical diagnosis

However, it was my lecture in 1981 at the Townsville College of Advanced Education's Race & Culture course, on 'Racism in School Textbooks', that saw the die cast. During a day or two spent in the city and at the James Cook University of North Queensland I had occasion to visit some Aboriginal families in their homes, and I have an explicit memory of being given a cup of tea in a badly chipped and black-rimmed teacup. I dismissed the impulse to decline it or surreptitiously pour it out, preferring simply to trust the Lord. *It proved to be the pivotal moment for the rest of my life.*

Back in the long Canberra winter I battled a particularly virulent and protracted head and chest cold. After some weeks of below-par performance I went to see my G.P. Suspicious, he ordered some tests and referred me to Dr Olver, the Government Medical Officer specialising in infectious diseases. His first comment was, "So you've just come back from the Third World?" After a pause I ventured, *"Er... yes, you could say that. I've been in far north Queensland, working amongst Aborigines."* Fingering my test results, he mused, "I'm sorry to say, you've caught tuberculosis" and observed that it was 10 times more prevalent among Aboriginal communities than in the general society. I was to report at once to Canberra Hospital, at that time still on its choice site on the Acton Peninsula jutting into Lake Burley Griffin. To the Infectious Diseases Ward.

Death sentence?

I was stunned. Tuberculosis was usually fatal. Or would I become a chronic invalid? And what of the family? What had happened to my future? Where was God? Till that moment I had enjoyed lifelong good health, having never been in hospital since my hernia operation at the age of six. It seemed unreal. Or was this merely the fashionable midlife crisis? Certainly, it proved to be the first and most brutal of several major transitions looming: from office desk to hospital bed.

But now things moved fast. Being so contagious, TB was not to be trifled with. I was in the hands of the health authorities. The whole family had to be tested forthwith and have a preventative shot, as did also the entire (though minuscule) staff of the Community Relations Office, from Al Grassby down. Fortunately, no one had become infected.

I needed to spend the first week in the isolation ward while the range of drugs now available was tried out to assess any allergies. Three were then designated to be my daily companions over many months, backing each other up: *aureomycin, rifampicin* and *isoniazid*, the last one having been developed only a few years earlier in Italy. To my huge relief, Dr Olver told me I would recover, though it would take time. How long he wouldn't specify. And I could stay at home rather than being put away, as in earlier times, in a remote infectious diseases hospital.

At home? And infect my family? In previous generations, home treatment was unthinkable because of the infectious nature of TB and the lack of effective curative measures. As formerly with leprosy, sufferers had to be excluded from society: *"Unclean!"* Sufferers spent the rest of their dwindling lives in a sanatorium with no real treatment. But I was reassured that prudent behaviour would ensure the family would be OK. Thank God for the new wonder drugs!

Heartwarming visitors

The week spent in Canberra Hospital was to become memorable for the stream of visitors to my bedside: family and close friends but also people from our Office, including Al Grassby, our church minister, people from our house fellowship and other church members, but also collaborators in our public campaigning for multicultural education and development in Canberra. At times, I found myself introducing to each other people around my bed drawn from a wide variety of contexts. Overall it was a great mercy of God's and in a time of stress a comfort, as I struggled with the big questions, not least of coming to terms with the stark transition from activist to irrelevant invalid whose future had evaporated.

Oddly enough I had no 'hours of pain'. I was told you can't feel anything happening in your lungs. If anything, it was all in my head. But that was the hallmark of the next few months, at home alone all day, musing about a future, worrying about the kids. I seemed to have no energy to contemplate anything: 'laid aside', as they say. I suppose the body had to concentrate fully on destroying the aliens within in order to offer any future at all.

After three months, despite my feeling neither better nor worse, Dr Olver ordered chest X-rays to check on progress – at first glacial. So the meaningless days slipped by; the highlight of many our youngest son David coming home from school. Later I was permitted to resume going to church on Sundays.

Not with a bang but a whimper

Meanwhile in our Office the end of all things was at hand: Al Grassby's term was finishing, and a senior (white) lawyer from the Department of Aboriginal Affairs with no experience of community activism had been appointed Acting Commissioner for Community Relations pending the full establishment of the Human Rights Commission. Our librarian Sylvia Gleeson delivered to our home sealed boxes of papers and documents from my filing cabinets, which I had diligently hoarded since the Office's inception and even earlier. It amounts to documentation of a crucial moment of Australian social and administrative history, the beginnings of multiculturalism.

'Where is God?'

Beyond three or four months of suspended animation, my mind was still turning over and over the basic question of where was God in what was happening to me. I fell to pondering the notion whether, by bringing my old life – and even the Office which was its context – to a close, God might actually be shepherding me towards a new working-life in a Christian context? Could it become, as C.S. Lewis put it, 'a severe mercy'? In any case, Grassby's Office was now withering on the vine and, despite my seven years of 'acting' at a higher level, I had no real job (not formally 'gazetted') in the Executive Service of the Commonwealth. So where would I belong on being pronounced fit to resume duty? Along the way, the Community Relations Office had been transferred from the responsibility of the Attorney-General's Department to the Department of Immigration & Ethnic Affairs. Back among my former sparring partners? Or could I contemplate a transition right out of the security of the Public Service?

It reawakened musings (and some negativity) about considering the Christian ministry, put aside 25 years earlier: I hadn't been a good enough Christian, or known much about personal holiness, besides I was committed to working off my bond with the NSW Education Department, and then to excelling in language teaching.

But now I gave my imagination freer rein. From the outset, the Churches had been faithful partners in our Office's quest for a fair multiracial society, a link which I sought to nurture both as a matter of principle and pragmatism. Grassby encouraged the links I was forging with the mainline Protestant Churches, since as Catholics he and George had no feel for this. In those final years, I was involved with specialist groups in several of the denominations, and also speaking at ecumenical conferences. I had developed wide-ranging contacts, especially within the Uniting Church: being a member of bodies promoting social justice or multiculturalism at every level: parish (local), Presbytery (district), Synod (State) and Assembly (nation). With the peak ecumenical body, the Australian Council of Churches, I had participated in workshops on race relations and Aboriginal issues.

But could I see myself in the ordained ministry: running church services, preaching sermons, teaching the faith, doing pastoral care? Scarcely. Yet I sensed I might contribute to the 'prophetic' role in the Christian community, like many of the people I had met during the Grassby years: specialists in social justice, Aboriginal and multicultural affairs, working within the State and national Councils of Churches. But did this amount to a call?

On good days, such positive thoughts preoccupied me, but more often I felt captive to a cloying inertia, peaking at the time of the monthly X-rays and sessions with Dr Olver. Then I would positively dread to hear his word about being fit to return to work. I seemed mesmerised, sloth-enwrapped, reluctant to venture into the community. But doubtless he was familiar with such mental patterns, as my body had its imperious say.

Towards the end of my house arrest, someone floated the wisdom of undertaking a lone 'retreat' to think and pray about God's will for the future. By then feeling more like facing new challenges, I drove down to my sister's weekend house near Sussex Inlet. For several days richly alone, reflecting, pondering, reading the Scriptures, praying – but always within the pictured over-arching context of the family.

After seven months out of action, I was finally spoken free by Dr Olver, then willing to confide that, when he had diagnosed my condition, with a hole in one lung the size of a 20c coin I had what would in former times have been called *'galloping consumption'* – incurable!

It gave me pause for thought: as St Paul observes, "Since we believe that Christ died for all, those who live [survive?] should no longer live for themselves but for him"[44]. What this might mean now needed to be explored. One early discovery was that – remarkably – the length of my illness had exactly matched the sick leave credits accrued over 19 years in the Public Service: *seven months to the day!*

---

[44] 2 Corinthians 5:15

CHAPTER 31: Explosion of Grace

The next 18 months were to prove an unsettled time as I groped fitfully at looming alternatives. But my lifelong identification with the Gospel of God's grace had ever accompanied me: in the years of teaching in Australia, England and Germany; in the transition to preparing textbooks for others to teach from; in proposing a national program for the education of migrant children; in researching ethnic group life across Australia – conferring a feel for the immigrant experience; in glimpsing the degree to which an alternative future for the country might emerge from the mutual recognition of broader European values than those inherited from the Empire framework; and finally in a wild ride over seven hectic years as insider to an outsider, travelling, writing, speaking, sowing a vision of equality in diversity.

The backdrop to the events on the public stage was our family's belonging to a vibrant community of faith at the O'Connor Methodist (later Uniting) Church. This dated from our first days in Canberra as a newly arrived family when the Minister, Rev. Perry Smith, was our first visitor. An earnest, though cheerful and kindly character, of English Methodist connections. Viewed in retrospect, the timing of this call was providential, leading us beyond our new area (where there were then no churches) towards a church with an amazing destiny waiting in the wings to usher in the remainder of my life-work.

Early days at O'Connor Methodist Church

From 1969 till 1983 through our years of raising the family, we belonged to this Christian community which grew exponentially during the period, reflecting the ever-increasing flow of newcomers to the national capital, bringing many Christian public servants and professionals, including some later well-known figures in public life: the Commissioner for Taxation, the Chief Justice of the ACT, and a future Prime Minister (Kevin Rudd during his student days at the ANU). The theological flavour of the church was evangelical in the fervent Wesleyan holiness tradition, with a commitment to Bible study and community service, backed by prayer.

Perry Smith was a man of boundless energy, an engaging preacher and a prayer warrior. In response came a spontaneous urge among the leaders to pray for God to empower and use the church. Early every morning there was a prayer time attended by a faithful few. Although a member of the 'Leaders' Meeting', I fear in that august company I contributed little to its strategising.

Close of an historic era

In 1974 a national vote taken across the membership of the Methodist, Presbyterian and Congregational Churches would lead to union. But unlike the other two Churches, the Methodist Church was committed to going out of existence if the majority of parishes supported union. They did, although we understand that the O'Connor Church voted more strongly against union than any parish in the land, such was the strength of its Wesleyan Methodist convictions and confidence in its leadership. But in June 1977 the Uniting Church in Australia came into being.

One outcome was that O'Connor sat loosely to its new affiliation and for its part, the ACT leadership of the UCA had little interest in what was happening there. A pity because it was now by far the most populous UCA parish in Canberra and its developing experience had much to contribute to the wider Church. Unfortunately, this official wariness confirmed its lone ranger status in its own eyes.

Transformational stirrings worldwide

But this also happened to be the era when church life around the world was beginning to experience a mysterious new dynamism, often quite transformational, which came to be known as the *charismatic movement*. It first came to our attention when we heard of a surprising phenomenon: a Roman Catholic revivalist group in Narrabundah. Next came an informal, fervent Protestant meeting spanning denominations and parishes, led by a loving and gentle Anglican minister. But for us the most significant of these early explorative encounters was with a newly established para-church in the making, led by an appealing Dutch migrant pastor, Tony, who somehow re-taught us everything we had learnt, but this time with a new perspective, depth and ... power!

Across the churches and denominations there was a new sense of community emerging, linked by the 'naïve' concept of a bond of love as all that mattered. In our 42 years, we had never encountered anything quite like this, and we sensed this was true for everybody involved. It was almost as if God himself had become our organiser, rendering all other categories meaningless.

Then an interesting, rather cosmopolitan American couple launched a sort of house church connected with Youth with a Mission, founded some years earlier in the USA, but from the outset an innovative, transnational, and largely unstructured agency training and deploying young people for strategic roles in world mission. Like Jesus, Claude 'spoke with authority and not as the scribes'[45], and this we found refreshing. Supplemented by the newcomers steadily arriving in the city, their non-denominational work exploded. Soon they had to shift camp and YWAM bought a former monastery on the northern outskirts of 'old Canberra' where three-month residential Discipleship Training Schools for young and older Christians were offered.

It was all beginning to stretch my categories for pigeonholing Christian groups. The pigeonholes themselves were melting into one. Now where had I heard of such a situation before? Could it be in the New Testament?

A new dynamic in the air

Back at the regular O'Connor services, something new was afoot. The numbers were climbing: we'd never lived through such a phenomenon. The more usual pattern was a slow decline as people aged. Moreover, from situations near and far, in all denominations, in Australia and beyond, we began to hear of similar developments. Was something stirring in the worldwide household of faith?

With a few others from O'Connor, on Sunday afternoons we began attending Tony's meeting, called the Christian Revival Crusade. What it offered we sorely needed: since our university days we had slipped back into the rather cloying routines of church life, in Canberra, in England and Germany, and then back in Sydney. Our evangelical faith

---
[45]Mark 1:22

was strictly 'head stuff' without much purchase on our daily lives. And, of course, these were too busy. With work and a young family, we had little energy to spare and church was actually de-energising – a travesty of what you read of the primitive church in the Acts of the Apostles. The worst of it was that we were quite unaware of any other possibilities, so that the sudden revelation of what church could become, and what resources the Faith really offered, took us by storm.

Encountering the Holy Spirit of the Triune God

Of course, the difference lay in the real presence and role of the Holy Spirit, the overlooked dimension of the Godhead. Like many, I had drifted into domesticating God, for our own and the church's benefit. Now we encountered the scary claim that the patterns of activity in the Early Church, miraculous dimension and all, far from being merely *'dispensational'*[46] as the Church had conveniently rationalised for centuries – without any scriptural warrant – were quite normative for every age. The sovereign God, "the nameless One though the Surname of all things", was revealing himself afresh as holy, but in grace and power. Indeed, in the depersonalised, technological age we were living in, manifestations of God's sovereignty had a unique capacity for getting under our guard. It was starting to look as if God himself had re-entered human society (since similar reports were coming to hand worldwide) in the person of the Holy Spirit whom Jesus had bequeathed to the church from the beginning, to continue his own ministry.

Teaching about the Gifts of the Spirit

Evidence for the miraculous was particularly manifest in the widespread experiences of spiritual healing being claimed, including in our own parish. In turn, these were set within the novel context (for conventional Christians like us) of the Gifts of the Spirit listed in the New Testament, particularly in Romans and 1 Corinthians.[47] Yet I could not recall ever having heard a sermon unpacking this basic teaching. Where had it been all my life?

---

[46] Applicable only to the apostolic age, not for all time.
[47] Romans 12: 6-8 and 1 Corinthians 12: 4-11.

At O'Connor Methodist, there was something of a low-key debate developing about the new claims. While some members were quite savvy biblically and theologically, and therefore averse to 'new' teaching as per se suspect, those of us more prone to recognise our need for greater reality in our Christian experience took a more pragmatic line. We needed it to be true! Ever the pragmatist – if not opportunist – I was hungry for whatever God was offering.

Secret of the new dynamism

The focus was often on a teaching we had heard from Pastor Tony called the 'baptism in the Holy Spirit' which is mentioned (but not often) in the New Testament, one evidence for which is to 'speak in tongues' (in a language unintelligible to the speaker), praising God. Certainly, many people appeared to be receiving this fresh baptism and manifesting this gift, sometimes noisily. But according to St Paul, to whom it was normative, it needed to be balanced by other more ministry-related gifts of the Spirit, such as service, healing and discernment.

Arrival of a familiar new minister

By the time Rev. Perry Smith left O'Connor in mid-1973, by his prayerfulness, enthusiasm and godliness he had well and truly laid the foundation for the church's remarkable future. He was replaced by Rev. Harry Westcott, who before ordination had been in my battalion in National Service at Ingleburn, and used to meet in the bush with a small group of us after 'lights out' to pray. A genial and open-hearted man, soon he was being courted by both groups of parishioners, but was wary of any commitment in either direction. With competition between the groups sharpening, his quandary deepened. As he was to testify later, on his appointment to the National Capital he had been in a blue funk – a man from a simple farming background and on transfer from a raffish mining town in the Pilbara where he had almost lost his faith. In despair, at daybreak one summer morning in 1974 he went across to the church and besought the Lord, confessing his sins and his emptiness, and crying out for a healing touch from God.

St Paul on the road to Damascus?

Harry received a remarkable answer. In a terrifying blaze of light, he heard the audible voice of God say, *"You are forgiven"* and felt baptised in the Holy Spirit: immersed in love, with faith and courage renewed, and filled with the desire to proclaim *'the full Gospel'* as he had now received it from the hands of God.

At once he shared his experience from the pulpit, as vulnerable as it might make him. Certainly, here was a man transformed, re-integrated and liberated, his latent gifts of love and boldness renewed. But a small group of the savvy withdrew, in apprehension of where the church might now be headed – into spiritual ratbaggery? The remainder were excited at the prospect of spiritual adventure in a new age marked by such manifestations of Holy Spirit power, and where the challenge was to experience a deepened trust in God's purposes for good.

God's gift of newness

There were great days ahead. The church grew spontaneously, with full house at both morning and evening services, great joy and informality in worship, and the advent of new popular hymns ('songs'), often very beautiful in melody and now played by gifted members of the congregation on various instruments rather than the organ (including on a harp), with scriptural words inspired by the Holy Spirit. A whole new people's hymnody was emerging from New Zealand and America and spreading across the English-speaking world. In Europe, I have encountered it since in both German and French translations. Doubtless there are endless others, particularly among the 'house churches' of China where an amazingly gifted woman *of peasant background,* Xiao Min, has become revered for her beautiful and godly hymnody (both words and music), especially in the underground churches spread across that vast land. With us too, worship was becoming a dialogue directly with God: no longer were we mostly singing *about* God, we were singing *to* God – and that from the heart rather than the head. I loved it. In O'Connor, overnight in a seamless transition the old had given way to the new, a process that in many traditional parishes took forever, with agonising disputes and distress. To us it was the gift of God and we received it in gratitude.

Preaching took on a new relevance to living, often supplemented with personal testimony about what God was doing in people's lives: animosities reconciled, relationships healed, illness cured. One memorable occasion was during a Communion Service when two 'enemies' from warring parts of the former Yugoslavia (Serbia and Croatia) found themselves kneeling side by side at the altar rail. Spontaneously the two men hugged each other, both of them in tears for the hardness of their hearts.

The worship services grew longer, at times lasting up to two hours – doesn't time fly when you're having fun? People simply didn't want to go home, so rich was the joy in worship and 'fellowship with the saints'. From just being the place that church people went to on Sundays, 'O'Connor' was becoming the integrating focus of their lives. Really the services didn't have a formal end but moved on into informal 'ministry time' when many individuals experienced wonderful, even miraculous, encounters with God from 'the laying on of hands' by the minister and un-ordained 'ministers', while the band continued in praise and worship songs. Many tears were wept, of liberation and joy and new beginnings.

Liberation from the clergy-focused church

In a significant development the whole renewal tended to become a people's movement, in which clergy participated but without directing. What joy: everyone was liberated from the age-old pattern of the clergy-focused church. It was not planned or devised, still less was it structured: it simply happened. While theological gifts were not to be despised, ministry gifts were of a different order, distributed more broadly across the congregation at the discretion of the Holy Spirit. No special favours for the ordained. It sufficed to be an earnest believer.

The people of God had been released into ministry! Some of our close friends now emerged in a totally new light as they discovered new personal ministries, some as prophet, some with the gift of (spiritual) discernment, others as revealing an amazing spiritual wisdom, and others as possessing a faith in the power of prayer 'to move mountains' – and all tending not to personal aggrandisement but to the upbuilding of the 'Body of Christ' – as the local church began to identify itself. Even I began to ponder whether, in some perhaps distant future, I might have gifts for ministry in the Church. Looking back from long afterwards, I suspect I was only identifying this as a calling to preach, but clearly Christian ministry is far broader and more demanding than that.

Some O'Connor people dared to wonder whether, after 2000 years, it might mean that the normative New Testament Church was starting to make a worldwide comeback. If so, this renewal was not associated with any one culture or people, still less one denomination – all of these now seen as worn-out old clothes to be shed. "Behold, I am doing a new thing." For a time, we had an auxiliary pastor fresh back from Vietnam who reported that, in the midst of the cruel war, a Christian revival of similar character was spontaneously afoot among the people. Indeed, recently I have read that today (36 years on, in 2011) it is all still happening like this in the underground churches (house churches) of China. What bliss to be part of it, a foretaste of the Kingdom of God rooted afresh in our workaday world.

Initiatives spontaneously emerging

With freedom conferred by a godly leadership team to explore new programs and structures, over the next five years innovative ministry initiatives were coming up everywhere like shoots out of dry ground: an 'open air witness' in Garema Place, City during the Friday night shopping hours, the launch of a Christian school, the formation of a Christian residential community, 'One Way House', adult baptisms by full immersion in the (at times icy) waters of Lake Burley Griffin, weekend lay ministry trips by teams into the surrounding countryside and later throughout Australia and even overseas, to PNG and the islands – exporting the renewal. A house was bequeathed to the parish, enabling the property opposite the church to be purchased for offices and meeting rooms. A recently retired public servant volunteered to work full-time as church administrator, and two schoolteachers 'left their nets' to work in the parish. In addition to these, the staff came to include a youth minister, office secretary, and soon a second ordained minister was called. *Until then we had never been in a church that employed more than the lone clergyman.* But over this period parish giving increased fivefold, reflecting the rapid growth in numbers and in devotion.

All this created *ex nihilo*[48] by the Holy Spirit deigning to use ordinary people transformed by love and gifted with a heart's desire to follow where Jesus led. As Harry Westcott put it once, it was "as if a bucket of love had been tipped out over the church." Even more than the charismatic gifts was this a convincing manifestation of the real presence of the Holy Spirit among us.

By 1977, the small O'Connor A-frame church was ready to burst at the seams as new people, having heard the rumour of God being there in power, turned up every Sunday, particularly ANU students, among them one Kevin Rudd.

A future Prime Ministerial ambition

On graduating from the ANU in 1979, Kevin Rudd confided to me one evening after church that he hoped to go into politics. I was caught by surprise at such an unusual plan, but knowing he came from Jo Bjelke-Petersen's perennial Country Party fiefdom of Queensland, I couldn't bear to ask which party. It had to be assumed that anyone hoping to build a career in Queensland politics would need to be from the Country Party.

Personal testimony

How did I relate to all that was happening at O'Connor? What about the baptism in the Holy Spirit? Despite our fervent prayers at the time, we were not to receive "power from on high when the Holy Spirit comes upon you", as Jesus put it, and as the charismatics were preaching as normative. Nor the gift of tongues – though arguably a *prophetic* gift ('speaking *forth*' on social issues, rather than 'foretelling' events), and for Marjorie the lifelong gift of helping others. Certainly, I was released from a humdrum Christian profession into an unanticipated new dimension of faith, hope and love. It also conferred great joy in

---

[48] 'Out of nothing', like the creation

worship, especially through the new music clothing scriptural words. My inward humming-life took up a new repertoire! More significantly, the 'melted heart' experience was to become permanent, with the 'repentance lag' after wilful forays increasingly reduced, and a real heart-desire to be less self-seeking. (Of course, such a claim can only be judged by others, especially one's children!)

A praise movement

On the other hand, there could be no doubt that the charismatic movement could justly be characterised as the *'praise movement'*, not only because of the emergence of so much creative new music in the contemporary idiom, but also because of the new joy Christians everywhere were experiencing in praising God together. It was God's world, he was our Father and we were his children – and the future was his! Whereas the traditional hymnody was grammatically expressed in the third person (singing thoughtfully *about* God) the new love songs were a balance of head and heart, often couched in the second person (fervently *addressed to* the Father or the Son or the Spirit, or even all Three).

... and also a 'prayer movement'.

A team of faithful prayer warriors began meeting to plead for God's Spirit to use the church. Like so many in the parish, I had a new urge to pray, pouring out my soul both privately and in corporate gatherings. Now an informal team was meeting weekly around Harry Westcott in his study, praying specifically for his ministry. In fact, everywhere prayer became one of the distinguishing features of the renewal, and remarkable answers to prayer were commonly reported. One Monday, after concerted, fervent prayer, the thief who had broken into the church and stolen the entire Sunday offering brought it back and *'laid it at the apostles' feet'*.[49]

During that turbulent epoch of social upheaval which swept the Western world in the 60s and 70s, characterised by discontent with old forms and solutions, the charismatic renewal was recognised as the God-dimension. Its hallmark was God's sovereign initiating of new life

---
[49] As recorded in Acts 4:37

and energy across the Western world: the old wineskins were bursting at the seams and spontaneous new expressions of worship, service and evangelism were everywhere apparent. Planners and organisers took a back seat. A new excitement was in the air. The sky was the limit: the Spirit was moving and we were convinced that prayer would change the world and imminently bring in the Kingdom of God. (And with a Labor Government in power, for the first time in 23 years espousing the cause of the poor and the needy, some of us had even fancied we could discern a small reflective factor there!)

Across the whole Body, an impulse for more fervent intercessory prayer was sensed: someone suggested an early-morning time be regularly set aside for prayer. Miraculously, I would be found in the church on midwinter Fridays – at five a.m! It had to be God!

But with the shocking dismissal of the Whitlam Government two years later, and the election that brought Malcolm Fraser to power, the following Sunday in a service at O'Connor I was to experience a poignant interface of Word and world. Kneeling at the communion rail next to my more politically conservative friend Tom, Pastor Harry paused in tender discernment to pray quietly over me in my distress, while Tom lovingly amen-ed. Amid bitter worldly division a moment of Spirit-given oneness.

... and even a heart-softening movement

Indeed, the charismatic movement was also the *'heart-softening movement'*. Many old allegiances and self-identifications melted away in the blaze of God's holy fire, just as willed by Jesus in his final prayer *("...that all might be one")*[50]. At large national conferences such as the one I attended at Sydney Showground, Catholics hugged Protestants, ecclesial distinctions dissolved: high church, low church, evangelical, liberal, Eastern Orthodox. No doubt the traditional differences were important, but they no longer mattered, *"...that the world might believe!"* Everyone was asked to find someone from an opposite camp and express a personal apology for our own part in perpetuating the rejections and

---

[50] John 17:20-21

hurts of the past. For me that was a powerfully liberating experience, which permanently eradicated the last roots of the old anti-Catholic animosity.

Open air preaching

So it was unsurprising that such a message should be taken into the community and preached: a new start with the God of new beginnings. I broke new ground personally by becoming involved in a team running an open-air rally in the city on Friday evenings in Garema Place – for such a wimp something unimaginable.

Friday by Friday, the Lord in his mercy vouchsafed an awesome sign of his presence: with the cumbersome PA system in our Falcon station wagon I would boldly drive straight to the first row of the huge carpark adjoining Civic Centre, select the most appropriate point in the serried ranks of parked vehicles – and move straight into a spot vacated by a car just leaving – week after week! Then one evening amid the surging crowd of shoppers, while I was actually 'preaching', I spotted Ted Charles passing by, my former boss and sparring partner at the Immigration Department. Now he would have good grounds for confirming me as a dangerous ratbag.

Not so a guy who would later become one of my closest friends, who paused to listen. Much later he would tell me that, in his despair at the death of his first wife, he had 'sacked' God and the church but that night, like St Peter at *Quo Vadis*[51] fleeing Rome, he heard the voice of Jesus within calling him to turn back.

Tender care

After one Friday evening's rally, I had a life-changing experience with a drug-addict, Glen, who had responded to the preaching. As he wept I was overcome by a surge of tenderness towards him, derelict and friendless as he seemed to be. Holding him closely and gently wiping the slobber from his nose and out of his beard, to me it became a sacred moment of identification with the world of suffering I'd never known before. Though unaware at the time, it was to be a portent for holistic ministry a decade later among the needy in Broadmeadows.

---

[51] Latin, "Where are you going?"

Small-group life

Also about that time, with three other families we experimented with a 'Family Cluster' as a natural milieu for imparting the faith to the next generation, spending many precious hours together, sharing the teaching and worship with each other and all our kids and in play. Twice we went away together on a holiday.

Such was the hunger for spiritual reality set over against people's real-life experience that there arose ten small-group meetings and home fellowships, so that the Sunday service became a joyful 'family' reunion, bringing together people bonded by friendship as well as devotion. In all our previous church life in three countries we had never encountered such an innovation. For years until we left Canberra we hosted a home group in Cook for praise and worship, study, sharing each family's concerns and problems, and praying for each other – deeply identifying with each other's struggles.

These 'cell groups' were actively promoted by the leadership, to become powerful incubators of experience and sharing. Actually, many of us felt they were more significant than attendance at the great Sunday services, because of their scope for confronting and tackling intractable personal issues that would hardly be addressed by the church at large. Certainly, we witnessed much blessing and some manifest healings in our home fellowship, a focus for permanently softened hearts, free from past hurts and negativities. It was from there that we were commissioned to go forth to Melbourne, taking up a ministry opportunity in their name.

On our last Sunday in the full assembly I was privileged to preach about my growing conviction that there was looming danger if the church didn't keep before itself the practical needs of the poor and dispossessed, as articulated in Jesus' two Great Commandments: love for God and love for our neighbour – the twin Gospel imperatives of personal salvation and social justice. On our departure, our house in Cook was designated as the residential base for the group of young O'Connor people previously living in Christian community in 'One Way House.'

The home fellowships were an integral part of the charismatic movement everywhere and conceivably its greatest ongoing legacy. In many ways, they recalled the pattern of the Early Church after being excluded from the synagogues and before there were any Christian buildings. It represented then, as in our day at O'Connor, a radical breach with organised religion. Unobtrusive initiatives in worship and fellowship in a home are hard to combat and can spread organically. This remains a vital factor in China today, where there are reputed on good authority to be many millions of new converts meeting in ('underground') house fellowships. It is also a manifestation of the church of the poor, thriving in the Third World and mostly with a charismatic dimension.

In our latest years in Canberra, we enrolled David in the O'Connor Christian School, launched in 1980. For a time, I was a member of the School Board. Today it is the well-endowed, independent Brindabella Christian College, an inter-denominational co-ed school of some 500 students from kindergarten to Year 12.

Grand gatherings Canberra-wide

At Harry Westcott's inspiration, large-scale Sunday evening outreach meetings were sponsored in the plush Lakeside International Hotel, under the showy title *'Another Night of Miracles'*, some featuring leading international charismatic preachers, and drawing up to 600 people from all over Canberra and beyond. Once the phenomenon was covered by the ABC television program *'Four Corners'*.

Subsequently one history of the parish[52] (but compiled by outsiders) reported that
> "By the late 1970s, O'Connor was widely known as a leading charismatic Uniting Church with an Australia-wide renewal ministry... Reputedly it was one of the fastest growing churches in the State *(sic)*. Its worship was noted for its profound sense of God.

---

[52] William and Susan Emilsen, 'Testing the Spirit': A History of O'Connor Uniting Church Parish, United Theological College, Sydney

There was a fine ministry amongst Canberra's burgeoning student population. Over the next decade, parish leaders often noted that O'Connor sponsored and supported more theological students than any other church in Australia. It was also known for its deep concern for the underdog. It was a church willing to pay the price of loving people. It was also a church that put into practice the Reformation notion of the 'priesthood of all believers'."

Significant though objective claims – and from my own perspective by no means inflated.

Advent of the glory days

After several years, Harry Westcott moved on to a preaching and evangelistic ministry, and a prayerful search brought Rev. Dan Armstrong, former Evangelist of the NSW Conference of the Methodist Church, to O'Connor as new senior pastor. Converted as a night-club entertainer, a sterling and appealing character, from his earliest Christian days he had a passion for sharing the love of God to anyone who would listen – from his class background retaining the common touch.

Dan was to preside over further growth in numbers and in breadth of ministry initiatives. When the O'Connor church building became quite inadequate the services were moved to the assembly hall of the nearby Lyneham High School where morning and evening services soon became crowded with large numbers of people praising and worshipping God.

In the next four years until we left Canberra, the worshipping community would grow stronger and more creative. Both monthly and quarterly parish publications were launched. The Christian School was an absorbing initiative, while street evangelism touched many lives. Parish mission teams moved ever farther afield, some for up to a week (for instance to Geraldton, WA), reporting some remarkable outcomes in renewal ministry. After much prayer, the leadership agreed that Dan should be released to exercise his God-given gift of evangelism on tours throughout Australia and overseas, while a newly appointed second minister would hold the fort back home.

Deep identification with Aboriginal Christians

One of Dan's prime concerns was for the Aboriginal people, for whom he had a deep love and understanding. He and Sue had an adopted Aboriginal daughter who now, 30 years later, is one of the strong women holding a Central Australian community together.

It was Dan's preaching at Elcho Island, off the NE tip of Arnhem Land, that would be a factor in the triggering of an unprecedented Aboriginal revival that swept across half the continent, as far as Leonora near Kalgoorlie, where the publican lamented that he was going broke for want of Aboriginal drinkers! The Yolngu community of the former Methodist Mission was deeply touched by the in-breaking of God's power, experiencing relationships restored, sick and oppressed healed, alcoholism beaten, lives cleaned up. In whole-community gatherings night after night for worship, prayer and praise, marked by a holy sense of God's presence, Aboriginal leaders like Rev. Djinyini Gondarra preached repentance and proclaimed God's love[53]. At the height of the renewal movement, as Aboriginal people across the north were experiencing God's healings within their broken communities, some of the Elcho Island leaders even hired a plane and undertook a missionary journey of their own far down into inland WA – St Paul in a Twin Otter!

Calls to ministry

Among the new people linked with O'Connor were a former public servant from my old car-sharing group. A year or so later, he and his family departed for Sydney for John to undertake theological study for the ministry – one of a considerable number of future ordinands from the parish. I well recall helping them clear out their home and load the hired van. As they and their family pulled away from their driveway, leaving their Canberra life behind them forever, I sensed a sort of epiphany foreshadowing – I felt both impressed but also a little anxious for them, and also envious: *so this is what comes in the package of responding whole-heartedly to God...?*

---

[53] See 'Fire in the Outback: the Untold Story of the Aboriginal Revival Movement that Began on Elcho Island in 1979' by John Blacket, Albatross, 1997

Two years later, in 1984, we too would pull away from our own driveway, embarking on a mission for Christ, never to live in Canberra again. But a good deal more was to unfold before that climactic departure would be fulfilled

During these years, a remarkable 'coincidence' occurred, reassuring us of God's ongoing practical presence. Negligently I had allowed our commitment to supporting Christian work in the parish and in the wider world to languish, to the point where it would require a sizeable disbursement of our income to rectify. Repentant, bur recklessly at one hit, I sent out a large number of cheques to meet overdue commitments, musing *'God will have to provide'*. A few days later, the fortnightly payslip seemed grossly inflated, to the point where I thought in all honesty I should report the obvious mistake. I was told we had all received an adjustment marking the protracted conclusion of a new pay deal with the Public Service Board. In my case the unexpected premium *exactly matched* the amount I had shelled out!

Epilogue: "Whatever happened to the Charismatic Movement?"

In any discussion of the charismatic movement of the 1970s and 80s, one salient question seems to emerge. Given its spontaneous manifestation around the globe in widely divergent Churches (historically, theologically, culturally) and its dynamism, why did it fade rather than becoming normative and permanent for all Churches everywhere? *So, whatever happened to the charismatic movement?*[54] Was it truly initiated by God? Or was it merely a passing phase, a fad even? Today in Australia relatively few of the mainline churches seem to have permanently integrated a distinctive charismatic flavour into their local congregation's worship or theological orientation.

Instead, while the high-water mark remains etched in the sands of time, the sea surges elsewhere. It seems that at the world level the liveliness and spirituality brought by the charismatic revival have

---

[54] In 2014 a religious program on ABC Television had this title, with a particular focus on the O'Connor story. Approached by the producer, I supplied the text of this chapter and a number of O'Connor contacts, ministerial and lay, making the point that the renewal was also (and still is) normative in many Third World churches. The outcome was disappointing: the program ignored much of this data in favour of a preconceived notion that it was all evanescent, now gone without trace. After screening, many O'Connor folk reported to me how disgusted they were with the cheap coverage. For me it was salutary evidence that the media pursue their own unbalanced agenda not always related to actuality.

indeed opened up an ongoing dimension in the life of the newer Churches, particularly in Africa, Latin America and China. Since many of these are quite recent foundations, there is no question of the charismatic dimension being an 'add-on', a new patch tacked on to a threadbare old garment. Rather it appears as simply one vital feature of newly emergent churches free to make their own response to the Holy Spirit, rather than being bound to historical patterns and structures imposed by Western missionaries.

Concluding from our O'Connor experience that the many innovations of the movement included a profound joy in praise and worship, a softening of hard hearts and the urge to pray, as well as a spontaneity in reworking tired old structures and a creative dynamism in outreach and service to the world – not to mention the manifestation of the Gifts of the Spirit, and most distinctively of healing – it is eminently imaginable that such a church newly planted in a culture previously unmarked by the Gospel would command respect and attention. It is, of course, highly likely that this was also the case with the Primitive Church of the first centuries. Certainly, the Acts of the Apostles and the New Testament Epistles provide numerous such glimpses. Did God mean this to be the timeless norm?

Moreover, many churches planted in recent years in Australian suburbia and larger provincial centres, and which appear to have thrived from the outset (sometimes by the infusion of dissatisfied worshippers from fossilising mainline Churches), almost invariably have a charismatic dimension. And this is also true from my own observations in the UK, in Germany and even in France, that largely ex-Christian society. They are often seen as 'Pentecostal', although this broad category has several strands. It almost seems to be the case that the vibrant churches in the West today have integrated a charismatic dimension with their 'orthopraxy'[55] Is this why they are so dynamic and grow so spontaneously?

My encounter a few years ago with a crowded, multiracial Pentecostal church based in a large Paris cinema in a working-class quarter, and in one of the most secularised countries of the post-Christian West, seems to confirm the trend. The elderly visiting evangelistic preacher was a Gypsy!

---

[55] Normative practices of worship and service

A passing fancy of our time?

But is the charismatic phenomenon so new? And is it merely contemporary? Or is it apparent across time as well as space? Certainly, in my lifetime and that of our parents it seemed unheard-of. But what are two or three generations in a pageant stretching back two millennia? As we observe its outer characteristics today, the movement reflects contemporary patterns of informality, spontaneity, and musical idiom, coupled with the use of hi-tech gadgetry, the whole project covered by localised authority – in all respects vastly different from my earlier experience of centralised, denominational church.

Yet *mutatis mutandis*[56], studies of church praxis throughout Christian history claim to have identified similar manifestations to the charismatic movement in many ages, sometimes related to surges of renewal and innovation occurring after long eras of stagnation, demoralisation and decline. Often the hierarchy opposed it. In the Wesleys' day, it used to be denounced as 'enthusiasm', as though true religion had to be lugubrious: *inter alia* they dared to co-opt popular tunes to grace the new hymns emerging. Tut, for shame! Though a learned Anglican divine and a failed missionary in the American colonies, John Wesley's own experience of the 'warmed heart' was to launch a revivalist ministry throughout Britain, sweeping untold numbers of working-class people into the Kingdom and, by 'class meetings', training a whole ministry force for what became the Methodist Church (though never intended as a separate church by John Wesley). It would become one of the largest in the English-speaking world, with its distinctive dual focus on evangelism and social justice. The Wesleys themselves exhorted the faithful to get involved in prison ministry with convicts, some later *'bound for Botany Bay'*. It all sounds like normative charismatic stuff.

But we may wonder whether today's ever-increasing secular consciousness is now making the traditional claims (and language) of faith increasingly disreputable, even unthinkable. The recent advent of an aggressive atheism, vigorously backed by media interests, may be a new factor in encouraging people merely indifferent to religion

---

[56]'All necessary changes having been made'

to become openly anti-Christian. But certainly we can assume that God is not fazed. Doubtless as the hymn puts it, he is *'working his purposes out as year succeeds to year'*. Conceivably the charismatic impulse could be his way of by-passing the intense secular-rationalist mindset in order to touch the deeper springs of our humanity and unleash creative processes of integration within, whereas the culture seems bent on fragmenting our inner life (recalling the old maxim of *'divide and conquer'*).

God's movement – or ours?

So what are the ubiquitous and perennial features of this renewal movement? In a few words, the refocusing of the Christian life from head to heart, from preoccupation with doctrine to the experience of the indwelling Spirit. From this flows the breaking down of barriers with Christians of other ilk, when they discover the new common experience they all share. So centuries of deep-rooted antagonism between Catholics and Protestants melt away within a few years, swallowed up in mutual respect and love for sisters and brothers in Christ.

And beyond these visible manifestations, the experience of inner healing resulting from greater self-acceptance, release from past hurts and ongoing anger, suspicion and resistance towards others, all subsumed by growing in Christlikeness – into holiness, as the Holy Spirit is afforded more sway. From this open-heart surgery may follow the Spirit's endowment of a ministry of healing and other gifts for the building up of the church as the Body of Christ.

And also, a greater responsiveness to God's concern for the wellbeing of his creation, both human and natural, but particularly for the powerless most in need of loving intervention. Such experiences lead to a fresh understanding of God's goodness and the power of his love, resulting in our release into deeper faith and trust. No wonder such joy and excitement and liberty can be manifest in public worship, eclipsing concerns about liturgical forms and ecclesial patterns.

Yet since God deigns to use human agency in shaping the life of the Church, the role of leadership must also be crucial. Too often this seems to be the point where human vulnerability enters the equation. Leaders of large, thriving church communities where the formal structures for ensuring accountability have been largely dispensed with, may become quite exposed. The fascination of power, the latent urge to dominate, the vanity to seek disciples, may subtly assert itself, gradually and insidiously, though perhaps rationalised away by appeal to strong Old Testament figures.

The people may also drift into a safe self-sufficiency: after all, the 'principalities and powers' are not inactive (as C. S. Lewis' *Screwtape Letters* graphically evokes). Sad to say, in a charismatic congregation the Gifts of the Spirit can become over time powerful tools for glorifying not only God. But God is not mocked, so that before long the glory may have departed, leaving the forms and the structures in place but powerless and sterile. Is this a familiarly unfolding pattern with churches?

Even if it were, we would not need to conclude that the charismatic initiative was the only string to God's bow, its decline or failure leaving his purposes thwarted. We are not his advisors. Our absurd aspiration to lock him into our rationality – our theological insights, our doctrinal formulations, our comfortable precedents – simply attests to the paucity of our imagination. We humans can scarcely understand our own bodies, let alone our minds and our spirits. How then can we aspire to fathom God, unless he reveals himself to us? Contemplating the boundless power of his grace,[57] the challenge for us remains to match our willingness to welcome him with his readiness to reveal himself to us.

The Creator of 2,000 species of butterflies on our planet is scarcely constrained in his creative options! But the grand sweep of his creation also spans a universe whose expansion is accelerating! Whatever its outward form then, our worship offered in sincerity and truth to the triune God: ineffable Father, cosmic Christ and life-giving Spirit, would surely beget in us joy at belonging in his world of wonder and delight, while pouring out our hearts in his praise.

---

[57] In biblical Greek 'charis' means grace

But I will not continue so foolishly to ponder imponderable questions of God's sovereign purposes and providence.

'The Lord is in his holy temple. Let all the earth keep silence before him.'[58]

---

[58] Habakkuk 2:20

CHAPTER 32: Transitions

Beyond tuberculosis, with my working life restored to me, I wondered which way to turn. At the age of 49, the first intimations of my mortality, conferring a salutary awareness of the finitude of our time on earth, had created the desire to make the rest of my life count for more.

Revisiting the past

And so, eight years after forsaking the Immigration Department for greener pastures, I found myself grazing once again in their home paddock – sheepishly. By then the old Department, resurrected and consolidated – minus some of the troglodytes – had moved to Benjamin Offices at Belconnen Town Centre.

But along the way, by my public forthrightness, I had made a few enemies (no admirers of Al Grassby or his cohorts) but who mercifully refrained from hubris. I was grateful to be appointed Class 10 in the Migrant Education section among a congenial group of urbane new colleagues. My work was with a new international phonetic alphabet for use in the adult English classes.

A few weeks afterwards, I was called to the office of the Acting Permanent Head of the Department whom I had respected from former days. He asked a favour of me: would I write at short notice an address he was slated to give to the Insurance Brokers' Council of Australia? I knocked it over promptly, pretty much off my head. A day or two later I was called in again: the speech had gone down well. He was indebted to me.

Opportunity knocks but once

The opportunity was too good to miss. Seizing the nettle, I boldly popped the $64 question: would he approve my formal application to participate in the current 'Public Service Exchange Scheme with the Private Sector'? Having discovered the Scheme in the *Commonwealth Gazette*, I had hit upon the idea that conceivably the Australian Council of Churches (ACC) might be deemed part of 'the private sector'. From my earlier membership of a specialist committee of the ACC I knew plans were afoot to establish a Churches' Commission on Community Relations, but without funds to realise it. His reply took me by surprise, "The Secretary wouldn't have approved it – he's back next week. But I owe you a favour. OK, you can go ... *you bugger!*"

Public Service decision-making at its crispest! It was to usher in the rest of my life, outside the Public Service, as the Shepherd opened the sheep gates and enticed me to enter. "See, I have set before you an open door, and no one can shut it; for you have a little strength ... and have not denied My name"[59].

Under the exchange agreement, a worker with the Australian Council of Churches would be attached to the Immigration Department in Sydney. The upshot came several weeks later, when the President of the Australian Council of Churches launched the Churches' Commission on Community Relations, based in Canberra, virtually to carry on the public educative work of the extinct Community Relations Office – now resuscitated within an explicitly Christian framework.

Churches' Commission on Community Relations

Commission members appointed by the ACC came from Melbourne, Sydney and Canberra, and its staff consisted of myself and a secretary, a young Finnish woman from O'Connor church. It was launched in the Woden Churches Centre where the Commission would have its office. A considerable crowd represented Canberra Churches, the ACT Ethnic Communities Council, the Australian Institute of Aboriginal & Islander Studies, the Immigration Department, local multicultural campaigners plus friends from the O'Connor church – with speakers including Professor Jerzy Zubrzycki and Al Grassby, to whom I replied. We had a modest operating budget for administration, given that my salary as Executive Officer continued to be paid by the Immigration Department at the existing Public Service rate. I used to joke that I must have been the highest-paid Christian worker in Australian history, promoted from my previous post as the highest-paid photocopier in the country!

---

[59]Revelation 3:8

Fading of Al Grassby

And what of Al Grassby? If I was negotiating an uneasy period of transition he, from the apex of his public career, went into a tailspin. Never again did he hold a statutory office but, to my mortification, ended up a controversialist, the subject of innuendos and insinuations widely believed in the general community, which greatly tarnished his credibility.

Never again was I to see Al Grassby in the flesh, although I have a recent photo of myself standing next to him, with my arm around his bronze shoulder. The life-sized statue stands in the foyer of the ACT Multicultural Centre in the Territory Government's headquarters in Canberra City, whither it had to be moved for its protection following a public outcry on its unveiling in the open forecourt outside. *Sic transit gloria mundi.*

Unproductive year

Regrettably, my period with the Churches Commission on Community Relations was to prove relatively unproductive. It was still the era of a few voices crying in the wilderness and, while State and national Church leaders needed no convincing, rank and file church members throughout Australia were unconvinced at best, mostly uninterested.

The Commission selected a few strategic areas of activity spanning the church/community interface: presentations at Church conferences: a model workshop on promoting community education on multiculturalism among local voluntary agencies; publishing articles in journals and submitting letters to newspapers; and responding to negative publicity. In this regard, I visited Nowra to pursue my letter to the editor of the local newspaper, following the controversial and very public banning of the Aboriginal flag by the town Council, and to consult with the local Aboriginal leadership from the Wreck Bay Community in the Jervis Bay enclave of the ACT nearby.

Also, I was invited to give the keynote address at a one-day conference on community education about multiculturalism convened by the new Anti-Discrimination Board of NSW at my old alma mater.

Kneeling before an Aboriginal

About that time, the ACC appointed its first Aboriginal development officer, to whom I paid my formal respects on a briefing visit to the Sydney HQ. It triggered an intense emotional experience: as I entered his office and he rose to greet me, a crippling surge of remorse welled up within me for all the trauma, dispossession and destruction wreaked on his people by my people. I fell at his feet, overwhelmed, broken, weeping, a priest making atonement for his people's sin but only able to stammer 'Forgive, forgive'. It was my personal epiphany on the road to Damascus, foreshadowing the nation's apology by Prime Minister Kevin Rudd 27 long years later, which Marjorie and I would fly to Canberra to experience and support. Likewise, on that occasion, few were the dry eyes by day's end. But *"O Lord, how long?"*[60]

Encountering the Churches of multicultural Australia

At the biennial ACC staff conference at Banyo Catholic seminary in Brisbane, followed by its General Assembly, I was able to encounter the leaders and animators of the national ecumenical movement, impressive figures covering a range of theologies – but with a liberal rather than literal bent. What struck me was that the evangelical wing of the Church (perhaps the most publicly conspicuous and active) seemed to be absent. Indeed, whole denominations were absent from the list of affiliated Churches: the Baptists, Presbyterians, Lutherans, Pentecostals on the one hand and the Roman Catholics on the other. But offsetting these was an exotic tapestry of 'migrant' Orthodox Churches which appeared to have virtually no other real presence in the ACC than appearing on the letterhead: Armenian, Antiochian, Coptic, Macedonian, Romanian, Syrian, Ukrainian and Malankara Orthodox Church from India.

On the other hand, the biblical justice orientation of the ACC worship sessions led into staff discussions earthed in a passionate commitment to human liberation and betterment, backed by a sober political nous. Overall it was a broadening experience to gauge the range and depth of Australian church life – a preview of the decades looming. But between those high-ridged contours of sun-dappled days to come would lie some clouded valleys.

---
[60]Psalm 13:1

De-commissioned!

At the end of my stretching exchange year with the ACC I was yanked back into harsh reality by being politely farewelled. To my surprise, the Churches Commission on Community Relations was 'de-commissioned'! With the end of my exchange year with the private sector, the money had run out. *Exeunt* from the Woden Churches Centre. In my *naïveté*, it had never occurred to me that there was no 'career path' in the Australian Council of Churches ensuring employment from year to year, nor stability of structures, but only an annual balancing act of jobs vs resources. Even the top functionaries had little security. Welcome to the real world outside the Public Service!

Returning tail between legs

For the second time, swallowing my pride, early in 1983 I trod the worn path back to the Benjamin Offices. For my pains rewarded with an Acting Class 11 position (still below my Community Relations glory days), I found myself in the Multicultural Affairs Branch of a department renamed by the new Hawke Labor Government *'Immigration, Local Government and Ethnic Affairs' (DILGEA)*, drawing on my knowledge of ethnic mentality and sensibilities, and answerable to a fellow-member of O'Connor Uniting Church. At least a nice symmetry there.

So the year with the ACC had offered a false start towards a new existence outside the Public Service. And a rather embarrassing one, since the over-hyped public launch of the new Commission had set up aspirations that could never be attained for want of resources. But maybe on the other hand it had amounted to something of a glorious failure, in that it did stake a historic claim by the Churches to participate, under God, in the shaping of a nation which repudiated racial superiority and espoused the oneness of humankind. In a country constitutionally marked by the smallness of its founding fathers' vision, perhaps this represented a useful step towards projecting some grander ideals. Probably grand ideals need a God-sanction: *'Under God ...'*

World Council of Churches 7th Assembly

The period conceivably also represented the high-water mark of the ecumenical movement in Australia, although some years later, in 1991, the 7th World Assembly of the World Council of Churches would meet in Canberra on the theme *Come, Holy Spirit, Renew the Whole Creation*. Marjorie and I would drive from Melbourne for the historic congress.

Standing in universal solidarity with the Aborigines in their ongoing plight would be a central focus of the Assembly. A preparatory document published by a group of international Christian experts on indigenous rights had raised the ire of Australian governments by reporting soberly on insights gleaned during their wide tour of Aboriginal situations across Australia. So it would become an historic and emotional moment when white Australian church leaders thronged to kneel at the feet of Aboriginal Christian elders to seek forgiveness, many in tears.

Travelling Australia on a Government Enquiry

Late in 1983, in the cloying security of DILGEA now under the Hawke Labor Government, preparing briefing notes for the Minister's visits to ethnic organisations and pondering ways of making local government councils more aware of the multicultural nature of Australia (even if manifest only by the local name of a dispossessed Aboriginal community!) I was still wrestling with the unfolding mystery of a life beyond tuberculosis, haunted by the rumour of a God who proposes. Of course, it only amounted to inchoate yearnings – but it was a smouldering that wouldn't die down.

Some weeks later, my boss informed me that the Government was about to announce a review of the Fraser Government's lovechild, the Australian Institute of Multicultural Affairs (AIMA) and that my name had been put forward as DILGEA's representative on the review panel. Later I was to learn that it was the panel's Chair, Dr Moss Cass, the Whitlam Government Minister for the Media and the Environment, who had asked the Department to appoint me for my knowledge of the ethnic scene nationwide, and in the interests of securing a genuine grassroots input to the review.

I was exhilarated, not only to become an agent of reform for the new Labor Government nor even to be valued for earlier achievements, but to be back 'on the track' around the ethnic communities so dear to me. Frankly, there was also a sense of poetic justice, of sitting in judgment on a controversial agency created by the same government that had swept away the Community Relations Office, to replace it by office-bound lawyers.

On a recommendation of the Galbally *Report on Migrant Services and Programs*, AIMA had been established in 1979 with the role of undertaking research, disseminating information, preparing educational materials and developing programs of community education, in addition to offering specialist advice to government. It was directed by Petro Georgio, a right-leaning academic sociologist from Melbourne University, who would subsequently become MP for Kooyong and, after the egregious *Tampa* affair, an internal critic of the Howard Government's asylum seeker policy.

Yet somehow by its academic aloofness AIMA had never managed to legitimise itself in the eyes of the broad ethnic communities, nor gain much respect from the public supporters of multiculturalism. It had never become engaged in the daily struggle. This seemed to be related to its management style, as being a personal fiefdom of Petro Georgio's (reminiscent of Al Grassby's *padrone* style – was it something of a Mediterranean syndrome?) Indeed, the Institute had managed to gather a considerable body of critics, many calling for its outright abolition by the new Government and replacement by a community-oriented centre for studies responsive to the ethnic communities' views.

Under the terms of its Act, in the previous two years or so AIMA had instituted an Australia-wide élite body of '100 Members' publicly recognised for their contribution to ethnic life or multicultural development. I was surprised to be named a Member – not from any surfeit of modesty (!) but because Petro Georgio and I were not sympathique to each other since the national conference *'Australia in the Multicultural 80s'* at which he was a speaker.

Twice the Members were summoned to an event, one in their State/Territory groups, and the other to a general convocation in Melbourne, a sort of staged 'junket', a command performance with no democratic process or outcomes at which Frank Galbally QC, the Institute's *éminence grise*, held court. To my surprise, at the Melbourne meeting, I found a cheque for $100 'for expenses' on the dressing table of my elegant bedroom in the Sheraton Hotel, as did all the other Members – in those days a sizeable largesse. It must be acknowledged however that the Members did include a number of outspoken critics (though I was not one, at least not publicly). Of course, it was safer for AIMA to incorporate them than to have them publicly excluded from recognition as the pioneering generation of Australian multiculturalism! The time-honoured device of 'co-opt and silence'.

Meeting a tough deadline

When the Review of AIMA was formally launched in mid-1983, it called for a report to be lodged with Parliament in three months. I was relocated to Melbourne, responsible for organising a nationwide field consultation to gather community views, and answerable to the secretary of the Review Committee. Informally I related more to the members of the Review Committee, mostly noted (and Labor-oriented) multiculturalists already known to me. I found it a most congenial challenge, though dogged by a ticking stopwatch. We worked with a will: the Committee appeared to have a covert mandate on behalf of the ethnic communities to damn the Institute on the grounds of compelling evidence (known in the trade as a *'hatchet job'*.) But, of course, we observed all the proprieties – and that, honourably.

For the duration, I moved into a migrant accommodation flat at West Heidelberg, accessible by the Commonwealth car allocated to me. My colleague in the community consultation process was Mike, a senior officer from the Melbourne Branch of DILGEA and a Greek-Australian. As we got to know each other, we became like blood brothers. He acknowledged me as an 'honorary ethnic', so much were we on the same wave-length. Our task was to locate people and agencies in the migrant communities across Australia who had been involved with AIMA and had some views to express, but we found this easier said than done. A basic finding of the Review was that there was only slight community contact because of the aloof operational style of the Institute with its rarified academic focus.

Nevertheless, we cast the net nationwide, mailing our documents to all the larger migrant bodies identified during my National Groups Survey 10 years earlier, and planning itineraries for the Review Committee to travel the Commonwealth to meet those who responded. Mike and I had the task of travelling ahead, liaising with the Department and arranging the encounters in all the State capitals, plus Darwin and Canberra.

The last few weeks proved tumultuous – inundated by reams of transcripts, truculent performances by the AIMA leaders, often bitter debates about the conclusions to be drawn, and Moss Cass in midnight conclave with political colleagues. The outcome was a two-volume report: an executive summary of the Committee's recommendations based on the evidence gathered nationwide in the field, and a second larger volume publishing the wide-ranging expert papers commissioned for the Review on what a revised Institute might look like.

Miraculously the Report got tabled on time in Parliament, duly calling for the Institute to be democratised, made accessible and accountable to the people, and restructured. This launched a tirade of opposition, orchestrated by Petro Georgio and godfather Frank Galbally, and the demand for a dissenting report. Magnanimously, the Government acquiesced. Lacking the resources of our Review team, it proved to be a thin and self-serving document but justice was seen to be done. Parliament received the two reports, commending them to the Government's tender mercies.

Several months later, the upshot of the Government's consideration was to sanction the restructuring of the Institute, under new management and with a revised charter, continuing in its historic, renovated colonial mansion on Queen Street, Melbourne. Of course, by then I had returned to Canberra and resumed our family life, though I had also been able to spend some weekends at home during the nationwide travelling circus.

A strategic new opening

Events in my professional life now continued to unfold at a bewildering pace. During the low period of January 1984, with the DILGEA offices in Belconnen half deserted and little urgency to address any of the half-baked development projects on hand, I received a phone call from the Director of the Migrants and Refugees Department of the Melbourne Anglican Diocese. She brought to my attention a grant of $70,000 made to the Victorian Council of Churches by the State Government under the 150th Anniversary of Victoria celebrations, enabling the employment of a Research Officer for two years to undertake an innovative project among the Member Churches: promoting a multicultural approach in their *programs for training their clergy*. She invited me to apply.

Could this be the decisive step towards the wisps of my dreams of full-time Christian service, or just another distraction appealing to a rolling stone? No way of resolving it other than by applying for the post, so a further trip to Melbourne – what was it now about Melbourne? The interview proved a mere formality: if I wanted the job, it was mine. Indecision not resolved.

Agonising indecision

I felt mugged by my fatal ambivalence. In one of the social developers' 'workshops' attended years earlier (actually a sort of 'Encounter Group') a doughty woman antagonist had once hurled at me, *"God, you're the most ambivalent person I've ever met!"* Touché. Now back in Canberra, in the wee hours of a climactic summer night I agonised, sleepless.

The stakes were high: if I accepted, it meant uprooting the family from their home in the city we had all come to love, and sundering the web of relationships we all lived within. Moss Street friends and boys' playmates, O'Connor church, our home fellowship group, Marjorie's social worker job at ACT Health Services, my colleagues and fellow-strugglers for multiculturalism – ah, but this project implied pushing a new frontier for that dream among the Churches. And in any case we were on the cusp of becoming a one-child family. Sarah-Jane had left home to go her own way, Christopher was off to university, having completed a gap year living in a Christian community in Adelaide and doing introductory theology study at the Uniting Church seminary, and Nicholas had gone to the United States under a student exchange scheme, *Youth for Understanding*. With David moving into year 9 at O'Connor Christian School it could be a relatively opportune time to make a radical change – and only for two years....

Desperate, sneaking out of bed that sleepless summer night, I crept out the front door and down the steep driveway, meandering aimlessly down Moss Street. By now quite frantic, and groping for strength, I took to hugging the gumtrees along the footpath, muttering in distress, "I can't leave. I can't! But I can't stay! ... God help me!" How much later I don't know, a car pulled up alongside and Marjorie invited me to get in and be taken home. If I really wanted to go she and David would come with me. It could be an adventure. Crisis resolved.

Confirmed from above

Impresssively now the arrangements fell into place: two years' Leave without Pay granted from DILGEA, a residential Christian community based at O'Connor Uniting Church to shift into our house, an agreement struck with the Victorian Council of Churches on the proportions of the project grant to be allocated to my remuneration (representing a salary cut of about fifty per cent) and to administration, and the acceptance of my request to devote three months of the twenty-four to an international study tour on the interface between multiculturalism and theological education overseas. And in particular, somewhere to live in Melbourne.

Our move south would correspond with the opening of the academic year. By now Chris had decided to study at La Trobe University rather than the ANU, so I planned to enrol him when I went down to locate a home for the family. Arrived in Melbourne, and then driving a car generously made available, I made for La Trobe University.

As I was crossing the Agora I was hailed by a stumpy little guy, *"Good God, Jim Houston! What are you doing here?"* I hadn't seen Tommy W. since we left Canterbury High in 1949, though I remember he was joining the Air Force. (He'd become Leader of the City of Melbourne Air Squadron, and was now retired). When I explained my purpose in Melbourne, he took me to his base as the university's staff housing officer. He opened a card index box (in those pre-computer days) and drew out the first card. A tenant was sought for the twenty-four months exactly corresponding to our needs by an elderly couple at Eltham, living on 'acres' with a mudbrick villa and a log cabin fitted out as an office. When I phoned, I noticed the lady's French accent. She invited me over *immédiatement*. They turned out to be a retired diplomatic couple who segued every two years between his charming lair at Eltham and her château in France. To our mutual satisfaction we did the instant deal – in French! *Mission accomplie*. Any fears and uncertainties about the future could be laid aside. As the sheep gate swung open we could all move forward with confidence into the new fold so graciously offered to us.

The Lord Almighty is with us; the God of Jacob (James) is our refuge. (Psalm 46:7)

Into the future – with trembling faith!

A few weeks later, as the Falcon pulled away from our drive, our hearts were heavy – yet expectant. Moss Street had been good to us. Friendships for all in a safe, neighbourly environment, the deep satisfaction of wresting a garden from a rock-strewn wilderness commanding views to two distant horizons. Above all, a love-nest on return from my ceaseless journeyings. Could it all now be at an end, or was this another family holiday, albeit a longer, working one?

This time however there was a new consideration: was God himself opening the door, murmuring 'This is the way. Walk in it'?[61] As in the scriptural motif of Abraham going forth in faith, not knowing where he was going? Or Moses leading Israel out of the secure hell of Egyptian slavery? And Joshua tremulously entering the promised land? If this were really true, would not God go with us too? Of course, none of them drove themselves to their destiny in a Ford Falcon. Melbourne and destiny, here we come! *"The journey of a thousand miles begins with a single step"*.

Farewell, Canberra! Theatre of our dreams, focus of our hopes, nurturer of our spirits. We've marked your growth from a cluster of prim suburbs, yet swelling with noble purpose, into a worthy national

---

[61]Isaiah 30:21

capital replete with the accoutrements of status and power, a budding metropolis. How we've loved your purple horizons dusted with wintry snow, your rolling grasslands and wooded hills, the sharpness of your distant vistas. And the mellifluous Molonglo, your friendly little stream, welling into a grand lake rimmed with monuments before escaping between the pines and the gumtrees. We'll miss the rhythm of your seasons: your riot of spring, your mellow autumns, your icy mornings portending a golden winter noontide. We thank you for the friends you brought us, the challenges of work, the return on our labours, the visions of God's new world a-birthing.

And above all, the promise of an eternal future in divine glory with our companions of the Way. How shall we forget you or fail to love you? Though we part we do not betray you, for you remain forever within our hearts. And maybe… yes… maybe, we shall return. But that rests in wiser hands.[62]

That late summer evening and through a long night, alternating at the wheel, we drove our Falcon to Melbourne, its four occupants (including Angus, our faithful black Labrador – doped to the eyeballs for the long trip.) Memorable still to recall him zig-zagging drunkenly through a park on a toilet break. Our task was to beat 'Tommy Tortoise's' purple pantechnicon to Eltham with its load of most of our furniture and household effects, and we managed this by a couple of hours. Our formal advent in Napoleon Street, then an urbanised dirt track, was marked by the high van carrying away the power cable to our neighbour's house.

---

[62]Strangely, in retrospect, my natural ambivalence about leaving (though the move was clearly affirmed) seems to have been marked since by recurrent dreams about continuing to live in our house – clandestinely, while the new owners are absent – though worryingly likely to return at any moment!

CHAPTER 33: Sorting out ITEMS

Eltham turned out to be a special place, an early rural village in rolling wooded country close to where Diamond Creek runs into the Yarra, 25 kilometres north-east of Melbourne, on Wurundjeri land whose native name is resurrected as Nillumbik Shire. It stakes a claim to be the green capital of Victoria, and certainly has some strong credentials.

Home among the gumtrees

A mudbrick villa, the house was sited near the Napoleon Street frontage of our two-acre block featuring mature conifers. Inside, the provincial French furniture and farmhouse kitchen made a self-conscious statement, proudly 1930s. Fifty metres away in the grounds stood a real log cabin of untrimmed radiata pine, crammed with shelves of books in English and French, and with a large old desk and a central wood-burning stove. A perfect gentleman's retreat.

The ITEMS Project

Working on my project, I was to report monthly to the Commission on Community and Race Relations of the Victorian Council of Churches, the State ecumenical body which, unlike its federal parent, included the Catholic Church. While really an employee, I was permitted to work from home. The VCC General Secretary, Sister Mary-Lou Moorhead, was squarely behind the project, as was Alan Matheson, then co-leader of the Ecumenical Migration Centre in Fitzroy, nursery of Australian multiculturalism. After the Public Service, I welcomed the novel ambiance of co-operation and goodwill, while enjoying professional freedom to develop the project as I saw fit.

Reflecting the guidelines endorsed by the Victorian Government's 150th Anniversary Board, I proposed the minting of the acronym *ITEMS* for my project, to signify *'Intercultural Theological Education in a Multi-faith Society'*. There were five emphases to be pursued:

- fostering a greater awareness in the theological arena and among the Churches of the new factor of *cultural diversity* transforming the context for urban ministry and mission;
- devising and implementing an accredited tertiary-level *course in applied cross-cultural theology* in a Melbourne ministry-training seminary;
- compiling, preparing and publishing a *textbook of cross-cultural theology and mission;*
- encouraging in the Churches an *understanding of other world Faiths and nurturing inter-faith contact and dialogue;*
- developing and publishing *multicultural study materials* for small-group use in Churches.

As an outsider, my first task was to get a feel for the principal denominations in whose vested interests I would be working. The Uniting Church I knew well – or so I thought. The Melbourne Anglican Diocese offered a tapestry of churchmanship, with the balance somewhat tilting towards the Anglo-Catholic expression. Of the Roman Catholic Church, through my studies in Latin and continental languages I had gleaned a modicum of understanding, updated by face-to-face encounter with Catholic charismatics in Canberra. But what of the Churches of Christ, the Salvation Army, the Quakers (Society of Friends) – not to mention the gaggle of ethnic Orthodox Churches, e.g. Greek, Romanian, Coptic? I had to shape something universally acceptable. The task looked more daunting than I had reckoned on, especially when I met the church leaders with their theological doctorates, while I could cite my NSW Methodist Local Preachers' qualification. Gulp!

On the other hand, I had not been selected for the task on any ground other than my assumed capacity for expressing the reality of multiculturalism to church theological educators. Of that I felt confident, perhaps brashly so. The challenge then was not only to plead the cause with the clergy educators themselves but also with the ultimate policy makers in the Churches' leadership. How could I know anything about the factors influencing the minds of church leaders? Yet was this not precisely what Al Grassby had advocated for years with professionals like medicos and lawyers and headmasters and broadcasters? Courage, my lad, in the face of prudence that would cry, *'Desist'*. Just do it!

Life-changing encounter

Early on I made an appointment to meet the Anglican Archbishop of Melbourne, Most Rev. Dr David Penman. I would start with him for several reasons: though only recently installed, he had already become the media's 'go-to man' for his accessibility on Christian social issues. He was knowledgeable and affable, with a PhD in Islamic Studies from Islamabad, Pakistan's capital, and prior experience as a Church Missionary Society worker in Lebanon. His background as an Arabic speaker with a love for the culture, and his experience in training clergy suggested that he could well be open to my approach. Moreover, in his public utterances he was already tackling intransigent community issues, among them racial prejudice and cultural diversity.

The encounter was literally life-changing. As I made my initial exposition he was all nods and when I finished he stood up before me, saying, "This is a really strategic project, and timely. It's high time all the Churches realised that Australian society is utterly different from the days when clergy training curricula were devised. I can give you an unqualified assurance that this Diocese will collaborate in every possible way. So, let's get down to business." Gobsmacked would be too anaemic a term to describe my reaction.

We talked of the unique situation of the Diocese with its two official seminaries, Trinity College with its traditional Anglo-Catholic orientation and Ridley College, the evangelical foundation. The differing curricula of both needed revision. Why didn't I draft a new subject, perhaps to be made compulsory at both, and requiring practical work in some migrant setting? We talked on and he offered his personal assistance in any way I needed to get the message across to Melbourne Anglican leaders. He asked me to keep him posted.

Then as we were winding up, we stood together and he put his arm around my shoulder and prayed for the success of the project and for me. At that instant, my heart was won. We had already decided to throw our lot in with the local Anglicans at St Margaret's Eltham rather than with the Uniting Church. After all, I had come to Melbourne to be an ecumenical worker. What better place to start than in our own churchgoing? The deal was clinched a couple of days later when the Vicar turned up at Napoleon Street to welcome us. For the duration, we were Anglicans.

The challenge of building awareness

Where to start? Why not with the most concrete of the four challenges of my task, if conceivably the most exacting: the cross-cultural theology course? The first step would be to produce a rationale and outline of the whole ITEMS project. Using the resources of the ecumenical movement, then in its heyday, we had 10,000 copies of an introductory brochure printed with the masthead *So many kinds of Australians. Who will minister the grace of God for their needs?* and distributed around local churches all over Melbourne.

My approach to the Heads of Churches bore fruit: to my joy all agreed to appear on the ITEMS letterhead as a Reference Panel. The fifteen names in the margin spanned eight Churches and also included a Jewish and a Buddhist leader. I followed up with a letter to State Government House and was rapt when the Governor, Sir Brian Murray, agreed to become the Patron of the project. The Office of the Labor Premier, John Cain, also expressed interest, albeit more low-key. Maybe the *seminary principals* might deign to consider the Project's claims?

Autumn 1984 found me pursuing a busy round of appointments at all the city's theological colleges and seminaries. But beyond creating goodwill, the challenge was to find an opening for an experimental course in theological study. Though theologians may be intellectually adventurous, open to revisiting traditional biblical insights, few at the time had shown much interest in the changing cultural context of the Church, and certainly not to the point of incorporating any reference to it in their courses. Though their towers are of stone rather than ivory, theological colleges scarcely resonate with the pulse of an ever-changing world. Indeed, some Anglican parishes turned out to be veritable time capsules of an Australia still unmarked by mass migration.

An academic innovation

Back in the log cabin, as our first Melbourne winter drew on, cosily ensconced by the wood-burning stove, I was drafting the substance of a course to open up the issues now confronting the Australian Church through its location within a pluralistic and multicultural society. In my view, the initial challenge facing students would be to develop a genuinely theological understanding of culture, and gain insights into:

- the intrinsic links between religion and culture: discerning the *'pearl of great price'* from the oyster shell of culture
- making caring contact with people from different cultures
- should the Churches speak out more? On what issues? Exploitation of migrant workers? Racism?
- identifying with the Aboriginal people's struggle
- encountering neighbours from other Faiths
- the national policy of multiculturalism & towards an Australian theology of multiculturalism: where does the Church figure?

To have integrity and humanity, the course would also need to include frankly the impact of European settlement on the Aborigines, and their place in Australian society – and in the national psyche – historically and until today.

The distinctive approach of the course would be its practical as well as its theoretical orientation. Instead of academic essay-writing, each student would gain practical exposure to everyday life within an ethnic community, devising how they could make a useful contribution in a specific situation while becoming acquainted with the realities of migrant life on the ground. Their report on this field placement would be assessed towards their final credit.

The other vital dimension of the course was the specifically theological perspective interwoven throughout, with particular attention to:

- understanding and ministering to people of ethnic backgrounds
- evangelism and nurture across cultures
- relating to ethnic congregations, within or separate from Anglo churches

- educating an Anglo congregation to understand migrant issues
- approaches to dialogue with people of other Faiths.

Class time: 2 hours weekly, plus field research and a placement in a minority group setting, concluded with a personal statement of any growth in attitudes and understanding over the period of the course.

Within the above dual framework, the specific content of the two-semester course would be:

First Semester

Basic concepts: culture, ethnicity, social class, the social and economic situation of ethnic minorities

The migrant family, (un)employment, health and housing, welfare services, the law

Language issues: learning English, maintaining home languages

Experiences of racism and discrimination, and the anti-discrimination legislation

Second Semester

Urban mission, Church welfare agencies

Orthodox Churches, inter-Faith contacts: Judaism, Islam

Mission across cultures: parish education, ethnic congregations

Aboriginal theology

Contextual theology and missiology: overseas and ecumenical initiatives

Of course, I was not competent to teach such a course – even in academia who could be? It would require both in-depth community experience across a wide range of settings, as well as a profound knowledge of the social sciences. But beyond that, there was need for a 'feel' for ethnic community perspectives: the outsiders' view of our society. Hence a unique feature of the course was the exposure, in class week by week, to established experts and community members sharing their insights, supplemented by field observations and audio-visual presentations. My task would be to initiate, launch and co-ordinate the course, making the contacts, providing the speakers, and arranging the field observations and – where I had real competence in areas of my personal experience – also by lecturing.

Such was the grand vision for the first pioneering course anywhere in Australia. But who would accredit the course, and which theological college would offer it? Ideally it would need to be held in an ecumenically-oriented institute so that students from more than one Church could take it as part of their studies.

Challenging the theological establishment

But these questions were not my responsibility to resolve. This was where the Melbourne ecumenical community offered its enthusiastic support for the project. The accreditation agency would be the Melbourne College of Divinity (an institution, not a building), jointly linked with the Anglican, Roman Catholic, Uniting, and Baptist Churches, the Churches of Christ and the Salvation Army, which since 1910 had awarded theology degrees obtained by study in its 'Affiliated Teaching Institutions'. There were several of these, some denominational, others inter-denominational or ecumenical. One of the latter was the Evangelical Theological Association, preparing students for ministry in both the Baptist Church and the Churches of Christ. It was a huge step forward when Dr Bill Tabernee, Principal of the Churches of Christ College, offered his seminary's hospitality for a trial teaching of the course in the 1985 academic year. It would be open to students doing a degree through any of the other affiliated teaching institutions of the Melbourne College of Theology to choose it as one of their subjects. It would be entitled *'The Strangers within our Gates: the Church and Australia's Multicultural Society'*.

I was exhilarated by the foretaste of success. Not only was there now a new and innovative course outlined in a theological college's *Calendar* for the coming year, but new horizons were opening up for me, beckoning me towards the rest of my life. We had weathered the transition to Melbourne. In a stimulating new metropolis, I had found more worlds to conquer, inheriting a ready-made network of Christian colleagues while still linked with my old secular multicultural network. And exploring the relevance of each to the other: 'the Christian response to Australian multiculturalism' sounded a stimulating project.

The icing on the cake

By September 1984, with the most demanding of the four ITEMS tasks bedded down until the College's first term opened next March, and with the other tasks yet to be broached, it seemed the time to plan the round-the-world study tour agreed upon with the VCC.

In Europe, with its guestworker economies booming, new initiatives in 'community relations' were being implemented in several countries between host and immigrant populations. There were ecumenical Christian and inter-faith initiatives to observe in the UK, Germany and in France. In the USA, immigration over the previous century had created the most multicultural society on earth. Some of the better-known theological seminaries, and also projects with Native Americans ('Red Indians') were strategic, and on the homeward leg, the Tao Fong Shan inter-faith study centre in Hong Kong.

From friends in the ethnic scene I had gathered a sheaf of contacts and invitations in Europe, while my ecumenical colleagues recommended many Christian agencies for observations and discussions. In all I sent some 60 letters abroad and planned my itinerary from the responses received, though my letters to the Vatican elicited courteous replies but no official consultations.

CHAPTER 34: Girdling the Globe

From my genesis as a romantic, dreaming of what the world offered beyond the heads of Botany Bay, I now felt confident and linguistically equipped, with my German and French and five years' experience of Europe, supplemented by courses in Italian and Modern Greek (not to speak of Russian and Turkish). Though versed in the fields of migration and multiculturalism, in matters theological I was a raw amateur – in any language. But that spring afternoon, as the jumbo-jet lumbered down the runway to leap off into the north-western skies, the lure of the far horizon was again working its magic.

In my pocket a round-the-world air ticket and rail passes for Britain and the Continent, together with an itinerary covering the old world and the new. To say the least, it was intensive, admitting no built-in rest days and also thrifty, accommodation all in non-tourist venues. It would certainly call for concentration!

But arguably the three months that followed would offer the most richly concentrated days of my life, an avalanche of experiential learning tinged with sheer enjoyment – and with an amazing bonus at the end.

Lands of faith

First and most powerful emotional experience: traversing the diminutive Holy Land. Tel Aviv, Jerusalem, the *Via Dolorosa* – did Jesus' feet touch these actual paving stones? Bethlehem, Sea of Galilee, and in Nazareth guest of an Arab Anglican canon who had once stood in vain for the Israeli Knesset. Intransigent, these antagonists, irreconcilably sundered by faith, ethnicity, history, politics. Oppressors and oppressed locked into a devil's dance of mutual resentment and hatred, there in the world's most volatile flashpoint, tendering no hint of resolution this side of the return of the Jewish Messiah to be hailed Universal Lord. Till then, God help them all!

Then the dramatic contrast of the Greek Orthodox 'Holy Mountain' of Mt Athos, haven of spiritual peace untouched by the Renaissance, its 20 mediaeval monasteries clinging to the rugged coasts of a thin peninsula of virgin forests where bison are still rumoured to roam. Arranged by the Greek Bishop of Melbourne encountered in my national groups survey, I was monk for a day. I was a failure. I found it positively alien: joyfully praising God at four o'clock in the morning? And living on olives, beans, nuts and wine? No one spoke any English, though I did meet a non-communicative German novice, and my Modern Greek wasn't up to it. Mercifully I came across another visitor, an American, the Athens correspondent of the *New York Times*, who took pity on me by offering human contact. An altogether exotic experience! How pathetically we cling to the familiar and shrink from the challenge of the unknown – or even the universal!

Breaching the Iron Curtain

Back to the familiar in a Sunday service with an evangelical Greek church in Thessaloniki, and then into the communist world beyond the Iron Curtain, in a Macedonian *Methodist* village (Melbourne inter-church contacts again) from where I took a sack of red peppers to a relative in Skopje, then entrained for Belgrade on the grey Danube, then *Yugoslav* but now Serbian capital.

The next goal was Bucharest, as guest of the Patriarchate of the Romanian Orthodox Church for a six-day program of celebrity treatment arranged through the Melbourne priest. Squired about by a clever budding bishop with an American doctorate – focused on the Methodist Church! – we were to prove kindred spirits, though spanning many worlds. Beyond a reception at the Patriarchate marking the former national day of St Dimitru (James) and attending Sunday liturgies in city churches, the highlight was to address the faculty of the Orthodox theological school on the church scene in Australia. The diversity and freedom of the Churches in Australia beggared their imagination, as did the concept of a multicultural society. Viewed from eastern Europe in 1984 we must have seemed a weird hybrid, libertarian society utterly beyond comprehension.

In the absence of the capitalistic gloss familiar in the West, Romanians under the ruthless dictator Ceauşescu came across as a down-at-heel society, glum and plodding. But my final night of 'carousing' in the home of a renegade priest (speaking atrocious French) was memorable for its relaxed humanity and irreverent candour about the Communist regime. Farewelled on the night express to Budapest my feeble protest was to bunk down in a *first-class* sleeper.

Routine paranoia

But the night was to become hideous, thanks to a paranoid Communist officialdom. After midnight, our sleep was rudely shattered by grinding of brakes, jolting of wagons, barking of orders, doors wrenched open and slammed shut, demands for papers, passports, visas. Welcome to Hungary, the tourist paradise! And no concessions to non-speakers of Hungarian. A mobile office walked into my sleeping compartment, in the form of a fold-down desk hanging from a uniformed neck, complete with stamps and stamp pads, to which we had to submit our documents for verification: guilty until proven innocent! To me it all seemed outrageous – or a comic opera – but people didn't seem to turn a hair. Just routine.

Despite my brush with Communist rigidity on the train, I found Hungary the most relaxed of the five satellite states of eastern Europe that I traversed. I recall little public indication of heavy-handed authoritarianism.

Hellish transit to freedom

My route wended ever north and westwards, by rail spanning the five satellite states of eastern Europe under communism: from Yugoslavia (semi-independently minded), through Romania, Hungary, Czechoslovakia, and into the German Democratic Republic (East Germany). All variations on the same drab themes: down-at-heel people, in the absence of any religion little sense of human dignity, propaganda signs and flags everywhere but no sense of celebrating anything, and few cars on the streets. And shabbily restored buildings after the wartime destruction, with an occasional site of a splendid historic church marked by neatly stacked piles of numbered stones awaiting resurrection.

To minimise costs, I would prowl the capital cities by day and travel on by overnight sleeper. But in 1984 only foreigners could pass through the Iron Curtain. In the East German overnight train, stopped in no man's land, I was asked by a border guard whether I was hiding anyone under my seat. Obligingly I got down on hands and knees to check: *"Nein. No one there".*

At the West German border, all hell broke loose. If the crossing into Hungary had been a comic opera, this was a full-scale Wagnerian epic, with night turned to day by the blaze of high-powered floodlights. The few international travellers crossing into the West sat for an unconscionable time while German travellers were interrogated by security police, papers checked and re-checked, police dogs led through the carriages, and the under-floor areas checked out from below by soldiers armed with searchlights, scouring all the axles and hiding-places because of the ingenuity of past escapees, several of whom had died in their desperate ploys. Finally, the train lurched into life again (presumably to dislodge anyone not yet detected underneath) and staggered through the invisible curtain.

Only one winner

The instant sense of relaxation was tangible. What was it about Communism that made its public face so harsh, so rude – so paranoid? Why never civil, never 'normal'– let alone humane – totally lacking in respect and the common courtesies? OK, they'd got rid of business with its self-serving greed and manipulative rapaciousness, and freed the people from the class-warfare it implied. But why couldn't Communism then treat people like brothers and sisters or even fellow-citizens with equal rights?

So as crazy as it may sound at this remove, in those Cold War years the contest could be a matter of life or death – for many, quite literally. The stakes were high: two incompatible systems of governance vying for the dominance that only one could achieve by bringing about the demise of the other. No expense was spared, even if it meant misery and deprivation for entire populations. Worse, it ensured the ongoing poverty and despair of the Third World by the squandering of resources that might have transformed their people's existence.

What greater evidence is needed that ours is a fallen world?

At the World Council of Churches

In Geneva at the world parent body of the Victorian Council of Churches I met with the directors of programs on migration, refugees, racism, theological education and non-Christian faiths. It triggered the perception of how unique is our Australian project of building a multicultural society in equal partnership with the ethnic communities, compared to lands where one single issue dominates the scene, e.g. guestworkers in Europe, street-level community relations in the UK, and tensions with Blacks and Hispanics in the USA. So the approach taken by the ITEMS Project was of considerable interest. (Perhaps other countries had never sought to initiate relationships with their 'National Groups' nor adopt a multicultural framework for their national life?) I left laden with specialist theological and social literature for presentation to the VCC library.

Consultations in French and German

In Paris, I attended a meeting of the *Fédération Protestante de France* convened to plan joint action by the Churches against anti-migrant racism. Invited to speak of the Australian experience of racism and our policy of multiculturalism, it was the first time I had ever used the French language for genuine communication on a significant theme. Later I would learn of a joint theological education initiative being considered in the Protestant theological faculty. Again, I brought home a bundle of materials on the struggle to create harmony across the racial/religious divide, especially with the large numbers of Muslims from North Africa.

In Frankfurt, Germany, I was invited to a dinner with two Lutheran pastors involved in Christian anti-racism campaigning, one of whom had just been appointed to a public post akin to Al Grassby's in the State of Hessen. While in Germany I took time out to re-visit Minden, re-living familiar scenes with dear Christian people and after 20 years paying a formal visit to the *Altsprachliches Gymnasium*, warmly received by the three teachers still there from my time, one of them now the Principal. An article in next morning's Minden daily got a couple of things right!

Consultations in England

In London, I met with the ecumenical unit for Racial Awareness of the British Council of Churches, also with the leadership of the Community Relations Committee of the Anglican Bishops' Conference of England and Wales, and with its counterpart in the Methodist Church.

Significantly I was also able to visit the Commission for Racial Equality, the government anti-discrimination agency properly empowered and staffed along the lines of the Whitlam Government's plans thwarted by Malcolm Fraser. Its commitment is to planning and implementing long-term strategies for community education against racism, based on rigorous research focused on rendering society more humane. I felt a poor relation indeed, with so little to report.

And, finally, some time with the Runnymede Trust, an independent think tank undertaking research and analysis at the civil society level. The lack of such a group in Australia leaves the field to economic rationalist and libertarian agencies, and the media and the Churches, endlessly circling over unresolved causes, especially in Aboriginal Australia.

My final visit was in Birmingham, with the remarkable consortium of the Selly Oak Colleges, education and training institutes of a variety of agencies from several different denominations. Over two days I met with leaders of institutes for Christian /Muslim Relations and the Cross-cultural Communications Centre, also visiting the Multi-Faith Resource Centre bringing together leadership from several world Faiths, exploring and sharing each other's perceptions of their community's life in Birmingham. At the close of day, I raised the possibility of the Centre's director, Sister Mary Hall, coming to Melbourne if we invited her under the ITEMS Project.

To the New World and beyond

On a bleak December afternoon, the transatlantic jet bore me aloft over the Irish Sea and the Emerald Isle, across a cloud-wrapped ocean and the desolate snowscapes of Labrador, before touching down at New York's La Guardia Airport. Fairly quivering with excitement, I peered through the cab 'windshield' towards Brooklyn Bridge, as the stunning façade of Manhattan loomed into focus out of the murk – The Big Apple! Home to the planet's most cosmopolitan population – the world's original melting pot – enshrining the very soul of modernity.

The next three nights, though spent in the not-for-profit YMCA hostel, proved to be the most expensive of my worldwide trip. So this was American life, with its high costs and refined tastes, its glitz, its infinite options of food, beverages, creature comforts, attractions and entertainment. Suddenly Australian standards seemed trite and our lack of style embarrassing. Moreover, my inherent parsimony was under constant siege. In 1984 American power and glory were undimmed while we amounted to a slightly upmarket Birmingham, solid enough but tasteless. If the image of London is of tradition and of Paris elegance, there is no missing the New York image: *naked power.*

Overawed by the heightened significance of everything, I reacted by setting a manic pace for myself. First a brief tourist visit to the UN Secretariat because it was close by and because it embodied a vision of internationalism far broader than the mawkish American patriotism on every hand. Then bussing and walking on southwards towards the tip of Manhattan Island marked by the soaring [pre-doomed] twin towers of the World Trade Centre, grossly out of proportion to their neighbours. But the heart-dropping elevator ride to the 107th floor of one of the twin towers rewarded you with a virtual aerial view over the Hudson River and New York Bay with the huge Statue of Liberty and Ellis Island where the immigrants landed in their millions.

But back on the ground (actually under) I was appalled at the graffiti-scrawled Subway, every wall, corridor and train inanely scribbled over – the era of self-expression gone mad. All the signs are bilingual, in English and Spanish. What about all the other languages?

Then 'uptown' to the skyscraper alley of swanky Fifth Avenue and the Avenue of the Americas, with the Empire State Building and the opulent shopping zone. Come Sunday, I worshipped in the immensely dignified Fifth Avenue Presbyterian Church and later the Episcopalian (Anglican) Cathedral of St John the Divine, both full of well-heeled parishioners, with robed choirs, great organists and fine preaching.

But what a relief in the heart of this pulsating ant-heap, to discover Central Park, so huge and natural that you could forget you were in the middle of a world metropolis. Its vast rectangle running no less than four km long and nearly one wide, in the epicentre of New York! I saw my first squirrels, scurrying bushy-tailed among the fallen leaves, and admired beautiful toddlers by the lake shores, and elegant poodles leading gorgeously furred dames along the curving paths.

But I would soon learn that this was not the full story. One night, emerging from a Subway entrance near Wall St to find myself the only survivor of the end of the world, not counting some huddled figures bedding down for a wintry night on flattened-out cardboard boxes, wreathed in clouds of warm steam rising from the Subway gratings beneath. Not a soul stirred. Pretty soon I sensed my vulnerability to a mugging. To avoid two rugged-up men approaching I crossed over and scuttled down another entry point to the Subway.

Then next morning I met with the urban affairs correspondent of the *New York Times*, my mentor from Holy Mt Athos, who drove me across the East River to Brooklyn. I was incredulous: it reminded me of an East Berlin post-war bombsite, with burnt-out tenement houses, shattered glass, boarded up shops, all graffiti-scarred, deserted – and in sight of the opulence of Manhattan just across the river. They had been like that for many years since large-scale urban rioting and, in his view, they might never be rehabilitated, since there is no money in restoring cheap rental housing in a Black ghetto. There's not much scope in America for losers. It was only under Democrat President Roosevelt in the Great Depression of the 1930s that the novel political idea was propounded that Administrations should govern for *all* Americans.

Consultations in the USA

This offered a salutary backgrounding for my consultations across the nation with seminary lecturers grappling with a theology with a place for poor Blacks and struggling Hispanics besides the well-groomed Republicans. But since most of the responses from Americans to my introductory letter had come from other cities, my only visit in New York was to the headquarters of the National Council of Churches of

Christ in the USA[63] near Columbia University. It was the massively funded ecumenical counterpart of our emaciated Australian Council of Churches linking no less than 38 Member Churches, 15 of them 'ethnic', and employing 28 staff members co-ordinating seven program areas.

My host, director of the Program on Racism (Americans are nothing if not kind) received me warmly and outlined for me a plan for visits in cities across the country with noted specialists in the theology of race and inter-group relations. Generously he allowed me to telephone all over the country. As it was Human Rights Day we attended a special service in the chapel, after which we adjourned to lunch with the other program directors, several of whom had visited Australia. Finally, laden with a bundle of relevant documentation, I was ready to fly on but the weather took an unexpected hand, with a shocking drop in temperature and a prodigious snowstorm. At 21 degrees below 0 it was the coldest I had ever endured (and without an overcoat!). All flights out were cancelled but I managed to horn in on a passenger negotiating a minibus ride to Philadelphia, my next destination.

Westminster Theological Seminary was not only a pioneer in urban mission geared to the life of the streets, but it also earthed initiatives in reconciliation across clearly demarcated ethnic neighbourhoods in the decaying inner areas: Blacks, Hispanics, Asians, and poor whites. The noted urban missiologist Harvie Conn was kind enough to spare me a whole morning. A helpful insight: avoid loaded theological terms *('swear-words')* in debates about the 'spiritual Gospel' *vs* the 'social Gospel'. Stick to the great scriptural words of the Faith: the issues are too crucial to be owned by either party. Focus on addressing actual needs of real people.

Next morning to Washington by an early flight. To Quaker House, a peace and disarmament lobby group targeting Congress as well as countering local apartheid: a *majority* of Washington's residents are Black!

---

[63]The member bodies of the National Council of Churches encompass a wide spectrum of American Christianity, representing traditions as varied as Protestant, Orthodox, Evangelical, Anglican, and African-American, historic peace churches and ethnic-language immigrant churches. These include more than 100,000 local congregations with 45 million members.

A black angel?

Inappropriately I landed at Chicago by night and took the elevated railway to the distant University Divinity School. Down at street level I found the suburban area dark and deserted. At once a taxi drew up and the Black driver hailed me, *"Hey, whitey, whaddya doin' here?"* On the way to the University he mentioned that anyone arriving in the Black quarter so late was just asking for trouble. It was the area where the young Barak Obama would become a community worker. Providential protection! Do modern angels drive taxis?

Next morning, I was with SCUPE (Seminary Consortium on Urban Pastoral Education) bridging 12 seminaries from different denominations seeking the shalom of the city by training leadership to *'view the inner city prophetically in all its struggle and pain'* while seeking justice for all, including minorities. More important than correct doctrine (middle class stuff) is to tune in to ordinary people's struggle. We should bring them with us, not keep them under us.

Nevertheless the *'pearl of great price'* is not itself divisible but needs a renewed 'oyster shell' around it: Hispanic worship style, Asian family loyalty, Black preaching – bringing aspects of truth overlooked in our individualistic suburban church life. The model is the Early Church pioneered in multicultural Corinth by the first urban missioner, Paul.

Agonising encounter

My next *leg* was to the Pacific coast at Los Angeles, where at the airport an unguarded moment crept up on me: putting my bag into the boot of a small car I was hit from behind and wedged between the rear bumper and a heavy 'yank tank' whose driver was waving to her arriving guest. I let out a yell and the small car driver let off the handbrake, so that the car edged forward. Though a sharp pain shot up my left leg I somehow sensed it wasn't broken. But neither was it OK.

Driven to the hospital, I encountered the American medical system: reams of paper work to be done despite my pain and my assurances that all costs would be met under my international travel insurance. Ultimately x-rays revealed a snapped posterior cruciate ligament behind my knee. But I had deadlines to meet. No time for the extensive bed rest required. Pumped full of painkillers, I bought the best crutches in aluminium and white leather pending an operation back home, and was driven to my host's, the mother of Brian Coulter, my Ceduna sidekick.

My three program engagements in the West were with two theological seminaries, in Los Angeles and San Francisco and a visit to a Native American reservation in the Arizona desert.

Fuller Theological Seminary in Pasadena, 30km north of LA and accessed by a terrifying six-lane freeway, was justly famed for educating specialists in world mission, including many Australian post-graduates. My contact was with Charles Kraft, a teacher/writer of international repute who had invited me to present a seminar about the ITEMS Project. Screwing up my courage I limped into the seminar room on crutches and (sort of) battled through. At the end, Charles Kraft said to me, "I couldn't bear to look you in the face. Would you let me pray for you?"

Though not a charismatic he prayed fervently and lovingly over me, a complete stranger. Later he told me he had never before prayed for anyone to be healed of an injury. Thanking him warmly I hobbled off to keep my rendez-vous in the desert, needing to be loaded onto a smaller plane by buggy and hoist.

With native Americans

At Phoenix, an amazing city of a million in a terrain drier than Alice Springs, I was met by a remarkable man of Native American and Black ancestry, teaching people's theology in a seminary specialising in training Native Americans for ministry across America. During an hour's drive further into the desert he provided a full backgrounding on the socio-political as well as spiritual situation of 'Red Indians' in the USA today. Despite the redneck culture of Phoenix evoking the all-too-familiar attitudes towards the first peoples, heartening advances had been made on Reservations owned under land rights legislation, with well-functioning community organisations and amenities (and a buoyancy of spirit) far superior to anything in Australia. Many were

Christians who had long since made their accommodation between the Red Indian world view and the Gospel. The elder statesman whose home we visited was a man of immense dignity.

It brought home to me again the terrible human toll that racism has exacted in Australia by beggaring the spirit of the indigenous people. In the USA, they seem if anything to be *resented* rather than *despised* and *rejected*. (Of course, it is the Blacks rather than the Indians who tend to be the racial scapegoats.) Perhaps the greater secularity of Australia dating from our dubious beginnings and the very marginality of early settler life had militated against the advent of such fundamental Christian attitudes as goodwill and respect for all, as equals in God's creation. And it is only in recent decades that an authentic Christian leadership seems to be emerging in many Aboriginal communities[64].

Back in Phoenix we visited the Indian leadership training school, and spent some hours discussing with the principal, a senior man of great discernment, the history and social situation of the Native Americans and appropriate models of theological education. On his shelves were several books on the Aborigines. Indeed, some Aboriginal Christian leaders were planning a study period there. Later we visited a retired director of Native Indian ministry, who had visited Elcho Island to become familiar with the Aboriginal people and their needs. I was given a bundle of documents about Native American ministry training, including one reporting on a lengthy consultation process sponsored by the National Council of Churches called *Goals for the Indian Ministry*.

Healing miracle

Next morning when I touched down in San Francisco further up the Pacific coast a miracle of healing was becoming manifest: the pain of my knee was abating remarkably and I was beginning to wonder whether I even needed the crutches. The San Francisco Theological Seminary was also a mecca for post-graduate Australian clergy. In fact, in my last year with the Community Relations Office in Canberra I had conducted a workshop on racism against Aborigines for a group

---

[64]Since 2010 a national gathering of emerging Aboriginal Christian leaders has been convened each year in Melbourne.

of local clergy doing an external doctorate there. Dr Gene Farlough, an Afro-American, had come over to supervise the students. His visit had led to the launch of an Aboriginal pastorate in Canberra through the fund-raising efforts of his doctoral students and their congregations.

Now with my arrival at the Seminary the wheel had turned full circle: he was my genial host for a productive two-day program. At a meeting with missiology faculty members in the charmingly gabled and turreted Seminary high above the city, I was indulged and blessed with a great deal of documentary material to take home.

On my final afternoon in the USA he drove me to the church he pastored in downmarket Oakland in a depressed Afro community across the Bay. Viewed from the Pacific coast with its Latino tensions this posed the other book-end to the dismal Black ghetto of Brooklyn on the Atlantic seabord. Indeed, several times I was told that by the 1980s, things were worse than before the Civil Rights movement began, because it had proven a failed dream now engendering cynicism.

Consultation in Hong Kong

After the high stimulation of the American program, the last few days of my study tour proved something of an anti-climax. Though interspersed with occasional days of tourism in sites of historic and cultural significance, my tour was bringing me to the brink of exhaustion from the intensity of meeting so many high-powered people, plus the constant alertness of mind and body demanded by the process of travelling alone.

Arriving at the 'Holy Carpenter Guesthouse' in Kowloon run by an Anglican Mission, I thankfully presented my now superfluous crutches to their disability unit. Mobile again on two legs. Healing miracle complete. Back home I never would need that operation.

The final encounter at the Tao Fong Shan Ecumenical Study Centre at Sha Tin first projected that focus on China that has enriched our later years. Its work seeks to build a bridge between the traditional, unadventurous churches of Hong Kong and the robust church emerging in the People's Republic of China, culturally authentic, committed to living simultaneously in two worlds, with all the tensions entailed.

Global study tour – gratis!

Providentially, the kerbside encounter at LAX airport opened the door to legal action against the negligent driver of the yank tank. Not that I would have thought of launching it. But my brother Max on one of his trans-Pacific flights 'happened' to be sitting next to a lawyer from LA who specialised in damages claims: *'lose the case, no charge; win the case, keep a quarter of the proceeds'*. I made contact with him, supplying all necessary documentation. On the day of the case the other party opted to settle out of court and I wound up receiving $US7,500 – my share of the damages. The total costs of my three-month round-the-world study safari had amounted to $US6,600. So the pain and discomfort endured had produced an overall *profit* of about $A1,000 on the study tour! Thank you, Father, truly *'Your ways are past finding out'!*[65]

The ultimate irony is that thirty years later the projected loss of use of my left knee – anticipated in the Melbourne orthopaedic surgeon's report clinching the case – has never transpired! Ironically a few months later it would be my *right* knee that would require an arthroscopy and become a handicap in older years, triggered by the exciting event of jumping down a 40cm gutter on an unmade Eltham street!

---

[65] Job 9:10

CHAPTER 35: Charting New Waters

With the mid-point of the ITEMS Project past, it was time to move purposively in grappling with its five tasks. The overall challenge was that, unless the Melbourne theological leadership could re-focus on the wider cultural scene, the major denominations could find themselves left behind in an evolving society. Actually, this prophetic insight was to prove true, as new and often charismatic churches bridging a wider cross-section of the community were already springing up, while many traditional Anglo parishes went into reverse.

It highlighted the cultural captivity of the Protestant Churches associating the Gospel with the status quo, rather than unchaining it to critique and transform every culture. Where were the prophetic voices? And the innovators in urban mission?

Introducing the pioneering course

The ITEMS centrepiece was the experimental course *The Strangers within our Gates: The Church and Australia's Multicultural Society* to be offered in 1985 in the Churches of Christ Theological College. Within theological circles it was arousing some interest but it was vital that it should succeed in order to demonstrate that an innovative pedagogy was possible in the conservative academic climate. To my immense relief enough students chose to enrol to ensure its viability. With no theological qualifications, I was not equipped to teach it (but neither would I be remunerated – it was part of my work commitment). Yet equally unthinkable was it that any theological teacher could cover the range of topics it covered. It amounted to a specialised course in *applied theology*, and I was determined that what it might lack in academic rigour would be more than offset by its social reality and its community authenticity. Certainly, it was no soft option.

Making history

In Australia, there had never been a tertiary course on the interface of church and the multicultural society. So its launch was something of a gala event, with the Theological College Principal present and a veritable spate of messages of goodwill received from the State Governor, the Premier of Victoria (who at my request had also written letters commending the course to the heads of the main denominations), the Minister for Immigration, the Victorian Ethnic Affairs Commission, the Ethnic Communities Council, Archbishop Penman and the Heads of other Churches, and a Jewish Rabbi.

I outlined the approach of the course, particularly the field visits and the challenge of relating to minority group people. The enthusiasm of the 15 students from three denominations was palpable, though perhaps somewhat tempered by the segment in the early weeks on learning Jiwarli, language of the Port Hedland Aboriginal people in which a retired missionary was fluent. It was of course a deliberately disempowering experience meant to convey something of the 'lostness' experienced by many migrants from non-English-speaking countries. We all felt appropriately lost.

Beyond my input in formal lecturing and holding it all together, in virtually every week's two-hour session we would have a visiting speaker offering grassroots experience of minority group life, or analysing authentic Christian responses. We also undertook a number of 'field exposure' visits. I remember a scary class visit to the General Motors engine-block factory, with chips of molten metal flying around, and later relating to migrant shift-bosses. And at the other end of the spectrum, evening lectures on Judaism at the Reform Synagogue and on Islam at the Preston Mosque, besides a lecture on Orthodoxy at the Greek church in North Carlton.

I found the lecturing task congenial, since I had personal experience of what I was teaching rather than it being 'head stuff.' Equally important was it, through exercising rigour in preparation and presentation, to ensure that it was no 'Mickey Mouse' course. As pioneers, the students were committed to proving the value of what they were studying and its relevance to their future ministry. At the end of the first semester their field reports on the face-to-face research projects undertaken within an ethnic or Aboriginal community, plus an account of their own cross-cultural journey, reflected their commitment to personal growth.

In the second semester, besides the formal program of lectures, the students undertook a field placement, e.g. in a public hospital, a Centrelink office or a relevant church location. The completion of the initial course was marked by the screening on SBS– TV of a segment in a news program.

An established future for the Course

Beyond 1985, Trinity College Theological School would offer the course in the following years. I was to lead it there for several years and later at Whitley (Baptist) Theological College. More significantly, in time this groundbreaking course would pioneer a broadening of the cultural focus of theological courses in seminaries in Melbourne and Sydney and around the country. To this time (2012) a version of the original course is still offered in Melbourne by Whitley College (Baptist) and a not dissimilar one at Ridley (Anglican) Theological College. Beyond the day of the 'inspired amateur', this area of theological training would become 'professionalised'.

Producing the theological textbook

Drawing on contacts made from Canberra during the Community Relations years with theologians interested in multiculturalism, we convened an advisory panel to determine topics to be explored and to choose appropriate academics to write the chapters of a book of readings on the interface between the Gospel and our increasingly pluralist community. It would be the first book in Australia to explore religion in the multicultural society.

I sketched out a schema for a book of readings with a dual focus – on theory and praxis – covering ministry issues posed by the presence of the minorities, both ethnic and Aboriginal, and circulated this, suggesting for each author a possible topic to be addressed. The response was immediate and enthusiastic, and the papers were forthwith commissioned. Archbishop David Penman contributed a Preface and I wrote a practical Introduction, and also prepared a 16-page bibliography, 'Guide to Further Reading: the Churches in a Multicultural Society'. We commissioned a book design featuring a stylised oyster shell with Jesus as the Pearl of Great Price.

In 1986 *The Cultured Pearl: Australian Readings in Cross-Cultural Theology and Mission*, of 294pp., was published by the Victorian Council of Churches, with a second edition published in 1988 by the Joint Board of Christian Education of Australia and NZ. We held a book launch at the VCC headquarters in Melbourne and another in Canberra at the Woden Churches Centre. It served as textbook for the ongoing lectures of the ITEMS course. The following year it would gain the award of *Christian Book of the Year* for 1987.

Among the subsequent reviews was one by Douglas Hynd in *Zadok Perspectives*[66] entitled "Towards an Australian Missiology":

"The editor is to be commended for his initiative in conceiving and bringing this volume to publication, the first-ever collection of readings focused on the Australian context for issues in cross- cultural theology and mission. Theological educators in Australia are in Jim Houston's debt for putting together a comprehensive agenda on a range of critical issues for both leaders and theological students. The theology of this volume is certainly public in its orientation. His activist stance seeks social transformation towards a more just and consciously multicultural society: a commitment to the Christian faith as world-transformative."

Another reviewer writes in *Intermesh*:

"The book is the first of its kind to be written by Australians about the Australian experience. It is an outstanding example of a book which can meet many different needs for the reader. It covers both a careful study of cross-cultural theology and a wide range of issues involved in cross-cultural mission. It is a resource which the reader will come back to many times.

The quality and usefulness of the book was recognised by the Australian Christian Literature Society, which awarded

---
[66] No. 17, March 1987

it 'Christian Book of the Year' for 1987. In the Foreword Archbishop David Penman wrote, "Christ, set in the midst of every culture, is himself the pearl, beyond price. He does not take over, or dominate local culture, but fills it with his own life and power. He enriches and interprets. He is implanted and rooted within every culture. He holds in himself the tension between the local and the universal."

Relating to other Faiths

With the approval of the VCC, I wrote to Sister Mary Hall at the Birmingham Multi-Faith Resource Centre, inviting her to be keynote speaker at a seminar to be jointly convened by a representative group from the Melbourne faith communities, funded from the ITEMS budget.

As the outcome of careful planning by a committee of representatives of the Christian, Jewish, Muslim, Buddhist, Hindu, and Sikh faiths, the Seminar *Faith in the Future* was held over a weekend at the Centre for Religions at Monash University, attended by 100 Melbourne religious leaders and their nominated delegations. It also figured as an official initiative for UN International Youth Year.

Its aim was not theological (still less *'imperialistic'*) but practical: to strengthen community solidarity by increasing all the participants' awareness of other people's faith-commitments, and in particular to acquaint Christians with a sound understanding of the other faiths practised in Melbourne, and to counter some historically incorrect stereotypes. It was significant that it was the representatives of non-Christian faiths who proposed that Christians should provide the largest contingent of participants, since they were the 'host faith' – and their divisions only too well recognised from outside!

The program provided for a paper to be presented by each of the six faiths, sharing concerns about the prospects of their children practising the faith when they grew up in the local secular climate. Could we learn anything from each other? In addition, all the faiths were responsible for providing a chairman for a segment of the program, and supplying appropriate food for the closing dinner (respecting the food taboos of all the other faiths!).

Significantly, an evening session was devoted to Aboriginal spirituality and experience, led by the Aboriginal Research Centre at Monash University. All the faith groups joined in honouring the land's first peoples, implying that there can be no respect for religious values in a society where the original cultural group is devalued or oppressed.

By mutual agreement, agendas about proselytising (even if subconscious) were to be excluded. Neither would there be any real dialogue between faiths: that would be for another time and place.

Catholic sister, Dr Mary Hall, director of the Birmingham Multi-Faith Resource Centre was sponsored by the ITEMS Project for her program in Australia, with engagements in Melbourne, Sydney and Perth. She recounted her UK experience of exploring common cause among people of the faiths in the face of racial and religious intolerance, and striving to build citizenship across the divisions, stressing shared action for the common good in real-life community situations in Birmingham.

The first recommendation from the closing session was to set up an interim committee to maintain the momentum from such a creative encounter, and explore ways of stimulating further contacts between the faith communities. I was asked to co-ordinate the process.

The ABC Radio's Division of Religious Programs had recorded the entire proceedings, leading to a later nationwide broadcast.

A sorry saga

But the initiative was to prove ahead of its time: on all sides energy was lacking. Presumably the vision had not arisen from any grassroots aspirations but from my esoteric obligation. Frankly, coming at the time of my own journey into Christian ministry, it was not a priority. Indeed, Archbishop Penman had advised me not to get involved.

Nevertheless, at a large follow-up meeting that I convened in December 1986 the 'Multi-Faith Resource Centre' had been founded on brave dreams, to be led by a representative committee of all the Faiths and my appointment as (unpaid) executive officer. *The Sun* pronounced the initiative as of greater significance than the Pope's recent visit to the Anglican cathedral!

But despite organising a couple of worthwhile occasions and later receiving a large grant from Canberra, the Committee remained dormant. At its first Annual General Meeting, the MFRC was to perish when a ferocious take-over bid (for a *multi-owned* agency) launched by *one* of the Faiths stacking the meeting would succeed – at the price of its demise! It would be all of 30 years before another multi-faith body would arise in Melbourne.

CHAPTER 36:
Journey to Parish Ministry

With the completion of the ITEMS Project, my two years' leave without pay from the Public Service almost spent, and the Eltham house lease running out, an uncertain future was looming. So was it time to slink back to Canberra?

Life-changing prospect

But isn't 'man's extremity God's opportunity'? I received a message from Archbishop David Penman: if I wished to stay on he would like me to work with him.

Wow! My visit to 'Bishopscourt' revealed the Archbishop's enthusiasm for multiculturalism and the wellbeing of minority groups. Being constantly approached by the media on social issues he needed an advisor: would I become his 'minder'? We could live in the flat attached to Bishopscourt when it became available. Once again, the pattern of divine grace shaping my decisive moments by offering prospects unsought!

In the next few weeks, I fulfilled several of his requests, resulting in my preparing briefing notes for his engagements and writing a keynote paper for him to present at a significant public conference.

Then late one night I received a call from him: he was under pressure from critics for recruiting people into significant positions who were 'not even Anglicans'. His reaction was typically feisty: would I mind if he ordained me? Had I heard aright? *Ordained?* I had never known of anybody being ordained at one fell swoop by the church hierarchy – though later in my Church History studies I would learn that in early times it was not at all unusual. Would I come to 'Bishopscourt' to see him?

Next day, pointing out that the founder of the Methodist Church, John Wesley, had lived and died an Anglican, he discussed the need for me to gain some basic understanding of theology by undertaking part-time studies in an Anglican ministry college. My (deferential) reply was that if I were to be ordained I would revel in the opportunity of gaining a proper degree by returning to full-time study. As a late newcomer to the Anglican Church I opted for Trinity College with its rigorous liturgical emphasis, so that I would become more confident in leading worship.

'Bloody idiot!'

When I called the Immigration Department in Canberra and boldly told the pay clerk to work out my entitlements: I was resigning, he expostulated, *"You're a bloody idiot!"* I had served for nineteen and three-quarter years. With 20 years I would be able to claim the full pay-out of my superannuation contributions plus the employer's component, payable either as a lump sum or as a (modest) pension for life. A long silence, before I stammered, "OK, thanks, I'll think about it".

How gracious of God to provide robust advice at the crucial moment. I needed to be shocked out of my manic hyperactivity. Common sense dictated that, with a considerable period likely to elapse before being on a parish payroll and while responsible for maintaining a family through expensive years still to come, proper attention needed to be given to the financial implications: I needed to find *three months'* further work in the Public Service.

Gaining insights for the future

Amazingly, the Archbishop fixed this problem too. A little earlier he had been appointed as the (part-time) Chairman of the newly restructured Australian Institute of Multicultural Affairs – a position publicly advertised. He was able to arrange for my appointment as the researcher to carry out an impending *three-months* study of a Melbourne suburban area known for its high concentration of migrants, for which Broadmeadows had been selected as probably the lowest rated socio-economic area in the whole of Australia.

The core of the task was to become familiar with the physical character, demographic composition, and economic and social issues of the area. In the early 1950s, it had been created on the hard basalt plains by slum-clearances from Collingwood and Abbotsford, plus later arrivals of unskilled workers from southern Europe offered low-quality housing as unskilled labour for the huge Ford plant. Overall the ethnic component made up a third of the population, mainly Turks/Kurds and Arabs – all Muslims, the first ever recruited. Many were rural workers who had come as short-term guestworkers intending to return home ere long but numbers of them, injured in the unfamiliar work environment, were now trapped by the unavailability of medical and social services back home.

The study required a balancing of the insights gathered in the field with the actual services provided by the welfare workers (social workers, community developers, interpreters, teachers, religious leaders) so as to draw objective conclusions based on my professional judgment. Beyond that, the study was concerned with taking the temperature of the inter-group relations in the area. For the young people, in times of economic downturn jobs were scarce so that youth gangs had become a feature, slugging it out on the streets: 'Broady Boys' vs 'Young Turks'. By 1986 it was clear that never again could Australia be a monocultural/monolingual society, yet my overseas study tour had established that no other country could offer a blueprint for Australia.

Even the physical aspect of the district struck me as depressing: bare parks with vandalised trees, graffiti, litter, few houses with lawns or gardens – some featuring abandoned cars. The locals were sullenly aware of the scant regard their suburb commanded in the eyes of Melbournians generally. For me, the 'coat of arms' of Broadmeadows could be a stylised barbed-wire fence draped with plastic bags blowing in the wind – cold in winter and searing in summer because unimpeded by hills, trees or higher buildings.

Researcher's paradise

Wryly, an early finding was that Broadmeadows was arguably the most-researched area of Melbourne! But despite all the penetrating studies, little seemed to have changed on the ground. Perhaps it was too hard. Or too late – the problems had become entrenched, now spilling over into the next generation. Yet the obvious solution had never been applied: adequate funding to meet manifest needs. The core reason was political: Broadmeadows would never elect a conservative MP, so Labor governments had no incentive to woo voters. Politically, the people had nowhere to go: classically disempowered, reminiscent of the Third Word poor.

One of my most insightful interview was with the vicar of the northern of the two Anglican parishes, St Mary Magdalene's (Dallas) whose church was an unprepossessing and unpainted besser-block box with a flat tin roof, set starkly on the bare corner paddock fronting the main truck route from Melbourne to Sydney.

Rediscovering the joy of learning

Our sons were now in tertiary studies: Christopher doing Sociology at La Trobe, Nicholas Arts/Law at Melbourne, and David a TAFE drama course. Sarah-Jane had gone off to England where she would later study TESL, the Teaching of English as a Second Language. We had bought a big timber house at Rosanna, renting our Canberra home to the O'Connor church residential community.

In the second week of first term 1986, belatedly joining the classes at the United Faculty of Theology within Melbourne University, it was to rediscover a half-forgotten world. The theological classrooms were strewn among the men's Colleges; teaching was by scholars from the three contracting Churches of the United Faculty of Theology: Anglican, Uniting and Catholic (Jesuits), all of them teaching the common faith, albeit tinged with their historic perspectives – in itself a paradigm of mind-broadening tolerance in the name of charity. The prevailing spirit was exploratory rather than dogmatic, evocative rather than didactic.

In a time when many retirees, both men and women, were taking up theological study I rated as one of the older students, though not all were seeking ordination. After half a lifetime, some 36 years, I marvelled at the privilege of this second chance of university study so unexpectedly opening before me. Though myself teaching in a theological college I was now focusing on the mainstream disciplines, and to me the lectures were a delight, bringing together and systematising the random strands of knowledge gleaned through a lifetime of hanging around churches. But now being geared towards my new calling, it also posed the challenge of reworking my sense of identity.

Before long the pleasure of being a spectator in the classes, not obligated to write the prescribed essays nor sit the examinations, began to pall: what sort of a minister did I intend to become? A cardboard cut-out? Next term I paid the full fee and saddled up for the long haul of a full Bachelor of Theology degree.

I was determined to play the serious, responsible student, atoning for the mediocre outcomes of my original tertiary studies (OK, I'd had a more important life-agenda then), and hopefully gaining commensurate recognition as well as the acquisition of learning. During the years of my study – a fulltime student only in the first year – I was to gain 'Distinctions' for every essay and in every exam. But to my chagrin never did I crack a 'High Distinction'. My degree covered the core disciplines of New and Old Testaments, Systematic Theology, Christology [who is Christ?], Christian Ethics, Church History and Pastoral Ministry – I was granted an exemption from New Testament Greek because of my earlier classical Greek courses at the ANU.

In particular I enjoyed Church History (at school I had had to drop history for German), covering the interface of Church and world for 2000 years. It was shocking to realise how our Protestant history leaps 1000 years from the Apostles to Martin Luther

In the final years (ultimately of ten!), long since an ordained clergyman, I opted to do some final subjects at Whitley College (Baptist) and the Churches of Christ College. I found the teaching no less rigorous. One Whitley course on American Church History was an eye opener on the historical development of non-conformist church life, and also for the intentional creation in the 1920s of the notion of advertising, a bane that has degraded the dignity of God's world to a market. It was in that era of woolly theological liberalism that the term 'fundamentalist' was coined defensively, simply to mean 'orthodox'.

My graduation as Bachelor of Theology in 1995 would prove a memorable occasion, with the Melbourne family foregathered to witness the public fulfilment of my vow to Archbishop Penman. But that was merely the formal recognition of having finally acquired the academic qualifications undergirding the practice of Christian ministry, some years after my ordination as a servant of the people of God – a task oriented to the heart rather than the head.

Ordained in the Church of God

On Saturday afternoon 29 March 1987 with about 12 other men and half a dozen women, I had been ordained deacon in a packed St Paul's Cathedral. During the study years I had learnt the historical background of 'Church Order', reflecting the apostolic threefold pattern of bishop, priest and deacon, appointed by the laying on of the hands of bishops. But like a good Anglican, at ordination I had to swear 'canonical obedience' to the *Archbishop* and allegiance to the Queen as titular head of the Church. (No one had ever mentioned this bit!) My strongest memory is of the immense weight of their hands on my head and shoulders, kneeling before Archbishop Penman and surrounded by a phalanx of clergy, practically forcing me onto the floor tiles before the altar – doubtless a salutary pose.

Of course, the profound personal significance of the occasion remains forever etched into my consciousness as I willingly took the vow to be set apart for the ministry of the Gospel, though also awed at the significance of the step I was taking, no longer to be merely a church attender but responsible for leading the worship of a congregation (in its Latin origin *'a gathered flock'*) and for the wellbeing of all the parishioners at every stage of life and unto death. It was a public role: henceforth every aspect of one's behaviour and family life had to be blameless as under the microscope of public scrutiny. And above all the holiness of the calling to 'work and speak and think' for God as his minister. *"Who indeed is sufficient for these things?*[67] *I thank God through our Lord Jesus Christ"*.

That early autumnal afternoon became one of life's grand moments, marking a total disjuncture from all my previous activity and ushering in the rest of my life. In a profound sense, my Employer was now the Lord, and the structure of my life became more focused than ever

---

[67] 2 Corinthians 2:16

on a narrowly defined task, *'the cure of souls'*.[68] My Duty Statement became to teach the Faith and to love people into God's Kingdom; my Work Hours became indeterminate: to be available and on call at all times; my Remuneration became the joy and privilege of being involved in so many peoples' lives, together with the appreciation they returned; and the Professional Development program became the Regional Bishop's supervisory group, plus the caring support of my far younger contemporaries in ministry.

It had also been a very public occasion with Anglicans from all over Melbourne present to celebrate its significance for the Church as well as for the new clergy. I was touched that several friends had travelled from far afield for the occasion, including from Canberra and Sydney. The final act saw all the new deacons gathered around the Archbishop on the cathedral steps for official photographs, plus family, friends and parishioners popping off flash bulbs.

In all, a life-renewing experience. Not merely a change of role – I'd been there before. But in a sense, I was returning to the teacher's role, but now of crucial truths of ultimate significance to our human existence. But more profoundly, I was embracing voluntary servanthood, my core identity now a servant of the poor, following hard after Jesus.

Curate of West Coburg

Archbishop Penman had appointed me deacon for two years in the parish of St Alban's West Coburg with St George's Pascoe Vale South, a lower middle-class area in the north of Melbourne, under the tutelage of the Rev. Ron Browning, some 15 years my junior but an experienced vicar with much to teach of Anglican lore. Because the parish lacked the financial resources, I was to serve half-time: Sundays and two weekdays.

My first appointed task was to visit patients identifying as Anglicans in the Sacred Heart private hospital nearby. I went in trepidation, only to find my first patient was a charming member of the congregation! At once she put me at ease. Really, she ministered to me. The hazard was overcome once and for all, and soon I came to find pastoral care

---

[68]From the Latin cura, 'care', cf 'curate'

congenial, so positive were the people, as I got in touch with my own unplumbed wells within.

More daunting initially was the challenge of conducting a worship service under the watchful eye of the Vicar, meticulous in his attention to the High Church proprieties. Though familiar enough with the newish *Prayer Book for Australia* from our two years in the Eltham parish, I had really never stood in front of a congregation other than to preach on one occasion at Eltham – on Aboriginal issues. The Prayer Book needed to become very familiar, but how long would that process take? Wisely Ron Browning took the line of throwing me in at the deep end: on my tentative first Sunday, I concluded the service with the misbegotten exhortation: "Go in peace to love and serve the world" ['the Lord']. No one turned a hair – perhaps they thought I meant to establish my credentials as a Christian socialist.

Gradually a work pattern started to emerge. The day would begin with our saying Morning Prayer together in the vestry, then my list of parishioners to be visited in their homes would be handed over, perhaps with a hospital call or two thrown in. Before every second Sunday, time out would be granted for sermon preparation, and the following Monday for evaluation of my halting efforts.

For me the saving grace was the natural growth of friendship with particular parishioners with whom I discovered common bonds – being of comparable age. Often, I would be invited for lunch and we would talk into the afternoon about the parish: its history, recent vicissitudes and current dreams. Also about their district. I surprised myself just how natural it all came to me, without the stiffness or awkwardness that I might have imagined. I found a good deal of common ground with the people, in background and status not unlike the Punchbowl Methodist members, though I was often surprised at the exaggerated esteem accorded my Anglican orders. (Non-conformist churches are noticeably more egalitarian.)

Early on I was to discover that Christian ministry, more than mere preaching, was mainly about loving people for Jesus' sake. And that began with exploring our common humanity and sharing our hearts' desires as well as our beliefs. In return, you encountered respect and kindness that triggered more joy in self-giving. Unlike relationships in the office or workplace, there was an underlying sense that we belonged to each other because we all belonged to Christ.

As I identified more and more with the parish, it became clear to me that I had no right to be living beyond its bounds. A parish needed its clergy to share the same community life as its people. Traditionally the vicarage was located beside the church. Marjorie agreed at once to my suggestion that we sell our Rosanna home and rent a house in Coburg. The thought was father to the deed, and by mid-year we had sold the house to the first enquirer (for a goodly outcome) and moved into an older weatherboard rented house just off Bell Street.

Because of my unusual story – changing professions in later life, decades older than my vicar, new to Anglicanism but anticipating a special role as advisor to the Archbishop - I had to serve two full years as Curate. The parishioners seemed to welcome the unusual arrangement of an older man learning what they had known since childhood, while modelling being humble and teachable (because so tentative!).

Surprised by joy

Towards the end of 1987 a letter from the Archbishop served notice of my impending ordination to the priesthood. My heart missed a beat – never had I anticipated being other than a deacon for the rest of my working life, a specialist but satisfying support role. And this further ordination involved appointment to be priest in charge of a parish! I had never considered such a prospect. Clearly, I was by no means ready for it. But always being one to let life unfold as it came, it seemed right to go with the flow.

The ordination service in the Cathedral followed the same lines as the deaconing, except that now I understood it more. I shall never forget the choir singing Stainer's beautiful anthem *For God so loved the world* as we took our priestly vows and experienced again the oppressive laying on of hands of Archbishop, Bishops and clergy friends.

My first duty, of conducting the main Parish Eucharist next morning (traditionally a signal occasion) passed off safely. I had finally 'arrived'. In 1988, towards the end of my second year when my long-suffering mentor announced his move to a parish across town, I took on added responsibilities.

As my term at West Coburg was drawing to a close, I was invited to Bishopscourt to discuss with the Archbishop my future area of service, in addition to being available for advising on multicultural matters. In view of my age and experience, he said, he wanted me to go to *'the worst parish in the Diocese'* and teasingly asked me where I thought that might be. After a couple of false responses, he announced, "No, Dallas". Of course – as former Chairman of the Council of the Australian Institute of Multicultural Affairs, he knew of my 1986 study of Broadmeadows and maybe even that I had interviewed the vicar in his house beside the church. Ironically, once during my time at West Coburg I had attended – but out of solidarity – a small gathering of local clergy convened by the vicar of that parish, on *'What can be done about Dallas?"* – a parish bereft of people!

I was to commence ministry at St Mary Magdalene's early in 1989 after taking the holidays due. We headed for the hills, making for Bright in the Victorian 'Alps'. Both 56, in rude health, and rarin' to go, our new life beckoned.

What's in a name?

The six-kilometre drive from Coburg to Dallas was remarkable for bringing about a profound change of identity from the curate to the embryonic vicar: I was farewelled as *Father Hughan* and arrived as *Reverend Jim!* Upon ordination, I had conceived the bold idea of marking my radical new life in ministry by a name-change: swapping my first for my second Christian name. I recalled my namesake in Scripture (Jacob = James) who after his night-long wrestle with the man of God (was it an angel, or even Jesus?) was renamed Israel (= *'who struggles with God'*). So, during the two years' curacy at St Alban's no one knew me as Jim. But ultimately it was to prove too late in life for such a radical change. Beyond the parish no one had ever known me as Hughan. I had never thought of myself as Hughan so the hope of doing so at the age of 56 was just a tad unrealistic: too hard to internalise. In the dismal end to the bold experiment I was stuck with Jim … or was it James?

CHAPTER 37: Sowing in Tears

Those who sow in tears will reap in joy

Could ever a new vicar have arrived with a better prior understanding of his district, having recently studied it full-time for three months? In addition, we brought a lifetime of experience: working class backgrounds transcended by education, professional training, 40 years' involvement in church life, parenting four children, commitment to social justice and my multicultural and multi-faith orientation – besides our failures, our woundedness and our need to look to God.

Noisy induction

On the great night, to our surprise, the little church building was virtually full – mainly with clergy of the area (including from other denominations) and many friends from West Coburg. I was installed by regional bishop, John Stewart, best comedian in the Diocese, preaching an encouraging sermon and commending us to the people of St Mary Magdalene's, all *sixteen* of them – though two were never seen again! It looked as if we needed to try a new approach to ministry....

After meeting the flock over a splendid supper in the hall we repaired to the vicarage. I counted *thirteen* jet aircraft flying literally just over the house, on the eastern approach to Melbourne Airport two miles away as the Boeing flies (and in those days far noisier planes than the more recent ones). No curfew for Melbourne!

The musical counterpoint was made more complex by the incessant flow, by night as by day, of semi-trailers past the church door on the main truck route to Sydney then from the western industrial suburbs, while the *obligato* of the *trio con brio* came in those sublime moments with the rhythmical *basso continuo* of a double-headed freight train half a kilometre long bound for Sydney on the rail lines 250m behind the vicarage. I had always loved the romance of transport – but this was ridiculous!

Afterwards, turning in for the night, I prayed, *"Lord, if you want us to stay here and function, please do something."* My predecessor had bequeathed me a bulging file on his vain representations with the Civil Aviation authorities about the terrible effects on the local community. But these would never be addressed.

After several bad nights, the Lord granted us the miracle of sleeping through the ear-blasting horror! ... or perhaps the planes stopped landing by night?? It was a wonderful reassurance that the God who had brought us here would also be our Shepherd.

Parish history

Later, as we met and talked with our mini-flock we learnt that from its inception the parish had struggled, founded by British migrants plus a few Anglo-Indians and Anglo-Sri Lankans, and even a few Aussies. Nearby at Broadmeadows Army Camp there had been a migrant hostel for newly arriving Brits.

We could detect no hint of celebration, nor that they had anything to offer the area in Christian service, nor even acknowledgment of other churches – let alone community outreach or a prophetic role for a church in one of the country's most marginalised suburbs. So initially, in such a demoralised parish, I had no idea of where to start.

The faithful few simply wanted their weekly Eucharist, providing comfort and security in a changing world, reinforcing their conservative values. Had the church ever challenged their values, opened them to the winds of change, even sounded Jesus' call to be self-giving, adventurous, *risk-taking ...?* Sadly, the church had no story.

Unlike other parishes, it had only ever survived on grants from the Diocese HQ. It appeared that no regard had ever been had to the urban poor or underclass of Broadmeadows, still less to the presence of newish migrants from the wider world. Under these circumstances it might even have been more practical for us to plant a new church with the money.

By contrast the Broadmeadows Uniting Church was structured as a 'Mission' with skilled professionals coming in daily, undergirded by wide publicity around the Melbourne parishes to elicit financial *and prayer* support. But the uninspired Anglican system was to make no concessions to the social character of the area ('one size fits all'), but to expect the heroic vicar to defy all the odds by triumphing single-handedly – sometimes as a celibate.

A further factor was the enormous extent to which the parish area had grown with the continuing expansion of Coolaroo West, leading to the huge new suburb of Meadow Heights and already the first neighbourhoods of the future satellite city of Roxburgh Park. This population doubled that of Mildura – did a lone Anglican clergyman minister single-handedly to Sunraysia?

But that is to overlook Marjorie's role as virtual 'co-vicar', more skilled and certainly harder-working than many a clergyman. She fairly bubbled with creative new ideas. And her social work background conferred people skills as well as impulses for community development – initially the central challenge. Oddly enough, no one ever asked – and we never mentioned – what training or work backgrounds we had both had. Still less my inner urge towards sponsoring cultural diversity. They didn't seem interested enough to ask. So, in the absence of any interest, let alone response, we could only go through the motions on Sundays while prayerfully waiting for God to turn up.

In an almost angry article that I wrote later for a theological publication I wondered "Is the Gospel actually a middle-class message – a thing of words? – as we hear it and transmit it and theologise about it in our Australian cities? If not, why has church life across these poor outer areas never flourished? And why does it flourish in the Bible belt?"

Perforce, our ministry was initially focused on the Fourteen, not all of them regular worshippers. The lack of a critical mass meant that our early worship services were pathetic and embarrassing rather than life-enriching, though we did stress the importance of the after-church fellowship time over a cuppa.

Where to from here? The only expedient was to get to know the gallant few in their home settings. That didn't take long! First visit was to the Vicar's Warden, who lived outside the area (as did the treasurer and the organist. It was the skills of these outsiders that had the place operational at all.). My suggestion of joining her weekly to pray for the parish and its people took her by surprise but she agreed, and this would continue for the next seven years. Another early home visit was to Alan and Gwenda, genuine locals with real social skills who had opted in to bless the area with their commonsense, sharp insights and dedication. Throughout our years in the parish they would be of indispensable support.

One early decision was to dedicate the vicarage to the service of the people, as well as being our home, with Vestry and other church meetings held in the lounge room and (later) teenagers playing on our early-model computer. At different periods, we had Nigel living with us after years of developmental work in Nepal, to help in our ministry as a volunteer and Mary-Rose, an ample Cook Islander, eating us out of house and home.

Aesthetic considerations

From the outset, I was perturbed by the visual impact of the 'church plant'. Though in a residential area of cheap privately-built housing, it could have been a small flat-roofed factory of unpainted concrete blocks, with little indication of church and a vacant block of land beside it, tree-rimmed but not used for anything. But my brainwave of planting it out as a garden came to grief when I borrowed a rotary hoe which broke its tynes as soon as they hit the rocklike, black, summer-baked clay. Welcome to Broadmeadows! Symbolic?

Another early project sought to soften the harsh lines of the blank street façade by planting a dense row of purple-flowered NZ hebes across it, backed by two scarlet-flowering bougainvillas climbing up V-frames on the front wall. The centre of this was highlighted by a large wooden cross. Finally, in the front lawn we planted two trees flanking a heavy-duty wooden sign, varnished and angled both ways with the church's name deeply engraved in yellow letters to address passers-by. I had renamed the church *'St Mary Magdalene's Anglican Church, Dallas-Coolaroo'* since Coolaroo on the other side of the road was far larger and more recent (and privately built) than most of Housing Commission Dallas. I was delighted when a local contact not involved in the parish installed a timed watering system!

First token of hope, since to this point the fourteen local parishioners, none of them involved in the beautification activity, continued to eye us without much interest: clergy came and went, but nothing ever changed. I suppose the jury was still out. After all, they knew we were not from Melbourne but Sydney, a semi-unpardonable sin.

A gracious love-gift

From the outset, I formed a close link with the other Broadmeadows parish of St Michael's near the station and 'town centre'. Praying together weekly I was much encouraged by their more experienced vicar. An early upshot was that a team of his laymen *painted* our whole church, inside and out, as a love-gift! This transformed the 'feel' of the church and its public image. In its new, crisp cream tonings it now positively burst out of its long obscurity as though emerging from shame. Given that civic pride was in such short supply, maybe this might lift the spirits of the mini-congregation.

But the new clean look was then out of kilter with the rubbish and traffic droppings incessantly lying or blowing around the unpaved church carpark, necessitating my regular 'emu-bob' to pick up every can, bottle and scrap of paper. Years afterwards a friendly neighbour would report that the Turkish family opposite had marvelled at the love the *hodja* seemed to lavish on the surrounds of his unlovely building.

Gleams of hope

Gradually the people were thawing out and ... miracle! one or two newcomers were appearing, from a variety of cultural backgrounds. It marked the beginning of transformation in the parish. What brought them?

Initially, the desire of some young parents to have children baptised. Using recommended preparatory material, which included an audio-visual, I made it my business to pay a home visit as soon as I received such a request, in order to ensure that parents understood the implications of baptism, which included providing a spiritual home in a church for raising the child. To my joy, upping the ante like this worked: several families responded positively to the challenge of coming to our worship services for a month as a prerequisite. Several of them stayed on, leading to young families becoming involved in the life of the church! Over the years baptisms were to bring many quality people into the parish. A classical model of church growth.

But this called for a new openness on the part of the 'chosen few'. To break down the *club mentality* seemed essential if the church were to grow as a public institution truly serving its local community. Surprise! With baptisms, enter children into the parish, a phenomenon apparently not seen for years past. The timing was favourable. We had concluded a deal with St Andrew's Hall, training college for the Church Missionary Society, to attach missionary candidates with children to our parish on Sundays for them to gain practical downmarket experience, and so we were able to launch a Sunday School with skilled teachers. Praise be, this was to become the joyful story of the following years.

Devastated!

But in October 1989, a body blow floored me with the all-too-early death of Archbishop David Penman, in only his fifth year of leadership. He had crammed an amazing amount of activity and achievement into his 53 years. At the 2nd World Conference on Evangelism, convened in Manila by the Lausanne Movement where he was presenting the Bible Studies, he had suffered a major heart attack and never regained consciousness[69]

My longer-term dreams lay in ruins. After gaining the necessary parish experience at Dallas I had expected to be appointed to his office as advisor in multicultural and Aboriginal affairs, thus completing

---

[69]His biographer, Alan Nichols, writes:
"David Penman was a strong supporter of multicultural ministry and in 1985 chair of AIMA. His leadership was also crucial in marshalling support for the ordination of women in Melbourne. He continued his commitment to the wider church, in 1988 becoming President of the Australian Council of Churches.
He was an acknowledged world expert in Middle Eastern and Islamic matters. In five years as Archbishop, David Penman changed the definition of church leader, making positive statements on government policies and community attitudes. He was a forthright commentator with a unique capacity to dialogue with multicultural groups in Australia while holding faithfully to his own religious convictions. He offered Jesus Christ to the Australian community in a way that was non-offensive even to people of other religious convictions. His faith was unshakeable, and his essential commitment to ecumenical bridge-building, peacemaking and social justice marked him out most distinctively. His selflessness and tireless dedication led to his premature death at only 53.

my transition from the Public Service to the Church, and offering my knowledge and experience for the Kingdom of God. I mused, *"But God must have other plans. Am I to remain in parish ministry? And at Dallas for the long term?"*

Inspired by David Penman's example, in time I felt genuinely able to say, "So be it, Lord." Now I felt the least I could do to honour the man who had been God's minister to me, recasting my life in a way unimaginable, was to plant an evergreen alder at the church door with a small bronze plaque worded *In loving memory of David Penman, Archbishop of Melbourne 1984-89.* After church one Sunday morning we consecrated the memorial, the costs met from my own pocket.

The beginnings of outreach

As the parish now grew in numbers and in socio-cultural diversity it became more appealing to other newcomers, including some recent arrivals in the area such as Army families. We tried to get them involved in new ways. This opened up prospects of diversifying our ministry beyond simply running worship services.

For example, Friday lunchtimes would see a queue forming outside the Hall door waiting for the free Food Bank distribution. One of our new men would drive his van over to the warehouse to collect the produce and groceries returned from supermarkets because of damaged packaging or approaching 'use-by' date. We had our regular customers, though I doubt that any of them ever came to church. But didn't Jesus say that whatever we did for the least of his brothers and sisters we did for him?

Soon it became quite an operation with a team doing the unpacking and re-parcelling, chatting with the customers, trying to make the supply go round as fairly as possible. Of course, sometimes there were a few charlatans prone to abuse the system but we weren't into playing favourites. Besides, in a stressed community where there were many casualties requiring caring support, it challenged the local Christians to see some of these literally on their church doorstep and, by responding to human needs, to grow into more than 'Sunday Christians'.

Creating links with local churches

From the outset, we had sought to build links with the area's other churches: Baptist, Catholic and Uniting – although our original parishioners seemed unexcited at the prospect.

But in an unchurched local community set within an indifferent if not hostile society, we clergy were all in the same game together. In particular we became close friends with Peter, pastor of the Baptist Church by the Dallas shopping precinct. Established around the same time, how dramatically different from St Mary Magdalene's had been its story, from the beginning responding to community needs: sponsoring the first medical clinic in the new suburb, moving into child care, an Opportunity Shop and a hardware store selling home maintenance materials at cost price. (Actually, it had been planted as a mission outreach by keen Christians moving into the area.)

Peter initiated the Broadmeadows Inter-Church Council which, as well as linking clergy in prayer and mutual support, would later organise some creative worship and outreach projects. The Easter Festivals became a feature of the local scene, bringing Christians together at the Dallas shops to serve free Easter eggs and sizzled halal sausages (free from pork – a love-gift for the Muslims), and with a sunrise (Sonrise) service on Easter morn in Broadmeadows Town Park. Some of our newcomers joined in heartily.

We also related warmly with the Catholic parish. There, in a combined service marking the Week of Prayer for Christian Unity, I actually served the elements of the Holy Communion to Catholics as well as Protestants! We also borrowed their parish hall for our Bush Dances. In the same spirit, one St Mary Magdalene's Day, Fr Barry preached the sermon.

One of Marjorie's latent interests was in liturgical dance. For great occasions, she trained a group of junior girls to present graceful and simple movements evoked by a modern worship song, such as we had been gradually introducing into the services to complement the hymnbook. The colourful dresses were generously lent by a Catholic parish.

Religious education in schools

After a few years we offered to teach Christian Religious Education at our local primary school, Dallas North, where Marjorie had been one of a team teaching an annual course on sex education. But the staff were not very sympathetic to religious teaching, since so few of the pupils (or teachers!) had had any connection whatsoever with any church – though far more children had connections with the Turkish mosque nearby.

When the Principal checked it out with the Education Department, he was told to conduct a survey with Muslim parents before a decision on Christian teaching could be made. When this elicited support for Islamic teaching to be introduced through volunteers, it was agreed we could all make a start – but in each child's case, only after parents had given their written consent.

So, every Tuesday afternoon several classrooms would ring with the rhythmical din of rote learning, with the Koran being chanted back and forth in a language foreign to the Turks (ancient Arabic that no one can speak today), while two small knots of pupils participated in a contemporary approach to Christian education, according to the Agreed Syllabus of all the Churches, using glossy learner's books and teacher's materials prepared by the Council for Christian Education in Schools.

One day, after I had occasion to rebuke an oversized Pacific Islander boy for disruptive behaviour in my class, I found the tyres of my Corona slashed. The Bishop agreed with my claim that it was suffered in the course of my duties and the Diocese paid. One Easter time a Turkish boy (oddly enough in Marjorie's class), on hearing about the Crucifixion, cried out in alarm at the enormity of the claim: *"God can't die!"* What a pity that modern Aussies mostly find the stupendous claim so ho-hum.

Ocker ministry

Besides this community-oriented activity, there was already a small group of women loosely linked with the church meeting weekly in homes for morning coffee, set up by the previous vicar. Nurturing this group, before long Marjorie found some newcomers joining in, so that it too became a point of growth.

It also attracted a desperately needy family consisting of a grossly non-coping mother of several children from serial fathers, whose Housing Ministry home was truly disgusting inside. In fact, there was a strong case to be made for maternal neglect leading to the children being fostered out. But over the years, despite the prodigious love and care invested by Marjorie and others, there was little to show for their labours, though the ragged little girls often came to Sunday School and the mother to church.

Blessing beggars

From time to time, people in crisis would call at the vicarage door begging for money to tide them over an emergency. The Bishop provided a small fund to draw on for this purpose, so on principle we never turned anyone away. Of course, the word would get around and inevitably some go-getters would try their luck. From time to time there would be Aborigines seeking petrol money 'to drive up-country to grandmother's funeral'. On one occasion, I drove to the service station behind a caller and, to his chagrin, filled his tank. The fluid he was craving wasn't motor spirits!

For our original parishioners, the encounter with marginal people was something new: what did that have to do with religion? But for some, for the first time, the experience did bring them face to face with the unmet needs of their area.

What then were the needs of a challenged area like Dallas, and how might a small, under-resourced church go about confronting them? Of course, like all human communities, the basic need is for meaning, security and hope – including beyond this life. So the central task of any church is to present and model God's dream of a Kingdom of forgiveness, love and justice, earthed in Christ, to be both personally experienced and collectively shared. From this should flow action, both through repentance leading to personal renewal and restored relationships, but also practical outcomes geared to blessing and benefiting others – a creative focus based on Jesus' dual commandment to love God and our neighbour.

So when one of the original Fourteen objected, "Jim, you're filling the church with broken-down people!" the only response had to be, *"Wouldn't Jesus?"*

CHAPTER 38: Reaping in Joy

One evening a tall, well-built Aboriginal man and white wife knocked at the vicarage door, not to beg, but to seek pastoral assistance in joining the church community! Touched, we ministered to the need they confessed as they opened their life to Christ, and the next Sunday Phil and Lynne duly showed up with their three girls, twins of about 13 and a four-year-old (affectionately nicknamed *Shithead*). We were awed: was the Lord sovereignly building his church from the truest locals?

Advent of team ministry

On the other hand, after they had come to church for two or three Sundays, he confided to me that with their little formal education they couldn't make much sense of the service. But we had another option up our sleeve. Some time earlier, a bright-looking young couple had turned up at the morning service, joining in heartily and singing the songs with zest. Afterwards, preoccupied with passing the time of day with those leaving the church, I missed having a word with them. When I realised this, I tore out of the building, to see them walking off 100 metres away. White clerical garb streaming out behind me I managed to catch up with them, breathless.

The conversation marked the launch of a ministry relationship with Ian and Ruth which continued while ever we all lived in the area. The couple had a passion for Christian witness and ministry with ordinary working people, though Ian had been a high-school teacher. Later when we shared with them the background of our struggles and prayers for the parish, they agreed to throw their lot in with us. Certainly, they were to prove a godsend to the ministry *of* (though not necessarily *at*) St Mary Mag's.

Launch of a 'house church'

We agreed to launch a small house-church, meeting fortnightly over dinner and rotating between their home in Coolaroo West, the vicarage and Phil and Lynne's place. How we came to revel in these occasions, all of us. They featured typically knockabout humour masking ever deepening relationships of honesty and intimacy, accompanied by good plain Aussie fare (and mountains of it), followed by a simple, practical Bible-teaching segment with frank questions and discussions. There followed prayer for all our concerns, often very practical ones about employment, making ends meet, and raising kids (the five of them always present). In time, another needy family or two joined in. As offbeat as these encounters undoubtedly were, there was also something holy about them. As we honoured each other in his name, Jesus deigned to join us.

But over some years, with moves into new rental housing along the way, Phil's old life was to resurface. Once he was summonsed to appear in court for having committed the heinous crime of relieving a supermarket of a stick of glue. I found it hard to believe that the justice system worked like that, or was it only in the case of Aborigines? Or the poor? Or both? In high dudgeon I went to the hearing in the Broadmeadows Court of Petty Sessions and put in a passionate plea for leniency, observing that Phil had needed the glue to hold together a model of St Mary Magdalene's Church that he was giving me, laboriously made out of matchsticks. The magistrate promptly threw the case out of court with costs awarded against the police. The model church still has pride of place here in my study.

But Phil's next court appearance was for real: it had come to light that for some time past he had been molesting his twin step-daughters, now young teenagers. Possibly this had been the reason for his initial call at the vicarage that first night seeking absolution for his sins. I had taken it very seriously but without knowing the full details. Believing him to be genuinely repentant, we had sought to build him into the support network of the church, a potent factor in his desire and attempts to go straight. But the power of his damaged past was too insistent, and this time there could be no leniency. He was sent to a newly opened prison for sexual offenders at Ararat, segregated from other prisoners for their own safety, where we later visited him in the name of Christ.

CHAPTER 38: Reaping in Joy   349

Monthly community news publication at Cook, ACT

'The Cultured Pearl: Australian Readings in Cross-Cultural Theology & Mission'

With pioneer of multiculturalism, Walter Lippmann (right), and others

Speaking at launch of 'Let's End the Slander' in Ballarat, 1979

With my son David at a Mexican pyramid

The front of our church (St Mary Magdalene's, Dallas-Coolaroo) with new garden and signs and son Nicholas

In the People's Republic of China, with a police officer, 1990

CHAPTER 38: Reaping in Joy 351

Our Golden Wedding 2006

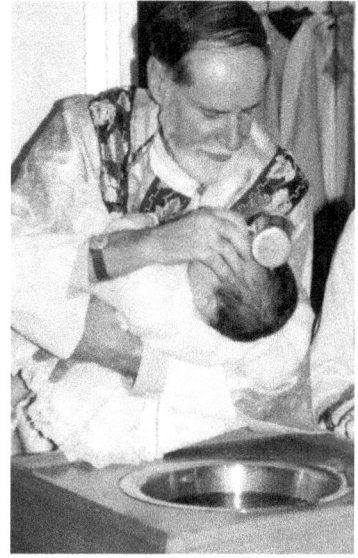
Baptising a baby

Our family home in Canberra overlooking the Molonglo Valley and the Brindabella Ranges

With two leaders of the Chinese unofficial church 1990

Graduation as Bachelor of Theology from Melbourne College of Divinity, Melbourne University

In a silver mine at Broken Hill

At daughter Sarah's graduation, Macquarie University

Easter message to the community passing along the main truck route from Melbourne docks to Sydney

Breaking the old mould

Clearly a structured team ministry was called for in the parish, interweaving varied ages and talents and gifts, working to individuals' strengths, supporting and backing each other, and with permission to experiment, change and adapt, even to reject some of the traditional approaches.

The nearest we could approach to this was to draw on Ian and Ruth's energy and wisdom, supplemented by the St Andrew's Hall missionary trainees, and inviting lay witness teams and clergy from other parishes to visit us occasionally for special Sundays. Twice teams from St Mark's Niddrie conducted 'missions' in our parish, and once the St Andrew's Hall trainees, led by their Principal, conducted a total letterbox-drop of Coolaroo West outlining St Mary Magdalene's range of activities and inviting people to join in our down-to-earth services. Significantly, not one person responded to this scattergun approach!

Green shoots from the baked black clay

Some of our new local families were social casualties. Jane, loud-mouthed mother of three boys by her disabled partner, was quite devoid of social graces, let alone attitudes appropriate in church. Arriving at the service with her herd she was prone to shatter the contemplative peace and quiet by giving voice to quite unprintable remarks made at maximum volume. To be sure (putting it mildly): the older boy was 'behaviourally challenged'. We ministered quite intensively to this family, often visiting in their home. I baptised the baby, Timmy, in their chaotic living-room from a washing-up basin balanced on top of a space heater flanked by two candles. Later her aunt who was a keen (but equally mouthy) Christian from another church threw her lot in with us, joining the home fellowship group. Ian worked in a sheltered workshop nearby. Some years later he was to drown in the Murray, perhaps while having a fit.

Another Ian was utterly challenging – though about him we had no illusions. A notorious identity around the Dallas shops, he had been banned from the Catholic parish for interfering with children in the toilet, and had done time in youth reformatories. He was an epileptic, with a mental age of perhaps ten, though well built, strong – and voluble. To protect the children, we had to supervise him constantly around the church building. One Sunday in the after-church fellowship, as I was talking with him, without warning he suddenly crashed insensible to the ground at my feet, with a great heart-rending crack of a skull against the parquetry floor. I also built quite a close relationship with his father, grateful for a new focus in Ian's life. In our last years, I would take him once a week to the Turkish men's *kahvehane* (coffee house), way out of bounds to non-Turks, but they were aware of his needs and kindly accommodated us.

A multicultural church emerging

Of particular joy to me was the widening cultural diversity of the growing congregation, reflecting the changing identity of Broadmeadows from a place for 'little Aussie battlers' into a multicultural hub. After some years, among our regular parishioners we had (unsurprisingly) some Anglo-Australians, but also English, Scots, Indians and Anglo-Indians, Sri Lankan Burghers and Sinhalese, Germans, an Italian, a Maltese, El Salvadorans, a Vietnamese, a mainland Chinese, a Lebanese, a Maori, Cook Islanders, a Mauritian, an Iranian, a Turk and an Aborigine. Not all were Anglicans by any means, coming also from Catholic, Eastern Orthodox and non-conformist backgrounds but in a new land happy to be worshipping together. A hint of the Kingdom of God, and a heartening one. In God's good plan, I was feeling in my element.

Who would not be touched by the personal stories of such special people as the El Salvadoran family and the lone Iranian?

Mario had been a young teacher in El Salvador when it was hell-bent on staving off a budding people's revolution against the five families who owned the country. One day some Government-paid assassins came to his school and in front of the class in the next room shot the teacher dead, mistaking him for Mario, the union rep. A gentle, peaceable man, he freaked out and fled into the jungle and was later able to emigrate to Australia through a special humanitarian program initiated by a Labor Government, subsequently sponsoring his wife and four little girls to join him. Nominal Catholics, they made no bones about joining St Mary Magdalene's and became among the most faithful worshippers, celebrating by having a fifth girl baby. One day I met another El Salvadoran and invited him to come to our church too, but when I reported this to Mario I was shocked at his vehemence: *"Father, if that guy comes, we're out of here! He was our village headman, strutting around with a revolver in his belt, and he wasn't shooting scrub turkeys!"*

Phillip was an Iranian Christian who had fled his country after Ayatollah Khomeini came to power in the Islamic revolution that overthrew the Shah of Persia in 1979. A lecturer in the Naval Academy, he had always had a Cross on his desk until the day a colleague said to him, *"You'd better get rid of that now, or they'll kill you."* Not doubting it, he fled into the mountains on the Iran-Turkey border and for some years linked up with the Kurdish rebels. Once standing on the skyline, checking the valley below for signs of military operations, his companions on either side of him suddenly slumped to the ground with bullets in them. He fled across Turkey and for some years lived in Istanbul from where he ultimately made his way to Australia with a Turkish wife. He too was traumatised by his experiences, suffering from recurrent nightmares and at times exhibiting really quirky behaviour.

A growing sense of community

After our first few stumbling years, once God began sending us people, a community development prospect loomed as feasible. But moulding people as middle class, or weaning them away from their old frameworks didn't figure among our aims. In fact, the range of new and group-focused activities that arose at St Mary Magdalene's in those years were all *ad hoc* responses to particular situations rather than figuring in a grand design. We simply sought to be available and respond to the people God sent us, with general guidelines in the back of our minds.

Such experiences brought home to us how inappropriate for such an area was the Anglican model of parish ministry, implying a sole and multi-talented vicar available for all, parishioners and the community:

visiting, counselling, caring, preaching, planning and administering while maintaining his equilibrium, kindly, unflappable, a veritable icon of Christ – until he suffers the inevitable burnout and breakdown. (There are said to be 10,000 ex-clergy in Australia.)

Focus on group life

With new personnel resources and a critical mass of parishioners, it was now time to create specialist activities focused on age, gender and interests. The Sunday School was functioning, the Food Bank was blessing some of the hungry in the general community, the house church was nurturing hitherto rank outsiders, the women's morning coffee group of about twelve was offering friendship to some who never came to church, while through the Christian Religious Education program (later also extended to Coolaroo South school) new families were coming into the church.

Of course Marjorie had now come into her own, with multiple talents and aptitudes, full of ideas and as game as Ned Kelly, blessed with a queen-sized heart for building and modelling loving relationships across the parish. She also launched a parish magazine entitled *Mary Mag's Mag* appearing monthly with newsy and inspirational articles, to build up the sense of a parish community. By ourselves we were a team ministry!

There had always been a problem of isolation from public transport. Now that the church had gone down-market we needed to ensure transport for many of the less well-off newcomers living in the far-flung reaches of the parish. Initially Marjorie and/or I (with our two cars) would pick them up for church and drive them home but later we managed to persuade other parishioners to divert from their route to do the same, which helped to integrate the growing congregation of sixty or more.

The well attended Sunday morning worship now took on a new fervour and even joy. I sought to make the preaching more informal and life-related. No longer were we bound to the formal Prayer Book services, incorporating innovations such as singing (instead of saying) the Creed to the tune of a popular song. Mostly we sang songs related to everyday life and faith, though the organist often had to be placated. Sadly, she couldn't adapt and ultimately withdrew. But we never had any instrumentalists (poor people don't learn music).

Youth ministry

In order to nurture young people of secondary-school age we launched a youth group, which took off like a rocket. At its height, it was drawing 40 (mostly quite unchurched) teenagers to the church hall for the Friday evening program! The word had quickly got around the kids in the local community, starved of a forum for meeting outside school. Borrowing the minibus from Broadmeadows Family Services at Glenroy, I would weave my way around the suburbs, picking up and delivering the precious cargo.

The group enjoyed a balanced program of Christian and 'fun' activities, with the girls being trained in liturgical dance by Marjorie. In particular we resonated with a German family with two teenage sons. In my frequent visits to their home I was delighted to have the opportunity to speak about the Gospel with the mother and grandmother in German. From their dormant Lutheran background, soon they all became regular worshippers.

For another boy, we facilitated a transfer to a new school after he was bullied at Upfield High School with its majority of Turkish students, and later collaborated in his gaining a scholarship into Ivanhoe Grammar School. This changed his life forever: he would become the only university graduate from the parish, and that through accessing a *New Zealand* university under more favourable HECS arrangements, where in his Arts degree he would study theology!

But what of the men?

Made possible by the skills of a newcomer to the church who was a chef, the monthly Men's Dinner became something of a legend, bringing a number of outsiders into the parish life. In Tony, I had a loyal offsider, a knock-about bloke who had done time for affray but later became a Christian. I appointed him the *'verger'* (how Anglican! but honorary of course), to look after the property and its facilities, a rouseabout always on hand and willing to try anything. While Ronny officiated in the hall kitchen, heating massive trays of luscious dishes he had cooked at home or brought from work, Tony and I would turn on the heating, and arrange the elegant table setting.

And how appreciated it was! No way any of us would have got such a great feed at home. No wonder numbers climbed into the 20s, each man paying only a token contribution but revelling in the raucous humour of the night, becoming bonded by the experience. We had hit upon a winner. There was always a speaker, sometimes from outside, sometimes one of us with something to share of our background or life experience. Our twin objectives: sharing faith & and building community.

Growth in spirituality

Strangely enough, until this point we had never had any small group specifically focused on stimulating growth in faith through fellowship, Bible study or prayer. Sensing the sluggish spiritual pulse of the place (one token Eucharist on Sundays), I had hesitated to launch a white elephant. But now we judged the time ripe and a Sri Lankan lady was glad to open her home. We used Bible study materials geared to the needs of new believers that encouraged trust in God and sharing with others.

Celebrations

In 1992 St Mary Magdalene's parish celebrated its first glorious quarter-century. We had a number of special events but also saw steady growth around that period. People were simply turning up, some from baptismal obligations, some moving into the area (the new suburb of Meadow Heights was growing apace), still others from my contacts within the multicultural community as I moved around the Broadmeadows suburbs, always backed up by continuing home visitation. I developed the conviction that this was the *sine qua non* of effective parish ministry, as rarely as it seems to be done now in more upmarket parishes. Of course, much of it had to be done in the evenings.

Now after early years of struggle, the parish was starting to embrace the central task of the Church: to model God's dream of a Kingdom of forgiveness, love and justice, earthed in Christ, to be both personally experienced and collectively shared. From this flows the action, both through repentance leading to personal renewal and restored relationships, but also practical outcomes geared to blessing and benefiting others – a creative focus based on Jesus' dual commandment to love God and to love one another.

Today, such a model of God's radical good news is in fact being incarnated in poor communities around the world. I had witnessed some of this in the north American urban mission initiatives. But Dallas too needed to see it and experience its power and opportunities. But the key resource required, even more than what money can buy, is people. Local people to be sought out, welcomed, loved, hopefully touched by the Gospel, integrated into an accepting community, nurtured and built up, and encouraged to serve the Lord within their own situation. A grand vision, demanding both time and workers.

Personal learnings

After our early stumbling years, once God began sending us people, a community development prospect was becoming feasible. But moulding people as middle class, or weaning them away from their old frameworks didn't figure among our aims. The longer-term objectives and outcomes remained in God's safe hands – as assuredly did the power to attempt them. Sensing that I had little aptitude for leadership after the classical model, I sought to major on love: acceptance of people just as they were, respect for their humanity and their personhood, 'love covering a multitude of sins'. At the time, we didn't have all this thought through and tabulated: we simply sought to be available and respond to those God sent us, with general guidelines in the back of our minds.

For example, Ken who had organised the painting of our church moved into our parish, becoming my right-hand man: diligent, supportive, godly, my prayer companion, advisor and best critic. Soon I nominated him and Alan, Chairman of the Vestry, to the Diocese to be licensed as Lay Readers with authority to lead worship services and preach, a role which they both took very seriously. Now occasionally we could take time out for a week or so, confidently leaving them in charge, thus avoiding paying for outside help to be supplied by the Diocese.

But often the innovations seemed to arise spontaneously, as if their time had come. Of course, they amounted to gracious answers to the regular, ongoing prayer that undergirded the parish and its people. Rev. Rick and his wife Jessica, originally from Hong Kong, offered to help us between parish placements. So, for some months I had a reliable Associate Priest sharing the Sunday duties of leadership and preaching, and being a sounding board for our dreams and aspirations. It would lead to a lasting friendship, and finally to that exquisite chapter of our lives represented by our love affair with China.

The glory days

Undoubtedly in St Mary Magdalene's 26-year history these were the glory days. The struggles were now memories, the present was vibrant and the future assured. The proof was in the financial record. I had made it a matter of spiritual principle never to harry parishioners over money: never did I preach a sermon on giving. We never ran a stewardship campaign. (I doubt that the Early Church did either.) It just seemed unacceptable for me to be burdening people almost invariably with incomes lower than ours – indeed a high proportion of them living on Social Security. Instead, with our prayer companions we looked to God to supply our needs, bearing in mind the missionary dictum: *"The work of God, done in God's way, will never lack for God's resources"*.

The only point I ever made about money was made, not to the congregation but to the Vestry, which in the later years agreed to my suggestion to distribute a tithe (10%) of the church's regular income to Christian work *beyond* the parish: the Anglican Board of Mission, the Bush Church Aid Society, the Brotherhood of St Laurence, the Bible Society, etc. To the quite rational objection, "Vicar, this is crazy, we're a poor parish, we need the funds here", I would reply with conviction, *"Look, God can do more with nine-tenths of our income than we can do with ten-tenths!"*

And that was precisely what we experienced: we gave it away, God gave it back – with interest! So much so, that in our last year we were contemplating telling the Diocese to forget their subsidy. (My monthly stipend was received from the Diocese. Marjorie was unpaid.) We had come of age. The poor are more generous than the rich. It's no wonder God has a heart for them.

During our later years, Marjorie had set up not one but two Op Shops, in old Broadmeadows and in Dallas. They had been her love-child, thriving in both dimensions. Several of the voluntary workers with no links to the church enjoyed the fellowship of the busy 'workplace' enhancing the shape and meaning of their lives.

Building community understanding

In order to build wider understanding across the local community, we ran a series of learning sessions in the vicarage about Islam. I did an evening adult-education course to learn Turkish, subsequently tutoring the newly arrived Turkish *hodja* in English in his mosque house (by reading the Psalms together – part of Islamic sacred writings), and explaining Australian multiculturalism through an interpreter. Frequently we rented our parish hall for Turkish women's pre-wedding parties. Occasionally I would call at the (Government-funded) Migrant Resource Centre to maintain contact with the local Migrant Settlement Network of professionals. The unifying motivation was, by modelling the patient seeking of openings for friendship and Christian witness beyond our own Anglo-Celtic comfort zone, to build parishioners' confidence in forging community links.

St Mary Magdalene's now had a functional team ministry serving the needs of a growing congregation, with Ian and Ruth, lay readers Ken and Alan, and Marjorie and myself all planning, praying, and working together. One Sunday I published in the 'pew bulletin' a complete list of all the activities of the parish, with the names of all those responsible for them. To my surprise it turned out to be almost a complete list of the parishioners, demonstrating the holistic ministry of the Body of Christ at Dallas.

Telling the story

About this time, I wrote a candid article on ministry in Broadmeadows, published in a Christian magazine, *On Being*. It raised more questions than answers, broaching the issue of how the Protestant church in Australian cities had become locked into the middle-class, having little or no contact with people of lower socio-economic status – except as recipients of their 'charity'. In view of Jesus' ministry among the poor and the needy, this was a disturbing situation. Further, there was little if any awareness in 'successful' middle-class parishes of the unequal struggle of under-resourced ministry just across town in industrial or poor neighbourhoods, with a high proportion of newcomers of other cultures and faiths, beside the customary social casualties. Subsequently my specific appeal for resources to the Diocese's most successful and wealthy parish of St Hilary's Kew landed a high-quality second-hand piano – but what I had in mind was some ongoing financial or personnel support, such as in later years would actually be provided by St Jude's Carlton to an inner-northern parish. It seemed I was ahead of my time.

Marjorie also wrote an article published in the Christian periodical *National Outlook*, entitled "Hard Labour in the Vineyard", and there was a report in the national Anglican newspaper *Church Scene*, as the feature article of their section *The Inside Magazine*, "Why is my church not flourishing?" illustrated by four wretched photos of the underbelly of Dallas and Upfield. Another outcome of these articles and a number of speaking engagements that followed was for groups of ministry students from various seminaries to visit Dallas for a colloquium in the vicarage and a conducted tour of the district, in its residential, industrial and Islamic dimensions. Mostly the middle-class students appeared suitably shell-shocked.

Sadly, it demonstrated the wealth-segmented character of contemporary urban life, reinforced by the insidious media coverage geared to making wealth the norm and ignoring the existence of the poor. Sadly, there were more forces working to maintain the chasm than to bridge it. All our cherished rhetoric about the Australian way of life and the fair go remained just that. The 'have nots' languished while the 'haves' enjoyed their fortune. As Al Grassby was wont to say, *Australia's greatest ghetto is Sydney's North Shore [or Melbourne's inner east?]*

CHAPTER 39: Dreams and Visions

Alas! The glory days were not to last. There arose a quite external factor ultimately destined to affect the whole equilibrium of the parish. At the neighbouring church of St Michael's Broadmeadows, the world had turned. After long years of successful ministry in an equally challenging parish to ours, my praying colleague Geoff had departed, honoured and sung. The Bishop had appointed a young minister, Rev. John from a small country town, decreeing that henceforth the two Broadmeadows parishes should collaborate closely in a joint ministry. Initially this worked well enough: we led services and preached in each other's church and would sometimes hold a joint service, in which the Dallas people were a clear majority.

The newcomer suggested a bold expedient: rotate our church layout clockwise! Instead of a long, narrow arrangement of the pews facing the front, it became a wide but shallow seating plan, crosswise – more contemporary, more intimate, more congenial. It worked well. By then the diehards had either *died* (i.e. gone), or come to terms with the new stage of parish history which actually filled the church, mostly with people unaware of and unconcerned about its traditions. For a while we even tried two morning services, the traditional Eucharist early and contemporary worship later. But in the absence of a band for the contemporary songs it languished.

A prophetic word?

One morning preaching at St Michael's, I remember issuing a solemn warning after hearing that the congregation was peevishly objecting to the antics of half a dozen rough country youths whom Rev. John had brought to Melbourne and set up as a Christian community in a rented house nearby. They had the charming habit of standing on the pews during a service to belt out the modern songs loudly and raucously. The Gospel reading for the day included the ominous verse, *"Every branch in me that does not bear fruit my father prunes ... and they are cast into the fire"*. Citing this, I warned the congregation that in God's

Kingdom people rate more highly than furniture or the proprieties. But the congregation was heedless and soon the youths, frozen out, had vanished and the community house fell through. At St Michael's it would indeed mark the beginning of a steep decline in spirit – and in numbers. So much so that, about this time the Regional Bishop closed the church altogether and the remnant of its congregation joined our parish, with Rev John appointed as my associate priest.

Grandiose dreams

Ironically, this was the period when we were raising the prospect of reconfiguring Anglican ministry across the whole rapidly expanding Broadmeadows area. Our dream encompassed an approach by the Bishop to the billionaire tycoon who owned (and was planning to extend) the large shopping complex at the Station, in the hope that he might be persuaded to allocate a corner section of his land for the building of an Anglican Centre for worship *and community service.* We had even roughed out a plan for a modern building with an internal courtyard garden setting. Convinced as we were of the unsuitable location of St Mary Magdalene's on its down-at-heel Dallas site on the wrong side of the tracks, we could not envisage it ever being likely to attract upwardly mobile people from the new, higher quality and swiftly growing suburbs to the north-west, bereft of a church of any description, though blessed with a mosque and an Islamic Centre. After decades of reworking its social identity and experiencing increasing numbers of Muslim migrants, the city centre of Broadmeadows was a strategic hub for multicultural Christian witness.

One day, I picked up the telephone in my study to hear the billionaire tycoon himself, the late Richard Pratt, on the line enquiring about our project in positive terms. My heart leapt within me: the veriest voice of power! *[Name it and you can have it?]*

What did we need? How would the project be realised? I passed the call on to the Bishop, but later discussions were to prove fruitless, I suspect, because the Diocese simply could not come up with its share of the funds required. Certainly, our unsophisticated parish had little to offer from the sale of its church plant, even if the new site was gifted by the philanthropist owner of both the shopping centre and the huge Visyboard manufacturing plant nearby. In the event, the outcome would be a large office for Centrelink built on that choice corner block.

The dream had been a mirage, shimmering away in an uncertain future, but during our later optimistic years in the parish our fantasy had begun to spawn grandiose visions of a Christian advance in the newer areas. Having by then set aside my earlier aesthetic prejudices about the district by becoming increasingly identified with the people, I actually began to savour my evolving 'feel' for Greater Broadmeadows and its future. For her part, Marjorie loved the Broadmeadows people so much that she declared her desire to retire there.

But with the area becoming increasingly Muslim, there were simply too few Anglicans – and, in many cases, those associated with our parish were non-viable. What *was* needed was not bricks and mortar on strategic sites, but human and spiritual resources to staff a Mission. Reality bites!

Incarnating urban mission?

The episode underlined the essential mismatch between Church perceptions and community realities. Doubtless there were 'little Broadmeadows' happening all around the growing edges of a metropolis of over three million, with a population drawn from around the globe bearing allegiance to a number of faiths. As members of the prim and proper Church of the Founding Fathers, Anglicans were (unwittingly) becoming increasingly concentrated in a band of affluent suburbs to the city's east and south while the population diversified elsewhere, unmatched by the slender resources of a Church unwilling or unable to transform its strategies from *'maintenance' to 'mission'*.

Yet our experience had offered another dream: it *was* possible for the Gospel to win its way into the lives of people of all cultural backgrounds by incarnating the approach to urban mission glimpsed in the depressed inner-city communities of America. Though at the time testing yet tumultuous, our seven years at Dallas had seen our community of Christian worship grow exponentially, with the church full on many a Sunday morning.

Yet would that prove to be more than a momentary glint of light on the dappled sea of eternity? Ultimately only God can make that call. Our task was *'to be found faithful'*. Certainly, for us, those years in our early sixties would prove the most satisfying and joyful of our professional lives.

CHAPTER 40:
Seeds Blowing in the Wind

Such was the backdrop against which Archbishop Keith Rayner invited me in 1993 to take on a not unfamiliar challenge: over the next six months to examine the progress made in the Diocese in developing multicultural ministry and mission. This echoed the claims voiced at recent annual Synods by our vibrant multicultural campaigners. Since at the time I was still teaching the ITEMS course on Multicultural Church each year at Trinity College or at Whitley Baptist College, I had a continuing awareness of the evolving Melbourne scene. He suggested that I work half-time on this project, over a period of six months (at my request later extended to eight).

This came as a surprise to the Vestry and our people. A couple of senior leaders wondered aloud whether I knew anything about that esoteric field. I smiled knowingly. My involvement in the project was only feasible because Rev. John was now available to work fulltime among the people of the merged parish, and I considered him well able to hold the fort for the next six months.

In 1984, Archbishop Penman had set up a Commission of Enquiry into Multicultural Ministry & Mission to grapple with the reality that *'the Anglican Church is a monocultural Church in the midst of a multicultural nation, and this implies the need for very considerable change'*. It had produced *A Garden of Many Colours*, a brilliant charter for the future as envisaged by David Penman, projecting the vision which he had recruited me to help him realise. But reactionary diehards had distracted him from the task: by 1989 few of the 99 recommendations had been realised. Now, ten years later, the situation was to be reviewed, though the new Archbishop had never shown any interest nor even known of me.

Setting up office in St Andrew's Hall in Parkville, assisted by Rosemary, a recently returned missionary, we wrote to all clergy and parishes, as well as Anglican agencies (in welfare, education, chaplaincy) and sought specific interviews with knowledgeable people, especially the ethnic clergy. We commissioned 19 specialist papers, received 36 submissions, interviewed 75 people and gathered 73 documents from wider sources (Anglican Dioceses and other denominations). The heartening response would have dwarfed many a government enquiry. The challenge was to persuade the Diocese as a whole to make a commitment to addressing the increasingly multicultural Melbourne scene with a practical and loving concern.

Framing recommendations

Drawing on my experience with governmental enquiries I prepared a comprehensive report covering the demographics of Melbourne, the current multicultural scene, the history of the Diocese's work with migrants and ethnic minorities, a call to a cross-cultural theology and engagement in mission, concluding with specific recommendations for action.

At my own expense, I commissioned the publication of the Report, a book of 135pp entitled *Seeds Blowing in the Wind: Review of Multicultural Ministry & Mission*, with the imprint of the Anglican Diocese of Melbourne, also submitted to the National Library in Canberra for cataloguing in the national archive. Its title wryly but deliberately evoked the previous report of 1984, *A Garden of Many Colours*, implying that the garden had never really taken root within the Diocese.

I had some misgivings at having produced such a blockbuster of a report laying down the gauntlet so provocatively – as cogently reasoned and professionally documented as it was. The early pages brought home how seriously the Diocese was out of step with the society, immured in its restricted social class and its ethnicity – only 8% of parishioners were from non-Anglo backgrounds (and these mostly from the British Empire connection.) And in particular, there was minimal involvement with migrant workers (indeed with workers in general!)

The Melbourne Anglican scene

Another indicator was the number and range of 'ethnic' congregations worshipping in their own language. Whereas in the Melbourne Catholic Archdiocese 52 ethnic priests were conducting Masses for congregations speaking their languages, our Diocese had five congregations: Tamils, Persians, two Chinese, and Japanese. Further, in contrast to the Catholic schools, Anglican schools seemed to be bastions resisting change. Their replies to our questionnaire produced little ground for hope.

Among the factors for the Diocese's minimal response to the *Garden* blueprint, I identified our inward-looking preoccupation, the chronic unavailability of financial resources, our competing liturgical/ theological emphases, and leadership – the Uniting Church and the Salvation Army were now drawing up blueprints for reform. "Basically, not enough of us have any knowledge of, nor interest in migrants".

Too often in the parishes, conservatism and stuffiness ruled while the Church declined. Nor were we always seen as a particularly outgoing or friendly denomination, with our firm ideas of doing things decently and in order, rather than making adjustments to today's community. Indeed, we seemed to be 'polarised and paralysed'. The challenge was to move beyond our own comfort zone in responding to Christ's Great Commission.

> *"We desire to be modern Australians, oriented towards the future and not so much the past! And we have discovered that the vast richness of human cultures presage for us the wonder of belonging to the Kingdom of Heaven, of which our staging camp in this world is but a pale foretaste".*

Responding to the official policy of multiculturalism

The Anglican Church needed to base its policies on the most objective statement about multiculturalism, published in the 1989 Federal Government document *National Agenda for a Multicultural Australia* whose philosophical underpinnings reflected *Christian values* of respect, equality, justice, and social responsibility.

Multicultural policies were based on the premise that all Australians of whatever background should have *an overriding commitment to Australia, and accept the basic structures and principles: the Constitution and rule of law, tolerance and equality, parliamentary democracy, freedom of speech and religion, equality of the sexes, and English as the national language.* Multicultural policies conferred rights and imposed obligations, including the equal right of all to express their views, to be protected from discrimination, to share their cultural heritage, to acquire and develop proficiency in the English language, and to enjoy equal life chances.

Actually, it was largely the prudence and sanity of the evolving multicultural policies of governments of both stripes that had enabled our integration of more than six million migrants since 1950 to be so harmonious – world's best practice. But for Christians, migrants were also 'our neighbour' and the 'strangers within our gates'.

* * *

Multiculturalism under a critical spotlight

However by 2017 a new phenomenon would arise in western Europe, with the public questioning of multiculturalism on reasoned grounds following an unprecedented social situation: the arrival over four or five years of a million and a half refugees from Muslim-majority lands. Commenting on the unexpected street violence, the German Chancellor, Angela Merkel, would observe that *"multiculturalism has utterly failed"*, while UK Prime Minster David Cameron would argue that *"all must commit to values underpinning tolerance and equal rights"*. In both lands (and certainly equally, if not more so, in France), this consensus had broken down, with *sharia* courts functioning in some UK Midlands industrial cities and much of Marseilles a 'no go' area for the gendarmerie because in the hands of extremist Muslim leaders.

In Australia, some radical Muslims would become the only ethnic group ever to flout normative Australian values, for instance by espousing such practices as child brides, female genital mutilation, and treating women as second class citizens, while calling for adjustments to be made across our whole community life in order to accommodate *their* desires: e.g. for *'halal'* certification in all supermarkets to be purchased from stipulated Islamic organisations, and for the celebration of Christmas to be removed from the public sphere as offensive to *them*. Such a mindset clearly subverts the central thrust of multiculturalism as building a co-operative, open-minded future based on respect for Australian values and mutual acceptance. One incidental outcome of these extraordinary demands has been a quite understandable hardening of public attitudes towards multiculturalism among many Australians, particularly in country areas and among One Nation supporters.

* * *

Blueprint for a new future for Melbourne Anglicans

Back in 1993, in my report to the Diocese, *Seeds Blowing in the Wind*, after a theological chapter on concepts of Mission and the Kingdom of God, and exploring the relationship of Gospel and culture, I had proffered suggestions for the way ahead, starting with the two theological colleges. But sadly, the questionnaire that I had distributed around diocesan agencies had elicited *no response* from them! Subsequent discussions would prove fruitless.

The ultimate challenge was to encourage and empower more Christians to get involved, and this at their local parish level. At Dallas, twice we had held a Multicultural Night, where all the parish cultures, including the Anglo-Australians and the Brits, shared their traditional foods, music, song and dance. The best coverage of possibilities in this field was the chapter 'Educating the People of God: Multicultural Awareness for Parishes and Clergy' in *The Cultured Pearl* – a treasure trove of practicable ideas.

To address these challenges, to gauge the present and inspire the future, we convened a one-day consultation of 60 parish and agency representatives, with input from Sydney Diocese (far down this track) and other Churches. Sydney Diocese experience was that the energetic embrace of cross-cultural ministry triggered life and growth – and released the needed resources.

The formal recommendations put forward in the Report included:
- formal commitment by diocesan leadership
- creation of a Cross-Cultural Ministry unit
- clergy education and in-service training
- promotion of cultural sensitivity in the parishes
- adapting parish life to incorporate ethnic newcomers
- facilitating ethnic congregations
- co-ordinating ESL teaching programs; and
- (tongue in cheek): "For detailed proposals, see the recommendations of *A Garden of Many Colours*, 1984 - but never implemented.

We despatched *Seeds Blowing in the Wind* gratis to every parish and agency and eagerly awaited outcomes.

A deafening silence

I might as well have saved myself the trouble. The silence of the Diocese and the parishes was deafening. Was the Report too polemical? But so was the *Garden of Many Colours*. It was well-reasoned, amply backed by evidence, and literate. After eight months' work, would a mealy-mouthed response have been more appreciated? Now that I think of it, I cannot recall receiving any letter or word of appreciation for my labours (and expenses) from anyone in authority.

A few weeks later, the Diocesan Synod passed a motion that I proposed, calling on all parishes and agencies to study the Report. Our group of clergy multicultural enthusiasts produced an appealing leaflet to publicise the book.

Since the Report was ultimately addressed to the Church leadership, presumably it must have been discussed at Bishops' meetings and dismissed – by the Archbishop? His antipathy alone would have spelt its demise. Or were the Diocese's financial resources so limited that nothing could be afforded. I shrugged it all off as a lost cause, kept a copy as a souvenir, and re-immersed myself in the ministry of St Mary Magdalene's.

Unexpected if belated outcome

The best part of a year later in 1994 a letter arrived from the Archbishop offering me the role of Director in a new Department of Multicultural Ministry – *half time!* Had my earlier reaction merely reflected the old Public Service mentality about prompt action rather than the Byzantine process of Church decision-making? All I know is that when I re-read the criteria for a Director put forward in the Report, I found myself looking into a mirror.

CHAPTER 41: The Heartache of Parting

Though now attached to the Division of Community Services in the diocesan headquarters, I still maintained my role as (half-time) leader of the team ministry at St Mary Magdalene's, then undergoing an exciting phase of growth. The place was abuzz.

Before long it became clear that this duality distracted me from the real vicarage-based people ministry. The two tasks shared no common ground. Clearly the twin strands of my existence needed to be teased apart. Gladly, I accepted the offer from St Matthew's Glenroy to set up an office in their under-utilised late-Victorian mansion, where I spent half my week devising policies for earthing the multicultural vision across Melbourne parishes. But the few months of working alone in such an isolated, sterile setting brought home to me that, really, I needed to be physically as well as notionally integrated in the Diocesan Services team. Either all in or right out. But was the half-time arrangement the real issue?

The agony of choosing

I wrote to Archbishop Rayner, outlining the dilemma. Kindly, he offered me free choice between the two options. If I chose parish ministry I would continue full-time at St Mary Magdalene's. But if I opted for the diocesan cross-cultural ministry the resources would only permit half-time employment. Torn between two loves, I appealed for guidance to the chaplain of Retreat House in Cheltenham, moving in for a day or two to contemplate the pattern of God's good guidance throughout my life, and trying to envisage which future path might release the most creative energies. I was referred to the famous maxim of Ignatian spirituality, *'Go deeply into thine innermost being, and profoundly and prayerfully examine both options until one begins to speak of desolation and one of consolation, one of death and one of life'.*

As the light on the path grew stronger, the shadows began to edge back. On the one hand, at St Mary Magdalene's I had poured my heart into a ministry among poor but choice people whom I had come to love. Inevitably, the issues of multicultural ministry had receded, yet over time the parish had come to reflect the culturally diverse character of the area, probably more so than any parish of the Diocese. Moreover, by their respect, warmth and love the people of the church had powerfully changed us (particularly me!). So how could I turn away to pursue a private agenda? And where would that leave Marjorie, the beating heart of our joint ministry?

But on the other hand, hadn't there been a passion running like a crimson thread through my life about the challenge of diversity? Different languages, different cultures, different lands, different peoples...? In my quest, I had travelled the world – observing, contemplating, dreaming. My long work life, in three professions and in three lands, had focused on facilitating connections for people retaining their identity while coping with a new environment: kids growing up, students learning a new language, migrants acquiring new ways of surviving, governments broadening their social concerns, parishes seeking to draw in unchurched outsiders.

But more specifically, couldn't my experience and political savvy now be turned to good account for the Diocese? Wasn't that why God had guided us to this moment? With this new prospect on offer, would it be right to ignore the opportunity by focusing only on the small-scale project in Dallas? Besides, deep within, wasn't there a passion stirring? It seemed good to...

I informed the Archbishop of my choice to pursue the cross-cultural ministry role – on the half-stipend. I withheld from him that I would in fact be working full-time, since half-time would be unthinkably ineffectual. And over the next four years that was to be the story, incomprehensible (if known at all) to the bean-counters but to me deeply gratifying. If you believe in your work that's already half the battle. Let the other half be remunerated!

So where would we live? There was no house that went with the job and we had no home of our own in Melbourne. Providentially (funny thing that) a vicarage became vacant beside one of the oldest churches in Melbourne, St Stephen's on Richmond Hill built in 1851, within walking distance of the Cathedral Offices.

Gut-wrenching farewells

With their expressions of sadness and affection, our final days at St Mary Magdalene's would be poignant indeed. No one in ministry had ever forewarned me about the pain of such a dismal scenario, with its looming betrayal of friendship. Most of our parishioners had no comprehension of why we were leaving or what cross-cultural ministry meant. We had never mentioned it, simply practising it as the membership diversified. Actually, we were quite burnt-out, and at 62 should probably have been thinking of the long-service leave becoming available. What was it that St Ignatius had to say about *desolation?*

In October 1995, our farewell Holy Communion service was memorable for the full house and the emotional charge. Referring to our own servanthood in the parish, I preached on Luke 17:10 where Jesus told his disciples: *"Likewise with you, when you have done everything you were told to do, you should say, 'We are unprofitable servants, we have only done our duty' ".*

Later circulating among our friends over a copious morning tea in the church hall, we were bidden by Vicar's Warden, Ken, to close our eyes and when we re-opened them, there sat our Regional Bishop, Andrew Curnow, ensconced in all his episcopal finery.

We were touched: there was no expectation, let alone obligation, for the Bishop to favour us. The ensuing speeches were a touching mix of ockerish sincerity and maudlin emotion – culminating in the whole congregation trooping outside to stand in broad array across the front of the building while Alan, photographer *extraordinaire*, recorded the moment for posterity- – the print now framed and hanging on our walls. If we had begun our ministry at St Mary Mag's with 14 or so diffident locals, after seven wonderful years we were privileged to be farewelled by some 130 affectionate friends.

"To God be the glory for the things he has done..."

At Dallas, we had reconnected with working-class and unemployed people, and were recognised as being on their side. But we also brought them the precious gift of the Gospel of hope that we had encountered and internalised many years earlier, and at times had the joy of seeing a growth in grace and maturity. Mostly we were spared the heartache and tragedy – often an inescapable cost of ministry – and making our final farewell, albeit with the pain and loss of parting, we rejoiced in the goodness of God and the loving warmth of a special band of his faithful people.

In retrospect

Now in pensive retrospect we view the Dallas years as the most gratifying and fruitful time of both our working lives. To be sure, the parishioners made large demands on us – we were learners in their school – but, on the whole, we managed to rise to their challenges. We worked hard and long. For instance, once feeling utterly drained, on checking back in our diaries we found we had worked 21 consecutive days without a break!

At such times, I would freak out and, while Marjorie might sometimes plug on indomitably, I would go bush alone into the Dandenongs and after an indulgent lunch in a tourist venue, spend a lush afternoon in a quiet spot along a mountain road, reclining in the laid-back driver's seat of our station waggon – transported by the beauty of a Dvořak symphony or lost in the healing power of a baroque oratorio, the glories of music and of nature blending together to pour a soothing balm over my soul.

CHAPTER 42:
Challenging the Church Establishment

Having previously written the handbook for the task, late in 1995 I took up my full-time calling to encourage and facilitate the development of cross-cultural ministry across the Diocese. My base was an upper-floor room in the neo-Gothic Cathedral Building overlooking the City Square. While able to draw on some clerical support, it was simpler to use my own (then new-fangled) word processor, forerunner to the desktop PC.

Our new home in a former vicarage of St Stephen's brought us our only taste ever of inner-city living. So stylish and convenient, close to the mecca of the three east-west shopping strips of Richmond with their world-spanning cuisines. And across the Yarra close by: Prahran market, and in bike-riding distance of Southbank, Albert Park, Port Melbourne and St Kilda. We both took up new posts in the Anglican Centre, Marjorie joining me in the Department of Community Development to research the provisions for disability in the Diocese while supervising the field placement of a social work student.

My initial emphasis was on the nurturing and integrating of the ethnic clergy, bringing them together for a festive lunch at the vicarage. They didn't really know each other: what else would bring a Chinese and a Japanese face-to-face? It would become a regular feature, moving later to the Chinese church of St Matthias North Richmond. Equally important was to visit all of them from time to time in the Sunday worship services they held in a variety of languages.

My prime emphasis was to encourage the traditional parishes to see and relate to the overseas migrants living all around them, though many were oblivious to the currents of diversity lapping around their doors. Mostly they were into *ministry* rather than *mission*, self-focused rather than outward-looking. I met with Vestries, organised regional workshops, took part in consultations, wrote articles for church papers and preached. Once I was the preacher for a formal Sunday evening service in the Cathedral.

Above all, for the Diocesan Synod each year, our ginger group of multicultural activists would scheme together about how best to make a plea for the allocation of resources, but to little avail. It was the time when the Diocese had hit its nadir: in numbers, resources and energies. And in hope.

Promoting English-teaching to migrants

The most productive outcome of these years was the promotion of English teaching to migrants, as a means of parishes making initial contacts and offering a strategic service to newcomers. For me it evoked earlier experiences of language teaching and preparing study materials, but I realised to my shame that I had never actually taught a migrant English. Well aware of Sydney Diocese's major emphasis on this area, we organised a two-day seminar featuring their experts which triggered several Melbourne parishes taking the plunge.

A bridge too far?

Sometimes I have wondered whether my appearance (by invitation) before the Bishops' Council didn't actually prove counter-productive. Having presented a compelling case based on immigration statistics and social indicators from the Census, backed by Scriptural imperatives about 'making disciples of all nations', I made so bold as to issue a final challenge along the lines of *"Gentlemen* [they were all men], *unless the will to respond is present in this room, we will see no change across the Diocese"* or some such impertinence – as true as it was. I was icily thanked and departed in disarray. Just slightly injudicious?

Going national

In 1997, the Anglican General Synod (national congress) set up a Multicultural Committee to advise the Church across Australia on how it might relate more sensitively to the full range of the population. As one of a handful of Anglicans in Australia working full-time in the field I was invited to join and became the secretary. The other members were church dignitaries. Meeting in Sydney, our initial task was to prepare a background paper for discussion at the next General Synod.

Though at times having to debate the issues with more conservative members, over a year the Committee produced a document conveying a strong case for profound change in attitudes and practices church-wide, together with a compelling brochure for mass distribution, *Disciples of All Nations*, pleading for the Church to transcend its English origins and orientation to mirror the ethnic mix of the population, while taking action at parish level in worship and outreach, and at diocesan level in clergy recruitment and training.

Alas! After six hundred years, Church Order is not lightly transcended. The General Synod Office failed to get the documentation into the hands of Members. As an elected Melbourne representative to General Synod, I attended the Adelaide meeting, a prepared speech in my pocket for the motion on Multicultural Ministry. I never got to speak. On the last of five days the agenda was bogged down so that a final resolution referred all unfinished business to the Standing Committee – that is, relegated to limbo. To say I was disillusioned would be the understatement of the season. I have never heard whether that national multicultural policy was ever adopted by subsequent General Synods.

Pity the pioneer

However, by 2016, Melbourne's five 'ethnic congregations' would grow to 40, drawn from 20 ethnic groups and linking 3,000 worshippers. The Diocese would have been shocked into action by the advent of south Sudanese Anglicans, accompanied by clergy, fleeing Muslim persecution in a civil war. Eight of these congregations would speak Dinka, and other Sudanese congregations five further languages. Newer ethnic congregations would also speak Arabic, Pakistani languages, Karen, Bahasa Indonesia, a Filipino language, Maori, Tongan and Samoan.

Looking back to 1995, it seems clear that in several respects I was cast in the gloomy role of a prophet ahead of his time, a voice crying in the wilderness, but whose vision had to bide its time. It would require the exotic recruits from Africa to carry the day.

Dodging retirement

On completion of my four-year term, at the young age of 66 still healthy and active and enthusiastic for further service for the Kingdom, we faced the ultimate dilemma: where to live now? Return to our home in Canberra? But we were quite unknown to the Canberra Anglicans, and beyond retirement age. Actually, the thought of retirement had never occurred to me.

Pondering and praying, a new work option came into focus, upon Marjorie's appointment as Pastoral Worker in the English and Cantonese-speaking parish of St Michael & All Angels, Bennettswood in East Burwood near Deakin University. I offered to assist Rick Cheung in his ministry, focusing on the ageing and dwindling English-speaking congregation, freeing him to concentrate on building the Chinese-language congregation. Early in 1999 I was appointed Associate Priest, largely honorary. The commitment would continue for the next eight years until 2007, by the age of 74 completing 21 years of ministry in the Melbourne Diocese.

Also in 1999, we sold our Canberra home for a goodly sum and began the search for a new Melbourne base. Not excited by the outer eastern suburbs (older housing on barely undulating land, and too dear) we recalled the pleasant wooded hills of the Hurstbridge line and, beyond a cancelled auction, were able to buy a modern house from a Christian family through a private sale. Once again, *Jehovah-jireh*.[70]

Set on a hillside overlooking a wooded urban valley, elegant and partly two-storeyed, it boasted a splendid multi-tiered garden, rock-edged and densely planted with a huge variety of exotic trees, shrubs and ground cover, all overshadowed by some ancient eucalypts, its drive and walkways all paved in redbrick. Charming and harmonious ensemble, thirty minutes' drive from Bennettswood.

In the Queen's Birthday Honours in 2001 I was to receive the Medal of the Order of Australia (OAM), citing my *'contribution to the development of our national policy of multiculturalism and of cross-cultural ministry within the Anglican Church of Australia'*.

---

[70] Hebrew for 'God will provide' (the lamb), originally God's promise to Abraham when releasing him from the testing command to sacrifice his own son Isaac on Mt Moriah (today's Temple Mount in Jerusalem) close to the hill of Calvary where God's own Son, Jesus the 'lamb of God' would later be sacrificed 'for the sins of the world'.

CHAPTER 43:
Promoting Multiculturalism across the Churches

By the late-1980s, ethnic congregations had been established by the Baptists, the Lutherans, the Presbyterians, Churches of Christ, the Salvation Army, the Uniting Church, the Catholic Archdiocese and even the Jehovah's Witnesses. Anglicans had the fewest. I had persuaded my former Department of Immigration's Melbourne branch to conduct a Melbourne-wide survey of the congregations.

Sadly, these tended to be sidelined and patronised rather than sharing in the normative ministry of their denominations. The Baptists grouped them together under the archaically styled *New Settlers' Federation*. It amounted to managing expectations rather than rethinking the holistic ministry of the denomination *in the presence of* the ethnic clergy, whereby everything might be up for review.

Returning missionaries accustomed to the indigenous leadership of churches in former mission fields were challenging local leadership to recognise that, in a sense, the *'mission field had come to Australia'.*

Stirring the Churches

In 1992, one of these former missionaries, the Baptist Charles Wilcox convened a Melbourne-wide meeting about ethnic congregations across the denominations which I attended to review common issues, assess resources and consider making common cause. The outcome was the launch of the Inter-Church Network for Cross-Cultural Mission, later undergirded with staff and financial support by the School of World Mission at Whitley College.

As the only paid worker across the Churches specifically tasked with developing multicultural approaches to ministry and mission, from the outset I served as the secretary. For the next 15 years or more we would meet as a ginger group of up to 20 clergy of several denominations: monitoring progress, compiling a database of local churches, co-publishing *Multicultural Horizons – a Newsletter and Digest*, and organising in-service training opportunities for clergy of all Churches. We conducted two adult education courses over three or four nights at Moonee Ponds and Kew, attended by some 200 church members, for which I gave the introductory lecture.

But our most distinctive public activities were quarterly pastors' breakfasts convened all over Melbourne in churches with a multicultural ministry – to Japanese, Koreans, Chinese, Russians, Germans, Slavs, Hispanics, Vietnamese, Arabs, Indians, Karens, Islanders and Aborigines, as well as churches with multi-ethnic ministries. Over a breakfast prepared according to their own ethno-specific cuisine, the host pastor would describe his ministry and project his vision. Over the years attended by several hundred clergy, these were a delight for the richness of their ethnic texture and the warmth of their common humanity universally redeemed in Christ. A veritable foretaste of the heavenly banquet. And a feast of inspirational ideas. In recent years the ageing and decline among the mainline Churches has been to an extent offset by the intensely multicultural character of the Pentecostal mega-churches.

To promote the normalising of cross-cultural approaches across them all, the Network's final initiative was the compiling and distribution in 2000 of a Manifesto addressed to the Churches of Victoria. The moving spirit in this initiative, as of the earlier in-service training days offered church leaders, was the late Ross Langmead, professor of world mission at the Baptist Theological College.

A MULTICULTURAL MANIFESTO TO THE CHURCHES OF VICTORIA

It had a glance at the past – in gratitude for the great souls who had sought to reach out across boundaries of race and culture – but in penitence for acts of violence, cruelty, and neglect and for arrogance and racial superiority.

It addressed the present – the diversity of the society but not of our Churches, the growth of ethno-specific churches and multicultural churches, but the maldistribution of resources and of training opportunities.

And it surveyed the future – we live in a post-Christian, pluralist society: a missionary environment. So we call for affirmative action by church leaders and decision-making bodies in regard to:
 appropriate theological curricula and training;
 reforms to empower NESB people through involvement in decision- making, and recognition of the gifts they bring;
 their access to church facilities, financial and human resources;
 encouragement for the use of a multiplicity of languages and appropriate forms of worship;
 support for 'incarnational ministries' among the marginalised and vulnerable (including asylum seekers and refugees) motivated by unconditional love;
 an appeal for Christians of all backgrounds and Churches to work together for God's Kingdom.

It concluded "Knowing the transforming power of God's love, we commit ourselves to addressing these issues in our church life, in the living power of the God who acts".

The *Manifesto* was also laid out in liturgical form for use in covenanting services.

Late in 2008 after a period of quiescence, the Network was formally wound up. We judged its pioneering role to have been influential in the change of climate across the Anglo Churches, and felt privileged to have been able to play a strategic role.

But what of the ecumenical movement?

Over the twenty years since we had come to Melbourne for my ITEMS Project with the Victorian Council of Churches (VCC), I had continued as a member of its Commission on Living Faiths & Community Relations, initially as a paid worker and later as one of the nominated Anglican representatives. In 1985, I had helped organise the VCC's annual conference at the Romanian Orthodox Church on the theme *The Church is Multicultural* as a speaker and small groups co-ordinator. At their request, I had also compiled and published a small handbook *Accents of Faith: the Churches of the Victorian Council of Churches* in consultation with their leadership.

But whereas the Inter-Church Network was basically composed of evangelical Churches working with ethnic congregations at the grassroots level, the VCC was the State component of the National Council of Churches of Australia (NCCA) – the 'ecumenical movement' with its more liberal theology and fading dreams of organic unity. In recent years, worldwide, it has gone into decline. Why? Maybe because its theology is now seen as rather unbalanced – stressing social justice and development to the detriment of 'new life' (conversion) and 'holiness' (sanctification) following the holistic scriptural paradigm. Moreover, several Churches had never joined (Presbyterian, Baptist, Lutheran, Pentecostals). However, since the 70s, evangelicals worldwide have broadened their focus also to embrace development and social justice (the Lausanne Movement, World Vision, TEAR).

During my 20-year membership of the VCC Commission (as longest-serving delegate) its focus increasingly moved from multicultural ministry towards relating to other Faiths, to the decline of interest in community relations (despite the One Nation 'Asian Debate' triggered by Pauline Hanson and the advent of black African migrants and refugee policy tensions). My resignation reflected an inability to challenge this drift. That I had in fact outlived my relevance came as a sobering realisation. But of course, my real focus had long since shifted from inter-Church relations to the privilege of serving God through ministering to specific congregations of Anglican Christians.

Bilingual/bicultural ministry

For eight years we served the dwindling English-speaking congregation at Bennettswood, as members of Rick Chung's bicultural ministry team of five. For us all it proved an enriching growth in mutual reliance, bridging languages and cultures. Occasionally, I would preach at the Cantonese service via a Chinese interpreter. The Early Church must have been like that with its Jewish and Gentile converts making common cause, albeit not without tensions, as *The Acts of the Apostles* makes clear.

Early on, we launched English classes for international students from Deakin University and others (one of whom in all modesty identified himself as Prime Minister of a tiny Pacific island nation!) Saturday mornings would see some 40 learners milling around the church facilities: Asian undergraduates, Chinese grandparents recruited to care for grandchildren, post-doctoral fellows, European migrants who had never really learnt the language. I delighted in the challenge. Over the years, in my class I had taught a young Spaniard, a long-term Greek migrant, a Korean couple, a Japanese, an elderly Taiwanese, a Chinese doing his second PhD and an older couple who were to become our closest Chinese friends.

Twice we took my class away for a holiday break to clergy vacation units at Pt Lonsdale and Phillip Island, memorable for the web of cross-cultural relations. Before heading out for the day, a morning lesson would focus on simple materials I had written in learner's English, perhaps a parable or a Gospel episode. Once sauntering along a beach together, my arm around his shoulder, Chun would observe, *"I never thought the day would come when I would have a Western friend."* Precious memory. Ever since, the two elderly couples have met regularly for a linguistically adventurous lunch.

Ministry to our fellow-elderly

Our old Dallas teamwork now came into its own with warmly appreciated pastoral visiting of homes, hospitals and retirement villages. In the absence of a focus for ministry to the men, we launched 'Mike's Mates' as a rather sumptuous monthly breakfast with wide-ranging speakers. After fifteen years or more it is still thriving, now in the impressive new complex built following St Michael's merger with a neighbouring parish.

In 2001, to mark St Michael's 50 years, I had put together parishioners' written reminiscences, updated to the present scene in the small book *Journeying on Together: the Inside Story of a Bicultural/Bilingual Parish in an Australian Suburb*, with final evaluative and challenging words from the two clergy. Over our years there it had been heartening to experience the progressive thawing out of relations between the two widely divergent cultural/linguistic age groups comprising the parish.

University English tutoring

In our final years, we became involved in weekly tutoring of Chinese postgraduate scholars and students at Deakin University, practising *everyday conversation* – not included in the austere requirements set in China for aspirants to study overseas.

In turn, this would result in our later visiting several of them in China on their return, drawing to an end that fascinating chapter of our lives of tutoring university lecturers and senior-year students in English conversation in the Chongqing University of Technology.

Belated entrant to university teaching

About this time I received an invitation to teach a semester course on 'Religion in Australian Society' at the Australian Catholic University, standing in for the regular lecturer. I had to devise and teach the course, a compulsory subject for young people training for the teaching profession – and more academically oriented than the ITEMS course. I enjoyed doing the historical research and preparing the teaching material which also drew on my lived experience. Two generations younger than me, the class seemed to lap it up. After half a lifetime's involvement in adult education, this experience represented the fulfilment of a long-held conceit about one day becoming a 'proper' university teacher.

Publications

Over the years in Melbourne, I had written a number of Christian and secular publications, with 'Seven Years in Broadmeadows' in *Church Scene*, and 'Hard Labour in the Vineyard' in *National Outlook*, a Christian monthly magazine. Beyond our own writings I had edited several books: two for son Christopher, an academic anthropologist; two for an Italo-Australian historian, and a comprehensive biography of a distinguished Aboriginal leader in Arnhem Land for a colleague. Marjorie had also burst into print several times. See Appendix on Publications.

So, the long Melbourne years had been distinguished as much by networking with diverse people in and beyond the Anglican Church as by our commitment to the parishioners we had loved and served day by day. Of course, with older years, community activism has perforce given way to an ongoing identification with issues rather than a practical involvement.

Finally, in 2010, in the face of a virtual ten-year drought that saw the beautiful Montmorency garden dying because of watering restrictions, we moved to our present home in east Eltham. A few months earlier the dreadful Kinglake/Marysville bushfires had claimed 173 lives. Finally, the crippling national drought would end spectacularly with severe flooding across several States. Truly ours is a *'land of drought and flooding rains'.*

CHAPTER 44: In Search of Meaning

The world into which we were born is no more. Many things we once loved have passed away, some now characterised as *'museum pieces'* (as are we?). Others have been transfigured through innovation, while unimaginably new creative solutions have emerged. The ever-shrinking world, instant communication, the digital age, space probes, the explosion of scientific knowledge, including of vastly expanded medical care, cures for once intractable diseases, widespread affluence, financial security, cheap travel, social media, creature comforts beyond credence, even ten more years of life expectancy. Impressive catalogue reflecting a single lifetime!

In such a rapidly evolving world, what are the underlying factors that have shaped the climate of our lives? What are the competing values systems within which we have sought to find personal meaning? They span the physical, economic, social, artistic and spiritual dimensions – all of them transformed during our longish journey. Eighty-five years confer a useful vantage point.

Social (in)security

First, the socio-economic dimension shaping our daily existence. Compared to our childhood and the lean post-war years, the 1960s and 1970s had seen the progressive transformation of our society through sustained prosperity, with the advent and maturing of the welfare state and the humanising of service provision to meet the needs of the whole community. Australia was often hailed as the most egalitarian nation on earth.

But in the late 1980s, with the demise of communism in Europe, history would go into reverse, as hard-nosed economic rationalists would take power in the UK and later in Australia.

A new economic model would be developed by the economic élite to *benefit* the economic élite. Since that decade we have been subjected to the sweeping triumph of neo-liberalism and globalisation, embraced by both sides of politics, swamping the wellbeing of whole sectors of the community and – like the emergent neo-capitalists of Russia and the socialist bloc on the fall of the Berlin Wall, daring to purloin and sell the people's crown jewels: our public utilities providing water, electricity, telephony, public transport, public works and infrastructure, airports, port installations, hydro-electric projects, the people's bank, public housing, our systems of personal services, health insurance, even our medical research institute, while privileging private schools and private hospitals over public.[71]

All justified by invoking the primacy of private ownership, while claiming to be responding to a concocted phobia of deficits and indebtedness. But such debts had ever been the universal norm! – whereby each new generation had benefited from the services inherited while making provision for the generation to follow, for instance by building significant infrastructure (by *Public Works* Departments) without invoking private enterprise with its profit motive and sometimes overseas ownership. A functional system – and well worth paying for through the annual interest bill on the borrowings.

Today the most egregious example in Australia: the Victorian public transport system privatised in the 1990s by Premier Kennett under the promise that government subsidies would diminish. Almost two decades later, subsidies have more than doubled, leaving taxpayers to foot the bill for lucrative private profits to be sent offshore (in some cases to other governments!) while our transport assets fall into disrepair. To vaunt the benefits of an 'open market' is to naïvely ignore the actual collusion of marketers whereby everybody pays more. Democracy becomes government of the gullible by the greedy, while the whole society comes under ever-increasing stress.

Neo-liberalism is the philosophy of the unfettered self, freed from the tiresome constraints of allegiance to the local community. The new digital *Übermensch* is the epitome of capitalist entitlement that believes only in the things it has created. *"There is no god but Mammon and the media is its prophet"*. But an eminent contemporary economist, Thomas Picketty,[72] has given the lie to the folly of neo-liberalism, pointing out that the surplus budgets so extolled actually *entrench*

---

[71] A 2016 opinion poll found that more Australians now oppose privatisation than accept it.
[72] 'Capital in the 21st Century', 2014

unemployment, put the brakes on *real wages growth*, and ultimately *shackle* the economy. But, of course, this serves the oligarchy, the real 'owners' of the world economy.

And sadly, there is no lack of politicians of all stripes prepared to do their bidding by conniving at their *'debt-phobia'* – as commonsensical as it may initially sound to the layman. But what is the nation-state for, if not to protect us and our culture from enemies without and wreckers within? By 2016 the 'little people' of the UK, cynical and disillusioned, would have their say in voting down the supra-national economic structure of the European Union while the USA, in a backlash against globalisation, would reject the political class in favour of President Trump. Though boosting the wealth of the rich, the Western economic heresy had effectively beggared the entire Third World, entrenching poverty through a more exploitative version of 19th century colonialism. The essential principles of moral integrity and the pursuit of the common good have been forfeit. In actual fact, *globalisation* had undermined *globalism* in the international arena: the UN system, the free flow of ideas, and the worldwide benefits of the civil society.

Local impact of economic rationalism

In the 1980s, by the thousands Australian jobs had been exported to China, India, Bangladesh and other Asian countries with low-wage economies. With the removal of tariffs whole industries closed, notably the footwear and garment industries in Melbourne's inner north. In Victoria at one stroke Coalition Premier Jeff Kennett cut the public payroll by sacking *10,000 teachers!* And closing schools galore – *three* of them in our long-suffering parish of Dallas, a heartless assault on Australia's poorest suburb!

Civil society became increasingly constrained as the arena of big business expanded exponentially, unchecked, untameable. Competition ruled, profits soared and affluence increased for some, while stress levels rose for many from threatened unemployment and forced early retirement, especially in the Public Service that I had known, now decimated by the outsourcing of projects (and hence jobs).

Security of employment fell dramatically as workers were all too often pushed onto contracts making them no longer employees with rights protected at law, thus creating many areas of precarious, insecure work as inexperienced 'contractors'.

Finally by 2017 the Australian automobile industry which had been building cars for 60 years would be forced off-shore. All of which outflanked the role of trade unionism with its traditional mantra of *'unity is strength'*, by putting a largely non-unionised workforce at the mercy of management's drive for increasing productivity and profits. Within a new class warfare, 'divide and conquer' prevails. This factor alone has undoubtedly multiplied social stress and undermined community cohesion and confidence. We have all paid the price in a heightened struggle for personal meaning.

Simultaneously we have lived through the progressive decline of *service* as the traditional mode of interaction within our society. The DiY revolution, now universal at supermarkets and petrol stations, as well as in department stores, has seen the end of being 'served' as a right. Business had pulled off a massive coup by recruiting the *customer* as an honorary *staff member!* In Broadmeadows unemployment amongst non-English-speaking migrants sky-rocketed. For those still working, job pressures grew and hours of work lengthened. At 7 o'clock in the evening suburban trains were now crowded by home-going office workers, many having worked extra hours – unpaid.

As the economy was deregulated, governments found themselves impotent in the face of a growing tide of insecurity, disaffection and pessimism. The atomisation of society meant that many of the community bodies (churches, trade unions) that people once turned to for support no longer existed as they had. Family life came under threat, and community organisations of all kinds went into a tailspin: with leisure in decline we became a nation of non-joiners, including of the Churches. Elite sport was professionalised. By way of dulling the pain the commercial media peddled trivia and soporific entertainment

Unchallenged, from its Temple in Wall Street, Mammon[73] was exacting a terrible price from its rabid worshippers. As I Timothy 6:10 observes, *"the love of money is the root of all evil"*. Greed had

---

[73]Jesus said, 'No one can serve two masters....You cannot serve God and Mammon.' (Luke 16:13)

triumphed over humanity and common decency, scornfully favouring competition over co-operation. The resulting casualisation of labour triggered intermittent and under-employment, implying the inability to acquire one's own home, forever the great Australian dream. To be sure, a tiny élite had entered into wealth unimaginable: in the world 85 mega-rich individuals now owned more than the rest of the seven billion put together[74], and six Australians more than all the rest of us. The architect of privatisation, ALP Prime Minister Paul Keating, has since acknowledged his misjudgment. Indeed, are we now starting to glimpse the terminal decline of capitalism with the every-increasing concentration of power into fewer hands? It raises the basic issue: is the global system there to serve people, or are people there to serve the global system, owned by so few?

The most recent OECD figures show that, while in the past two years Australia has ranked as the world's richest country in per capita wealth (largely because of our high rate of home ownership – now in sharp decline), one in six children are living below the poverty line! In the *land of the 'fair go'?*

The legitimacy of business

Of course, with private enterprise *per se* there need be no argument – my encounter with Soviet socialism had demonstrated how bleak was its assessment of human dignity. Doubtless, trading must be the oldest mode of human interaction, saving us all from living as hunter/gatherers, pioneering sociality, engendering the town, begetting relational skills, fathering culture, progress and innovation.

And Jesus did not disapprove of business activity. Among the characters in his parables was the shrewd manager commended for putting his master's funds to productive use – but also Dives (Latin for *'rich man'*) eternally judged for scorning the needs of the poor. While Zacchaeus, diminutive tax collector, would spontaneously respond to Jesus' appeal by offering *fourfold* restitution for his ill-gotten gains. Already another tax collector, Matthew, had forsaken his toll-booth to join the wandering preacher as a disciple, subsequently recording his experience of the three years with Jesus in the Gospel that bears his name.

---

[74] According to the head of the International Monetary Fund, Christine Lagarde, 2016

Indeed, over the millennia no other durable option appears to have been devised. The reality is that we all depend on business for our daily bread as well as to safeguard and grow our money. At best business works for the benefit of all involved, whether as manufacturers, suppliers, distributors, sellers or consumers, and the creative energies released can be explosive agents of progress. By their energy, flair and enthusiasm, talented entrepreneurs have made their mark in shaping the Western world, while the prudent investment of surplus profits meets emerging needs and strengthens the system for all.

Papal infallibility?

However, this is a far cry from the *'gnomes of Zurich'* playing with other nations' currencies or US investment banks collapsing from frenzied trading in tranches of worthless loans. It is this yielding to greed and megalomania (the worship of the Golden Calf) that Pope Francis deplored in his 2015 Encyclical *Laudato Si'*:

> *"Once capital becomes an idol and guides people's decisions, once greed for money presides over the entire socio-economic system, it ruins society, it condemns and enslaves men and women, it destroys human fraternity, it sets people against one another and, as we clearly see, it even puts at risk our common home, sister and mother earth.*
>
> *The first task is to put the economy at the service of peoples. Human beings and nature must not be at the service of money. Let us say 'NO' to an economy of exclusion and inequality, where money rules, rather than service. That sort of economy excludes. That economy destroys Mother Earth.... The economy should serve human beings and nature, and ensure a decent life for the poor and a respect for the environment. Working for a just distribution of the fruits of the earth is a moral obligation. For Christians, the responsibility is even greater: it is a commandment. It is about giving to the poor and to peoples what is theirs by right. It is a reality prior to private property. Property, especially when it affects natural resources, must always serve the needs of peoples. I ask you, in the name of God, to defend Mother Earth."*

Global environmental crisis

But a tiny coterie of corporate moguls from Wall Street and their bankers, together with the arms manufacturers trading in human flesh, are holding the planet's future to ransom. The looming environmental crisis is hastened by the reluctance of national leaders to commit to the global action required to impede the warming of the planet towards the point of no return: escalating climate change, rising sea levels, deforestation, desertification, loss of species,[75] and inevitable food and water wars.

Commenting on this, Pope Francis summed up that the Earth is *"exploited by human greed and rapacity"* and that *"humans have slapped nature in the face. Well might we ask, 'How is it possible that the most intelligent creature ever to walk the face of the earth is conniving at its destruction? We are standing on the wrong side of history'."*[76]

Offering resistance

But hope springs eternal. In a film screened here recently by a local civil society group, *'The Wisdom to Survive – Climate Change, Capitalism and Community'*, we learnt that lateral thinking, ingenuity, humour, the power of the arts, and above all widespread collaboration can outwit the dire predictability of the boardroom planners.

Now in our 80s, Marjorie and I have taken to the streets in four demonstrations: resisting the Government's *dismantling* of environmental provisions (an action unique in the world); opposing the disproportionate impact of a Federal Budget on needier people; marching with 60,000 Melbournians calling for real action at the Paris Climate Conference; and appealing to the Government to offer refuge to the Christian community resident in northern Iraq since 100AD but now being driven out or massacred.

---

[75] The ABC Radio National's 'Science Show' claimed that one third of all species of wildlife animals are now threatened with extinction (2014), while the BBC has indicated that the greatest extinction since that of the dinosaurs 65 million years ago is in view, with so many species of wild animals now among the 'walking dead'.
[76] From an ABC Radio National broadcast in August 2014.

A few years earlier, in a mobilisation against the meeting in Melbourne of the world trade cartel, in a shoving match with the police I was felled to the ground. The view of a demo *from the underside* is not for the faint-hearted! But as long as we are able, on public issues of conscience we aim to offer our mini-contribution.

A new world evolving

But there is another side to the coin. Thank God, all is not doom and gloom. It is still God's world that we live in. Despite the media's assiduous reporting of crime and sleaze – tending to obscure the presence of decency and kindness, and even normality in the world – over our lifetime real progress has been made by the civil society in 'humanising' the Western world: liberating multitudes from past inequities, expanding social welfare coverage, defining and extending human rights, combating discrimination on many grounds, identifying and countering racism, caring for the disabled, guaranteeing freedom of conscience and generally making the rule of law more comprehensive. Significantly, this liberal breakthrough had never been on the capitalist agenda of ignoring the injustices of the status quo while pursuing higher profits.

Surely it has been God's Holy Spirit inspiring such advances – all of them reflecting Christian understandings and compassion at the local and the international levels, exemplified particularly in the emergence of the United Nations system of global co-operation and solidarity, backed by international specialist agencies for health, food and agriculture, education, science and culture, labour relations, human rights, refugees and the environment. Moreover, throughout the Third World numbers of young Western expatriates, many of them Christians, daily brave fearsome odds in seeking the wellbeing of disadvantaged communities. Without their presence, some of the Western financial aid programs would be unworkable.

Indubitably today's is an immensely complex world, unrecognisable from the one we lived in at the height of the Cold War in the mid-'50s (despite all its uncertainties), though there is still far to go in countering poverty and inequality.

The 'end of history'?

Beyond the end of the Cold War – hailed by Francis Fukuyama as heralding 'the end of history' and the triumph of the civil society – today's world is actually more fraught with violence, suffering and despair than at any other point in our lifetime except between 1939 and 1945. I have just read that 'the world is full of tears and blinded by hate'. Certainly, there are now millions more refugees in the world (over 60 million) than ever in human history because there are more armed conflicts using ever more sophisticated weapons, in more ruthless hands and backed by more ruthless ideologies - not to mention the arms industry, the world's arch-villains.

The distinctive factor is the escalation of military violence around the world, together with the advent of an all-embracing religious ideology motivating many alienated young Muslims by the vision of a worldwide Caliphate, serving Allah by spreading Islam through *jihad* – and ultimately destroying the *'Rûm'*.[77] *Armageddon*, the term in both the Bible and the Koran for the conflict to mark the end of time, in the Muslim understanding is to be launched from Dabiq[78] in eastern Syria.

The race relations scene

In our own land, though considerable progress towards racial equality has been registered, it could not be claimed that the chasm between the First Australians and descendants of the immigrants has been bridged. In the wide-ranging spheres of community life perhaps sports (and particularly football) offer the most encouraging evidence of significant gains, no doubt because of the level playing field in strength and skills.

In education and occupational life, considerable progress has also been made – in the cities. Today there are over 200 Aboriginal doctors, with some 30,000 Aboriginal university graduates: academics, teachers, community workers, lawyers, a surgeon, writers, artists, film makers, choreographers and politicians, a federal Minster, State

---

[77]Traditional Islamist term for Rome/ New Rome (Constantinople)/ America and the West – together seen as Christendom.
[78]Site of a crucial battle in 1516 which established Ottoman rule over the Arab lands, and today the name of the ISIL news magazine.

Ministers, Shadow Ministers, plus a former national president of the Labor Party.

Legally, the greatest step forward has been in land rights, thanks to the powers of the *Racial Discrimination Act* being upheld in 1992 by the High Court of Australia in the Eddie Mabo case, focused on the unbroken possession of Murray Island (Mer) off the tip of Cape York Peninsula. (So much for the sneer about it being a 'puny' champion!) The subsequent enacting of the *Native Title Act* by the Keating Government applied the ruling throughout Australia wherever unbroken possession could be proven. Further claims are pending, though the current Turnbull Government is again seeking to water down its scope.

It had only been with the passage of the *Racial Discrimination Act* by Gough Whitlam in 1975 that Aborigines were formally recognised under Australian law. Today Aboriginal people own over one third of the total area of the Australian landmass! But this legal reality does not materially affect the lives of Aboriginal people living in the remaining two-thirds of the continent, which includes all cities, towns and areas 'settled' by non-Aborigines. Today, the First Australians comprise only some 7% of the national population. But I would like to think that the multicultural density of our cities has also boosted Aboriginal stocks by breaking down the original mono-Anglo stereotype that had ever prevailed as the norm. Conversely, in remote and rural communities, the absence of this factor sees anti-Aboriginal animus still going largely unchallenged.

On the other hand, how encouraging is the measure of peace, harmony and mutual respect achieved within our multicultural society, perhaps the Western world's most diverse, with 17% of the population now from Asian backgrounds. Probably this is the greatest single achievement during the fair slab of Australian history that we have lived through and, compared to the prevailing social attitudes of our childhood, it is nothing less than dramatic. And that I should have had the privilege of a strategic involvement in shaping this outcome brings the utmost satisfaction.

What of the arts and culture?

Regrettably, the home I grew up in placed little emphasis on high culture, beyond that occasionally encountered on the radio. The ABC (launched a few months before I was born) had two radio stations in Sydney: 2FC for everyday information and entertainment and 2BL for highbrow culture, but our mother favoured the commercial stations with their inane chatter.

Apart from my discovery of classical music through learning the violin from Jewish maestro Mischa Dobrinski in the city in 1941-2, aborted by our move to the philistine outer suburbs, the first performances I attended were with our Opportunity C Class at two Gilbert & Sullivan operas, and later the memorable demonstration of the instruments of the orchestra under Sir Bernard Heinze at a schools' concert in Sydney Town Hall. Then I had to wait till my student days in the 1950s to attend the ABC Youth Concert series with the Sydney Symphony Orchestra.

Captured for life by the majesty and power of a symphony orchestra in full voice, in later life I would satisfy the craving by holding season tickets for concerts of the Canberra and later Melbourne Symphony Orchestras, and the years have brought untold musical delight in the dim recesses of the Llewellyn and Hamer Halls. But choicest of all would be the midsummer evenings spent with dear friends in the warm darkness of the Myer Music Bowl, held spellbound by Tchaikovsky. I have probably imbibed a good deal of the entire classical repertoire – although at times affronted by contemporary cacophonies. Sometimes in retrospect I have taken to wondering whether my truest calling might not have been to music in some form. Certainly, I had made a good, if precocious start – but it petered out for lack of funds and teachers. But I cannot contemplate living without music – my soul's wellbeing is intertwined with it. Moreover, my whole Christian experience has been reflected in music: hymns, modern songs and choruses, both words and music forever coursing through my brain. And invariably I write here against a background of classical music on FM radio.

Crisis in classical music?

But sad to say, today classical music seems to be in steep decline, rarely if ever presented on television or on commercial radio – hence never encountered by the great bulk of the population, but particularly the younger generations. The threatening demise within one lifetime of European musical traditions spanning five centuries is quite alarming. And what does the future hold for choral singing when young people seem to be mostly tone deaf?

Doubtless the realm of music offers something of a barometer for the changing social climate: is there some parallelism between moral and aesthetic anarchy? Both dimensions seem to have lost their rootedness in the classical norms practised in the West for centuries and profoundly undergirded by Christian values. Today the universally humanising component of melody seems to be under siege from disharmony, with the overwhelming domination of percussion ('noise') intermittently broken by snatches of melody. No longer are pop songs *whistlable*. And what can be more cringe-worthy than hearing the cacophony of a victorious football team 'singing' its club song on a tuneless monotone, or a crowd 'singing' the national anthem?

Even church music has succumbed to canned music so that hymns or worship songs are barely 'sung' in church any more but rather swamped by the electronic power of a band's booming percussion. So the poetic beauty and people's theology of the classical hymns, with their memorable melodies, reflecting almost two thousand years of the life of faith, have now largely been replaced by tuneless ditties clothing trite (and often archaically expressed!) spiritual clichés.

In most churches, the inevitable response has been to corral the older generation apart from the younger ones into separate worship services (earlier, of course) but this offends against the universal vision of the one worshipping people of God. Again, it reflects the uniquely fractured nature of Western society, united only in our brokenness.

However, in our current parish base at All Saints' Greensborough, with one of the best modern organs in Melbourne and a master organist presiding, early on Sunday mornings a churchful of older worshippers sing not four but five traditional hymns reflecting the biblical theme of the day, led by the excellent choir that also models the chanting of an ancient Jewish psalm. Truly uplifting!

No doubt critics of my musings will be tempted to dismiss them as nothing more than the jaundiced maunderings of one who has outlived his cultural day. To be sure, I do struggle against the negativity of so much around us in today's world: brutal reality or merely media projection? But the long perspective reflects that awareness that only older people can bring, having lived through 'the past' not shared by younger generations.

With other fine arts (theatre, ballet), regrettably I have little experience, other than occasional Aboriginal drama recommended by son Dave from his wide contacts, and of course his own performances.

Museums and Galleries

On the other hand the visual arts have ever made a huge appeal – chiefly perceiving reality as I do through the eyes. I recall lengthy visits to Le Louvre and to the Musée d'Art Impressioniste in Paris, to the Neue Pinakothek in Munich and the Museum of Art History in Vienna, as well as to galleries in London and Istanbul. Stimulating have been the many hours spent in museums spanning history, the arts and technology: the Victoria & Albert in London, the Museum of Wales in Cardiff, the 'Spanish Riding School' in Vienna, the Pergamon Museum in East Berlin, and museums of archaeology and antiquities in Cairo, Istanbul, Ankara, Budapest, Chongqing, and Quito, plus traumatic evocations of the wartime destruction wrought upon Würzburg, Hiroshima and Nagasaki. All of them recording the peoples' search for meaning in the face of such horror.

Not to speak of the splendid palace complexes in Windsor, Versailles, Vienna, Potsdam, Hanover and Dresden, as well as in Istanbul and Beijing. In fact, it is the architectural glories that have captivated me the most. A huge proportion of the countless colour slides and photos taken around the world turn out to be of impressive buildings: cathedrals, castles, marketplaces, half-timbered houses, urban vistas.

Delights of world travel

Of profound significance have been the opportunities for worldwide travel, visiting sites such as the Pyramids and Sphinx, Pompeii and Mt Vesuvius, the Colosseum, the Catacombs, the Acropolis, the ruins of Ephesus and Troy, le Pont du Gard, Hadrian's Wall, Stonehenge, the Mexican pyramids, Machu Picchu, and Lake Titicaca with its floating islands. And in the Holy Land: Jerusalem, Bethlehem, Nazareth, the Sea of Galilee. Also, the Vatican City, Holy Mt Athos, Mt Ararat, the 'Iron Curtain' and the Berlin Wall, Red Square and the Kremlin, Hiroshima and Nagasaki, and the Great Wall of China. Meccas for world tourism conferring memories to cherish lifelong.

Along the way, a gratifying factor has been the inverse relationship between the worldwide range of these travels and the minimal outlays on creature comforts while mostly adventuring alone. It would become a matter of honour, building self-reliance and reflecting a delight with languages. Over my lifetime, I have travelled to 42 countries worldwide. Few have seen and done so much while expending so little.

Love affair with China

Undoubtedly, apart from our years in Europe, the most significant outcome of these travels was our discovery of China. The taste was originally acquired from my brief holiday in 1989 with daughter Sara-Jane in Hong Kong and Guilin, wryly climaxing in a gallant motor-cycle outrider of a People's Army unit coming a cropper at our feet while affecting to bow to the blonde maiden – triggering a series of rear-end military clashes! Instantly we melted into the ubiquitous throng.

Then in 2003 I was to join a small team of Australian teacher volunteers under the aegis of a Christian professional service agency (descendant of the 19th century China Inland Mission), training younger academics and senior students in applied English in the Institute (later University) of Technology in Chongqing, one of 14 in this huge regional metropolis of SW China with its 10 million people – wartime capital under the Japanese occupation of the east. In my pocket, the *Expert's Passport* backing my Australian passport in gaining privileged access and a designated, honoured role in the People's Republic of China.

In the following two years, facilitated by the Institute's International Office, working in a relaxed political climate compared to the earlier decades, for periods of three months we both took up the mantle as volunteer conversation partners' with trios of lecturers and of advanced students. I had prepared and gained approval of a syllabus of topics for discussion, widely covering contemporary life and thought. Sharing our personal stories led to cordial relationships, at times expressed in surprisingly frank expressions of opinion on social issues. What a privilege to be taken so freely into their confidence and accorded such respect, reaping the benefit of our wrinkles and grey hair.

And what better way of accessing and seeking to fathom the four thousand year history, culture, lore and daily life of China's people than by enjoying creative relationships with so many knowledgeable and sophisticated observers – along the way fostering the emergence of confident speakers of English in a city with few esoteric contacts. To us two it brought sheer joy.

A role of honour

Setting up home in a self-contained suite in the university's Academic Visitors' Centre we became part of the local economy, buying our supplies at local supermarkets modelled on Western ones (but at derisory prices!) and preparing meals on a 'magnetic cooker'. Weekday mornings we would be woken by a martial air ringing out across the residential campus – in China all tertiary students live within their university, residing in separate multi-storeyed dormitories.

As guests of the International Office, on several occasions we were taken on excursions such as an evening cruise on the two mighty rivers that converge in the centre of Chongqing, and out into the countryside to places of historic interest, such as Deng Xiao Ping's home town and family villa. Of course, at weekends we explored the metropolis and, to escape the dense industrial smog limiting visibility to a few hundred metres 24/7, we would venture further afield into nearby mountains, once staying the weekend at the Visitors' Centre of the University for Posts & Telecommunications. Sundays would see us worshipping in English at a Foreigners' Church that met in an upmarket hotel with fellow-teachers and other professionals from SE Asia and North America, pastored by an Australian attached to the International School. We were both given the honour of preaching to the diverse congregation.

At the end of our second three-months' stint a student asked me out of the blue in a discussion period, *"Tell me about Christian"*. He had responded to an impromptu international missionary venture by a few young Chinese-American students who had turned up to practise basketball on campus before inviting contacts to an evening meal in a city hotel, with a Christian presentation. As a result, he wanted to be a Christian. Deeming it an appropriate response to his request (about an issue which I had never mentioned earlier) I responded positively but discreetly. Providentially the following year, in a far-off city where he was then working, we were to make further contact, arranging for an older Chinese Christian friend to spend an afternoon sharing the Faith with him.

On another occasion, when his discussion partner failed to show, an older lecturer asked me what Christians believed. I judged his enquiry to be genuine. Later he invited us to join his family at home for dinner (unheard-of in China, where people sense they would be 'shamed' in front of visitors for the meanness of their quarters). But doubtless he also felt it inappropriate to be discussing such a topic in a public place. I had bought him a bilingual New Testament in a city church I knew of, and together we read the Parable of the Good Samaritan. He was so impressed at the ethical implications of the story that he proceeded to expound it impromptu (in Chinese) to his family. Who knows the ultimate outcomes of such chance encounters?

Towards the end of our second stay, I had written up our tutoring methodology for the Professor of English who subsequently published it as an article in the national linguistic journal. Later we were called up to the International Office where – in appreciation of our voluntary efforts – we each received a towering wad of *yuan* banknotes reimbursing our airfares to China.

Swansong

Our final visit saw us travelling to several provinces at the invitation of friends made during our tutoring of post-graduate students at Deakin University, as well as bidding final farewell to colleagues and friends in Chongqing. We had also spent a few days in Jiuzhaigo, a pristine wilderness of gorgeous forests and lakes backed by snow-capped ranges, sparsely populated by an ethnic Tibetan minority, where the jetliner landed on an airfield consisting of the tops of two peaks sliced off to fill the intervening valley! China today: land of stunning infrastructure foreshadowing a future rimmed in hope. And home to an earnest, talented and disciplined people fulfilling an ancient destiny.

For me the travels worldwide had brought the ultimate fulfilment of the childhood dream – beyond all imagining. Now forever resolved, the old mystery of the Botany Bay Heads!

Our diversifying homeland

An essential dimension of my quest for meaning and fulfilment, intensifying over the decades, had been my interest in monitoring the evolution of Australia within the broader world, as our population quadrupled from six to twenty-four million in my lifetime! Apart from the endless frustrations (and occasional triumphs) of party politics, my interest has been excited by the physical environment, the architecture, the townscapes, town planning and the urban scene, the development of public transport, motoring and aviation, rather than the boring, underlying (but indispensable) technology – not to mention the inner workings of the economy –- which remain closed books.

But beyond this, my sharpest focus had been reserved for the human dimension of our national development: who are we Australians? In my childhood, from coast to coast the answer would have been unequivocal: people from British backgrounds. Later censuses would show that the 1930s had been the least multicultural period since the First Fleet. Through my schooldays, I only knew of one boy who was half-Chinese, two Jews and one classmate with an Italian-sounding surname. Only at university would I meet holocaust escapees studying (of all things!) German. And, of course, I was barely aware of the scope of the White Australia Policy for excluding Asians ('coloureds') from the country – rather, we sensed we were a branch of the British Isles somehow transposed to the Antipodes and with no local regional connections required. Yet the great romance of my life would become bound up with facilitating the diversification of cultures destined to create the Australia we know today, where every second Australian is overseas-born or has one or both parents born overseas – including all our children's partners and all four of our grandchildren!

And of course, we have enjoyed the great good fortune of living out our lives in a stable, secure society far from the world centres of conflict marked by the arms race, the Cold War and the balance of terror, and today's Islamist excesses. Beyond our parents' soul-destroying experience of two dreadful wars interspersed by the near-total collapse of national economies, our generation in Australia had been privileged to live through an era of peace and reconstruction, with full employment, growing prosperity and social mobility. And in later years through an amazing technological evolution that has transformed human existence in the West – although within which there was still some continuity of earlier moral and religious values.

Thus we have living memories of a church life which for so many Australians claimed centre stage, both in the public realm and in satisfying the personal quest for meaning through offering a faith to live by. The stability conferred on our lives by these factors stands in stark contrast to the sense of multi-level crisis pervading the community today and casting a long shadow over the future.

The domestic scene

In retrospect, the travel motif also seems to have symbolised the three serial forays of my life's journey: into education and teaching, into public service research and community development, and into Christian ministry, each seamlessly contiguous. All three of them focusing on human betterment rather than competitive or commercial gain – a tremendous privilege which I never foresaw, let alone sought. In the ongoing pilgrimage, there was often a sense (if at times only dimly perceived) of a divine guide quietly unfolding the purposes for my existence in his world. Regret has barely tinged the onward way.

And how much have I treasured the understanding, support and love of my life-partner Marjorie, despite the changing scenes we have explored together and the burdens I have laden her with. Her patience and loyalty in the face of misgivings, her courage in venturing into the unknown, and the diligence of her physical caring for our family is all exemplified in the portrait of the remarkable wife and mother whom we meet in Proverbs chapter 31 in the Jewish culture of the Old Testament:

> *"A good woman is hard to find and worth more than rubies. She's diligent in home-making, quick to assist anyone in need, reaches out to help the poor. When she speaks she has something worth hearing and she always says it kindly. Her children respect and bless her. Many women have done remarkable things, but you've outclassed them all!"*[79]

But, of course, she has also led her own creative life within and beyond the domestic setting, bringing her finely honed skills to the task of counselling and blessing people, within a community development context, as well as raising and nurturing four children, often under the testing circumstances of my frequent and at times lengthy absences on demanding work assignments. And in our ministry phase, she was in reality 'co-vicar', humanising our Broadmeadows parish by being ever available to all, initiating creative activities for all ages.

In recent years, she has become active in spiritual direction ('soul companioning'), completing a three-year diploma and working under the close supervision required of practitioners. Beyond this she is currently co-ordinator of the women's network of Renewal Retreat Ministries in Victoria which sustains women in professional ministry by offering mutual support over a three-year cycle of residential retreats.

In 2016, we celebrated our sixty years of life together. But at this remove, mulling over what it has all meant through a lifetime, maybe I can claim to have seen the scriptural promise fulfilled, that *those who seek shall find*. I have indeed 'found': peace in my home and among my family, a faith to live by and the prospects of eternity, the joy of

---

[79]Excerpts from Proverbs ch. 31 in 'The Message: The Bible in Contemporary Language' translated by Eugene H Peterson, Navpress, USA

belonging to God's people and using my gifts for serving among the worldwide company of believers, the pleasure of children successfully launched into the world and our four dear grandchildren growing apace in a land still marked by hope, despite many indications of retreat and gathering darkness.

And on every hand the enticing wonders of creation, the promise of every new dawn – and peace at the end.

CHAPTER 45: Core of my Heart

It has taken a lifetime to plumb the implications of living *in* and *by* faith – and still I've a way to go. Yet along the path, the God dimension has increasingly captured my imagination. Without such an ordering principle, life would remain inexplicable. As a teenager in Sydney Town Hall reacting to a call to *'Come to Christ'*, my discovery was that God is for real, that we are created as spiritual beings, and that through love he has taken the initiative of self-disclosure, desiring to be accessed by us mortals.

During the next decade, though blessed with opportunities for education unheard-of in my extended family and the opening before me of professional life – not to mention the joys of friendships and ultimately love – I seem to have been a slow learner. In my adolescent years, I never knew how to converse with peers: I would agonise that I had nothing to say, and would muse about how people managed meaningful conversations. Only decades later, through involvement in personal growth groups, would I grasp the basic (and obvious) principle that meaningful encounters flow from tuning in to your conversation partner's life and concerns as well as being preoccupied with your own. Walk a mile in their shoes!

Among the naïve rationalisations of the 1960s/70s social upheaval was the dismissal of traditional conventions and of earlier didactic approaches, replaced by an exciting new prospect of *non-directive* learning. There was even a modish theology around suggesting that Christians should never 'name the Name' but let their own integrity and inner wholeness carry the day. (In retrospect, it probably meant that for the most part nobody noticed anything!) I feel sad about having consciously acted out this misguided approach to parenting adolescents, in essence weakening the essential link between faith and life.

Moreover, it was only after internalising the belated insight about focusing on others that the possibility of involvement in Christian ministry could start to become thinkable. As it happened, years afterwards and beyond professional training, as a parish minister I did seem able to invest myself in people and to handle pastoral care with warmth. Indeed, I can claim to have actually grown into enjoying it. It had taken all of 55 years.

Primacy of grace

As a young adult, what I hadn't inwardly grasped was the veriest core of the Good News: the unbelievable truth of the *scope and plenitude of God's grace* (goodness, kindness, generosity) – of course all unsought and undeserved – and the efficacy of the redemption purchased for humanity once for all on the Cross and freely offered through a love-relationship with Christ. To be accessed simply by our inward identification with it (taking God's promise seriously and accepting it inwardly). And even that act of faith on our part itself a gift of God's love: the ability to internalise the liberating notion that Christ has done it all and offers the unspeakable gift of God's lifelong friendship and guidance.

The setting for these early struggles of mind and will was my involvement in the Sydney University Evangelical Union (in ultimate retrospect, producing the most transformational outcomes of my years of tertiary study), and subsequently in Methodist and Anglican parishes, supplemented by the broader experience of churchgoing in England and Germany. Along the way had come the dawning awareness of the dualistic character of Christian identity – personal faith *and* commitment to others, especially the neediest. Of course, the two dimensions are interwoven, because discovering the reality of God immediately implies relating with local fellow-believers in fellowship and worship. But the pity is that this fellowship can so satisfy us that we may not take the next step to 'serve the present age'.

Throughout church history, times of renewal and revival have been marked by the rediscovery of this dualistic message: God's favour *proclaimed* with new conviction but also demonstrated through relevant social action, for instance in the combat of poverty and industrial exploitation, slavery, child labour, treatment of prisoners, discrimination against women and the disabled; opposing racism, war, the arms race and nuclear armaments; and seeking justice for indigenous people, refugees and asylum seekers – besides the wellbeing of the environment within which it all happens – to cite some of the perennial causes in Western (Christian) society often lacking elsewhere.

God's worldwide strategic initiative

Amidst the social upheaval of the '60s and '70s, God appeared to have launched a wave of spiritual liberation around the Christian world, softening hearts and empowering believers, in retrospect now recognised as preparing the church for the coming age of tribulation that we call the 21st century – yet within two or three decades a church to be widely (and justly) reviled and shamed for its public sins and its traditional hubris. Does it betoken a countdown to the scriptural promise of Christ's appearance at the end of the age in a welter of apostasy, confusion and conflict?

Recently I encountered the disturbing claim that the 20th century had witnessed a wider persecution of Christians than the previous 19 centuries put together, with no less than 100 million victims! The pace of the countdown is quickening. A bloody persecution of Christians is now escalating in many parts of the Muslim world and in North Korea – with scant succour (or even interest) from the once-Christian West. Is this also an end-time marker?

Forsaking the faith

Certainly, within my lifetime, in Western society the widespread abandonment of virtually two thousand years of Christian belief has come about at a bewildering pace and at marked social cost, in little more than one generation – leaving a vacuum of values, a moral void in politics, and a legacy of libertarianism, confusion and anomie. Not to speak of rampant evil manifest across our society and throughout the world. I am desolated at the accelerating rate of abandonment of the core verities underlying Western civilisation.

Of course, from the 18th century Enlightenment period and more intensively in the latter half of the 19th century, many European philosophers, political thinkers and scientists were positing a new scientific-rationalist understanding of life and society which dispensed with the need for a divine creator or agent of 'progress'. To many, modernity and humanism offered appealing alternatives. So for the first time many of the *educated élites* grew up largely untouched by the rumour of God or the sanction of his holiness – or the power of his love. With the new factor today of the silencing of Christian opinion in the media and often in academia – and the feckless abdication on the part of so many of us Christians – God seems to be written out of his creation.

But conceivably the decline of Christian faith *among the masses* during the 20th century in Europe (reflected in the Antipodes) was also attributable to the crises of competing capitalisms masquerading as nationalism, which triggered unprecedented conflicts killing 80 million human beings in two barbaric World Wars (the greatest in human history) and demoralising entire populations. On both sides, the majority of Church leaders had allowed their national loyalty to eclipse their loyalty to the Prince of Peace: where was God when both sides were claiming a monopoly on him? Why had he not responded to the heart cry of millions, especially the mothers? Or had he too wept over such freely endorsed human wickedness culminating in the Holocaust[80] that smote the descendants of the 'Chosen People' with the genocide of six million?

So over the post-war generations, the drift from the Churches of the West would escalate into a stampede. Would this amount to the greatest (and *swiftest*) mass apostasy from any faith in human history? Certainly, it seems unprecedented. Are the issues now so cosmic that even the most faithful of us can make so slight an impact on our communal environment of disbelief?

A recent survey found that 49% of Australians now hold that there is no God, spawning the massively subjective turn of today's Western culture. '*I shall decide for myself, thank you!*' The new focus on individualism and self-actualisation has at best led to a 'believing without belonging' but more broadly to a brutal materialism portending the end of civility and the widespread rejection of authority – replaced by the search for authenticity, expressivity and self-fulfilment. Of

---
[80]The Hebrew word for 'burnt offering'

course, it also reflects the increase in prosperity and the benefits of the welfare state, as well as consumerism and greater social mobility – all of them manifestations of modernity and in some cases Christian gifts to society. But it has come at a price: a collective amnesia threatening the loss of our spiritual history, our truest identity and our ultimate destiny.

As UK Rabbi, Jonathan Sachs has said in a TED talk

> *"The old marriage of religion and culture has ended in divorce. Today the secular West has largely lost the values that used to be called the Judeo-Christian heritage. Instead it has chosen to worship the idols of the self — the market, consumerism, autonomy, rights, individualism, and "whatever works for you" — while relinquishing the codes of loyalty, reverence and respect that once preserved marriages, communities and the subtle bonds that tie us to one another, moving us to work for the common good."*

A gathering darkness

With both the motivations and sanctions of religion lost, the search for personal meaning becomes a daunting challenge, perhaps inducing confusion and despair or leading to a headlong embrace of provocative and self-destructive behaviours reflecting social disintegration and nihilism. Welcome to today's Western society!

At the personal level, to dispense with a faith to live by and the guidance it provides for discerning good from evil, and to spurn God's indwelling Holy Spirit who empowers daily living, seem to amount to acts of folly. And when such acts are widespread across society, it must trigger an erosion of moral and ethical standards once perceived as normative, but now more likely to be ignored, even derided. Further, when this drift occurs within one single generation – as we have experienced – it amounts to the society losing its moral compass, to become the plaything of sinister forces bent on sidelining God and actively encouraging agnosticism or even atheism. *'No God, no master!'* rang the catchcry of rebellion in the 1970s.

Whence do these forces arise other than from the cosmic powers of evil loosed upon the earth? In the Western world, the all-pervasive media and entertainment colossus, whether intentionally or subconsciously, has moved into a new crusade to dismiss God from his creation and subvert residual Christian ethics by libertarian campaigning. Its success is attested by the current generation's scepticism of religion as simply irrelevant to living.

The cynical role of the commercial media has recently been starkly exemplified in its conniving with predatory capitalism to *undermine public health and physical wellbeing* through unconscionable advertising of food products reeking in sugar known to promote obesity with all its attendant and life-shortening ills. Our expanding silhouettes tell the story. More than half of Australians are now over-weight or obese, and this is rapidly becoming a major health concern worldwide, clearly related to dietary intake. In a series of recent television programs, these strategies were clinically dissected, revealing the shameless behaviour of captains of commerce, actually *backed by* conservative, business-oriented governments – even though their refusal to act is triggering escalating healthcare budgets!

A counter-indication on the world scene: explosive Christian growth

But despite the current decline of Christian faith in Australia and the Western world, statisticians of world religions envisage Christianity still being the globe's major faith in 2050, with the overall percentage of *'unbelievers with no religion'* actually in decline! Of course, it must be noted that today it is only in the secular West that Christianity is in such sharp decline. We live in an amazing window of history where it is being reported that more people are being swept into the Kingdom of God (including via the Internet) than ever in recorded history. Recent decades have seen millions turning to Christ in Africa and Asia and Latin America relatively unaffected by Western post-modernism and hedonism, so that today the dynamic in world mission is coming from countries like Korea and Nigeria. For instance, one third of the population of South Korea are now Christians, while in

Nigeria alone there are more *Anglicans* in church on Sundays than in England, America and Australia put together! In 1900, there were said to be six million Christians in all of Africa (the great majority of them the Copts of Egypt). Today, Africa-wide, Christians comprise 50% of the continent's total population. Indeed, many are putting their lives on the line at the hands of Islamist terrorist movements. In Iran, by way of reaction to the excesses of the harsh Shia Muslim regime of the Ayatollahs, it is said that one fifth of the population have become Christian. Across the world it is a similar story of new converts risking persecution in many countries where Christian missions had planted churches.

And academic estimates by leading Chinese universities put that country's Christian population variously between 54 and 130 million. Difficult to substantiate because of the explosive growth of the 'underground churches' gathering in farms and rural villages out of the public eye. A recent official statistic puts the number of Christians for the first time as exceeding the national membership of the Communist Party (88 million), triggering random localised reactions such as the forcible removal of crosses from the roofs of large church buildings and the bulldozing in 2014 of a newly built Catholic cathedral in Wenzhou in Zhejiang Province.

Overall, the decline of Christian faith in the West, balanced by its growth in the non-Western world, may effectively dissolve the European captivity of the Gospel: from the beginning the faith was not a Western phenomenon, although early in Christian history it had become domesticated under the centralised power of Rome and later of New Rome (Constantinople), and subsequently it informed European culture for a thousand years, culminating in the missionary movement from the 16th to the 20th century within the framework of colonialism which made the Christian faith the world's foremost religion – the only one practised in every land on earth.

So today's Western scepticism stands in sharp contrast to the norms of religion across the face of human society down all ages and until today – its ubiquity, its intensity and its devotion. Particularly its capacity for offering devotees, in an often meaningless world, a sense of belonging. My recent reading of several modern scholarly novels set in classical antiquity has confirmed just how drenched with religion that world was, despite the disdain of its élites. So it is scarcely surprising that Christianity's current decline in the West is not matched elsewhere in time or place. Nor is it matched by rejection of any of the other great world faiths in their homelands e.g. Islam in the Middle East, Hinduism in India, Buddhism in Tibet, or even Confucianism and Taoism in Communist China. Nor among their settler groups in Australia.

It is even claimed that the rest of the world is becoming more religious – ominously so in parts of the Middle East! *The West may yet wind up as an effete push-over for a looming religious militancy currently brewing beyond its borders.*

Power of the media

By way of a conspiracy theory, one might premise that a principal function of the *commercial* media is to deflect people from ideologies – and especially faith – in the interests of consumerism. Traducing truth for trivia. Buy! Conform! ... to the media's take on issues, precluding any other opinion. Why? To dumb down the functioning of a discriminating civil society by substituting the bread-and-circuses mentality?

Of course, the 'circuses' of today are the products of a highly professional, ingenious, compelling entertainment industry, spinner of dreams of which we are all passive consumers in our own homes. One of the leading figures an (ex)-Australian media mogul, sometimes cited as the world's most powerful figure, to whom even leaders of nations defer. As an insightful comment in the preface to a contemporary autobiography put it: *"The media today is obsessed with the moment, so memories get cancelled out in a generation".* This factor could account for the astonishing loss of Christian insights on how we might publicly address the intractable dilemmas of our day.

Indeed, a future Martian explorer of our Western world might be forgiven for concluding that religion was of merely historic interest. By its unrelenting negativity, cynicism, carping criticism and intentional neglect of other ideological standpoints (especially with a religious sanction) the media also contribute to the growing contempt for democracy, with politicians shrinking from moral leadership and merely acting in the role of managers of the status quo. It is the media that ought to be under the spotlight. But for all their self-obsession, media operatives seem incapable of self-criticism.

Areas of social distress

So to the specifics: what are the most serious areas of distress characterising our community life today? What are the losses challenging our societal wellbeing – not to speak of personal meaning and contentment?

It comes to mind that society is paying dearly for the wholesale disdain of the worldwide and timeless bond of matrimony – *a committed lifelong partnership with a religious and social sanction*. In Australia, the universal concept of the family as the nest for raising the young is in retreat. A recent media report acknowledges that the majority of cases of violence against women are occurring within non-marital relationships, with a growing number of disgruntled, angry and sometimes vengeful ex-partners, maybe from serial relationships – and sad, lost children. The federal government has recently declared domestic violence to be a 'national crisis': each week across Australia two women are murdered and three hospitalised with brain damage, while among Aboriginal communities the rate is forty times higher! Some States now have a Minister for the Prevention of Family Violence.

In today's explicitly sexualised and violent society, changes in the realm of sexual ethics make pornography virtually inescapable by children from primary school level, thus subverting parental responsibility. Despite commissions of enquiry in Europe and America and a Senate Enquiry in Australia on the 'Sexualisation of Children in the Media', no action appears to have resulted. Indeed, in the Victorian Parliament the porn merchants are represented by the Sex Party which professes to be countering 'the *increasing influence* of religion in Australian politics'!

There is also a crisis in gambling on the ubiquitous poker machines, reflected by the advent of a federal political party specifically dedicated to combating them. But sadly, attempts to seek restrictions come to naught because of advertising on television and at sporting venues, including opportunities for gambling on every second kick or cricket shot – and with governments addicted to the revenues at stake.

Apart from the ongoing and worsening drugs crisis, mental health concerns include the growing incidence of depression, now experienced in the lives of 45% of Australians – and higher among Aboriginals – triggered by a raft of factors, including brutal competitiveness and loss of the scaffolding of a belief system other than the worship of the dollar.

For Australians under 44, suicide has become the commonest cause of death – among young Aboriginal people a veritable epidemic. It seems clear that the moral fabric of our society is starting to unravel at an accelerating rate. A US magazine reports that the children of parents caught up in the '60s sexual revolution with its flouting of boundaries are now becoming a generation killing themselves in unprecedented numbers. And today comes a call for *all teachers* to be trained in suicide prevention.

'Post-God Nation?'

In a new, well-argued book, former barrister Roy Williams refutes the wilful blindness of the narrative now promoted by libertarian secularists, and reflected in the new national education curriculum, claiming that Christianity has exercised only a minimal or even malign influence on Australia's development. The advent of this curriculum Australia-wide must profoundly undermine the transmission of Christian values to the next generation. But while not overlooking the many failings of Christians and the Church, Williams meticulously catalogues the cavalcade of men and women of faith over two centuries who have contributed in every area of community life, more than balancing out the larrikin spirit associated with our dubious beginnings.

He demonstrates that the First Settlement was devised in England by strategically placed Christians, and early Governors were almost invariably devout men, particularly Governor Lachlan Macquarie, who with his far-seeing vision led NSW from penal colony to free society.

> "All social welfare, healthcare and education was done by the Church and Christian volunteers. Without people motivated by their faith the early colony could not have survived. Though rough and irreverent, the colony would not have got through its early years without descending into impoverished barbarism. And over this period, saving the indigenous people from total extinction may be the Churches' most important achievement, though much evil was perpetrated on its frontiers."

Roy Williams details how the colonial legislatures brought together many Christians in leading roles imbued with the ideal of service rather than personal advantage, while Christians also played crucial roles in the discussions leading to Federation. Since then, the Churches have played a vital role in shaping modern Australian society. Meticulously recording our 200-year history, he challenges atheists, agnostics and believers to a genuinely open debate about the power of Christian faith to change society. But he warns that there is a limit to how long our society can go on drawing down its Judaeo-Christian patrimony.

He suggests the Churches would find more allies on the Left, where the well-meaning idealists reside while the Liberal Party, once the preserve of the 'moral middle class', has been hijacked by neo-liberals to become the populist party of the super-rich and the go-getters, with its senior ranks dominated by shallow, market-driven secularists and selectively doctrinaire Catholics who endorse the Vatican on narrowly dogmatic issues but not on the macro-level issues of war, the environment, poverty, social justice, or refugees. In the process, the Party has become less benevolent.

Of course, Williams acknowledges openly that the Churches have also lost influence through such societal issues as prosperity, scientism, nationalism, war, sex and gender but he claims that, if they could become more open to change, they could yet restore their tarnished image and project an attainable moral vision for Australia. He concludes that there is little doubt that it is becoming harder to be a Christian in today's Australia.

The Cosmic Christ

But beyond Australia, what of the future for humanity?

The recent identification of a possible counterpart of Earth in a galaxy some nine trillion kilometres away, graced with the fetching name of *'Kepler 186f'*, is said to have further shifted the goalposts. Travelling at 300,000 km per sec – the speed of light – we could circle the earth seven times in one second. Had we set off in Columbus' day and maintained that goodly speed, by now we would be nearing our Kepler destination!

It must take a robust 'non-faith' to hold that life on earth in all its intricacy, complexity and beauty, with 8.7 million species identified (and still counting!) – from single-cell organisms to the human brain with its infinite inventiveness, within the context of an inter-dependent world of wonder and delight, on a planet spinning through space at 500,000 mph within a solar system of impeccable timing – all this simply materialised, out of nothing. Nothing? *Come on...* Astronomy reveals that there are 200 *billion* stars in the 'Back End' of the Milky Way visible from Australia.

The very notion that God should have *conceived of the idea of creating* seems mind-blowing, not to speak of the further implication that without the Christ *"nothing was made that was made"*.[81] Or did it all just happen by chance, without a Cause or an Intelligence? Let alone a Maker of infinite power and majesty? What are the odds on that?

Or again, that a Creator would have no interest in his human creation, loftily indifferent to its fate? Most ordinary Australians are not so sure. Too often we are overtaken and held spellbound by the morning magic of a misty glen, the riotous greens of a rainforest, the wonder of a desert night sky, the soaring harmonies of a symphony, the glory of a life laid down for another.

By definition, God must be *unimaginable, incomprehensible, indefinable*. Is theology foolish then in essaying to corral God into the constraints of human thought? But if indeed God exists and created everything for his own pleasure, then, clearly, he is invested in his whole creation – including us and our environment in our time –

---
[81] John 1:2

and must be granted the equally incomprehensible condescension of disclosing himself by seeking us out for a conscious love-relationship. If God, the father of all, chooses to reveal himself to humankind through wrapping himself in the human clay he had created, is it folly to explore the offer? Doesn't the alternative: of dismissing unexamined a claim that might make sense of our human condition, seem hubristic – to say the least?

God's future – and ours

But it is not what we humans think of God that counts, but what the holy, infinite, all-loving and self-revealing God purposes to do in the ongoing story of his world, let alone his cosmos. What we learn of God through his self-disclosure might lead us to understand that he is not fazed by hard human hearts as much as grieved because so many lost people decline to be 'found'. What might God's intentions be? And what sort of future could this betoken for the Western world?

The only indication can be the future outlined in the Scriptures: that the Reign of God, from the beginning of the Christian era growing in the world in embryonic form among the 'household of faith', will be publicly vindicated and universally ushered in by the personal return of Jesus the Christ in triumph, in an era of cataclysmic worldwide conflict (nuclear?) termed Armageddon, beyond which God's values and God's truth will reign. Hence we pray in the Lord's Prayer, *"Your Kingdom come, your will be done"*.

From as far back as the widespread persecution of Christians in the Roman Empire the Church has looked and yearned for the 'Day of the Lord' to come soon, expressed in the traditional sigh of prayer in Aramaic, the language of Jesus: '*Maranatha*': ('O Lord, come'. Come quickly).[82] Come and end the world's suffering and anguish.

This is the one hope that unites and sustains Christians around the globe, including Syrian and Iraqi Christians facing death at the hands of enemies hell-bent on their eradication, and also us beleaguered ones in the West held in the thrall of a godless affluence. While secular

---

[82] Both 'soon' and 'quickly' are implied in the word.

Westerners may view our regional 'civilisation' as the apex of human achievement, God's schedule relates to a universal scenario and indeed favours the 'insignificant' parts of the world. According to Jesus' timetable: "The Good News must first be preached *among all nations* [people groups] before the end shall come."[83]

Only in our time has this condition looked like being met, with churches, groups of believers or missionary activity now found in every land on earth (even including Saudi Arabia). And around the world Scripture translations being made into tiny minority-group languages.[84] So the times appear to be rapidly ripening towards God's decisive intervention in history.

But, of course, contemporary Western scepticism scorns God's perspective that humanity is fatally flawed, dogged by evil without and sin within – the latter term cringe-worthy indeed to our enlightened belief in human perfectibility through knowledge and education (despite the eloquent verdict of history – and this morning's newspaper!). Such scepticism precludes the acceptance of God's redeeming love-initiative: his merciful condescension in visiting our planet divinely wrapped in human flesh, bringing the sublime ethical insights offered our race with their potential for creating one worldwide family. But our Father is *good*: to spurn his love-initiative is to defer to the powers of evil – sadly, an all too present reality in our world.

In recent years, in our ever-darkening world of tears and fears still doggedly dismissive of God's solution for human brokenness, at times I too struggle to maintain hope. I find it truly saddening to think of militant atheists and honest agnostics despising the love of Christ on the cross as he whispers, *"Father, forgive them. They know not what they do"*. Yet against this backdrop of human unbelief reigns the unchanging, eternal God, throughout and beyond the cosmos. Irrespective of human scepticism his Son offers our conflicted world the unique hope of reconciliation – with each other and with God, across all barriers of fear and hate. Of course, only God's Holy Spirit can open closed minds and soften hardened hearts to comprehend and

---

[83] Mark's Gospel, 13:10 and Luke 24:47.

[84] It is significant that, around the world, the Wycliffe Bible Translators alone initiate one new translation into minority group languages every week.

receive such love. So in the face of my despair at the world's rampant evils, the challenge comes to continue to watch and pray, both for the world's little people suffering at the hands of the ruthless, the cruel and the greedy, while still pondering our Lord's incredible challenge to forgive – and to pray – for our enemies... *even ISIL!*

'Thy Kingdom come'

The Kingdom of God was the unifying focus of all Christ's teaching. Prophesied in ancient Jewish writings over the previous five hundred years, the Reign of God (in Jesus' words also characterised as the 'Kingdom of God') would initially be ushered in through the Messiah's birth,[85] his peerless life, his sublime teachings, his atoning death, his wondrous resurrection and his exaltation to glory – the pivot of world history. For the whole race, reconciliation achieved through the Cross: this world matters – love has won!

But while God's rule is not yet manifest as a visible reality in the world, nonetheless over the past two thousand years of his grace, unfailing love and patience, it has been inwardly experienced in myriad human hearts, as well as humanising once-Christian societies. To conventional thinking the values of God's Kingdom will prove upside-down: status hierarchies reversed – *"putting down the mighty from their seat and exalting the humble and meek"* so that *"the first shall be last, and the last first"*. This order is incompatible with the ways of the world. Indeed, the wisdom of the world is exposed as foolishness. The coinage of the Kingdom will not be wealth and power but humility and love. No wonder during Jesus' public ministry 'the common people heard him gladly'.

So the Kingdom of God that Christ has brought into the world is *'already – but not yet'*: that is, ineradicably planted and in embryo growing over the past 2000 years, now finally spanning the globe but yet to be made manifest in majesty and awe at the revelation of Jesus as the cosmic Christ, the Lord of all creation, and the Judge of all the earth who "shall reign for ever and ever". Until that great day, Christians dwell simultaneously in two worlds: the so-called 'real

---

[85]The Messiah (in Hebrew) or The Christ (in Greek) was long prophesied in the Old Testament as God's Anointed and Chosen Leader –deliverer of Israel and of the human race.

world' and the unseen, inwardly experienced world of the Spirit, living in daily communion with Christ.

His appearing will spell the defeat of evil and the vanquishing of death, bringing renewal of the whole creation, with a new heaven and a new earth finally restored in harmony with their Creator. So God *"will be all in all, and His Kingdom will have no end."*[86]

Until God chooses to fulfil that enticing vision, the bidding of Jesus rings down the centuries to make disciples among every nation. And to strive to be hope-bearers in a world marred by negativity and violence and the worship of the 'Golden Calf'. *"Occupy till I come"*. [87]

From my late eventide perspective, I offer my gratitude for God's sovereign initiative in loving, calling, forgiving and receiving me. And for his ever-patient companionship during the ride of a lifetime: his steadily unfolding purposes for my life, his gifts of health, home and family love, of work callings, of adequate resources, of friendships, of encouragement in perplexity, in worldwide travel adventures and dramatic rescues. And for the assurance, as Jesus has explicitly promised[88], that he has prepared a place to be where he is.

Meanwhile I remain grateful to be living in God's world of beauty and wonder. And to be watching for the dawn.

Maranatha – Come, Lord, come quickly!

---

[86] I Corinthians 15: 28 and Luke 1: 33
[87] Luke 19:13 (King James Version)
[88] John 14: 1-4

APPENDIX: Publications

'An Antipodean looks at the King's School', article in *The Elean*, Lent and Summer Terms, 1960, No 134 (new series), magazine of The King's School, Ely, Cambridgeshire, England

Let's Speak French: a Course in Four Parts, Part Four, by Neile Osman, James Houston and Michel Bocquet, Students' Book 390pp and Teacher's Source Book 512pp, Angus & Robertson, Sydney, 1970

Le Jour J, in French, in Reader Series for *Let's Speak French*, Part One, Angus & Robertson, Sydney, 1966, 32pp

Cook's Endeavour (as founder and editor, backed by committee of Cook Primary School Parents & Citizens), community news periodical for residents of the new suburb of Cook in Canberra, 11 issues in four volumes of (mostly) three issues, each up to 24pp, 1969-72. [Lodged in National Library at its request]

Chapter in *A Charge to Keep: an Evangelical Symposium on the Christian Life Curriculum*, ed.Brian Hill, Aldersgate Fellowship of NSW, Sydney, 1971

National Groups in Australia: A Directory, separate Directories for all six States and the ACT/Queanbeyan, compiled from field data and observation, Australian Government Publishing Service, Canberra, 1975

A Multicultural Society for the Future, Immigration Reference Paper, Australian Government Publishing Service, Canberra, 1973 [Paper presented at Cairnmillar Institute's symposium, 'Strategy 2000: Australia for Tomorrow', Melbourne, by A J Grassby, Minister for Immigration]

Foreign Languages in Australia, Immigration Reference Paper, Australian Government Publishing Service, Canberra, 1974 [Paper presented at conference of Qld Modern Language Teachers Association by A J Grassby, Minister for Immigration]

APPENDIX: Publications 427

Australian Schools Commission's Report for the Triennium 1976-78, chapter 8: 'The Education of Migrant Children', Australian Government Publishing Service, Canberra, 1975

The Schools Commission, [Prototype of the Gonski Committee, was established 'to develop a funding system for Australian schooling which is transparent, fair, financially sustainable and effective in promoting excellent outcomes for all Australian students'. In both cases recommendations would not be implemented by an incoming Coalition Government

Let's End the Slander: Combating Racial Prejudice in Teaching Materials, Office of the Commissioner for Community Relations, Commonwealth of Australia, 1979, 124pp

Our Multicultural Capital: Community Conference Report, co-editor with Don Phillips, Canberra, 1978, 129pp

The Galbally Report in the ACT and the Prospects for Multiculturalism, Report and resolutions of Community Workshop, convened in Canberra Nov 1978

Chapter 'Racism and Ethnocentrism in Textbooks' in *Multicultural Education: Issues and Innovations'*, ed. John Sherwood, Creative Research, Perth, 1981

Australian Multicultural Society: Identity, Communication, Decision-Making, co-editor with Don Phillips, Drummond, Melbourne, 1984, 206pp [36 papers presented at the National Conference on 'Australian Society in the Multicultural 80s' convened in Canberra by the Office of the Commissioner for Community Relations in 1980]

Monograph *A Tale of Two Towns: Report on a New Initiative in Community Education in Rockhampton and Kempsey*, Community Relations Paper No. 15, Office of the Commissioner for Community Relations, 1981, 33pp

Regional Ecumenical Course with Clergy and Aboriginal People (RECOCAP), print materials to accompany audiotapes of study course for clergy of Central Queensland, Unit 1: Regional history of inter-racial conflict; Unit 2: Traditional Aboriginal culture and the ongoing implications for race relations; Unit 3: Current situation of Aboriginal people, and

Government policies, state & federal. 1981. Total 169pp

Statement 'A Christian Response to the Situation of the Aboriginal People' concluding with a three-pronged proposal for Christian action, sent to the leadership of every denomination in every State, 1977 [without response]

Article 'Crossroads – The Aboriginal Situation and the Church' (9th Hobson Memorial Lecture), in *St Mark's Review*, No 98, June 1979

Article 'A tale of three generations: a multicultural audit for the International Year of the Child' in *Growing up in a Multicultural Society*, report of 5th annual cultural conference, Goulburn College of Advanced Education, 1979

Article 'Educating for Justice and Human Rights' in *Journal of Christian Education*, Papers 65, July 1979, 14pp

Contribution to symposium 'Conform or Transform: Community Intervention in Educational Policy' in *Journal of Christian Education*, Papers 78, Nov 1983

Article 'How neutral is neutral? Towards a Christian Perspective on Public Service Impartiality', 16pp, in *Private Values and Public Policy: The Ethics of Decision-Making in Government Administration*, Zadok Centre, Canberra 1983, 197pg

Accents of Faith: the Churches of the Victorian Council of Churches, directory compiled for the Victorian Council of Churches, Melbourne, 1985, 55pp

The Cultured Pearl: Australian Readings in Cross-Cultural Theology and Mission, Victorian Council of Churches, 1986, 294pp (Australian Christian Book of the Year for 1987) Republished by Joint Board of Christian Education, Melbourne, 1988

Seeds Blowing in the Wind: Review of Multicultural Ministry & Mission, Anglican Diocese of Melbourne, 1993, 133pp

Journeying On Together: The Inside Story of a Bicultural/Bilingual Church in an Australian Suburb, St Michael & All Angels, Bennettswood, 2001, 85pp

Report on Seminar conducted on 'Church, Gospel and Evangelism in a Multicultural Setting' sponsored by Scaffolding Inc. and the Baptist Home Mission Society, Sydney, 20pp [principal speaker] in *Intermesh, Urban Mission Journal: Resourcing Clergy, Church Leaders & Lay People*, Vol 9, No 11, Apr. 1991

Report on seminar *Dying with Dignity: Ethical, Religious and Cultural Perspectives. Implications for Health Professionals*, jointly convened at the Royal Melbourne Hospital, Aug. 1988 by Multi-Faith Resource Centre, National Association for Loss & Grief (Vic), and Centre for Applied Social Research in Health [Marjorie Houston and I co-organisers on behalf of MFRC and NALAG.]

Article 'Some Perspectives on Religious Pluralism', in *2nd National Congress Report*, FECCA (Federation of Ethnic Communities Councils in Australia), 1988

Article 'Midwife to Multiculturalism?' in *Australian Mosaic*, journal of FECCA, Issue 23, Oct. 2009

Article 'Towards a Constitution for a Multicultural Republic' in *National Outlook: Christian Perspectives on Contemporary Issues*, March 1998

Article 'Where have All the Foreigners Gone?' in *National Outlook: Christian Perspectives on Contemporary Issues*, August 1998

Article 'Australia's Policies on Cultural Diversity: Secular and Christian Perspectives' in *South Pacific Journal of Mission Studies*, No 23, April 2000.

Article 'How Multi-Cultural is God in Australia?' in *AFES Graduates Fellowship Papers on Biblical & Current Questions*, Issue 32

Article on 'God – Alive and Well, and Living in the Eastern Suburbs?' in *Australian Ministry: Quarterly Journal for Clergy and Church Leaders*, Vol 4, No 3, Aug. 1992 [on ministry challenges encountered in Broadmeadows]

Feature article 'Judaea, Samaria and the Ends of the Earth' in *On Being, Christian monthly magazine*, Vol 7, No 11, Jan.1981

Article 'The Strangers within our Gates' in *On Being*, Vol 11, No 10, Nov.1984

Feature Article 'The Message We Don't Want to Hear: A Report on the World Council of Churches Assembly, Canberra, Feb. 1991' in *Renewing Australia: Encouraging Ministry and Renewal*, No 23, Sept. 1991 [Aboriginal issues]

Article 'Once you were no people' in *Contact: Magazine of Reid Uniting Church*, Canberra, Aug 1982

Article 'Multiculturalism – A Christian perspective: Celebrating Diversity and Doing Justice' in *Tyndale Papers, Vol XXIX*, No. 3, July 1984 [Prepared for and presented by Archbishop David Penman]

Chapter on 'Cross-Cultural Ministry in the Anglican Church of Australia' in *Report on First International Network Forum on Multicultural Ministry*, convened by National Assembly of Uniting Church in Australia, Sydney, Nov 1999

Essay no 5 'Australian Faces: Christians in a Multicultural Australia' in *Bicentenary publication of the Commission for Mission of the Uniting Church in Australia*, Sydney, 1988 [including a half-page listing of points of tension in our multicultural society calling for Christian action for social justice]

Main feature article 'Still Room for Repentance over First Australians' in *The Melbourne Anglican* newspaper, Melbourne, August 2016

www.ingramcontent.com/pod-product-compliance
Lightning Source LLC
Chambersburg PA
CBHW051932290426
44110CB00015B/1955